感謝
KANSHA

感謝

KANSHA

Celebrating Japan's Vegan & Vegetarian Traditions

ELIZABETH ANDOH

Photography by Leigh Beisch

TEN SPEED PRESS
Berkeley

Library of Congress Cataloging-in-Publication Data
Andoh, Elizabeth.
    Kansha : celebrating Japan's vegan and vegetarian traditions /
Elizabeth Andoh ; photography by Leigh Beisch.—1st ed.
        p. cm.
    Includes index.
    1. Cookery, Japanese. 2. Vegan cookery. I. Title.
    TX724.5.J3A525 2010
    641.5952—dc22
                        2010021768
ISBN 978-1-58008-955-5

Printed in China

Design by Toni Tajima
Food styling by Karen Shinto
Prop Styling by Sara Slavin
Photography assistance by Kate Robison and Sean Franzen
Food styling assistance by Fanny Pan

The publisher and author would like to thank ceramic artists
Catherine White, Warren Frederick, and Romig Streeter for the
generous loan of their work.

10 9 8 7 6 5 4 3 2 1

First Edition

CONTENTS

ACKNOWLEDGMENTS

THE THEME OF THIS BOOK is *kansha*—appreciation—and I use the word here to express my deep gratitude to those who worked with me on this project.

From the start, I saw *Kansha* as a collective, cooperative undertaking and sought like-minded others to join me in creating a different sort of cookbook—one that would encourage and enable readers to experience *kansha* cooking in their own kitchens as they prepared their daily meals and shared nourishment with others. Although the specific recipes—and the guidance I provide in making them—are deeply rooted in Japanese food traditions, I believe that the notion of *kansha* is universal in its appeal and its application.

Lisa Ekus-Saffer, exemplary literary agent, fervent advocate, and enduring ally, patiently helped me hone my proposal and place the *Kansha* project with Ten Speed Press. Publisher Aaron Wehner, whose superb editorial skills had enabled me to bring forth *Washoku* five years ago, now paired me with Dawn Yanagihara. From our first exchange of e-mails I knew she was everything I wanted my new editorial partner to be—sharp and savvy, precise but patient, dynamic and determined. In turn, Dawn made sure that the same terrific team that worked on *Washoku*—art director Toni Tajima, copy editor Sharon Silva, proofreader Karen Levy, indexer Ken DellaPenta—would again contibute their talents to *Kansha*. All struggled with my densely cross-referenced manuscript, steamlining and formatting it into the elegant yet practical book you hold in your hands. Such masterful work, and so well coordinated

by Dawn! She and I practiced our own editorial version of *kansha*—appreciating nature (the time difference between California and Japan)—cleverly using it to our mutual advantage (as one worked, the other slept). Luckily, living in Japan gave me the advantage of "extra" hours to meet deadlines!

Leigh Beisch is also a kindred spirit in *kansha*: she works entirely, creatively, with the light that nature provides (a true challenge on drizzle-filled, winter-shortened San Francisco days). Her able and affable crew, studio manager Kate Robison and digital technologist (and hand model!) Sean Franzen, enabled our photo shoot to run smoothly. Styling the food with artistry, cultural sensitivity, and technical accomplishment, Karen Shinto, ably assisted by Fanny Pan, contributed immeasureably to *Kansha*'s imagery. Prop stylist Sara Slavin made sure we had a wide variety of stunning vessels from which to choose in setting our culinary scenes. The vibrant work of ceramic artists, Frederick Warren, Romig Streeter, and Catherine White inspires creativity in food presentation. I admire their individual talents, and collectively cherish their continued friendship.

Many others contibuted their support to *Kansha*. As I struggled to organize my ideas and select recipes, I sought—and gratefully received—the counsel of Gary Goldberg, Holly Kawakami, Halsey and Alice North, Yukari Sakamoto, Hiroko Sasaki, David Sculnick, and Jessica Wickham.

In the spring of 2008, I issued a call for volunteers through my electronic newsletter and was gratified to receive hundreds of offers to join my "advisory council." I began by selecting a few Tokyo residents (I dubbed them the "*Kansha* Club") who gathered periodically in my kitchen to help me work out kinks in recipe development and to help me correspond with and collate responses from dozens of others living outside Japan. I chose my advisory council members for their demographic diversity: single-career households, multi-generational families, people engaged in sundry occupations, and practicing a variety of dietary habits (a few vegans, most merely curious). The majority of council members had little or no experience cooking Japanese food. If these people could make and enjoy the food I wanted to include in this volume, I reckoned that readers anywhere could do likewise.

I am deeply indebted to my steadfast *Kansha* Club: Rachel Austin, Melinda Joe, Sarah Kelly, Amy Hamilton Lane, Jessica Sakuma, Laurel Swift, and Tiffany R. Toeda.

I am grateful for the candid comments and thoughtful feedback of my advisory council: William Francis Ahearn; Claire Baram; Sukey Barnhart; Annette Baron; Kim Bartko; Daniel and Linda Bogan; Kitty Bradshaw; Thomas Cali; Elizabeth Cheslock; Mark W. Dawson; Marie L. DeVito; David George; Sage and Jim Hagy; Torkil Heggstad; Cayce Hill; Karen Jull; Laurel Kao; Daniele Kay; Yoshiko Kuriyama-Imagawa; Thng Lay Geok (LG); Julie Lovins; Matthew, Naomi, and Lisa Miller; Nancy Moore Bess; Mitch Muroff; Wendy Savage; Risa Sekiguchi; Beverly Sing; Corona So; David Song; Hilary Snow; Jim and Phyllis Thrush; Eva Tiecke; Kay Hisae Tokunaga; Wendy Wasserman; Susanna Wellenberg; Kelly R. Wells; Jenny Winker; Cynthia Winter; Kirk Wright and Alison Lew; and Amanda Zimlich.

At first merely intrigued with Japan's food culture, I was quickly and deeply drawn in to its practice by the kitchen charisma of Kiyoko Andoh (aka *Okaasan*, my mother-in-law). Today, as I air-dry persimmon peels to add to my pickle pot, or stew *kombu* salvaged from yesterday's stock-making, I can hear her gentle chiding: nothing should go to waste. My sisters-in-law, Teruko, Nobuko (Okashita), and Yohko (Yokoi) continue the Andoh traditions and are my valued cooking comrades.

My formal training in Japan's classical cuisine began more than forty years ago under the tutelage of Master Toshio Yanagihara; his son, Kazunari; and daughter-in-law, Noriko. Today, the third generation, Young Master Naoyuki, carries on the family's commitment to culinary education, teaching at their Tokyo-based school and writing for Japan's leading publications. It is with pleasure and pride that I continue to learn from this multitalented family.

My mother, Caroline Saxe, encouraged me to be curious and seek knowledge. My daughter, Rena Andoh, continues to show me what focus and passion can achieve. And, if it were not for the ardent, adoring support of my husband, Atsunori, I could never have sustained the energy necessary to complete this project.

I am filled with appreciation to each and all.

Kansha, kansha. 感謝

INTRODUCTION

KANSHA MEANS "appreciation," an expression evident in many aspects of Japanese society and daily living. In a culinary context, the word acknowledges both nature's bounty and the efforts and ingenuity of people who transform that abundance into marvelous food. In the kitchen and at table, in the supermarket and out in the gardens, fields, and waterways, *kansha* encourages us to prepare nutritionally sound and aesthetically satisfying meals that also avoid waste, conserve energy, and sustain our natural resources.

A keen appreciation of food does not require anyone to choose a plant-based diet, but it is in keeping with such a mindset. *Kansha* is about abundance—of grains, legumes, roots, shoots, leafy plants (aquatic and terrestrial), shrubs, herbs, berries, seeds, tree fruits and nuts—not abstinence (doing without meat, fish, poultry, eggs, or dairy). It is about nourishing ourselves with what nature provides, cleverly and respectfully applying human technique and technology in the process.

Kansha as both a concept and a practice is well integrated into Japanese culinary tradition. Indeed, it is one of several aspects of *washoku*, the ancient and indigenous food culture of Japan. Based on the notion that balancing color, flavor, and method of food preparation enables

ICHI MOTSU ZEN SHOKU: *in the* kansha *kitchen, a daikon with greens (right, with tip to the side) is used in its entirety—greens dried (top center); tapered end grated (top left); midsection cut into thick half moons and wedges (center left), circles (center), and thin half-moons (on plate); peel from neck portion cut into sen-giri strips (to left of whole daikon), and midsection peeled* katsura-muki *style (bottom left)*

optimal nutrition and aesthetic satisfaction at table, the principles of *washoku* guide home cooks and food professionals alike to culinary harmony. As with my book *Washoku: Recipes from the Japanese Home Kitchen*, I want this volume to both stimulate your intellect and satisfy your palate. And, as is true of *washoku*, I believe that *kansha* as a guiding principle in procuring, preparing, and partaking of food is universal in its appeal and application.

A HISTORICAL PERSPECTIVE ON KANSHA

Buddhism, with its inherent respect for life that eschews consumption of animals, was first introduced to Japan by way of Korea in the sixth century. Among Japan's varied food traditions, *shōjin ryōri*, most often translated as "Buddhist cuisine" or "temple cookery," has become synonymous with vegetarian cooking. Indeed it is vegan, as no animal products are used. *Shōjin ryōri* became well established during the Kamakura period (1185–1333), a tumultuous time in Japan's history as feudal warlords vied for power. No doubt life was particularly perilous, and therefore seemed even more precious.

SHŌJIN RYŌRI The word *shōjin* means "earnest commitment." *Shōjin ryōri* is not about dietary restrictions, but rather respect for nature's bounty and for the diligence and ingenuity of those who procure it.

As you might expect, the earnest endeavor to prepare food shuns the use of shortcuts. The time and energy required to assemble a classic *shōjin ryōri* dish such as *goma-dōfu*, a creamy sesame pudding, is part of the reason it appears on temple vegetarian menus. It is undeniably delicious when prepared in the traditional time-consuming and physically exhausting manner, but there is a simpler way to make the pudding: using *neri goma* (toasted sesame paste), rather than parching, crushing, and grinding the seeds yourself in a *suribachi* (grooved mortar), a roughly two-hour workout guaranteed to tone your upper arms. In this book, I will be offering you both ways: the classic method for those who wish to experience appreciation through their own effort and labor, and the modern method for those pressed for time or with physical limitations—in which case, your appreciation can be focused on the ingenious efforts of others. *Kansha*, in this example, would be gratitude for artisanally produced pure toasted sesame paste.

ICHI MOTSU ZEN SHOKU The need to use food and energy resources as fully and effectively as possible led to many frugal culinary customs in Japan. The ecologically and nutritionally sound practice of *ichi motsu zen shoku* (one food, used entirely) encourages the use of all edible parts of plant foods: peels, roots, shoots, stems, seeds, and flowers. Throughout the book, I will be alerting you to opportunities for making fine food from the trimmed-away bits and pieces of produce that inevitably accumulate as you prepare a meal. You will soon discover that nothing goes to waste in the *kansha* kitchen.

KONDATÉ-ZUKUSHI Another longstanding Japanese culinary practice, *kondaté-zukushi* takes pleasure in making a meal from a single ingredient. This custom of using seasonally and regionally available foodstuffs developed in response to cyclical abundance amidst otherwise limited food resources. The well-established Japanese notion that a single ingredient, transformed in myriad ways, can become the highlight of a complete meal was the driving force behind the original (and flamboyant) *Iron Chef* television program.

Ancient approaches that remain applicable and meaningful to modern society, *ichi motsu zen shoku* and *kondaté-zukushi* will be evident throughout this book. At the conclusion of this introduction, in the section called Practicing *Kansha*, I will walk you through the preparation of *Daikon-Zukushi*, a menu celebrating the full glory of a plump, snowy white, green-tufted radish.

RECENT DEVELOPMENTS

Since the 1970s, a number of social and dietary movements operating globally have combined to increase awareness of the benefits of adopting a vegetarian lifestyle. The modern macrobiotic movement, born in Japan and well traveled worldwide, has helped rekindle an interest in the ancient notion of food as medicine.

In Japan in the past decade, a growing consciousness of the importance of passing on Japanese culinary culture to future generations, combined with other food-related concerns, evolved into a grassroots movement known as *shokuiku*. The word itself, a combination of the calligraphy for "food" and for "education," was coined by a group of food journalists to describe wide-ranging goals. Those aspirations included defining (and encouraging the adoption of) healthful dietary practices, recognizing the need to monitor safety in food production and distribution, and the training of young people's palates to appreciate food prepared without chemical additives. In 2005, the *shokuiku* movement was formally recognized by the Japanese government's Cabinet Office (Naikakufu), which influences policy and legislation in several key agencies, including the Ministry of Health, Labor and Welfare (Kōseisho); the Ministry of Agriculture, Forestry and Fisheries (Nōrinsuisansho); and the Ministry of Education (Mombusho).

Current societal concerns with ecology (environmental pollution) and economics (pinched household budgets) have also led to a renewed interest in no-waste vegetarian cooking. In particular, a marketing concept known as LOHAS (Lifestyles of Health and Sustainability), which includes valuing organic farming over conventional methods, has become important in Japan's contemporary food supply and distribution networks. Combined with the recent advent of the Slow Food movement and its respect for old-fashioned ways that encourage artisanal production, even urban dwellers have access to excellent processed foods that support a healthful, plant-focused diet.

The Japanese have also recently embraced induction heat (IH) cooking, a flameless way to prepare food in which heat is produced by magnetic fields. IH cooking is thought to be safer, less costly (after the initial investment for the special countertop cooker), and kinder to the environment. It does, however, place special requirements on cookware: the outer surface of pots, pans, and skillets must be ferrous—no glass, ceramic, aluminum, or copper, for example—and must come in direct, flat contact with the IH cooktop. But these requisites have not slowed the spread of this new cooking medium.

PUTTING THEORY INTO PRACTICE

My goal in writing *Kansha* is to empower you to create wholesome, nutritionally balanced, plant-based dishes, easily integrating preparation of these dishes into your busy and, most likely, urban daily routine.

Being able to consider the relative merits of one foodstuff or technique compared to another requires a comfortable familiarity with a wide range of products and kitchen skills. I will help you build that knowledge base, expanding your culinary horizons and repertoire by introducing you to an array of possibly unfamiliar foods and

Tokyo, 1969, presenting a *kansha* bouquet to my new in-laws,
Kiyoko and Hisao Andoh, as my mother Caroline Saxe, looks on

techniques that were developed in tandem with Japan's vegetarian traditions. To help you become a practitioner-cook of *kansha*, I have included a detailed reference section, A Guide to the Kansha Kitchen, at the back of this book. It is divided into two parts, A Catalog of Tools and Techniques and A Catalog of Ingredients.

As a teacher of the Japanese culinary arts, I believe that the best recipes demonstrate how the culture as a whole approaches food preparation. My recipes will guide you to an understanding of *why* certain procedures are performed in the Japanese kitchen, then teach you *when* and *how* to do what needs to be done by advising you on timing, techniques, and relative proportion of ingredients to use. I will be encouraging you to adopt a mindful, considered approach to food preparation beginning with menu planning that eliminates unnecessary time and energy or superfluous foodstuffs.

PRACTICING KANSHA

Nothing goes to waste in the *kansha* kitchen. Putting this ideal into practice means fully using the food that nature provides, minimizing waste while maximizing eating pleasure.

Many fruits and vegetables come to market oddly shaped, slightly bruised, or a bit past prime, though still full of flavor and brimming with nutrients. What often ends up in the trash bin—seeds, fruit peels, vegetable trimmings, and misshapen or overripe produce—can be transformed into tasty side dishes. One approach is to mash, crush, grate, and/or blend the pulp of less-than-perfect produce to make soups, sauces, and aspics. Another approach is to finely shred or mince these usual castoffs, and make crispy fritters or crunchy pickles from them. You will find dozens of recipes throughout the book for using these usual kitchen scraps creatively, deliciously.

Packaged pantry goods such as soy sauce and miso do not spoil easily, though they do lose their aroma within a few weeks of opening. Refrigerating opened packages helps slow the loss, but after a month or so you'll find such products lack verve. That's when revitalizing them, changing them into flavor-enhancing condiments, makes sense. Having a jar of homemade Vegan Seasoned Soy Concentrate (page 131) at the back of your refrigerator will be a boon on busy days, and Robust Miso (page 132) will perk up rice or dress up sticks of raw vegetables in a pinch. Once you get the hang of it, you will be surprised at how much you can do to reduce waste and improve flavor and nutrition. Think of the resulting dishes as a bonus for your resourcefulness.

One way to experience *kansha* in your own kitchen is to build an entire meal around a single vegetable, using it fully. Consider constructing a menu to celebrate a glorious daikon you find at your local farmers' market. Title your meal *Daikon-Zukushi*: daikon in its entirety!

Different sections of daikon have different flavor and texture profiles. I suggest you use the leafy tops for making a confetti-like condiment to toss into cooked rice (Rice Tossed with Radish Greens, page 23). Then, divide the root portion into three segments: the neck (nearest the leafy tuft; this is often green), the midsection (usually bulbous and snowy white), and the tapered tip. Peel each segment and use the peels in various dishes, such as soup (Red and White Miso Soup, page 82) and a spicy sauté (Spicy Stir-Fry, page 122). Any leftover peels can be stored in a resealable bag and refrigerated for several days. To make a hearty main course, sear thick wheels of daikon from the neck portion in a skillet, glazing them lightly with a sweetened soy sauce before topping with citrus peel slivers or zest (Skillet-Seared Daikon with Yuzu, page 98). The midsection is perhaps the most versatile segment of the entire daikon. It can be seared, simmered, steamed, grated, shredded or thinly sliced and eaten raw or lightly pickled (Quick-Fix Pickles: Fruity, Sweet-and-Sour Daikon, page 196). The tip of the root is best when it is grated and used as a condiment or garnish with fried foods. One of my favorites is Crispy-Creamy Tōfu, Southern Barbarian Style (page 178), which would be a fine addition to our *Daikon-Zukushi* feast. Bruised or misshapen daikon roots are often shredded and dried (if you have a dehydrator, you can make your own shreds—any segment of the root, and peels, can be made into *kiriboshi daikon*—or you can buy shelf-stable bags of them at Asian grocery stores). For our *Daikon-Zukushi* menu, I suggest a sweet, spicy, and tart pickle (page 204) made from *kiriboshi daikon* (sun-dried radish shreds).

When planning a meal, you need not choose between *kansha* and *washoku* as menu-organizing principles: each complements and enhances the other. For those of you who have cooked from *Washoku*, rest assured that the *Daikon-Zukushi* meal I have just described meets the guidelines for balancing color, flavor, and preparation method:

white (daikon and rice), black (sesame seeds mixed with the daikon leaves and the soy glaze), red (carrots in the soup and the stir-fry), yellow (pickles and *yuzu* zest), and green (leafy daikon tops); sweet (sugar in the soy-glazed daikon and in the pickling brine), sour (pickles), and salty (soy sauce and miso), with accents of spice (7-blend spice, red chile) and bitterness (*yuzu* zest); raw (grated condiment), simmered and seared (soy-glazed daikon wheels), fried (crispy-creamy tōfu), and steamed (rice).

Kansha—appreciating good food and the efforts of those who make it—can be experienced and practiced at any age. If you have an opportunity to cook with, or for, young children, I encourage you to try your hand at making nutritionally balanced, aesthetically appealing, kid-friendly boxed lunches-to-go. The lunch pictured on page 168 features soy-glazed tōfu burgers (page 169) that youngsters adore. These protein-packed sliders could be served on small buns, with the salad greens tucked inside, American-sandwich style. But in Japan, where seasonal

Atsunori and me, entertaining as newlyweds

sensitivity is an important part of menu planning, cherry blossom–studded rice (page 25) would be enjoyed instead, *obentō* style, while flower-viewing in the company of friends and family. Serving fresh fruit is a great way to provide nutritional balance to a lunch menu, though whole fruit can be messy to peel and eat. Sliced citrus typically bruises, and the juice oozes, but these wedges of jellied grapefruit (page 232) are easy to make, pack, and eat.

MEAL PLANNING

Japanese meals are organized around a core of three foods: rice (or noodles), soup (clear, miso enriched, or puréed), and pickles. Greater volume and complexity are usually achieved by adding small dishes to this trio to round out the menu. Classic meal planning follows guidelines associated with Japan's native culinary culture, *washoku*. Such meals achieve culinary harmony by balancing colors, flavors, and preparation methods. Without having to stop and do cumbersome nutritional arithmetic, you are assured of getting essential vitamins and minerals in your daily diet when you choose colorful ingredients (red, green, yellow, black, and white) at every meal. Using different cooking techniques (simmering, searing, keeping raw, steaming, and frying) provides textural interest that contributes to a sense of satisfied fullness while actually consuming less food. Serving a range of flavors (sweet, sour, and salty, with accents of spice and bitterness) curbs food cravings that could lead to overeating.

I have arranged recipes into chapters that I hope will help you plan well-rounded menus. For those of you not yet used to balancing the nutritional requirements of a vegan diet, I suggest you first choose a rice or noodle dish (nearly all of them in this book include produce), and then add one dish from each of the following three chapters: Fresh from the Market, The Well-Stocked Pantry, and Mostly Soy. By including one dish that features fresh produce from the market or farm, another that relies on *kambutsu* (dried foods) from the pantry, and a third that contains significant quantities of plant-sourced protein (mostly tōfu in its many forms), you will have assembled a nutritionally balanced meal without complicated calculations. If you have chosen a substantial rice or noodle dish, then the other dishes can be sides or toppings to the rice or noodles. Your meal can be expanded by the addition of a soup, pickles (think of them as fully dressed "salads"), and dessert, each of which has its own collection of recipes in separate chapters.

SOME FINAL THOUGHTS

You do *not* need to convert to eating only Japanese food to practice *kansha*. Nor do you have to assemble your meals from Japanese foodstuffs alone. Many of the dishes in this book can be happily incorporated into—or adapted to—American, Mediterranean, northern European, or other Asian menus.

Some people elect not to consume any animal flesh, dairy products, or eggs for metabolic reasons. Food allergies and other health-compromising issues such as elevated cholesterol seem to head the list. Others might follow a vegetarian or vegan regimen as an ethical choice—their way of demonstrating respect for animal life. Still others have a concern for the ecology of the planet that compels them to eat plant-based foods exclusively.

If you are just embarking on a plant-based diet, or combining vegetarian dishes with small quantities of meat, dairy, eggs, fish, and poultry to feed yourself or others, you will find lots of dishes and menu suggestions in *Kansha* to help you transition to a primarily vegetarian diet. If you have already chosen a vegetarian lifestyle but are unfamiliar with Japanese food, you will discover exciting new dishes and ideas to expand and enliven your repertoire.

Dōzo, meshiagaré—Go ahead, eat up!

A NOTE ABOUT LANGUAGE

Writing about Japanese food in English is challenging. I often ask myself: What label should I use when describing a certain idea? What should a particular ingredient or technique be called? Should I use the Japanese word (sometimes long and awkward to pronounce), an English equivalent (often there is none), or a combination of both? There are no simple answers.

As with other aspects of culture, language is dynamic, a constantly changing tool used to convey information and discuss ideas. Since the publication of *Washoku* in 2005, I have reviewed and revised some of the choices I made when writing that volume. I have based my current decisions primarily on the advice and opinions of my international advisory council, a group of dedicated volunteers living outside Japan who tested recipes and provided me with exceptionally valuable feedback.

When it comes to identifying the proper ingredient in a recipe, I often find the need to combine English and Japanese. *Udon* noodles and fried tōfu are good examples of this. In the first instance, Japanese modifies English; in the latter example, the order is reversed. Because labels on commercially manufactured products vary, it is not possible to provide you with a complete list of every version you may encounter when shopping. Here are some general guidelines for how I determined what to call an item: When there is an obvious, uncontested, single, accurate (or fairly accurate) English name for something, I have used the English word as the primary word: soy sauce, not *shōyu*, and vinegar, not *su*, illustrate this well. When an English name is misleading, awkward, or unnecessarily unappetizing, I use the Japanese name to identify the item. *Shiso*, not perilla leaf or beefsteak plant, and *konnyaku*, not devil's tongue root, tuber aspic, taro jelly, or alimentary paste, are good examples of this decision.

Japanese names for some foods are becoming increasingly common outside the culture. Miso, not fermented bean paste; wasabi, not Japanese horseradish; and tōfu, not bean curd, illustrate this point, and I willingly—and gratefully—use the now-familiar Japanese.

Although I strived for consistency and ease in identification, all the choices I made are admittedly arbitrary. If you are having trouble locating an item in A Guide to the Kansha Kitchen, refer to the index beginning on page 286, where pages numbers will be listed for references to every item.

RICE

I COMMUTE FREQUENTLY BETWEEN Osaka and Tokyo via rapid Shinkansen service, and I cannot help but notice the change in seasons as the countryside whizzes past my train window. In Japan's central and Pacific coast areas, rice fields that are lush, vibrant green carpets in July and early August turn to gold by September. Once harvesting begins, sheaves of cut grain lay bundled in the fields, and anticipation builds among consumers eager to eat the year's new crop, or *shin mai*. As supermarket shelves begin to stock premium-priced, newly harvested rice, a fresh crop of cookbooks showcasing rice begins to appear in bookstores throughout Japan. On television, *kansha*, gratitude for a good harvest, becomes the theme of many shows. Culinary travelogues are especially popular, with footage of well-known television personalities visiting rice-growing areas, where they get restaurant chefs and local housewives to share their rice recipes with a national viewing audience.

Hopefully, you can obtain some newly harvested rice grown where you live. Japanese-style short- or medium-grain varieties are grown in California, Texas, and other areas of the United States. If locally cultivated rice is not available, you are likely to find Japan's *shin mai* in many Asian groceries. Whatever your source for new-crop rice, I want to expand your repertoire for cooking with it. In this section, I offer you more than a dozen ways to prepare and enjoy rice, nearly all of which are what would be deemed "featured" or main-course dishes, rather than "side" accompaniments. These are rice dishes around which you can plan a satisfying, nutritious meal.

In Japanese, the word *gohan* means both "cooked rice" and "a meal." Because rice is synonymous with eating in Japan, preparing it is an important kitchen skill. I begin this chapter with a thorough explanation of the mechanics of washing and cooking rice (white, brown, and mixed with other grains) and the classic technique for seasoning it to make sushi rice. Once you have a grasp of these basic procedures, the other recipes in the chapter will be easy to follow. My master recipes for cooking rice take into consideration three variables: the degree to which the grain has been hulled (polished), the vessel in which the rice will be cooked, and the type of heat used to cook the rice. All the recipes use standard American cups to measure both rice and cooking water. (For information about the two basic types of rice used in the Japanese kitchen, purchasing advice, and storage recommendations, turn to page 274 in A Guide to the Kansha Kitchen.)

For purists who are also practical, I provide detailed instructions for modern stove-top cooking. I recommend you use a straight-sided, stainless-steel or enamel-lined cast-iron pot with a tight-fitting lid. For cooks who prefer to employ the latest technology, I include directions for using an electric rice cooker. Models programmed with "fuzzy logic" (see page 241) are nearly foolproof. (If you are using an electric rice cooker and want to use the horizontal markings on the side of the rice-cooker bowl, you need to use the measuring cup that came with the rice cooker, not the cup measures in the recipes.)

For the best-tasting results, use filtered water or bottled soft water for cooking white rice, especially if your tap water is hard (contains an appreciable quantity of dissolved minerals). Salt is added to the water for cooking potassium-rich brown rice; the sodium counteracts any bitterness caused by the potassium.

COOKED WHITE RICE

SEIHAKU MAI

In Japan, the ultimate symbol of economic and societal well-being has traditionally been expressed by a single image: *Okaasan* (Mother) scooping tender, plump grains of steaming white rice from a pot, coaxing it lovingly, respectfully into a modest mound on a small plate, and then placing the plate before the ancestral altar in a gesture of appreciation—*kansha*—before serving *Otoosan* (Father) and other family members.

Whether *Okaasan* wears a traditional kimono or contemporary casual clothes, whether the cooking vessel is an old-fashioned *okama* (pot) set over a wood-burning stove or a modern automated appliance, freshly cooked white rice remains the Japanese culinary ideal—the evidence that family finances and the kitchen prowess of *Okaasan* can provide nutritional balance and satiety with the numerous other foods served alongside it. Indeed, plain white rice, cooked to tender perfection, becomes the perfect accompaniment to a variety of other dishes.

MAKES 2 CUPS COOKED RICE

1 cup Japanese-style white rice

1 cup plus 2 tablespoons water, soft tap or filtered

MAKES 3 CUPS COOKED RICE

1 1/2 cups Japanese-style white rice

Scant 1 3/4 cups water, soft tap or filtered

MAKES 5 CUPS COOKED RICE

2 1/2 cups Japanese-style white rice

Scant 3 cups water, soft tap or filtered

Wash the rice: The purpose of washing polished white rice is to remove excess starch and to discard any small pebbles or bits of straw (natural abrasives used to help separate kernel from hull in the milling and polishing process) that might be mixed with it. Place the rice in a deep bowl and cover it with cool tap water. Stir the rice vigorously. The water will become cloudy with the starch that coated the grains.

Many Japanese will not just swish and stir, but actually roll the rice between their hands, or their dominant hand and the side of the bowl near the bottom, to energetically remove excess starch. This action is known as *togu*, "to polish," and is used to describe knife sharpening, too. The resulting sound is a bit like a maraca being gently shaken. If you wish to follow suit, slightly bend and cup the fingers of your dominant hand to scoop up some of the water-moistened rice. Release it against either the flat open palm of your other hand, or against the side of the bowl, at the bottom. As you release the rice, gently roll the grains between the heel of your dominant hand and your palm or the side of the bowl. Rhythmically repeat this action several times. Add a bit more cold water to the bowl, swish, and drain the rice.

Save this cloudy, starch-intense, slightly oily first rinsing water, known as *togi-jiru* (page 242), for blanching vegetables and other foods. Store it in a lidded glass jar in the refrigerator. The starchy matter will settle to the bottom, forming a white, oily layer of sediment. Stir to recombine just before using. If you will be accumulating *togi-jiru*

(continued)

from several days of rice rinsing, date the original batch and use the combined *togi-jiru* within 5 days of the date.

Repeat the washing process with fresh cold water. Continue to rinse, roll, swish, and drain the raw rice until the rinsing water runs clear. This will probably require 3 or 4 washings. Drain the rice well after the final rinsing. You will notice that the rice has become slightly more opaque; the kernels have begun to absorb moisture from the washing process. Carefully transfer the rice to your cooking pot or rice-cooker bowl.

To cook on the stove top: Place the washed and drained rice in a sturdy, straight-sided pot. A 2- or 3-quart size will work well for the two smaller quantities, and a 4- to 6-quart pot is appropriate for the larger amount. Add the water. Ideally, the rice should sit in its measured water for 10 minutes before cooking, but if you are pressed for time, add a few extra drops of water and cook right away. Cover the pot with a tight-fitting lid.

Bring the water to a rolling boil over high heat. You will hear bubbling noises and see the lid begin to dance after several minutes. An onomatopoeic folk jingle that describes the cooking of rice refers to this bubbling stage as *choro choro*. Reduce the heat and continue to cook until the water is absorbed (about 5 minutes). You will know this point has been reached when you hear a low hissing sound (the folk jingle calls this *naka pappa*). If it is difficult to rely on the sound of the cooking and you must check visually on progress along the way, peek quickly and replace the lid immediately.

Raise the heat to high again for 30 seconds to dry off the rice. Remove the pot from the heat and let the rice stand, still tightly covered, for at least 10 minutes. Even if you wish to serve the rice piping hot, these final minutes of self-steaming (called *murasu*) are necessary to achieve the proper texture.

To cook in a rice cooker: Place the washed and drained rice in the bowl of your cooker. Add the water. It is important to use *cool* liquid when cooking rice in a thermostatically controlled appliance; using warm or hot liquid from the start will cut short the cooking cycle. Close the lid, press the start switch, and let the appliance do the cooking. The time required to complete the cooking cycle will vary with the appliance, but most models take about 40 minutes to cook 1 to $1\frac{1}{2}$ cups raw rice. After the active cooking cycle is complete, let the rice stand, still covered, to self-steam for at least 10 minutes, or for up to several hours if your appliance has a warmer feature.

COOKED WHITE RICE ENRICHED WITH MIXED GRAINS

ZAKKOKU MAI

Adding a mixture of other grains, such as millet, barley, flaxseed, amaranth, and/or quinoa (these last two are not native to Japan), to white rice enriches the nutritional value of the dish. It also makes the texture more varied, and the flavor more complex. Indeed, you may find that you prefer to include a mix of other grains in the rice that accompanies your daily home-cooked meals.

Mixed-grain rice does not work well for sushi rice, however. Other grains do not absorb the seasoned vinegar well, and too many textures detract from the fillings or toppings that accompany sushi rice.

MAKES 2 CUPS COOKED RICE

1 cup Japanese-style white rice

1 tablespoon mixed grains (see box)

1 cup plus 3 tablespoons water, soft tap or filtered

MAKES 3 CUPS COOKED RICE

1^1/$_2$ cups Japanese-style white rice

1^1/$_2$ tablespoons mixed grains (see box)

1^3/$_4$ cups water, soft tap or filtered

Follow the instructions for washing rice in Cooked White Rice (page 11). Place the washed and drained rice in a pot or rice-cooker bowl, add the mixed grains, and stir to distribute evenly. Add the water, then cook on the stove top or in the rice cooker as directed for Cooked White Rice.

ZAKKOKU MAI MIXTURES

Packets of premixed grains and of grains mixed with dried beans are sold in Japanese grocery stores under the name *zakkoku mai*. But it is a simple matter to create your own *zakkoku* mixture of millet (*hie*, *awa*, and *kibi* are three Japanese varieties), sorghum (*taka kibi*), barley (either flat *oshi mugi* or pearl), rolled oats, quinoa, and/or amaranth. Select at least three grains, measure 1 or more tablespoons of each grain into a small bowl, and stir to mix. To store the mixture, transfer it to a clean, dry glass jar with a tight-fitting lid and keep it on a dark, cool shelf in the cupboard.

COOKED SEMI-POLISHED RICE

HAIGA MAI

Despite a heightened awareness of the nutritional superiority of whole rice grains in recent years, polished white rice at table remains a status symbol in Japan. But *haiga mai* has become a middle-of-the-road alternative for many health-conscious households. The appearance and taste is close to that of fully polished rice, but *haiga*, the nutrient-rich germ, is left intact (though the hull has been removed). Greater care is needed, however, when washing the grains not to dislodge, and accidentally discard, the germ. *Haiga mai*, like *genmai* (brown rice), should be stored at a cool temperature to delay rancidity of the natural oils in the grain's germ. If you have a cool, dark pantry shelf, that's fine. If not, find a spot in your refrigerator (the freezer is too cold).

MAKES 2 CUPS COOKED RICE

1 cup Japanese-style semi-polished rice

1 cup plus 3 tablespoons water, soft tap or filtered

MAKES 3 CUPS COOKED RICE

1½ cups Japanese-style semi-polished rice

Generous 1¾ cups water, soft tap or filtered

Wash the rice: As already noted, great care must be taken when washing partially polished rice to avoid dislodging the nutrient-rich germ. Place the rice in a deep bowl and pour in enough cool tap water just to cover the grains. Using your fingertips in gentle swirling, swishing motions, rinse the grains for about 15 seconds. With slightly scooping motions, gently lift the grains once or twice, to ensure that water flows freely around each grain. Drain the rice. Use your hand or a fine-mesh strainer to hold back the rice as you drain off the water. Some people find it useful to line their strainer with *sarashi* (page 250) or a clean, low-lint kitchen towel. Carefully transfer the rice to a pot or rice-cooker bowl.

Add the water, then cook on the stove top or in the rice cooker as directed for Cooked White Rice (page 11).

COOKED BROWN RICE

GENMAI

When I first arrived in Japan in the 1960s, a stigma was attached to rice that was not fully polished: *genmai*, or brown rice, was associated with low social status and wartime shortages. In the last few decades, however, educated and well-to-do Japanese (many influenced by the macrobiotic movement) have begun to cook *genmai* at home and seek restaurants serving it when dining out.

Some rice cookers have a special setting for brown rice; some have very sophisticated thermostats that can "read" the need to adjust time and temperature controls when cooking brown rice. If your rice cooker has a brown-rice setting, use it. If it does not, you may find that using a two-stage cooking procedure is best, which I describe below.

For the home cook who will not be eating brown rice at every meal, it is important to store *genmai* under optimal conditions to preserve nutrients and fresh taste: a cool (50°F), dark, dry location. The crisper in your refrigerator is fine, but avoid harsh extremes (such as the freezer) and variations in temperature (shifting back and forth from a warm kitchen shelf to a cold basement pantry).

MAKES 2 CUPS COOKED RICE

1 cup Japanese-style brown rice

Scant 2 cups water, soft tap or filtered, if cooking on stove top

1½ cups plus ⅓ cup water, soft tap or filtered, if cooking in rice cooker (plus 1 tablespoon if using two-stage cooking method)

⅛ teaspoon salt

MAKES 3 CUPS COOKED RICE

1½ cups Japanese-style brown rice

2⅓ cups water, soft tap or filtered, if cooking on stove top

2 cups plus 5 tablespoons water, soft tap or filtered, if cooking in rice cooker (plus generous 1 tablespoon water if using two-stage cooking method)

Scant ¼ teaspoon salt

Wash the rice: The purpose of washing brown rice well is to remove any surface impurities and, more important, to make the grains more porous so they become tender faster (even so, cooking time will be extended compared to polished rice). Place the rice in a deep bowl, cover it with cool tap water, and rinse it once following the instructions for washing rice in Cooked White Rice (page 11). Since there will be little to no starch in the rinsing water, it will not perform as *togi-jiru* (page 242), but it's fine for watering plants. Drain the rinsed rice well and return it to the bowl. Cover with fresh water and let sit for at least 6 hours or preferably overnight. You will notice that the grains will become slightly more opaque and that they will begin to swell, absorbing moisture from the soaking. Just before cooking, drain the rice.

To cook on the stove top: Measure the cooking water into a sturdy, straight-sided 3-quart pot with a tight-fitting lid. Add the salt and bring the water to a rolling boil. Stir in the drained rice. When the water returns to a boil, reduce the heat until it is barely simmering, cover tightly, and cook for 40 minutes, or until all the water has been absorbed.

(continued)

Turn off the heat and allow the rice to stand, covered, for at least 10 minutes. When you remove the lid, you will notice small, craterlike depressions on the surface of the rice; this pattern does not appear when cooking milled white rice.

To cook in a rice cooker: Place the drained rice in a rice-cooker bowl. Add the water and salt and stir to mix in the salt. Close the lid, and press the start switch. (If cooking in two stages, this is stage one.)

When the cooking cycle is complete, unplug the appliance but keep it lidded. Let the rice stand for 10 minutes. Remove the lid. You will notice small, craterlike depressions on the surface of the rice; this pattern does not appear when cooking milled white rice. Fluff the rice with a *shamoji* (page 248), using cutting and folding motions. Do

a taste test: If the rice seems tender, you do not need the extra water or cooking time. Enjoy the rice right away, or keep it warm for a later mealtime if your appliance has a warmer feature.

If the rice seems tough, with an especially chew-resistant outer surface (tougher than al dente), proceed to stage two of cooking: Sprinkle the cooked rice with the additional water. Re-cover, plug in the appliance again, and press the switch to start.

When the second cooking cycle has been completed, fluff again with the *shamoji*. The brown rice is ready to eat, or keep it warm for a later mealtime if your appliance has a warmer feature.

CLASSIC SUSHI RICE

SU MESHI

Slightly sweet vinegar-seasoned rice called *su meshi* (literally "tart rice") is the basis for all sushi dishes. For optimal flavor and texture, use freshly cooked, still-warm Japanese-style short-grain white rice that has been rinsed thoroughly before cooking to remove surface starch. If you have it, add a small piece ($1/2$-inch square) of *kombu* to the water in the pot—lay it on top for easy removal after cooking—which will improve the flavor of the rice. As warm rice cools, it is particularly receptive to absorbing the seasoned vinegar (the reason freshly cooked rice is best). If surface starch remains on the rice because it has not been thoroughly rinsed, the cooked rice can become unpleasantly gummy and gluey.

It is difficult to make tender, flavorful sushi rice from brown rice. The hull of brown rice is tough, forming a barrier to absorption of the seasoned vinegar. If you are concerned with nutritional value at mealtime, I suggest you incorporate nutrients through other foods eaten in conjunction with your *su meshi*, rather than look to the rice to supply most essential nutrients.

That said, to add visual drama (an amethyst hue studded with darker spots) and a somewhat enriched nutritional content (polyphenols, iron, dietary fiber), you can add black rice to white rice for sushi dishes. Instructions for making black sushi rice seasoned with sweet pink plum vinegar and *aka-jiso* leaves is included in Festive Flower Sushi Rolls (page 33).

MAKES GENEROUS 1 CUP SEASONED VINEGAR

1 cup rice vinegar

2 tablespoons sugar

Scant $1/2$ teaspoon salt

$1/2$-inch piece kombu (page 266), optional

MAKES 3 CUPS SUSHI RICE

3 cups Cooked White Rice (page 11), freshly made and still warm

Generous $1/2$ cup seasoned vinegar

MAKES 5 CUPS SUSHI RICE

5 cups Cooked White Rice (page 11), freshly made and still warm

Scant 1 cup seasoned vinegar

Make the seasoned vinegar: Combine all the ingredients in a small pot; the addition of *kombu* will boost flavor. Place over low heat and stir until the sugar and salt dissolve. Remove from the heat and let cool naturally. If you will not be using all of the seasoned vinegar within an hour or so, transfer the unused portion to a lidded glass jar, with the *kombu* (if used). When the steam is no longer rising, cap the jar and refrigerate. It will keep for 1 week.

For the best results, transfer the freshly cooked rice to a *handai* (page 247). If you do not have one, use the widest, shallowest bowl you have (preferably not metal, as it retains heat and often imparts a metallic taste to the rice). A wooden salad bowl is fine, as long as it does not reek of garlic and/or olive oil.

Using gentle cutting and folding motions, toss the warm rice with a *shamoji* (page 248), while fanning it with an *uchiwa* (page 248). The fanning cools the rice rapidly without allowing condensation to form. A large, broad

(continued)

spatula and a stiff piece of cardboard can substitute in a pinch for the traditional equipment.

When clouds of steam are no longer rising, drizzle some of the seasoned vinegar over the warm rice. Start with just a few tablespoons. Continue to use gentle cutting and folding motions and to fan as you season the rice, adding the vinegar bit by bit. Taste occasionally to verify the seasoning, erring on the side of tart. Some of the vinegar evaporates as the rice continues to cool, making it milder than you might have first thought.

Cover the cooled seasoned rice with plastic wrap and keep it at cool room temperature until ready to serve, but no more than 6 hours. Avoid extreme cold: refrigerated sushi rice gets tough and crusty; frozen sushi rice becomes mushy when thawed.

BLACK RICE WITH GREEN SOYBEANS

KŌDAI KURO MAI TO ÉDAMAMÉ

Indigenous heirloom rice strains, known collectively as *kōdai mai*, have experienced a revival of sorts among Japan's younger population. Packages of both black and red rice can be found on many supermarket shelves. Black rice (*kōdai kuro mai*) cooked with (not instead of) white rice results in a marvelous purple-hued, nutritionally enhanced mixture. Studded with green soybeans and garnished with toasted white sesame seeds, this dish makes a stunning backdrop for any meal.

SERVES 4

> 1 cup Japanese-style white rice
>
> 1¹/₂ tablespoons black rice
>
> 1¹/₄ cups cold water
>
> ¹/₂ cup frozen édamamé in the pod or ¹/₂ cup fresh pods plus 1 teaspoon kosher salt
>
> 1 tablespoon white sesame seeds, freshly dry-roasted (page 245)

Wash the white rice, following the instructions for washing rice in Cooked White Rice (page 11). Briefly rinse and drain the black rice. Place the washed and drained white rice in a pot or rice-cooker bowl, add the black rice, and stir to distribute evenly. Add the water, then cook on the stove top or in the rice cooker as directed for Cooked White Rice.

While the rice is cooking, cook the *édamamé*. If using frozen *édamamé*, bring a pot of water to a rolling boil over high heat and add the still-frozen pods. When the water returns to a boil, scoop out the pods with a slotted spoon. (If using thawed pods, drop them into the boiling water and remove them after 15 seconds.) To preserve nutrients and flavor, do not refresh in cold water. When the pods are cool enough to handle comfortably, remove the beans; for a more attractive appearance, discard thin "skins."

If using fresh *édamamé*, place them in a sturdy plastic bag with the salt. Toss to coat the pods, and then rub to remove the fine fuzz on the outside of the pods. Bring a pot of water to a rolling boil over high heat, add the pods, and cook for 7 or 8 minutes. They are ready when a few of the pods look as if they are splitting at the seam. Scoop out the pods with a slotted spoon. As with frozen pods, do *not* refresh in cold water. When the pods are cool enough to handle comfortably, treat as you would frozen pods.

When the rice is fully cooked (for the stove-top method, this means all the water has cooked away; in a rice cooker, the machine typically flips over from the "cook" to the "warm" cycle), and just before it is allowed to self-steam, scatter the *édamamé* over the cooked rice. Re-cover the pot or cooker and allow the rice and beans to steam together for at least 5 minutes or up to 20 minutes.

Using a *shamoji* (page 248) or other paddlelike spoon or spatula, carefully mix the rice and beans. Use light cutting, scooping, and folding motions to avoid smashing the beans and mashing the rice. Scoop out into bowls, garnish with a sprinkle of the sesame seeds, and serve piping hot. Or, let the rice mixture cool before shaping into *omusubi* (see Hand-Pressed Rice with Fillings, page 45) or into log-shaped *tawara* bundles (see Rice with Salted Cherry Blossoms, page 25) to pack in a picnic lunch.

RICE WITH FRESH BAMBOO SHOOTS

TAKÉNOKO GOHAN

Many versions of this springtime classic add fried tōfu to the sliced bamboo to boost nutrition and provide a pleasantly chewy texture that contrasts to the tender-crisp shoots. I prefer to use bits of dried *yuba* instead, since the brittle sheets that inevitably break would go to waste otherwise.

SERVES 4 TO 6

> 3¹/₂ to 4 ounces boiled fresh bamboo shoot (page 92), preferably the tip or center section, thinly cut kushi-gata style (page 244)
>
> 1¹/₂ cups stock, preferably Basic Kelp Stock (page 75) or Sun-Dried Gourd Ribbon Stock (page 76)
>
> 2 teaspoons mirin
>
> 2 teaspoons light-colored soy sauce
>
> 1 sheet hoshi yuba (page 261), broken into confetti-like bits (about 2 tablespoons)
>
> 1¹/₂ cups Japanese-style white rice
>
> 10 to 12 sprigs ki no mé (page 2586), or ¹/₄ teaspoon kona-zanshō (page 258) mixed with a pinch of salt

To maximize the aroma of fresh bamboo shoots and to ensure they are tender, arrange the slices in a shallow pot or skillet, fanning them out to cover the surface in a single, or at most double, layer. Add the stock, mirin, and soy sauce. Place an *otoshi-buta* (page 243) or a circle of parchment paper directly on the bamboo shoots and bring to a boil over medium heat. Lower the heat to maintain a gentle simmer and cook for 2 minutes. Skim away any froth that appears with a fine-mesh skimmer.

Remove the pot from the heat, lift the lid or parchment, and scatter the *yuba* over the shoots. Replace the *otoshi-buta* or parchment and let the bamboo shoot sit until cool. It is during this slow cooling process that flavor is transferred to the *yuba*. When the cooking liquid has cooled to nearly room temperature, strain it into a measuring cup, setting aside the bamboo shoot and *yuba*. If need be, add more stock or water to the liquid to total 1³/₄ cups.

To cook the rice on the stove top: Wash the rice, following the instructions for washing rice in Cooked White Rice (page 11). Place the washed and drained rice and the reserved flavored liquid in a 3-quart lidded pot. Place the bamboo shoot and *yuba* on top of the rice. Cover the pot with a tight-fitting lid, place over high heat, and cook for about 5 minutes, or until the liquid begins to bubble. Adjust the heat to maintain a steady but not-too-vigorous boil and continue to cook, covered, for about 5 minutes longer, or until all the liquid has been absorbed. Remove the pot from the heat and allow the rice to steam with retained heat for another 10 to 15 minutes.

To cook the rice in a rice cooker: Wash the white rice, following the instructions for washing rice in Cooked White Rice (page 11). Place the washed and drained rice and the reserved flavored liquid in the rice-cooker bowl. Place the bamboo shoot and *yuba* on top of the rice. Make sure the liquid is at cool room temperature before pressing the start switch of a thermostatically controlled rice cooker. Close the lid and press the start switch.

When the rice is ready, with a *shamoji* (page 248) or other paddlike spoon or sqatula, use light cutting and flipping motions to distribute the bamboo shoot and *yuba* evenly throughout the rice. The bottom surface develops a slightly caramelized *okogé*, or crust, that is especially tasty. Garnish individual portions with *ki no mé* sprigs or a sprinkle of the *kona-zanshō* mixture.

RICE WITH MIXED MUSHROOMS

KINOKO GOHAN

Each season has its own culinary pleasures and treasures, but most Japanese would agree that autumn offers the greatest variety of foodstuffs. The phrase *aki no mikaku* (autumnal delicacies) includes a wide range of dishes made from fall foods, some cultivated, others foraged. One of my personal favorites is *kinako gohan*, a pilaflike dish infused with a rich, woodsy broth produced by briefly braising mushrooms that are later tossed with the rice. I like to balance the scent of the forest with the bracing aroma of the seashore by garnishing my rice with *ao nori*, a green sea herb.

SERVES 4

8 to 10 ounces fresh mushrooms (see box, page 22), cleaned and trimmed (page 272)

2 cups stock, preferably Basic Kelp Stock (page 75)

3 tablespoons saké

3 tablespoons mirin

2 tablespoons light-colored soy sauce

2 cups Japanese-style white rice

1 teaspoon ao nori (page 256)

The first step is to extract a flavorful broth from the mushrooms without totally depleting them of flavor. Pour the stock into a pot, season with the saké, mirin, and soy sauce, and bring to a boil over medium heat. Add the mushrooms and reduce the heat to maintain a steady, not-too-vigorous simmer. Use an *otoshi-buta* (page 243) to keep the mushrooms submerged as they cook, or stir several times to achieve the same result. Cook the mushrooms for 2 to 2¹/₂ minutes (they should be aromatic but not too wilted in appearance), and then strain the cooking liquid into a

measuring cup, pressing the mushrooms gently to extract as much liquid as possible. Add more stock or cold water to the liquid to total 2¹/₃ cups.

To cook the rice on the stove top: Wash the rice, following the instructions for washing rice in Cooked White Rice (page 11). Place the washed and drained rice and the reserved flavored liquid in a 3- to 3¹/₂-quart pot, then cook as directed for Cooked White Rice. When the rice has finished active cooking, remove the pot from the heat, toss in the reserved mushrooms, re-cover the pot immediately, and allow the rice to self-steam for 10 minutes.

Then, with a *shamoji* (page 248) or other paddlelike spoon or spatula, use light cutting and folding motions to distribute the mushrooms evenly throughout the rice. As you cut and fold, you will notice a crusty layer of rice on the bottom of the pot. When it is time to serve the rice, make sure that each portion includes some of this delicious *okogé*, literally "the honorable burnt bits."

To cook the rice in a rice cooker: Wash the rice, following the instructions for washing rice in Cooked White Rice (page 11). Place the washed and drained rice and the reserved flavored liquid in a rice-cooker bowl, then cook as directed in Cooked White Rice. When the active cooking cycle is complete, toss in the reserved mushrooms, re-cover the cooker immediately, and allow the rice to self-steam for 10 minutes. Then, with a *shamoji*, cut and fold the mushrooms into the rice as for the stove-top rice. There will be relatively less *okogé* when using a rice cooker.

Serve the rice hot, warm, or at room temperature. If you wish to keep the rice for several hours before eating,

(continued)

let it cool naturally to room temperature, then cover it with a clean, damp cloth and plastic wrap to prevent it from drying out and to trap in aromas. No refrigeration is necessary for up to 4 hours in a cool room.

If you do refrigerate the rice, "freshen" it briefly in a microwave (about 20 seconds on the "reheat" or "warm" cycle) or in a steamer (about 10 minutes over low, steady steam heat) before serving.

Whether you are serving the rice hot, warm, or at room temperature (this is a favorite picnic dish in Japan), garnish with *ao nori* just before eating. To heighten the seashore aroma of the sea herb, invite diners to rub a pinch of the *ao nori* briefly between their thumb and index finger before sprinkling it over the rice.

PRIZED MUSHROOMS

For a complex, full-flavored pilaf, use a combination of ruffled *maitaké*, black-capped shiitaké, pearly gray *shiméji*, ivory enoki, and/or golden chanterelle mushrooms. The most prized, and wildly expensive, wild mushrooms are *matsutaké*, redolent with the scent of pine trees near which they can be found. If you can source these near you (they grow in parts of Canada, the Pacific Northwest, and Scandinavia, in addition to Korea, Japan, and Mongolia), you are in for an extravagant treat: use just these.

RICE TOSSED WITH RADISH GREENS

NA MESHI

If you see daikon at your market with its green leafy tops still attached, I urge you to purchase the root whole (the bushier the top tuft, the better). As soon as you return to your kitchen, slice off the green tuft and set it aside. Wrap the root in damp paper towels and/or newspaper and store in a cool, dark spot. Over the next few days, you can enjoy the daikon in many preparations.

But now, turn your attention to the green tops. Although they can be blanched and eaten as you would any leafy vegetable, I like to use them to make *furikaké*, a seasoned, semi-dried, confetti-like condiment. The sprinkles are easy to dry in your oven, or you can dry them outside or with a dehydrator (see box, page 24). They are especially tasty tossed into steaming rice, a dish called *na meshi*, or "leafy rice."

Pictured on the front cover

SERVES 4, WITH LEFTOVER SPRINKLES

FURIKAKÉ

Large tuft of daikon tops, turnip tops, and/or other dark greens such as kale, collards, or beet greens, 4 to 5 ounces

¼ teaspoon salt

3 tablespoons black or white sesame seeds, freshly dry-roasted (page 245)

3 cups Cooked White Rice (page 11), freshly made and still warm

Make the *furikaké*: If using daikon tops, rinse well to remove any soil clinging to the base of the tuft. If using other dark greens, line them up so that their tougher stems can be tied together with kitchen twine. Bring a small pot of water to a rolling boil, add the salt, and blanch the daikon tuft for less than a minute, or until it turns bright green. Remove the tuft and immediately immerse it in a bowl of cold water to stop the cooking. Lift the tuft from the water right away, firmly squeezing out any excess water.

If using kale or other tougher greens, place the bunch of leaves, tough stems first, in the salted boiling water, holding the bunch by the leafy tops until you feel the remainder begin to wilt in the water (about 1 minute). Then press to submerge the entire bundle in the boiling water and cook for 2 to 3 minutes after the water returns to a boil. Remove the bundle and refresh in a bowl of cold water, squeezing out any excess moisture when cool enough to handle comfortably.

Wrap your greens in a kitchen or paper towel to blot up any additional moisture. Using a sharp knife, chop coarsely, then mince finely (a food processor or other machine tends to rip leafy fibers, compromising their flavor and appearance).

Set your oven to the lowest temperature (usually 200°F). Line a baking sheet with aluminum foil or parchment paper and spread the minced greens on it. Oven-dry for 20 to 25 minutes, turning the pieces every 7 or 8 minutes to expose all surfaces to the heat. As the greens dry, they will become quite brittle, much darker, and slightly aromatic.

(continued)

Once the greens are ready, rub them between your hands to break any clusters into finer pieces, then mix with the sesame seeds. You will have about ¹/₃ cup. Set aside 1 or 2 tablespoons for adding to the rice. Let the remainder cool completely, then store in a tightly sealed glass jar in the refrigerator for up to 1 month.

Sprinkle the *furikaké* over the hot rice. Using a *shamoji* (page 248) or other paddlelike spoon or spatula, gently fold in the sprinkles, distributing them evenly. The heat and moisture of the rice will be sufficient to rehydrate the greens. Serve piping hot or allow to cool to room temperature.

DRYING GREENS TWO WAYS:
OLD-FASHIONED AND NATURAL OR CLEVER AND MODERN

If you live in a dry, sunny climate, you might be able to dry your greens the old-fashioned way, on a sunny veranda or window ledge. Spread them out on a fine-mesh surface, then lightly cover them with a cloth to keep them from scattering in the wind (and to keep birds from pecking at them). The cloth must be open-weave muslin, gauze, or cheesecloth for proper ventilation.

But most people, myself included (Japan's climate boasts high humidity), will need to use an oven or special drying equipment, especially if they want to store the condiment for more than a few days. I find that an electric dehydrator with multiple trays or shelves is the most reliable and convenient way to dry the greens. If you own one, follow the instructions that came with your machine.

RICE WITH SALTED CHERRY BLOSSOMS

SAKURA GOHAN

Flower-viewing (*hanami*) parties in Japan date back to the eighth century, though in those days it was *umé* (plum), not *sakura* (cherry), that was the flower in the limelight. The shift to cherry blossoms took place in the spring of 1594, at an extravagant affair hosted by Toyotomi Hideyoshi at Yoshinoyama, in Nara. The guest list for the event was long (nearly five thousand names!) and illustrious, including Tokugawa Ieyasu, the warrior-statesman who became Japan's first shogun. The brief but beautiful blossoming of cherry trees rapidly became an apt symbol for the precious but fleeting nature of life under the shogun's feudal rule. A make-merry-while-you-can attitude encouraged an odd mixture of solemn reverence and outrageous sport.

Modern, urban *hanami* rituals continue in much the same manner. Groups of business colleagues, friends, and family spread out tarps or old-fashioned *goza* (woven reed mats) beneath flowering branches at public parks and proceed to eat and drink (excessively) together! Open-air *hanami* parties can become boisterous, though in a good-natured way.

Obentō are an integral part of Japan's food culture and *hanami bentō*, flower-viewing boxed lunches, are part of Japan's springtime culinary customs. This rice, the essence of springtime and a perfect *hanami bentō* menu item, is often shaped into easy-to-eat bundles. I have included instructions on shaping it should you wish to pack it into your next ode-to-springtime picnic hamper.

Pictured on page 168

MAKES 20 TO 28 BITE-SIZE BUNDLES

20 or more salt-preserved cherry blossoms (see box, page 26)

2 tablespoons white sesame seeds, freshly dry-roasted (page 245)

3 cups Cooked White Rice (page 11), freshly made and still warm

4 to 6 salt-preserved cherry leaves, optional

Shake off loose crystals of salt from the cherry blossoms. If the blossoms seem thickly crusted with salt, use gentle rubbing motions to help remove the excess. Do not soak or rinse the flowers in water. The delicate floral aroma is volatile and will be lost. The salt that clings to the blossoms after shaking is needed to season the cooked rice and to retard spoilage when served hours later at a picnic.

Select whole flowers that look pretty for garnish, setting aside several for each portion. Finely mince the remaining blossoms. Scatter the minced blossoms and the sesame seeds over the hot rice. With a *shamoji* (page 248) dipped into cold water (to prevent the rice from sticking to it), toss the rice to distribute the flowers and seeds evenly, using gentle cutting and tossing motions to avoid mashing the rice.

Serve the rice lightly mounded in rice bowls, and top each bowl with a whole blossom or two.

Or, form the rice into loglike bundles, a shape known as *tawara*, or "rice sheath." *Maku no uchi* rice molds (page 249) come in two sizes, yielding either 5 or 7 log-shaped bundles (the latter are slightly smaller) from the same quantity of cooked rice (about $3/4$ cup). Separate the mold into its three

(continued)

component parts: a rectangular frame and two strips. Each strip will have either 5 or 7 curved and hollowed "valleys," and 6 or 8 pointed "mountains." Soak all three of the mold parts in cold water to cover.

Lift the rectangular frame from the cold water and set it on your work surface (do not dry it off). Fit one strip, with the mountains facing up, into the frame. Dip your hands in cold water, then scoop up one-fourth of the warm rice and fill the mold with it, distributing it evenly. Take the remaining strip of the mold from the cold water in which it is soaking, shaking off the excess water. Insert it, mountains pointing down, into the frame.

With your thumbs, press down evenly on the top strip while gently sliding the frame up with your other fingers. Lift the frame off the rice and set it soaking in water for the next use. Peel off the top strip from the rice, invert the rice, and peel off the remaining strip. With fingers dampened in cold water, separate the bundles of rice. Repeat three times to shape all the rice into bundles.

If you have been able to source salted cherry leaves, use them to line your serving platter or individual lunch boxes. Rinse the leaves briefly in cold water and pat dry just before using, to retain as much aroma as possible. The leaves also help retard spoilage of the rice.

Arrange the rice bundles in rows, or stack them in pyramid-like mounds. Garnish some of the bundles with the whole blossoms. If you are making the bundles more than 30 minutes in advance of serving, cover them with plastic wrap to prevent the rice from drying out. The rice bundles will keep well at cool room temperature for up to 5 hours.

EDIBLE CHERRY BLOSSOMS AND LEAVES

The blossoms and leaves of certain varieties of *sakura* are made edible by preserving them in salt, in a process known as *shio-zuké*. Deeply colored *yaezakura* blossoms are especially prized, while the leaves of the pale-petaled *Somei Yoshino* are preferred.

Cherry leaves, and to a lesser extent the flowers, contain coumarin, a chemical compound that accounts for the distinctive sweet cherry aroma found in many plants (including cinnamon bark and chamomile). Consumed in large quantities, coumarin can be mildly toxic to humans, though many practitioners of *kampōyaku*, Japan's herbal medicine, make use of coumarin's anticoagulant properties.

The most common use of salt-preserved cherry blossoms (pictured on page 252) is to make a savory, tea-like broth often served at wedding receptions. They are also used in a wide variety of confections.

Blossoms and leaves are sold in vacuum-sealed bags; the blossoms are sometimes sold in glass jars. Their aroma dissipates quickly after opening, so always transfer unused blossoms or leaves to a container that can be sealed tightly and refrigerate. They will keep for up to 2 months.

SKILLET-TOSSED CURRIED RICE

KARÉ FUMI CHAHAN

Historically, the Japanese have adapted culinary practices from many different cultures, blending them into distinctively Japanese dishes. The sweet red peppers, red onions, and celery used in this dish first came to the Japanese table by way of American specialty-produce suppliers toward the end of the twentieth century; today all three are grown in Japan. Prominent Asian influences on Japanese cooking include India and China, and in this dish we see evidence of both culinary traditions: the Chinese practice of stir-frying already-cooked rice combines with Indian-inspired curry flavoring to make a spicy pilaf.

In most Japanese households, a generous portion of this rice dish would be served as a main course with soup—perhaps a creamy-textured one such as Springtime in a Bowl (page 87) and pickled vegetables such as Sour and Spicy Gourd Pickles (page 212).

SERVES 4 AS AN ACCOMPANIMENT TO SEVERAL SMALL DISHES; SERVES 2 AS A MAIN COURSE WITH SOUP AND PICKLES

1 teaspoon vegetable oil

$1/3$ cup finely diced red onion

$1/4$ cup finely diced celery

$1/4$ cup finely diced red bell pepper

$1/8$ teaspoon salt

$1/4$ teaspoon Japanese curry powder (page 257)

3 cups cold cooked rice, preferably Cooked Brown Rice (page 15), refrigerated leftovers are perfect

2 to 3 tablespoons stock, preferably vegetarian stock (page 76), or water

$1^1/2$ teaspoons soy sauce

1 tablespoon finely chopped celery leaves

Heat the oil in a wok or 12-inch skillet. Add the onion and stir-fry vigorously for about 2 minutes, or until aromatic, slightly wilted, and a bit caramelized. Add the celery and continue to stir-fry, tossing vigorously, for another minute, or until the celery turns slightly translucent. Add the red pepper, toss to combine, and then sprinkle the salt and curry powder over all the vegetables. Continue to stir-fry, tossing continuously to ensure even distribution of the seasonings, for about 1 minute, or until aromatic.

Add the rice to the center of the wok. Working quickly, break up any clumps with a broad wooden spoon or spatula, using cutting and tapping motions. Toss the contents of the wok thoroughly to ensure even distribution of the rice and curried vegetables until the rice is heated through.

Mix together 2 tablespoons of the stock and the soy sauce. Again working quickly, drizzle the mixture into the wok in a spiral pattern, starting from the outer rim and moving toward the center. The liquid will create a curry-flavored sauce. Toss the the rice and vegetables to coat them in the sauce. Add the remaining tablespoon stock or water if the rice seems dry.

To preserve aroma and texture contrast, add the celery leaves as you remove the wok from the heat, tossing the contents lightly to evenly distribute them. Serve the rice piping hot in deep bowls. Most Japanese eat this dish with a small shovel-like utensil called a *rengé*. A soupspoon makes a fine substitute.

MINI MEAL IN A BOWL

MINI-DON

Tableware is an integral part of Japanese meal planning and service. The name for a type of food and the dish on or in which it is served are often the same. *Domburi*, often abbreviated as *don*, illustrates this point: the word describes both a deep (usually) ceramic bowl and the food set atop rice in the bowl.

Domburi dining is casual fare, often making use of leftovers from previous meals. A handful of the recipes found in other chapters of this book are suitable *donburi* candidates (see box on page 30 for suggestions). This recipe assembles already-cooked food that can be reheated and then garnishes it (dresses it up) with fresh cucumbers and radishes. Here, I chose the playful Glazed Eel Look-Alike to show you how to create this type of meal in a bowl.

If you have small Japanese rice bowls or large tea cups without handles, they are perfect for serving this dish. Small plates with a flange or raised edge can also be used.

SERVES 4

8 to 12 strips Glazed Eel Look-Alike (page 188), without glaze applied (but glaze made and kept warm)

3 cups Cooked White Rice (page 11), freshly made and still warm

2 teaspoons white or black sesame seeds, freshly dry-roasted (page 245), optional

1/2 teaspoon kona-zanshō (page 258)

GARNISHES

2 small red radishes, cut into thin sticks

1 small cucumber, preferably Japanese cucumber, sliced lengthwise, then cut into thin slices on the diagonal

Use warm, freshly fried eel strips or reheat ones that were previously fried. To reheat the eel strips, use a toaster oven or a conventional oven. If you have refrigerated fried strips, reheat them cold. If you have frozen fried strips, you will have greatest success if you reheat them directly from the freezer.

If using a toaster oven, place the strips, nori side up, on a broiler pan that fits about 2 inches below the toaster coils. Toast for 1 minute on a medium-high setting. Flip them over (nori side down) and toast for 45 seconds to 1 minute. Blot away any moisture with paper towels and let the strips sit for 2 or 3 minutes. Then, toast the strips again for about 1 minute on each side and about 1½ minutes if they were frozen. If it appears the edges may scorch, loosely cover the strips with aluminum foil after flipping them over.

If using a conventional oven, preheat to 200°F. Place the eel strips on a rack set over an aluminum foil–lined baking pan. If you are heating refrigerated strips, bake them for 2 to 3 minutes, or until warm and dry. If the strips are frozen, bake them for 3 to 4 minutes. If necessary, cover the strips loosely with foil after 1 minute to prevent the edges from scorching.

(continued)

Assemble the mini meal: Loosely fill 4 small bowls with the rice, putting about ³/₄ cup rice in each. Sprinkle the sesame seeds over the rice, dividing them evenly. One at a time, dip the eel strips in the warm glaze and place over the rice in a bowl; arrange 2 or 3 strips on each rice bowl. Or, spoon, drizzle, or paint (with a pastry brush) the glaze over the eel strips before placing them on the rice. Sprinkle with the *kona-zanshō*. Garnish each serving with a few sticks of radish and slices of cucumber. Serve at once.

SUGGESTED PAIRINGS OF RICE AND TOPPINGS

- Cooked Brown Rice (page 15) topped with Heaven-and-Earth Tempura Pancakes (page 109)
- Rice with Mixed Mushrooms (page 21) topped with Crispy and Creamy Kabocha Croquettes (page 118)
- Rice Tossed with Radish Greens (page 23) topped with Soy-Braised Kabocha and Wheat Wheels (page 139)
- Rice Tossed with Radish Greens (page 23) topped with Two Kinds of Tōfu, Amber Braised with Carrots (page 174)

TEMPLE SCATTERED-STYLE SUSHI

GOMOKU SHŌJIN CHIRASHI-ZUSHI

Most people associate sushi with raw fish, and indeed sushi dishes that make use of fresh fish abound. But the ingredient that truly defines sushi is the vinegar-seasoned rice, and many delightful vegetarian sushi dishes are popular. One that is often served on celebratory occasions at home, rather than in a restaurant setting, is *chirashi-zushi*. The name means "scattered," and the platter recalls a pilaf or paella that has ingredients both tossed with the rice and decoratively arranged on top of it. The version I offer here is decorated in the *bara*, or "random," manner, and is an impressive dish to set out on a buffet. It is also an excellent vehicle for clearing the refrigerator of bits and pieces left from previous meals (see box on page 32 for ideas).

The various subrecipes for toppings and items for tossing with the rice make use of several other recipes. Preparing everything from scratch on the day you want to serve this dish would be a formidable (though not impossible) task. Instead, I urge you to make the subrecipes, a few at a time, days in advance. Enjoy the items, such as gingery enoki mushrooms with carrots, first as an appetizer, setting aside a larger cache for the sushi presentation a few days later.

Or, make your *chirashi-zushi* a communal project: ask your guests to make a component dish (much as you might for a potluck dinner) and assemble the sushi together. Only the rice needs to be cooked and seasoned on the day of your party, ideally a few hours before you plan to serve it.

SERVES 6 TO 8

OMELET LOOK-ALIKE (TAMAGO YAKI MODOKI)

    5 or 6 sheets hoshi yuba, softened (page 261)

    1/2 to 2/3 cup stock, preferably Basic Kelp Stock (page 75)

    1 tablespoon saké

    1 teaspoon sugar

    1 teaspoon light-colored soy sauce

    1 kuchinashi no mi (page 269), cracked, or a few drops yellow food coloring

    1 tablespoon white or black sesame seeds, freshly dry-roasted (page 245)

    5 cups Classic Sushi Rice (page 17)

    1/3 to 1/2 cup Granny's Sun-Dried Radish (page 142), well drained and coarsely chopped

    5 to 6 feet plum-infused gourd ribbons (see Festive Flower Sushi Rolls, page 33)

    2 large dried shiitaké mushrooms, prepared as instructed in Pom-Pom Sushi (page 43), well drained and thinly sliced

    12 to 16 snow peas, strings and stems removed, blanched for 1 minute, and cut into narrow strips on the diagonal

Prepare the omelet look-alike: Lay the softened *yuba* sheets in a nonstick, enamel-lined, or other nonreactive saucepan or skillet large enough to hold them without tearing or folding them. Stacking the sheets is fine as long as the top sheet will be covered by liquid. Add the stock, saké, sugar, and soy sauce.

If you have been able to source *kuchinashi no mi*, place a cracked pod in your pan and let it soak for 5 minutes, or until the liquid turns bright yellow. Remove the pod (save in a closed plastic bag in the refrigerator for another use within 1 week), and allow the *yuba* sheets to soak in the yellow liquid for 2 or 3 minutes longer before applying

(continued)

heat. If you are using yellow food coloring instead, add the drops to the liquid just before placing the pan over the heat. Cover with a circle of parchment paper (a wooden *otoshi-buta* would stain yellow).

Place the pan over low heat and bring the liquid to a simmer. Cook gently for 2 minutes, or until the liquid is reduced and just barely moistening the *yuba* sheets. Remove the pan from the heat and allow the sheets to cool, still covered with the parchment, in the pan. It is during this cooling stage that most of the delicate flavor of the simmering liquid is absorbed and the color intensifies. Transfer the sheets to a lidded container if not using immediately.

When ready to use, remove the *yuba* sheets from the remaining liquid and blot gently on paper towels. Cut the sheets in half lengthwise, and then stack the halves. Slice the sheets thinly, creating shreds. Set aside to use as a garnish for the finished dish; cover with plastic wrap to prevent them from drying out.

Sprinkle the sesame seeds over the sushi rice and, using a *shamoji* (page 248), toss well to distribute evenly, using light folding and cutting motions. Scatter the sun-dried radish over the rice and again toss with light folding and cutting motions to distribute evenly.

Lightly mound the rice mixture on a large platter or tray. The dish can be assembled to this point 3 to 4 hours in advance of serving. Cover it snugly with a clean, damp cloth and/or plastic wrap and keep it away from extremes of hot or cold.

When ready to serve, scatter the *yuba* shreds across the seasoned rice, allowing some of the white rice to peek out from under the yellow shreds. Loosely tie the gourd ribbon in knots at 2-inch intervals, beginning at one end and working your way to the other. When the knots are uniformly shaped, pull each slightly to make it snug, then cut between them to separate. Scatter these randomly across the platter. (The pink color may bleed a bit, so do this just before serving.)

If the shiitaké slices seem too moist, blot them with paper towels, then scatter them across the platter. Finally, scatter the snow peas across the platter. (Green vegetables turn brown with extended exposure to vinegar, so do this just before serving.) Serve at room temperature.

OTHER OPTIONS

In lieu of Granny's Sun-Dried Radish, consider one or more of the following, each drained and coarsely chopped, to total about 1/3 cup:
- Gingery Enoki Mushrooms with Carrots (page 127)
- Successivley Simmered Kōya-Dōfu and Vegetables (page 140)
- Hijiki with Thick Fried Tōfu (page 146)
- Tricolored Vegetables Rolled in Fried Tōfu (page 182)

In lieu of, or in addition to, snow peas, consider one or more of the following as a garnish:
- Briefly blanched shelled fava beans or *édamamé*
- Briefly blanched green beans or asparagus, sliced on the diagonal into thin slivers
- Coarsely chopped or shredded fresh herbs such as *shiso* (page 258) or mint

In lieu of, or in addition to, plum-infused gourd ribbon, consider store-bought pink or red pickled ginger, drained and clustered decoratively on top.

FESTIVE FLOWER SUSHI ROLLS

MATSURI-ZUSHI

A specialty of Chiba Prefecture near Tokyo, plump *matsuri-zushi* rolls appear on family tables at holiday time and at many community events. This sort of decorative culinary art was most likely developed to showcase the bounty of the Chiba region, especially sheets of nori from the local aquatic plantations off the coast of the Boso Peninsula. The eye-catching patterns have captured the interest (hearts and appetites) of many Japanese, including blogging home-makers wanting to make cute *obentō* lunch boxes for their children. A subculture of decorative rice dishes known as *kazari-zushi* (literally "decorative sushi") has emerged that applies many of the same techniques.

In creating these festive rolls, I have taken several standard components of the decorative sushi approach and added a few original (and slightly quirky) twists. I offer a vegetarian flower roll using three types of tartly seasoned sushi rice: classic white, pale pink (dyed and scented with plum vinegar), and darker pink, made with black rice (the color is more amethyst than onyx). Instructions for constructing the patterned rolls follow a "logic" that will seem familiar to anyone who knits or embroiders using pattern books: patience and practice will produce impressive results.

MAKES 8 ROLLS, 24 OR 32 PIECES

PLUM-INFUSED GOURD RIBBONS

 1 package (³/₄ ounce, 20 grams) kampyō (page 262), about 20 feet, preferably uncut

 1-inch square kombu (page 266), optional

 1 to 1¹/₂ cups water

 ¹/₄ cup sugar

 2 tablespoons plum vinegar (page 284) or the deep pink liquid surrounding uméboshi (page 283) that have been pickled with aka-jiso leaves

 2 tablespoons rice vinegar

 10 or more salt-brined yukari (aka-jiso) leaves, the kind found packed with uméboshi

 ¹/₄ teaspoon kosher salt

SEASONED RICE VINEGAR

 ³/₄ cup rice vinegar

 3 tablespoons sugar

 Scant ¹/₂ teaspoon salt

 1-inch square kombu (page 266), optional

 1 bunch mitsuba (page 257) or watercress, about 2 ounces

 2 cups cooked black rice (Black Rice with Green Soybeans, prepared without the soybeans, page 19) freshly made and still warm (or zapped in the microwave for about 20 seconds)

 3 cups Cooked White Rice (page 11), freshly made and still warm

 8 full-size sheets yaki nori (page 267)

 Soy sauce for serving (optional)

Prepare the plum-infused gourd ribbons: Put the *kampyō* and *kombu* in a glass jar, add the water, and set aside to soak for at least 30 minutes. Remove the *kampyō* and the *kombu* from the water. Reserve the soaking water to use as a flavorful stock in other recipes; it will keep in a lidded glass jar in the refrigerator for up to 3 days. The *kombu* can be saved and used to make Rice Friends (page 152).

(continued)

Mix together the sugar, plum vinegar, rice vinegar, and *yukari* leaves in a small nonreactive pot. Apply the salt to the softened *kampyō*, rubbing as though you were trying to remove a spot from clothing. The gourd ribbons will become much softer and somewhat velvety to the touch. Rinse off the excess salt. Bring a saucepan filled with water to a vigorous boil, add the gourd ribbons, and boil for 2 minutes. Drain, and while the gourd ribbons are still warm, transfer them to the pot holding the plum vinegar mixture.

Place the pot over medium heat and bring to a simmer, stirring to dissolve the sugar and ensure even color distribution throughout the gourd ribbons. Remove from the heat and allow the gourd ribbons to cool, naturally, in the pot. It is during this cooling-down process that the plum flavor is thoroughly absorbed. Transfer the gourd ribbons, with the liquid remaining in the pot, to a glass jar, letting it cool before covering and chilling for at least 30 minutes. The cooled marinating liquid will be used to season the pink sushi rice.

Rinse the small pot and use it to prepare the seasoned rice vinegar: Combine all the ingredients in the pot; the addition of *kombu* will boost flavor. Place over low heat and stir until the sugar and salt dissolve. Remove from the heat and let cool naturally. When steam is no longer rising, transfer to a lidded glass jar, including the *kombu*. Chill for at least 30 minutes.

Prepare the *mitsuba*: Line up the *mitsuba* stalks so that the stems can be tied together with kitchen twine to make a neat bunch. Trim the tough stem ends so that the remaining stalks are completely edible. Bring a small pot of water to a rolling boil and remove it from the heat. Holding the bunch by its leafy end, dip the stem ends into the scalding water until they turn bright green and wilt ever so slightly. Release the bundle, allowing the leafy tops to be briefly submerged in the pot, and then scoop them out right away. Rinse the greens briefly under cold water, then squeeze gently to remove excess moisture. Snip the string and divide the stalks into 8 portions, keeping them aligned.

Make the black sushi rice: Following the directions in Classic Sushi Rice (page 17), season the black rice with slightly less than half of the seasoned rice vinegar. The rice will turn an amethyst hue as the vinegar is absorbed. Divide the rice into 8 portions (each about $^{1}/_{4}$ cup). Divide each portion in half, and shape each half into a cylinder. Set the 16 black rice cylinders aside on a flat plate, and cover with a damp cloth and/or plastic wrap until ready to make the rolls.

Make the white sushi rice: Season $2^{1}/_{2}$ cups of the white rice with the remaining seasoned rice vinegar, following the directions in Classic Sushi Rice (page 17). Divide the rice into 8 portions (each about 5 tablespoons), and shape each portion into a cylinder. Set the 8 white rice cylinders aside on a flat plate, and cover with a damp cloth and/or plastic wrap until ready to make the rolls.

To make the pink sushi rice: Drain the gourd ribbons, setting aside $^{1}/_{4}$ cup of the pink plum vinegar. The remaining vinegar can be stored in a tightly capped glass jar in the refrigerator for up to 10 days. Blot away excess moisture from the gourd ribbons with paper towels. Cut the ribbons into 6-inch lengths. Each of the 8 rolls will use 5 of these ribbons; set them aside. Finely mince enough of the remaining gourd to make 1 teaspoon and toss it into the remaining $^{1}/_{2}$ cup cooked white rice. Use light cutting and folding motions to distribute the gourd pieces. Season the rice with the reserved $^{1}/_{4}$ cup pink plum vinegar, following the directions in Classic Sushi Rice (page 17). It will color the rice pale pink and add a distinct plum aroma. Divide the rice into 8 portions (each about 1 tablespoon), and shape each portion into a cylinder. Set the 8 pink rice cylinders aside on a flat plate, and cover with a damp cloth and/or plastic wrap until ready to make the rolls.

Roll the sushi: Each of the 8 rolls is constructed with an inner roll at the core (rolled to create a swirl pattern) and an outer layer that envelops that core (rolled to create a bull's-eye effect).

Begin by making the inner rolls. Using scissors, cut each nori sheet in half crosswise to produce a total of 16 pieces, each about 7^1/$_2$ by 4^1/$_4$ inches. To keep the cut sheets dry, place them in a lidded container or set on a dry cutting board and cover with a tray or baking sheet. Set aside until ready to use.

Lay a *sudaré* (page 249), smooth side up, on a clean, dry work surface, arranging the mat so the slats run horizontally. If only one edge is tasseled, position it farthest away from you. Arrange 1 nori sheet, rough side up, on the mat. Line up the sheet so the edge nearest you (the short side for these fancy rolls) is almost flush with the mat.

Set a small bowl of water to the side of your work area. You will need to moisten your fingers and palms with water often to keep the rice from sticking to them. But you must be careful not to splash water on the nori.

Take 5 pink-tinted gourd ribbons and arrange them vertically, one next to the other, to cover the nori. With moistened fingers, place 1 black rice cylinder horizontally on the gourd ribbons, and spread it to make a horizontal stripe near the edge of the nori nearest you. Be careful not to extend beyond the edges of the nori on the right and left sides. Moisten your fingers again and, using 1 pink rice cylinder, make a stripe just behind, and parallel to, the black rice. Moisten your fingers yet again and, using a second black rice cylinder, make a final stripe behind, and

(continued)

RICE

parallel to, the pink rice. Be sure to leave an ample border beyond the second black stripe with no rice.

Place your thumbs under the near corners of the slatted mat. Hold the edges of the nori in place by pinching with your index fingers. (This will leave three fingers "free" on each hand to hold fillings in place as you lift and roll away from you.) Lift up the edges of the mat and flip the nori over the stripe of black rice nearest you, aiming to make contact just beyond where the pink rice begins. Press gently to seal. Lift the mat to nudge the roll over the stripe of pink rice and continue rolling to make a swirl pattern, enclosing the second stripe of black rice. Just before sealing this inner roll at the far end, take a a few grains of rice from the cylinder of white sushi rice and place them on the far edge, squishing them so they become a pasty "glue."

Check the side edges of the roll to make sure they are not overflowing. If necessary, moisten your fingertips and press gently on the outer edges to make the rice flush with the edges of the nori. Let the roll stand, seam side down, for a moment to let its own weight (and the moisture from the rice) help seal it closed. Repeat to make a total of 8 inner rolls. Set these aside, seam side down, on a flat plate.

Construct the outer rolls: Lay the *sudaré*, smooth side up, on a clean, dry work surface. As before, make sure the slats run horizontally and the tasseled edge is away from you. Arrange 1 nori sheet, rough side up, on the mat. Line up the sheet so a short edge is nearest you and is almost flush with the mat.

With moistened fingers, place 1 white rice cylinder horizontally in the center of the nori sheet. With moistened fingers, spread the rice to cover the center two-thirds of the nori evenly. The rice must be flush with both the right and the left edges of the nori, and the empty borders at the top and bottom should be even.

Moisten your fingers again and press the rice to make 2 horizontal channels to hold the *mitsuba*, which will become the "leaves" of our flower. Arrange them parallel

to each other and about 1/2 inch in from the top and bottom edges of the white rice. Divide 1 *mitsuba* portion in half, and place half in each channel, with the leafy ends pointing in the same direction. Place 1 inner roll between (and parallel to) the 2 *mitsuba* rows, using the greens as guidelines. Once the inner roll is in place, the greens will be barely visible. With your dominant hand, lift the mat (with inner roll set on top of the outer roll) and set it in the cupped palm of your nondominant hand.

Most plump sushi rolls are rolled on a flat work surface, but these are formed while being held above the board. Bringing the fingers of your nondominant hand together to encircle the rolled sushi, seal the top with a few grains of the white sushi rice that will be exposed at the edges of the nori.

Check the sides of the roll to make sure they are not overflowing. If need be, realign with one edge flush to the mat and then press gently with moistened fingertips to flatten. Turn the roll to flatten the opposite edge the same way. Let the roll stand, seam side down, for a moment, to let its own weight (and the moisture from the rice) help seal it closed. Repeat to make a total of 8 rolls.

Slice the rolls: You will need a very sharp knife, preferably pointed and with a blade at least 6 inches long. To prevent sticking, you will need to wipe the blade clean after every stroke. Have a tightly wrung, damp, low-lint kitchen towel next to your cutting board for this purpose. The blade of your knife will also need to be "lubricated" with a few drops of water before each cut, so have a small bowl of water nearby. When it is time to cut, dip the point of the knife blade into the water, then lift up the blade so the water dribbles down its sides. If the blade is too wet, swipe it lightly across the towel to absorb some of the moisture.

Set 1 finished roll parallel to the long edge of your cutting board. Place your *sudaré* loosely over the roll, aligning it so that about 1 inch of the roll is visible. Use the edge of the mat to guide the placement of your knife and to distribute pressure as you slice through the roll. The cut is made as the blade is pushed *away* from you, ideally in a single stroke without flexing your wrist. To cut completely through the roll, you may need to realign your blade a couple of times, especially if the blade is short. Avoid sawing motions. Instead, apply no pressure as you pull the blade back toward you before slicing *away* again. After the final stroke slicing away, draw the tip of the knife blade toward you to separate the slice. Try to avoid wrist-flexing, elbow-rocking motions, as they tend to tear and compress the rolls. Then, as directed above, wipe the knife clean after each slice, and moisten the blade before the next slice.

Repeat to finish slicing the roll. You should end up with 4 even pieces, each about 1 inch long. If you are a novice, you may find it easier to wrap your finished roll in plastic wrap before slicing it. A sharp knife will easily cut through the plastic to make a clean, flat edge. After slicing, remove the clear wrap from each piece. You may also find it easier to cut the roll into 3 pieces until you have mastered the cutting motion. Experienced cooks typically dispense with the mat: they cut each roll in half, line up the halves, and slice again to yield the 4 even pieces. Repeat with the remaining rolls.

Arrange slices on a platter to display the flower pattern, cut side up. Serve at room temperature with soy sauce for dipping, if you like. The rolls themselves have a complex and balanced flavor of salty, sweet, and sour, making the soy sauce unnecessary.

A NOTE ON YIELDS: Because decorative rolls are served on special occasions, the yields reflect the need to feed a small crowd. And, quite frankly, the amount of work needed to make a lot of these rolls is no more than to make just a few. That's why this recipe provides instructions for making 8 plump rolls that yield 24 slices (if you are new to sushi rolling) or 32 slices (if you are experienced in the art).

EGGPLANT SUSHI ROLLS

NASU NO BATTERA-ZUSHI

The classic version of *battera-zushi* is made with fillets of pickled mackerel set on logs of tartly seasoned rice; most renditions are topped with *shirata kombu*, a tissue-thin slice of kelp that has been cooked in a sweet-and-sour sauce. The cylindrical sushi is then sliced into bite-size pieces and served with soy sauce on the side. Thin slices, or young stems, of pink pickled ginger are often included as an accompaniment.

One summer day when I had an abundance of eggplant on hand, I experimented with making a vegan version of *battera*. After the long, slender, deeply purple egglant was seared in a skillet and marinated in soy, it looked somewhat like the bluish silver mackerel. Although definitely vegetal in flavor, the eggplant worked well, indeed.

If you want to add a hint of the sea to your eggplant sushi, look for *tororo* or *oboro kombu* in an Asian supermarket. Both are shelf-stable vinegar-marinated kelps that have been finely shaved (the core of kelp that remains becomes *shirata kombu*, a difficult to source, to-the-trade specialty product, even in Japan). Information on purchasing, storing, and using *tororo* or *oboro kombu* can be found on page 266.

MAKES 4 ROLLS; 24 BITE-SIZE PIECES

Scant 1 teaspoon salt

2 1/2 cups water

2 large Japanese eggplants, each about 4 inches long and 5 ounces

Scant 1 teaspoon aromatic sesame oil

2 to 3 tablespoons soy sauce

1 to 2 tablespoons stock, preferably Basic Kelp Stock (page 75)

1 tablespoon white sesame seeds, freshly dry-roasted (page 245), optional

1 1/2 cups Classic Sushi Rice (page 17)

1/4 cup shreds oboro kombu or several gauzy pieces tororo kombu (optional)

1 teaspoon wasabi paste

Soy sauce for dipping (optional)

Prepare the eggplants: In a bowl, dissolve the salt in the water. Trim away the sepals and slice each eggplant in half lengthwise. Arrange the 4 halves, flat side down, on the cutting board, and slice each half in half holding the knife so that the flat side of the blade is parallel to the cutting board. This will yield 8 slices, each about 1/4 inch thick. You will have 4 slices with dark skin on one of their sides, and 4 pale yellow slices rimmed with dark skin. Slip the slices into the warm salted water and top with an *otoshi-buta* (page 243) or flat plate (avoid a metal lid) to keep them submerged. Allow the eggplant to soak for at least 10 minutes or up to 1 hour. The liquid may turn brown, but the eggplant slices should not darken.

Drain the eggplant, rinse under cold water, drain again, and press lightly to remove excess moisture. Pat the eggplant dry with paper towels.

Warm the sesame oil over medium heat in a skillet large enough to hold the 8 eggplant slices in a single layer. When the oil is aromatic (about 30 seconds), place the 4 slices with the dark skin, skin side down, in the skillet and sear until the deep purple color becomes more vivid, about 1 minute. Add the remaining slices to the skillet.

(continued)

Use the *otoshi-buta* or a broad, flexible spatula to press the slices so they sear evenly (the flesh may brown a bit). Flip the slices after 1 minute, then press again to ensure even contact with the skillet surface. Sear for another minute.

In a shallow glass baking dish large enough to hold the eggplant slices in 2 layers, mix together 2 tablespoons of the soy sauce and 1 tablespoon of the stock. Lay the still-warm eggplant slices in the marinade, arranging the pieces with dark skin on top. Ideally the eggplant will be barely covered with the marinade; if need be, add a few more drops of soy sauce or stock. Allow the eggplant to marinate for 10 minutes while you shape the rice.

Season and shape the rice: Sprinkle the sesame seeds over the sushi rice and, using a *shamoji* (page 248), toss well to distribute evenly, using light folding and cutting motions. Moisten your fingers and palms with water to keep the rice from sticking to them, then divide the rice into 4 portions (about $1/3$ cup each). Coax each portion into a 4-inch-long loglike cylinder. Set the cylinders aside on a flat plate, and cover with a damp cloth and/or plastic wrap until ready to use.

Assemble the rolls: Lay a *sudaré* (page 249), smooth side up, on a clean, dry work surface, arranging the mat so the slats run horizontally. If only one edge is tasseled, position it farthest away from you. Set a small bowl of water to the side of your work area. You will need to moisten your fingers and palms with water often to keep the rice from sticking to them.

Cover the entire mat area with plastic wrap. In the center of the mat, horizontally align 2 eggplant slices, 1 with dark skin, 1 without. Place the slice with dark skin farthest from you; lay the slice rimmed in dark skin parallel to the first slice, closer to you.

If you want to enhance the briny flavor of this dish, place a few pieces of *oboro kombu* over the eggplant. A little bit will go a long way in enhancing the flavor; too much will overwhelm the dish.

Place 1 rice cylinder over the eggplant. With moistened fingers, gently press and slightly flatten the rice, spreading it to cover the eggplant. Place your thumbs under the near corners of the slatted mat. Hold the edges of the plastic wrap in place by pinching with your index fingers. (This will leave three fingers "free" on each hand to hold the eggplant in place as you lift and roll away from you.) Lift up the edges of the mat and flip it over the rice; several inches of rice should be visible after flipping.

With one hand, hold the top flap of the mat in place while tugging back slightly on the rolled portion of the mat. This will ensure that the eggplant is snugly enclosed. Continue to roll, lifting up the top of the mat and gently pushing the sushi away from you at the same time. When the roll is complete, twist the plastic wrap closed at the right and left sides to ensure a snug log shape. Set the roll aside and shape the remaining 3 rolls. The rolls should sit, seam side down, for a few moments before you slice them.

Slice the rolls: You will need a very sharp knife, preferably pointed and with a blade at least 6 inches long. To prevent sticking, you will need to wipe the blade clean after every stroke. Have a tightly wrung, damp, low-lint kitchen towel next to your cutting board for this purpose. The blade of your knife will also need to be "lubricated" with a few drops of water before each cut, so have a small bowl of water nearby. When it is time to cut, dip the point of the knife blade into the water, then lift up the blade so the water dribbles down its sides. If the blade is too wet, swipe it lightly across the towel to absorb some of the moisture.

Set 1 finished roll, still wrapped in plastic wrap, parallel to the long edge of your cutting board. Place your *sudaré* loosely over the roll, aligning it so that about $3/4$ inch of the roll is visible. Use the edge of the mat to guide the placement of your knife and to distribute pressure as you slice through the roll. The cut is made as the blade is pushed *away* from you, ideally in a single stroke without flexing your wrist. To cut completely through the roll, you may need to realign your blade a couple of times, especially if the blade is short. Avoid sawing motions. Instead, apply no pressure as you pull the blade back toward you before slicing *away* again. After the final stroke slicing away, draw the tip of the knife blade toward you to separate the slice. Try to avoid wrist-flexing, elbow-rocking motions, as they tend to tear the rolls. Then, as directed above, wipe the knife clean after each slice, and moisten the blade before cutting the next slice.

When the entire roll has been sliced, remove and discard the plastic wrap from each slice. Dab a small amount of wasabi on each piece of sushi. Think stingy: too heavy a hand will mask the delicate flavor of the eggplant.

Serve at room temperature with soy sauce for dipping, if you like. The rolls themselves have a complex and balanced flavor of salty, sweet, and sour, making the soy sauce unnecessary.

POM-POM SUSHI

TEMARI-ZUSHI

Like many frugal Japanese women who managed house-holds in the early and mid-twentieth century, my mother-in-law, Kiyoko Andoh, practiced thrift in and out of the kitchen. She saved bits and pieces of cloth, turning them into quilted cushions and throws. Odd lengths of thread were transformed into charming ornaments called *temari*, made by winding colorful strands in patterns around a spherical core. And in the kitchen, my mother-in-law was a master at transforming bits and pieces of food into sumptuous meals.

One of her tricks was to take thin slices of pickled or soy-stewed vegetables and place them on tiny spheres of tart sushi rice, making what she called *temari-zushi*. Although not especially fluffy, the pert, plump, bite-size sushi balls with colorful toppings reminded me of pom-poms, and that is how I would call them. In this recipe, I combine classic and modern ingredients and offer a trio of toppings: fuchsia-colored radicchio (or *myōga*), ebony-hued shiitaké, and sunny green avocado.

MAKES 36 PIECES (12 EACH OF 3 FLAVORS)

BLUSHING PICKLES

3 or 4 small radicchio leaves or 4 myōga bulbs, prepared as in In-the-Pink Pickles (page 198)

SHIITAKÉ MUSHROOMS

3 large dried shiitaké mushrooms

1¼ cups water

1 tablespoon saké

Scant 1 tablespoon sugar

1½ tablespoons soy sauce

AVOCADO

½ ripe avocado, pitted, peeled, and brushed with lemon juice

3 cups Classic Sushi Rice (page 17)

Wasabi paste

Fresh shiso leaves (page 258) or mint leaves (optional)

Soy sauce for dipping (optional)

Prepare the blushing pickles: Remove the radicchio or *myōga* from their sweet-and-sour marinade, drain, and pat dry. If using radicchio, cut each leaf in half lengthwise, trimming away any tough edges or center core. Cut 12 pieces each about 1 inch square and set aside. Finely mince any tough bits for tossing into the rice and set aside. If using *myōga*, peel back the top layers, and set aside 12 of the most vibrantly colored outer leaves. Finely mince the remaining *myōga* for tossing into the rice and set aside.

Prepare the shiitaké mushrooms: Snap off the stems of the mushrooms and set them aside for making stock on another occasion. Soak the mushroom caps in the water for at least 1 hour. It is best to apply weight with an *otoshi-buta* (page 243) or a small, flat plate to submerge the mush-rooms in liquid completely as they soak.

When the mushrooms have softened, drain them, reserving the soaking liquid. Rinse the mushrooms to remove any gritty material, and squeeze out the excess liq-uid. Slice each cap, *sogi-giri* (page 244) style into 4 flattish slices (1 slice for each pom-pom). Resoak the slices in the strained liquid for 5 to 10 minutes (the caps must be fully

(continued)

reconstituted before cooking). Drain again, reserving the liquid; you should have a generous cup. (This softening procedure can be done a few days in advance. Refrigerate the mushroom caps in their strained liquid.)

Place ³/₄ cup of the mushroom liquid in a small saucepan or skillet, add the saké, and bring to a simmer. Add the mushroom slices and cover with an *otoshi-buta* or a circle of parchment paper to keep the mushrooms submerged in the liquid. Cook for 7 to 8 minutes, maintaining a steady but gentle boil. If, at any point, the mushrooms appear in danger of scorching, add more water to keep them barely submerged in liquid.

Skim away any froth with a fine-mesh skimmer, then add the sugar and the remaining ¹/₄ cup mushroom liquid. Re-cover with the *otoshi-buta* or parchment and cook for 3 to 4 minutes, stirring occasionally. Add water only if needed to keep the mushrooms from scorching. Add the soy sauce and cook for 2 to 3 minutes, or until the mushrooms are glazed. Remove from the heat and allow the mushrooms to cool in the pan. It is during this cooling-down stage that seasonings are fully absorbed. (The mushrooms can be made several days or even a week in advance. If making ahead, transfer cooked and cooled mushrooms to a clean glass jar, cover with plastic wrap to seal tightly, and refrigerate.) Set aside.

Prepare the avocado: Cut the avocado half lengthwise into 6 slices. Cut each slice in half crosswise to yield 12 pieces total. If you wish, slice each piece into thin strips and realign to make a fan; each fan will top one nugget of sushi rice.

Shape the rice: Set a small bowl of water to the side of your work area. You will need to moisten your fingers and palms with water often to keep the rice from sticking to them. Divide the sushi rice into 36 portions, and shape each portion into a small spherelike nugget. Set the nuggets aside on a flat plate.

For each of the 3 different toppings, you need a separate flat work surface (such as an inverted baking sheet). Cover each work surface with a sheet of plastic wrap. Depending upon the size of your surface, you may need to make the pom-poms in batches, covering with plastic wrap for each batch.

Shape the radicchio- or *myōga*-topped pom-poms: Place the radicchio or *myōga* slices in 2 rows, about 3 inches apart, on the plastic wrap. Pick up a nugget of rice and press it on top of a radicchio or *myōga* slices. Repeat to make 12 pom-poms total.

Shape the shiitaké-topped pom-poms: Place the shiitaké slices in 2 rows about 3 inches apart, on the plastic wrap. Pick up a nugget of rice, dab a bit of wasabi on it, and place it, wasabi side down, on top of a slice of shiitaké. Repeat to make 12 pom-poms total.

Shape the avocado-topped pompoms: Place the avocado pieces (or fans, if you have formed them) in 2 rows, about 3 inches apart, on the plastic wrap. Pick up a nugget of rice, dab a bit of wasabi on it, and place it, wasabi side down, on an avocado slice (or fan). Repeat to make 12 pom-poms total.

With scissors, carefully cut the plastic wrap between the pompoms to separate each into a small rectangle about 3 by 4 inches. Gather up the far corner edges of the wrap over each of the nuggets of rice. Twist lightly to compact the rice and form each nugget into a perfect sphere. Keep the nuggets tightly wrapped until ready to serve. They will keep at cool room temperature for up to 6 hours.

Unwrap the balls of sushi and stack them toppings facing up, in a bowl. Or, lay the *shiso* leaves on a flat platter and arrange the sushi on the leaves. Serve with soy sauce, for dipping, on the side if you like.

HAND-PRESSED RICE WITH FILLINGS

OMUSUBI

Making *omusubi* is a bit like sandwich making, using rice instead of bread. Sandwich fillings are usually spread or layered on the bread, but *omusubi* stuffings are buried, like treasure, in the center of the rice. The word *musubu* means "to tie" or "to bring together," and it aptly applies to these ubiquitous Japanese rice "sandwiches" that bring disparate flavors and textures together into a neatly portable, delectable package.

Most *omusubi* are coaxed into a triangular shape, though many are chubby cylinders, a shape the Japanese call *tawara*, or "bundle of harvested rice." Or, sometimes they turn up as round balls or oval patties. Kids' lunch boxes are increasingly packed with elaborate molded rice sculptures of comic-book heroes and impossibly cute stylized animals (think Hello Kitty!).

In this recipe, I have gone back to the basics, showing you how to fashion a simple triangle with your hands or with the aid of a measuring cup. For fillings, I have chosen a robustly spiced dark miso and a tart and sharp pickle, though I offer further suggestions on page 47. For wrappers, I use classic strips of *yaki nori* in addition to *oboro kombu*, a pale green, gauzelike shaved kelp that may be new to you.

MAKES 4 OR 6 RICE TRIANGLES

¹/₈ teaspoon salt

3 cups Cooked White Rice (page 11), freshly made and still warm (or zapped in the microwave for about 20 seconds)

1¹/₂ tablespoons Good Fortune Pickles (page 207), well drained

1¹/₂ tablespoons Robust Miso (page 132)

¹/₂ sheet yaki nori (page 267), cut lengthwise into 2 or 3 strips

¹/₂ ounce oboro kombu (page 266)

Rice will stick easily to your hands. From start to finish—while salting the rice, dividing it into portions and shaping it, stuffing it, and wrapping the *omusubi*—have a small bowl of water and a tightly wrung, damp, low-lint kitchen towel within easy reach. Arrange your workspace so that water, as you lift your hands from the bowl, will not drip over the food.

Sprinkle the salt over the warm rice. The salt not only perks up the flavor of the rice but also helps retard spoilage. Some home cooks will salt their hands in addition to the rice, especially if they know the *omusubi* will be eaten many hours later. Using gentle cutting and folding motions, toss the warm rice with a *shamoji* (page 248) while fanning it with an *uchiwa* (page 248). The fanning cools the rice rapidly without allowing condensation to form. A large, broad spatula and a stiff piece of cardboard can substitute in a pinch for the traditional equipment.

Divide the rice and begin to shape the *omusubi*: Although most Japanese home cooks shape *omusubi* with their hands alone, if you have little experience in handling and shaping rice, using a ¹/₂-cup measure (made of metal or sturdy plastic) will make it easier. When you use a mold such as a measuring cup, you tend to compact the rice a bit more than if you shaped it with only your hands. Because of this, if you are using a mold, I suggest you make a total of 4 *omusubi* from the 3 cups salted rice.

Dip the cup briefly in cold water and shake off the excess moisture. Immediately fill the cup with one-fourth of the salted rice. Moisten your hands with water and press firmly to level the rice just below the rim of the cup. Invert

(continued)

the cup, tapping lightly to release the rice onto your other hand. Using both hands (they should be moistened with water), apply light pressure to shape it into a sphere.

If you are hand-shaping *omusubi* from the start, make 6 spheres from the 3 cups salted rice. Moisten your hands frequently to keep the rice from sticking to them.

Prepare the filling and fill the *omusubi*: Finely mince the Good Fortune Pickles, making them about the size of sesame seeds. Gather together into mounds, squeezing gently and blotting up any resulting liquid. Divide into 2 portions, if making 4 *omusubi*, or 3 portions, if making 6 *omusubi*. The Robust Miso is thick and easy to spoon out into 2 or 3 portions.

Take a single sphere of rice in your moistened, non-dominant hand. With dampened fingers of the dominant hand, make an indentation in the center of the rice ball. Place a single portion of one of the fillings in the space you have created. As you press the filling in place, cup the hand holding the rice to enclose the filling. Using both hands, apply light pressure to enclose the filling completely, reshaping the rice into a sphere. You will no longer be able to see the filling. Repeat to fill all the rice spheres.

To form the spheres into triangles, take a filled sphere in your moistened, nondominant hand. Bend the dampened fingers of your dominant hand to form a V-shaped "roof" over the top of the rice ball. Exert gentle pressure with this top hand to mold the rice—this "roof" becomes one of the triangle's pointed tips. Use the extended fingers of your bottom (nondominant) hand to flatten the sides of the triangle. With your cupped (top) hand, roll the rice ball toward you, flexing your wrist to turn your hand up. As you do this, the rice ball will flip so that the edge that previously was formed against your top hand now rests on the flat palm of your bottom hand. Exert gentle pressure again to form the second pointed tip on top. Repeat the roll, press, and flip motion to complete the making of the triangle. Shape the remaining *omusubi* in the same manner.

Although there are no hard-and-fast rules about which wrapper goes with what filling, I suggest the classic *yaki nori* with the miso filling, and the gauzy *oboro kombu* with the pickles. Nor are there special rules regarding how the wrapper gets wound, but I like the look (and ease of nibbling later) the kimono-style drape for *yaki nori*.

To attach the *yaki nori* wrapper, kimono style: Place a miso-stuffed *omusubi* on a dry cutting board so that one point of the triangle is on top (looks like a mountain). Take one strip of nori and, holding it horizontally, place the center of the strip flush against the broad triangular area closest to you; the ends should extend like tabs, right and left, somewhat like the top of a T. Fold down the right tab first, pressing it to the rice on the far, or backside, of the triangle. Repeat with the left tab. Turn the triangle around so that you can see the V neck of the kimono, with the right flap lying over the left. The kimono, for men and women, is always worn this way; only bodies prepared for burial are wrapped in the reverse. Flip both tab ends of nori under the flat base of the triangle to complete the wrapping.

To attach the *oboro kombu* wrapper: Because most packages of *oboro kombu* contain more shreds than full sheets, it is easiest to spread the contents out on a dry surface and gently tug and stretch to make 3-inch squares. You can patch up areas that have little or no *oboro kombu* by laying extra tufts on top, and you can pull some away from an area that seems too thick. Should you need to trim and cut, scissors will be easier and more effective than a knife. You will need a 3-inch square of gauzy kelp for each *omusubi*.

Stand a pickle-stuffed *omusubi* (like a mountain) on a square, aligning it in the center on the diagonal. Now, gently tap on the *omusubi* to knock it over; it should fall with its point touching a corner of the square. Because the rice is moist and somewhat sticky, the *oboro kombu* will cling immediately. Flip the *omusubi* so the other side falls on the remaining *oboro kombu*; it will also cling easily. Stand the *omusubi* up and press excess shreds against the sides of the "mountain" to finish enclosing the *omusubi*. (The very top may be white, depending on the size of your *omusubi* in relation to the kelp.)

The *omusubi* will keep well at cool room temperature for up to 6 hours. If you want to hold them for more than 30 minutes, wrap them in plastic wrap, either individually or covered on a platter, to prevent them from drying out.

If you know you want to hold the *omusubi* for longer than 6 hours, do not wrap them in either *yaki nori* or *oboro kombu*. Instead, wrap them in plastic wrap and refrigerate for up to 24 hours, or freeze them for several weeks. Chilled or frozen *omusubi* are perfect for making toasted hand-pressed rice following the directions for Toasted Hand-Pressed Brown Rice with Hijiki (page 48). You can always add *yaki nori* after toasting the *omusubi*—the heat will make the wrapper a bit limp, but also aromatic (I happen to adore the slightly chewy texture and seashore aroma that results). Similarily, the *oboro kombu* will go limp and will seem to melt with the heat of the toasted rice (I actually prefer it this way!).

OTHER FILLINGS, COATINGS, AND WRAPPERS FOR OMUSUBI

You can also fill your hand-pressed rice triangles with Rice Friends: Peppery Kelp Squares and Plummy Kelp Squares (page 152); Home-Style Purple-Pickled Eggplant (page 202); Sweet, Spicy, and Tart Sun-Dried Radish (page 204); or Sour and Spicy Gourd Pickles (page 212).

Although *yaki nori* and *oboro kombu* make easy-to-hold-and-nibble packages, some home cooks prefer to coat or wrap their *omusubi* differently. You can roll them in dry-roasted sesame seeds (page 245), *yukari* (page 259), or *ao nori* (page 256). Or, if you have large leaves of pickled cabbage, drain them, pat dry, and wrap your rice sandwiches in them.

TOASTED HAND-PRESSED BROWN RICE WITH HIJIKI

HIJIKI GENMAI YAKI OMUSUBI

Toasted rice, especially brown rice, is yummy—and even more so when bits of soy-simmered *hijiki*, a mineral-rich sea vegetable, have been tossed into the rice before shaping and toasting it. These *yaki omusubi* make a terrific snack or light lunch.

The old-fashioned method of toasting *omusubi* on an *ami* net placed over a stove-top burner has been abandoned by most Japanese city dwellers. With the advent of new technologies such as induction heat and microwave and convection ovens, clever new gadgets have been invented. But for most American apartment dwellers, it makes sense to toast *omusubi* in a skillet or in a toaster oven (preferably one with coils top and bottom). I have provided you instructions for both methods. Of course, if you have a backyard grill, that's wonderful, too: just wrap your *omusubi* in foil like you would a baked potato.

MAKES 4 OR 6 RICE TRIANGLES

> ¼ to ⅓ cup Hijiki with Thick Fried Tōfu (page 146), made without the fried tōfu
>
> 3 cups Cooked Brown Rice (page 15), freshly cooked and still warm (or zapped in the microwave for about 20 seconds)
>
> ½ teaspoon aromatic sesame oil
>
> 1½ tablespoons Vegan Seasoned Soy Concentrate (page 131)
>
> 1 tablespoon vinegar for brushing, if using toaster oven

If your Hijiki with Thick Fried Tōfu was made with the longer stem pieces (*naga hijiki*), chop them first into ¼-inch lengths (the buds, *mé hijiki*, will be the right size without chopping).

Sprinkle the *hijiki* over the warm rice. Using gentle cutting and folding motions, toss the warm rice with a *shamoji* (page 248) to distribute the *hijiki* evenly.

Following the instructions in Hand-Pressed Rice with Fillings (page 45), divide the rice into 4 or 6 portions and shape each into a triangle. Allow the rice triangles to cool completely before proceeding. Chilling the *omusubi*, loosely wrapped, for 5 to 10 minutes in the refrigerator will actually make them easier to toast. If you wish to set some, or all, aside for toasting at a later time, carefully, completely, and snugly wrap each one in plastic wrap. Label with the date and refrigerate for up to 24 hours or freeze for up to 2 weeks.

Toast the hand-pressed rice in a skillet: Lightly coat a cast-iron skillet or griddle with the sesame oil. Slowly heat over low heat until you see the oil shimmer; be careful not to let the oil smoke. Place the *omusubi* in a single layer in the pan, making sure the heat is at the lowest possible setting. Let the rice toast slowly, crusting over so that it will release easily. If you are toasting frozen *omusubi*, you may want to place a cover on the pan to trap and concentrate heat, which will aid defrosting. Under any circumstances, patience is required.

After 5 or 6 minutes, try slipping a spatula under one of the *omusubi*. If you are able to dislodge it easily, flip it. If not, wait another minute or so before trying again. When you are able to flip it easily, do so, and then allow the other side to crust slowly, about 5 more minutes.

Once all the *omusubi* have formed a thin crust on both sides, paint the top surface with a pastry brush dipped in the soy concentrate. Turn off the heat under the skillet and flip the *omusubi* over so that the soy-slathered surface sizzles and becomes aromatic. Wait for 1 to 2 minutes as the *omusubi* brown with retained heat. Remove with a spatula. Eat warm.

Toast the hand-pressed rice in a toaster oven: If your toaster oven has coils top and bottom and a removable mesh or net tray, you can toast the *omusubi* directly on the tray. To discourage sticking, brush the cool tray with vinegar. Lightly brush the top and bottom surfaces of cold (or frozen) *omusubi* with vinegar, too. Place the *omusubi* on the tray and set your toaster to a medium-high setting for 2 minutes (4 minutes, if the *omusubi* are frozen). The vinegar will evaporate and not add any sour notes to the rice; you may smell it, however, as it heats in the toaster.

When the toaster-oven cycle is complete, let the *omusubi* rest for 1 minute. Use that time to soak a paper towel with sesame oil and wipe the tip of a spatula with it. Use the spatula to pry and lift the *omusubi* from the tray. If there is resistance, toast for 1 minute longer, let rest for another minute, and try again. Once you are able to release the *omusubi*, paint the top surface with a pastry brush dipped in the soy concentrate. Retoast for 1 minute, or until aromatic and lightly browned. Eat warm.

NOTES ABOUT YAKI OMUSUBI

Because it is difficult to cook small quantities of rice, people living alone or in small households inevitably cook more rice than can be eaten at one meal. Next time you make brown rice, shape the leftovers into *omusubi* and freeze them. They defrost and toast at the same time!

I am especially fond of the *hijiki* and brown rice version of *yaki omusubi* I offer here, but other leftovers, such as Gingery Enoki Mushrooms with Carrots (page 127) and Granny's Sun-Dried Radish (page 142), can be minced and tossed with the brown rice instead.

NOODLES

WHEN A JAPANESE REFERS TO his or her *furusato*, or birthplace, it is spoken of in wistful tones, especially by middle-aged urban dwellers whose formative years were spent in *inaka*, "the countryside" (yet another nostalgia-laden Japanese word). Although I was born and bred in the big city (New York), my adoptive *furusato* is a small coastal community on the island of Shikoku in the heart of Sanuki, a region famous for—in fact, synonymous with—*udon* noodles. When it comes to my own noodle identity, I admit I can become as maudlin as any Sanuki-born matron when I extol the virtues of the local noodles. I did try to take a more geographically (and emotionally) balanced approach to this chapter by including a few *soba* (buckwheat noodle) dishes, a specialty of central Japan's Nagano Prefecture. But then I cheated a bit: *sōmen* (thread-thin, white wheat noodles) are also a Shikoku specialty.

In order to simplify instructions in each of the noodle recipes, I have started this chapter with master recipes: everything you need to know about cooking *sōmen*, *udon*, and *soba* noodles.

PURCHASING AND STORING NOODLES

Japanese *udon*, *soba*, and *sōmen* are vegan; most *ramen* noodles use egg as a binder. Because buckwheat is a gluten-free grain, some *soba* noodles will use *yama imo*, a sticky mountain yam, or a combination of *yama imo* and wheat flour as a binder. Check the label carefully if you have an allergy to wheat products. Depending on the type of noodle—fresh, dried, or other shelf-stable forms—storage recommendations differ.

DRIED NOODLES (*kan men*) Store all dried noodles as you would dried pasta, on a cool, dark, dry shelf. Once you have opened the package, transfer any unused contents to a lidded glass jar, canister, or sealed bag (include the packet of drying agent that came in the original package). Label the container with the date the package was opened, and use the product, if possible, within a few months, though spoilage is rare even a year later.

SEMIFRESH NOODLES (*han nama men*) Before you open the package, these semidried, somewhat soft and pliable noodles are shelf-stable, again on a cool, dark, dry shelf. I suggest you keep them in a lidded sturdy container to prevent heavier boxes, bags, or cans stored nearby from accidentally crushing them. Packages will have a sell-by date stamped on them; use within a week of that date. Once you open the package, the noodles must be cooked (preferably on the same day) or refrigerated for up to 2 days.

FRESH NOODLES (*nama men*) Store all fresh noodles—homemade and store-bought—in the refrigerator. If the noodles were refrigerated when you bought them, you will need to continue to keep them under refrigeration. Be sure to consume them on or before the sell-by date stamped on the package. Do not freeze purchased fresh noodles unless you bought them frozen and can maintain that temperature between the store and your home. You can freeze homemade fresh noodles, but that must be done within an hour of making them. Once frozen noodles have been allowed to thaw, do not refreeze them.

COOKING PROCEDURE

Cooking methods and times for Japanese packaged noodles vary enormously according to the type (dried, semifresh, fresh, and frozen-precooked) and the kind (*udon, soba,* or *sōmen*). It may sound obvious, but look first to see if instructions are provided on the package. If so, follow the guidelines printed there for timing, but note that any measurements for quantities may be different: the Japanese use metric measures; some "translations" take this into consideration and others do not. A Japanese cup is 200 cc (cubic centimeters), the equivalent of a generous ³/₄ cup American measure; a liter is slightly larger than a quart. If no guidelines are available or you are having trouble deciphering the instructions, follow the basic procedure outlined here.

Use plenty of water and a deep pot. A pot that has a tight-fitting lid will be more fuel-efficient (water in a lidded pot will come to a boil faster). The lid will also trap heat in the pot after cooking, if the noodles need a bit more time to become tender. Always allow at least 2 inches of headroom (the distance between the rim of the pot and the water level), or more if you are cooking *sōmen*.

Bring the water to a vigorously bubbling boil over high heat before adding the noodles. Poke dried noodles, if necessary, to keep them from sticking to one another. Leave fresh and frozen precooked noodles alone until the water returns to a boil. This is the point at which you begin counting your cooking time. If cooking *udon, soba,* or other thick noodles, adjust the heat to maintain a steady, but slightly less vigorous boil. When cooking *sōmen* or other thin noodles, use the surprise-water technique (see box, page 54). Ideally, noodles will cook through (no hard core) but still be firm, what Italians call al dente or the Japanese call *koshi* (substance). If the noodles are too firm, follow the directions in each recipe for cooking them longer.

When the noodles are done, scoop them out with a strainer or skimmer. Or, if using a pot with a pasta insert—a fine-meshed insert particularly useful if cooking thread-thin *sōmen*—lift the insert from the pot, leaving the boiling water behind in the pot. When cooking *udon* and *sōmen*, do *not* dump out the water if you will be serving the noodles hot; the cooking water can be used to reheat the rinsed noodles before serving. The nutrient-rich water from cooking *soba* is *always* saved and used to thin the dipping sauce into a warm soup.

RINSING COOKED NOODLES

Surprising as it may sound, rinsing freshly cooked noodles—all types of noodles—in cold water is common Japanese kitchen practice. It removes surface starch so the noodles won't be gummy. The Japanese adore noodles that slither and slide when they slurp them, and rinsing cooked noodles aids in achieving this. Later, if the rinsed noodles will be used in a hot dish, they can be dipped briefly in boiling water, and the bowls can be warmed with boiling water. Similarly, precooked noodles are rinsed in cold water if serving them chilled.

SERVING NOODLES HOT

After cooking noodles, use the very hot water that remains in the pot to warm your serving bowls and reheat the noodles. Ladle some of the hot water into each bowl and leave the bowls on your counter while you bring the water in the pot back to a boil. Place your cooked noodles in a colander or strainer that will fit inside the pot. The Japanese use a deep bowl-shaped strainer with a vertical handle, similar to but larger than a *miso koshi* (page 250). Bring the water in the pot to a rolling boil and lower the colander into it. Immediately remove the pot from the heat. Allow the noodles to sit undisturbed in the colander for about 30 seconds, then stir them and lift the colander from the pot. Tap or shake to drain off the excess liquid. Pour off the hot water in the bowls and slide in the rewarmed noodles. Add toppings, ladle in hot broth, and slurp away!

COOKED SŌMEN NOODLES

Thread-thin *sōmen* noodles are cooked using the *bikkuri mizu* (surprise water) technique (see box).

MAKES ENOUGH FOR 4 SERVINGS

6 bundles sōmen noodles, about 1¹/₂ ounces each

2 cups cold water

Fill a large pot with at least 4 quarts water, leaving at least 2 inches of headroom to allow for the addition of more water later. Bring the water to a rolling boil over high heat. Remove the band from around each bundle of *sōmen* noodles and scatter the noodles over the water. Stir once to make sure they separate into individual strands.

When the water returns to a boil, immediately add 1 cup of the cold water (this is the *bikkuri mizu* or surprise water). Continue to cook the noodles over high heat, adding the remaining 1 cup cold water just at the point when the water begins to boil again. When the water returns to a boil for the third time, remove the pot from the heat and test for doneness.

Lift a few noodles from the boiling water and plunge them into a bowl of cold water. Ideally, the noodles will be firm but tender and slightly translucent. If the noodles have a hard core or look opaque, place a lid on the pot to trap the heat for 30 seconds, then test again. Continue to cover, wait, and test at 30-second intervals until the noodles are tender. If you will be serving the *sōmen* noodles cold, drain them in a fine-mesh colander. If you will be serving the *sōmen* noodles hot, scoop them out with a fine-mesh strainer and reserve the water in the pot to reheat them.

Rinse the noodles quickly but thoroughly under running cold water to remove surface starch, then immediately drain. The noodles tend to stretch and become soggy if allowed to sit in water for too long. If serving the noodles cold, give them another quick rinse under cold water just before serving, if necessary. If serving the noodles hot, reheat them and warm the bowls as directed on page 53.

SURPRISE!

Cooks unfamiliar with the ways of the Japanese kitchen are often surprised to learn about *bikkuri mizu*—literally "surprise water"—a technique used to control water temperature as noodles cook. In the case of thin *sōmen*, the noodles are "surprised" by two additions of cold water. (This method is also known as *sashi mizu*, or "adding extra water," but I prefer surprises.) The cooking process begins when noodles are added to vigorously boiling water. But the delicate strands cannot stand up to such harsh treatment for long, so when the water returns to a boil, it is time for a pleasant surprise—*bikkuri mizu*—that cools the boil to a gentle simmer. Heat is retained at the core of each noodle, however, continuing to make the noodles tender. This method works very well with any thin noodle.

COOKED UDON NOODLES

A large, deep pot and steady high heat are needed to cook thick *udon* noodles to slithery, tender-but-chewy perfection. Because a great deal of starch is thrown off to the cooking water as you boil the noodles, you may want to swap out pots with fresh boiling water (or cook in two pots simultaneously) if preparing more than 4 portions at once.

Whether you plan to serve the noodles hot or cold, you will need to rinse them well under running cold water to remove surface starch, then drain them. Cooked *udon* noodles can be used immediately, or set aside until ready to eat (they can be held for 20 minutes at room temperature, or for several hours loosely covered and refrigerated).

MAKES ENOUGH FOR 4 SERVINGS

> 4 portions (7 ounces each) refrigerated or frozen precooked udon, Home-Stomped Whole-Wheat Udon Noodles (page 61), 14 to 16 ounces semifresh udon, or 4 (3-ounce) bundles dried udon

Fill a very large pot with at least 5 quarts water, leaving at least 2 inches of headroom. Bring the water to a rolling boil over high heat.

Depending upon the type of *udon* you are preparing, the length of time in boiling water will vary. If preparing refrigerated or frozen precooked *udon* noodles, add them cold or frozen to the boiling water. Do not stir right away. Instead, wait for a few moments until the hot water has had a chance to circulate around the clumped noodles, then stir gently to encourage them to separate. Wait for the water to return to a boil.

If cooking fresh homemade or semifresh *udon*, gently shake off excess flour, then lower the noodles into the boiling water. Cook fresh *udon* at a steady boil for 5 or 6 minutes; cook semifresh *udon* at a steady boil for 8 or 9 minutes. Stir the noodles occasionally as they boil.

If cooking dried *udon*, remove the band from around each bundle and scatter the noodles over the water. Stir once to make sure they separate into individual strands, then cook at a steady boil for 10 minutes. Stir the noodles occasionally as they boil.

Remove the pot from the heat before testing for doneness. Pull a noodle from the pot and plunge it into a bowl of cold water. It should be translucent and firm with no hard core. The outer surface will be slippery but not overly soft. If necessary, return the pot to the heat and continue to cook, checking doneness every 45 seconds or so.

When the *udon* noodles are tender, remove the pot from the heat. If you will be serving the noodles cold, drain them in a colander. If you will be serving the noodles hot, scoop them out with a fine-mesh strainer and reserve the water in the pot to reheat them.

If serving the noodles cold, give them another quick rinse under cold running water just before serving, then drain them well. If serving the noodles hot, reheat them and warm the bowls as directed on page 53.

COOKED SOBA NOODLES

Soba yu, the nutrient-rich water from cooking soba, is always saved. When serving the noodles cold, *zaru soba* style, *soba yu* is brought to table in a pitcher to add to the dipping sauce, making a warm broth to drink after finishing the noodles. When *soba* is served hot, the *soba yu* is used to reheat the noodles.

MAKES ENOUGH FOR 4 SERVINGS

4 portions (about 6 ounces each) refrigerated or frozen precooked soba, 4 portions (about 4 ounces each) semifresh soba, or 4 bundles (2¹/₂ to 3 ounces each) dried soba

Fill a very large pot with at least 5 quarts water, leaving at least 2 inches of headroom. Bring the water to a rolling boil over high heat.

If preparing refrigerated or frozen precooked *soba* noodles, add them cold or frozen to the rapidly boiling water. Do not stir right away. Instead, allow the water to return to a boil. Use long chopsticks or a long-handled wooden spoon to gently poke and separate the noodles. When the water returns to a boil, scoop out the *soba* noodles with a fine-mesh strainer. A quick swish through boiling water is sufficient for heating precooked *soba* noodles. Reserve the cooking water, or *soba yu*. Whether serving them cold or hot, transfer the noodles to a bowl of ice water. Swish to cool them down rapidly and rinse away any surface starch, then drain well.

If preparing semifresh *soba* noodles, gently shake off any excess flour before lowering them into the boiling water. If preparing dried *soba* noodles, remove the band from around each bundle and scatter the noodles over the water. Use long chopsticks to gently poke and separate the noodles. When the water returns to a boil, adjust the heat to maintain a steady but not particularly vigorous boil and begin counting the number of minutes listed on the package. If there is no indication of time, start with 1 minute for semifresh noodles and 4 minutes for dried noodles.

Remove the pot from the heat before testing them for doneness. Lift a couple of noodles from the boiling water and plunge them into a bowl of cold water. Ideally, the noodles will be firm but cooked through. If necessary, continue to cook, checking doneness every 30 seconds for semifresh noodles and 1 minute or so for dried noodles. If the noodles are still not tender, remove the pot from the heat and cover it. This allows the noodles to "self-steam," what the Japanese call *murasu*. Test a noodle again, then extend the self-steaming time, if necessary.

When the noodles are ready, scoop them out with a fine-mesh strainer. Reserve the cooking water, or *soba yu*. Whether serving them cold or hot, transfer the cooked noodles to a bowl of ice water. Swish to cool them down rapidly and rinse away any surface starch, then drain well.

If serving the *soba* noodles cold, give them another quick rinse under cold water just before serving, if necessary. If serving the noodles hot, reheat them and warm the bowls as directed on page 53.

WARM SŌMEN NOODLES, SHOWERED WITH MUSHROOMS

NYŪMEN NO KINOKO AN KAKÉ

Say "*sōmen*" to any Japanese and it is likely he or she will conjure up a swirl of slender noodles bobbing about in deep glass bowls filled with glacierlike chunks of ice. Indeed, in the heat of summer, most *sōmen* are served "on the rocks" with condiments and a seasoned soy dipping sauce. But when the first chilly evenings of autumn arrive, thoughts (and appetites) turn to hot noodle dishes, and this *nyūmen*, with its mélange of fall mushrooms, becomes comforting fare.

SERVES 4

2 dried shiitaké mushrooms

2 cups water

1¹/₂ ounces enoki mushrooms (page 272), trimmed and cut into ¹/₂-inch lengths

1¹/₂ ounces maitaké mushrooms (page 272), trimmed and hand shredded into ¹/₂-inch lengths

Pinch of salt

2 tablespoons Vegan Seasoned Soy Concentrate (page 131) or generous 1 tablespoon soy sauce mixed with scant 1 tablespoon mirin

Cooked Sōmen Noodles, for serving hot (page 54)

1 tablespoon cold water

1 teaspoon cornstarch

¹/₂ teaspoon grated fresh ginger and/or daikon (optional)

Extract a stock from the dried shiitaké mushrooms: Break off the stems and set them aside for making stock on another occasion. Here you are using only the dried shiitaké caps to make a stock (and to cook later with the other mushrooms). Soak the caps in the water in a bowl for at least 30 minutes and preferably for 1 hour or more. Remove the caps from the water and rinse them to remove any gritty material, then squeeze gently. Pour the soaking water through a fine-mesh strainer (or disposable coffee filter) into a clean bowl to remove unwanted bits that may have settled at the bottom of the bowl. Set the stock aside. Slice the dried shiitaké caps into very narrow strips.

Place the shiitaké, enoki, and *maitaké* mushrooms in a saucepan with the reserved mushroom liquid. Set over medium heat and bring to a simmer. Skim away any froth with a fine-mesh skimmer. Season with the salt and soy concentrate, then keep warm over the lowest possible heat while the noodles are cooking.

Select 4 shallow soup bowls or 4 plates with a flange or raised edge and warm them. Divide the noodles among the vessels.

In a small bowl, mix together the cold water and cornstarch to make a paste. Increase the heat under the mushroom mixture to high and bring to a simmer. Add the cornstarch mixture and stir until the sauce thickens and turns clear. Spoon the piping-hot sauce over the noodles to cover them completely. Garnish each portion with a small mound of ginger and/or daikon. Or, coax a bit of both into a single mountain, with the daikon as the base and the ginger as the peak.

Each diner stirs his or her own serving to mix the condiments with the noodles and warm sauce. Japanese table manners encourage slurping, but if you prefer less noise, use a soupspoon and fork Italian style, swirling the noodles into easy mouthfuls.

SLITHERY SŌMEN NOODLES

NEBANEBA SŌMEN

Mouthfeel (the way a food feels in the mouth), more than flavor symmetry (balance of sweet, salty, and sour tastes), helps define a food culture. We often speak of people who have "acquired a taste" for a food that was at first culturally alien to them. Actually, acquiring a mouthfeel for a food is even more challenging.

Many non-Japanese have acquired a taste and mouthfeel for sushi and sashimi, overcoming their initial reluctance to eating raw fish. The distinctive texture of fresh fish—usually silky, often unctuous, occasionally springy—is decidedly different from the flaky quality of cooked fish. The notion of consuming raw flesh may be intellectually demanding to some diners, but the real challenge will more likely be mouthfeel than philosophy.

Most Americans love things crunchy (think potato chips, crisp apples, cornflakes, and granola) and creamy (especially ice cream). The Japanese, however, favor slithery, slippery stuff that can be easily slurped. They describe these foods as *tsurutsuru*, essentially "slick" or "polished." Slithery, slender *sōmen* noodles are a good example.

The Japanese also have an affinity for sticky, viscous items that string, calling them *nebaneba*, from the verb *nebaru*, which means "stick" or "cling." *Nebaneba* describes sticky, tacky, clinging things such as okra and *nattō* (fermented soybeans).

This chilled salad combines *tsurutsuru* noodles with *nebaneba* toppings, and may be a new and possibly challenging slurping sensation for you. I urge you to try it, though, especially on a muggy summer day. It is surprisingly refreshing and, thanks to the *nattō*, packed with nutrients.

SERVES 4

DIPPING SAUCE

2 tablespoons Vegan Seasoned Soy Concentrate (page 131)

2 tablespoons stock, preferably Basic Kelp Stock (page 75), or cold water

TOPPINGS

Gingery Enoki Mushrooms with Carrots (page 127), chilled

3 packages nattō (page 273), about $1^1/_2$ ounces each

8 to 10 okra pods

$^1/_2$ teaspoon salt

Ice cubes

Cooked Sōmen Noodles, for serving chilled (page 54)

CONDIMENTS

1 small knob fresh ginger, about $^1/_2$ ounce, peeled and freshly grated

3 or 4 fresh shiso leaves (page 258), stems trimmed, then leaves stacked, tightly rolled lengthwise, and cut crosswise into very thin shreds (optional)

1 tablespoon white sesame seeds, freshly dry-roasted (page 245), optional

Make the dipping sauce: Combine the soy concentrate and stock in a small bowl and chill for at least 30 minutes.

Ready the toppings: Have the mushrooms at hand. Open the *nattō* packages. If there is a plastic film covering the top, peel it back and discard; you can also discard the

(continued)

sauce and mustard that is usually packaged with the sticky beans; typically they are filled with preservatives.

To prepare the okra, rub each pod with some of the salt to remove surface fuzz; the salt will also ensure a bright color when blanching. Trim off each stem without cutting into the pod. Bring a small pot of water to a boil, add the okra pods, and blanch for 1¹/₂ minutes. Drain, but do not refresh in cold water (this will keep them flavorful and help control stickiness). When cool enough to handle, thinly slice crosswise.

Place a few ice cubes in each of 4 deep, individual bowls. Add just enough water to make the ice cubes stick together, then drape the noodles over them. Arrange the toppings—the enoki, *nattō*, and okra—on the noodles, but do not cover the noodles entirely.

Divide the chilled dipping sauce among 4 small, deep bowls. Place a small mound of ginger on each of 4 small plates; for greater flavor complexity, include a small tuft of *shiso* shreds, and a small pile of sesame seeds, too.

Each diner can nibble at the toppings before eating his or her noodles, though most prefer to stir them, especially the *nattō*, into the noodles from the start (much like tossing a chef's salad before eating it). Each diner seasons his or her own dipping sauce with the condiments to taste, then lifts the noodles from the bowl, dunks them briefly in the dipping sauce, and eats with gusto.

KITCHEN CULTURE: NOODLES AND LEGENDS

Prized as a refreshing hot-weather food, *sōmen* noodles are also associated with a midsummer festival called Tanabata. Celebrated on July 7 in most parts of the country (a few regions keep to the old lunar calendar, which puts the festivities in August), the festival marks the time when celestial movements bring the stars Altair and Vega together across the Milky Way. The Tanabata legend, adapted from an even older traditional Chinese tale, has a cowherd, Kengyū, as the star Altair, and a weaving princess, Orihimé, as Vega. So enamored were they of each other that their work suffered, and the two lovers were banished to opposite ends of the firmament. After frequently beseeching the gods to reunite them, their wish was granted. A brief meeting would be permitted once a year.

Although white *sōmen* noodles are sold at supermarkets year-round, in the summertime, you'll notice packages with all white noodles except for a handful of colored ones dyed a vivid pink (these are seasoned with *uméboshi*, or pickled plums), bright yellow (some made with *yuzu*, some with egg, and the color enhanced by the addition of *kuchinashi no mi*, or dried gardenia pods), or deep olive (from *matcha*, or powdered green tea). These colored noodles are meant to suggest the colored threads from which Orihimé weaves her cloth.

Sometimes *sōmen* noodles are tied into bundles at one end with kitchen twine before cooking, so that they appear to flow like the Milky Way.

HOME-STOMPED WHOLE-WHEAT UDON NOODLES

TE UCHI UDON

My life in Japan has been filled with cultural and culinary discoveries. During my first summer in Kanonji, a coastal township on the island of Shikoku, I learned how to make *udon* noodles from scratch. Not by hand, but by foot! This debut encounter with noodle stomping was under the tutorial guidance of Kiyoko Andoh, the diminutive but energetic woman who, several years later, would become my mother-in-law.

Made from high-gluten wheat flour and saltwater, *udon* dough is dense and stiff and requires tremendous strength to knead it—especially in hot weather when a saltier brine is used than in the winter. Stomping power is far more effective, and certainly more fun, than using your hands to work the dough.

Years ago, when my daughter, Rena, was just a toddler in Tokyo, we would often invite her park playmates to join us at home in a noodle-stomping session. During the early summer rainy season when outdoor activities were curtailed, making *udon* at home became a terrific rainy-day playdate, with lunch included!

MAKES 1 POUND; ENOUGH FOR 4 SERVINGS

- 1 tablespoon sea salt
- ³/₄ cup warm water
- 2 cups whole-wheat bread (high-gluten) flour, plus ¹/₃ cup for hands, rolling pin, and work surface

Dissolve the salt in the warm water in a small bowl (the mixture should taste briny, like the sea). Place the flour in a bowl. Pour in half of the warm salted water in a steady, slow stream, directing it around the outer edge of the bowl, rather than in the center. Using clean hands or a wooden spoon, gently stir from the outer edges to the center to mix the water with the flour. Gradually drizzle in more of the salted water, stirring until the dough forms a slightly crumbly mass. (The ratio of flour to water will vary with the weather; on a rainy day you will probably need less water.) Exert a bit of pressure to form the dough into a ball, then place the ball in a resealable plastic bag, seal the bag, and let the dough rest at room temperature for about 30 minutes. This resting time is needed to help ensure that the noodles will have a satisfying, chewy texture after cooking. If you prefer to make the dough ahead of time, you can refrigerate it for up to 24 hours at this point. (Bring it back to room temperature before continuing.)

Even after the dough has rested, it will be fairly stiff, which is why it is stomped by foot, rather than kneaded by hand. Although a *tatami*-matted floor is an ideal surface for the stomping, linoleum flooring works well, too. If your kitchen has a hardwood or flagstone floor, you will need a large bath towel to provide some cushioning. If foot stomping is not your style, you can use a mechanical kneading device, such as a dough hook on a stand mixer, a food processor, or a lasagna attachment on a pasta machine.

Sandwich the rested dough between lightly floured layers of clean heavy-duty plastic (a 6-foot plastic tarp, oil-cloth, or vinyl tablecloth folded in half works well). Place the plastic-enclosed dough on the floor (slide a bath towel under it if the floor is hardwood or flagstone) and stand barefoot on top of it. Press down with both feet, putting

(continued)

slightly greater weight on your heels, and gradually turn in a circular fashion, using small, stomping steps. As your body weight is applied, the dough will flatten out and stretch. Stop occasionally to remove and fold the dough with your hands, then sandwich it again between floured layers of plastic and repeat your foot-pressing activity. Turn counterclockwise occasionally to keep from getting dizzy. Sprinkle the dough and/or plastic with additional flour, as needed, to prevent it from sticking to the plastic.

After 4 or 5 minutes, when the dough feels elastic and has acquired a satiny sheen, do a final round of stomping to flatten the dough as evenly as possible.

Lightly flour a work surface for rolling and lightly dust a rolling pin. Place the dough on the floured work surface. Alternating vertical and horizontal strokes, roll out the dough into a large oval or oblong shape a bit thinner than 1/8 inch. If necessary, divide the dough in half and roll out 2 smaller ovals, each about 6 inches wide and 12 inches long.

Sprinkle the rolled-out dough liberally with flour, and fold it back on itself 4 or 5 times, like folding a paper fan.

Do not crease or press the folds. Use a long, sharp knife to cut the dough into 1/8-inch-wide ribbons (each noodle is slightly wider than it is thick). Lightly dust the noodles with flour, then lift them from the board and set them aside on a tray or other flat surface. They can be cooked immediately, or they can be covered loosely with a towel or plastic wrap and left at cool room temperature for up to 2 hours before cooking. If you wish to hold the noodles for later the same day or the next day, lightly flour them and place them in a resealable plastic bag in the refrigerator. (When ready to use, take them straight from the refrigerator and shake off excess flour before cooking.)

To cook the *udon*, see Cooked Udon Noodles, page 55; they may be served hot or chilled.

VARIATION: To boost the nutritional profile of plain *udon* and add flavor interest, mix a teaspoon of *yomogi* herb into the whole-wheat flour. The herb, rich in vitamins C and E, as well as antioxidants, is sold in powdered form, making it easy to blend with the flour. In English, *yomogi* goes by the rather unattractive "mugwort."

FLAT PLATE UDON NOODLES

SARA UDON

Throughout the southern island of Kyushu, but especially in and around the port city of Nagasaki, indigenous Japanese ingredients and cooking methods have long melded with foreign foods and ways to create some distinctive dishes. *Sara udon*, or "plate noodles," is a classic example of this tradition. Borrowing heavily from Chinese fare, it resembles the *lo mein* served in many Chinese American restaurants. In Japan, *sara udon* is usually made with slithery-soft noodles, rather than with crunchy panfried ones, and typically includes *kamaboko* (fish sausage) in the stir-fried topping. My vegan version of the Nagasaki dish is a quickly assembled, ginger-infused happy hodgepodge of thick slabs of deep-fried tōfu, cabbage, onions, stir-fried shiitaké mushrooms, carrots, and sweet peppers piled atop a mound of thick wheat noodles.

If you have made your own *udon* (see Home Stomped Whole-Wheat Udon Noodles, page 61), this is a fine way to showcase the noodles. If not, precooked frozen noodles are the next best option (especially if your local Asian grocery imports Sanuki *udon*). In a pinch, semifresh or dried noodles that you cook ahead can be substituted.

SERVES 4

2 dried shiitaké mushrooms

1 cup water

14 ounces thick fried tōfu (page 282)

1 teaspoon aromatic sesame oil

1 large yellow onion, about 7 ounces, cut into 1/4-inch-thick wedges

1/4 head green cabbage or hakusai (page 253), 6 to 7 ounces, coarsely shredded

1 slender carrot, about 3 ounces, scraped and cut into matchsticks

1/2 teaspoon sugar

1 tablespoon saké

1 red or green bell pepper, halved, seeded, and cut lengthwise into 1/2-inch-wide strips

1 teaspoon soy sauce

1/2 teaspoon ginger juice (page 246)

1 tablespoon cornstarch

2 tablespoons cold water

Cooked udon noodles, for serving hot (page 55)

Extract a stock from the dried shiitaké mushrooms: Break off the stems and set them aside for making stock on another occasion. Here you are using only the dried shiitaké caps to make a stock (and to cook later with the other vegetables). Soak the caps in the water in a bowl for at least 30 minutes and preferably for 1 hour or more. Remove the caps from the water and rinse them to remove any gritty material, then squeeze gently. Pour the soaking water through a fine-mesh strainer (or disposable coffee filter) into a clean bowl to remove unwanted bits that may have settled at the bottom of the bowl. Set the stock aside. Slice the dried shiitaké caps into narrow strips and set aside.

Blot away excess oil from the tōfu loaf. Draw the tip of a sharp knife through the loaf lengthwise to make 3 or 4 equal strips. Then cut the strips crosswise at 1/4-inch intervals. You should have a few dozen 1/4-inch-thick slices.

(continued)

Heat a wok or a large, heavy skillet over high heat. Toss in the tōfu slices and allow the pieces to sear for a moment until lightly browned in spots. Drizzle in half the sesame oil and toss to coat the tōfu pieces. Add the onion wedges and stir-fry for about 1 minute, or until they are limp, have colored slightly, and are aromatic. Toss in the cabbage and stir-fry briefly until it begins to wilt. Transfer the contents of the pan, including any liquid in the bottom, to a bowl.

Return the wok to high heat. Add the remaining sesame oil, toss in the shiitaké strips, and stir-fry vigorously for about 1 minute, or just until aromatic. Add the carrot and toss to mix. Sprinkle the sugar over the mushrooms and carrot, toss, and add the saké, scraping up any crusty bits that may be clinging to the pan. Lower the heat, add the reserved mushroom stock, and simmer for 3 or 4 minutes, or until the carrot pieces are tender but firm and the liquid is greatly reduced. Toss in the bell pepper and stir-fry vigorously for about 45 seconds, or until barely wilted.

Return the cabbage, onion, and tōfu to the wok, along with any liquid from the bottom of the bowl. Drizzle in the soy sauce and ginger juice and stir-fry vigorously to distribute seasonings.

In a small bowl, stir together the cornstarch and cold water. Pour the mixture over the contents of the wok and cook, stirring, until the liquid is thickened and glossy.

Divide the noodles among 4 warmed plates. Divide the vegetables and thickened sauce evenly among the plates and serve immediately.

UDON NOODLE SOUP WITH VEGETABLES AND TŌFU

KENCHIN UDON

Traditionally, the word *kenchin* is the name of a Japanese dish linked it to Kenchōji, a Zen temple built in Kamakura in 1253. Modern usage of the word on a menu conveys a much broader meaning, however: almost any stew, chowder, or soup noodle that includes at least one type of tōfu qualifies. In this version of *kenchin udon*, the topping for thick, slithery noodles is a hearty combination of two types of tōfu—slivers of thin sheets of fried tōfu (*abura agé*) and bits of dried *yuba*—and lots of root vegetables. The soup noodles are garnished with freshly grated ginger and chopped leafy greens and served piping hot—a meal in a bowl.

This dish is best when made with fresh, slightly chewy homemade noodles (see Home Stomped Whole-Wheat Udon Noodles, page 61), though semifresh or dried *udon* can be used instead.

SERVES 4

3 or 4 large dried shiitaké mushrooms

3 cups water

1¹/₂ ounces daikon tops, kale, or other leafy greens, loosely tied in a bundle with kitchen twine

3 sheets thin fried tōfu (page 282)

4 ounces fresh mushrooms, preferably maitaké (page 272), trimmed and hand shredded into ¹/₂-inch lengths

1 teaspoon sugar

1 tablespoon saké

1 slender carrot, about 2 ounces, scraped and cut into matchsticks

2 ounces daikon, scraped and cut into matchsticks

1 tablespoon mirin

1 tablespoon light-colored soy sauce

2 sheets hoshi yuba, softened (page 261) and coarsely shredded, or ¹/₄ cup finely broken hoshi yuba (¹/₄-inch bits)

1¹/₂ teaspoons soy sauce

1 tablespoon cornstarch

2 tablespoons cold water

Cooked udon noodles, for serving hot (page 55)

1 tablespoon grated fresh ginger

Extract a stock from the dried shiitaké mushrooms: Break off the stems and set them aside for making stock on another occasion. Here you are using only the dried shiitaké caps to make a stock (and to cook later with the other vegetables). Soak the caps in the water in a bowl for at least 30 minutes and preferably for 1 hour or more. Remove the caps from the water and rinse them to remove any gritty material, then squeeze gently. Pour the soaking water through a fine-mesh strainer (or disposable coffee filter) into a clean bowl to remove unwanted bits that may have settled at the bottom of the bowl. Set the stock aside. Slice the dried shiitake caps into very narrow strips.

Bring a small saucepan filled with water to a boil. Blanch the bundle of leafy greens for 30 seconds, or until they wilt and turn a vivid green. With long chopsticks or tongs pull them from the pot and set aside. Blanch the tōfu slices in the same pot for 1 minute, or until oil swirls on the water's surface. Drain, cut each slice lengthwise in half, and then cut each half crosswise into short, narrow strips. Blot away excess oil from the strips. When the greens are

(continued)

cool enough to handle, squeeze out excess moisture, chop coarsely, and set aside.

Heat a wok or a large, heavy skillet over high heat. Toss in the tōfu and allow the pieces to sear for a moment until lightly browned at the edges. Add the fresh mushrooms, then the slivers of softened dried shiitaké and stir-fry for about 1 minute, or until any excess liquid has evaporated and the mushrooms are aromatic. Sprinkle with the sugar and continue to stir-fry for 30 seconds longer. Add the saké and stir-fry until the pan is dry.

Add the stock (it will sizzle and sputter a bit, so be careful) and lower the heat to maintain a steady but not-too-vigorous simmer. Skim away the first large cloud of froth that appears with a fine-mesh skimmer. More froth will appear (this is normal when using shiitaké mushroom stock) as you continue to simmer. Cook for 5 or 6 minutes, then skim away the froth again.

Add the carrot and daikon, season the soup with the mirin and light-colored soy sauce, and continue to simmer for 2 or 3 minutes, or until the vegetables are firm but tender and the flavors are melded.

Add the *yuba* and stir to distribute, and then add the soy sauce. In a small bowl, stir together the cornstarch and cold water. Add the mixture to the pan, raise the heat to high, and stir until thickened and glossy. The final soup will have the consistency of a thin sauce.

Divide the noodles among 4 warmed bowls, then divide the soup evenly among the bowls. Top each serving with some of the chopped greens and a small mound of ginger. Serve immediately.

CHILLED SOBA NOODLES WITH MISO DIP

MISO-DARÉ ZARU SOBA

Noodle purists insist that *zaru soba*, boiled buckwheat noodles served on a slatted bamboo tray, is the benchmark by which all other *soba* dishes must be judged. Indeed, the complex, nutty aroma and texture of good-quality *soba* is shown off best without further adornment. The classic presentation today pairs the noodles with a wasabi-spiked, intensely seasoned soy dipping sauce that has been infused with smoky fish flakes. The vegan version I offer here harks back centuries, to a time when miso, rather than soy sauce, was the primary seasoning element in the Japanese kitchen. Be sure to reserve the *soba yu*, the nutrient-rich noodle cooking water, for making the dipping sauce and for transforming what remains of the dipping sauce into a broth for sipping, if you like.

SERVES 4

Cooked soba noodles, for serving cold (page 56), with soba yu reserved

MISO DIP

3 tablespoons Sendai miso (page 271) or other full-bodied red miso

1¹/₂ tablespoons sugar

2 tablespoons saké

2 to 2¹/₂ tablespoons soba yu

2-inch segment naga negi (page 273) or leek

2 to 3 tablespoons white sesame seeds, freshly dry-roasted (page 245), cracked or whole

2 cups soba yu (optional)

Ready the noodles, reserving the *soba yu*.

Make the miso dip: In a small, heavy saucepan, combine the miso, sugar, saké, and 2 tablespoons of the *soba yu*. Stir well. Place the pan over medium heat and continue to stir the mixture, allowing the sauce to thicken as it cooks. The sauce will bubble; be careful not to burn yourself as the bubbles burst. It is ready when you can draw a line on the bottom of the pan with a spoon or silicone spatula that remains visible for several seconds before it fills. Remove the pan from the heat. As the sauce cools, it will thicken further (you can thin it later when ready to serve).

Slit the segment of *naga negi* lengthwise to open it flat against your cutting board. Slice it lengthwise into fine, threadlike strips. Cut these strips crosswise into thirds. Immerse the pieces in ice water. In less than a minute, they will begin to curl slightly. Drain and set aside as a garnish.

Serve the noodles: Place the *soba* in a strainer or colander and run cold water over them to help loosen individual strands. Drain well by tapping the side of the strainer vigorously. Divide the noodles among 4 slatted bamboo trays. You can improvise by placing a *sudaré* (page 249) over an ordinary plate. Adjust the consistency of the dipping sauce by adding additional *soba yu* as needed. Divide the dipping sauce among 4 small, deep bowls.

Garnish each portion of noodles with a tuft of the *naga negi* and a scattering of sesame seeds. Set each place with a tray of noodles and a small bowl of miso dip. Place the 2 cups *soba yu* in an attractive pitcher and bring it to table. Each person lifts noodles from his or her tray and dips them in the miso dip. After eating the noodles, the *soba yu* can be added to what remains of the dip to make a miso-enriched broth that is drunk at the conclusion of the meal.

CHILLED SOBA NOODLES WITH PLUM-FLAVORED MOUNTAIN YAM SALAD

SOBA NO BAINIKU YAMA KAKÉ

The Japanese cultivate a wide variety of tubers, many of which boast a slithery, sticky texture (for most Japanese that's the best thing about eating them). Two varieties, *yama imo* (literally "mountain tuber") and *naga imo* (literally "long tuber") are especially viscous. In fact, they are grated and used as a binder in lieu of beaten eggs in the vegan kitchen. In this recipe, however, the mountain yam is sliced into slender matchsticks, tossed in a sour plum sauce, and then garnished with shreds of herbaceous *shiso*. The texture of the ivory-colored yam is both crisp (you will hear a crunch when you bite into it) and silky (well, maybe "slippery" is more accurate), and when you toss the saladlike topping with the *soba* noodles it will cling and coat them, making them easy to slurp—which is how the Japanese eat this dish!

SERVES 4

Cooked soba noodles, for serving cold (page 56)

4 cups cold water

1 teaspoon vinegar

8 to 10 ounces yama imo (page 276), sliced into 8 circles, each about ¹/₂ inch thick

Sour Plum Sauce (page 125)

4 or 5 fresh shiso leaves (page 258), stems trimmed, then leaves stacked, tightly rolled lengthwise, and cut crosswise into very thin shreds

Divide the noodles among 4 serving bowls.

Pour the water into a bowl and stir in the vinegar. Carefully remove the peel from each *yama imo* slice. The slices will be slippery, but peeling the skin in a single strip from around each slice is the simplest and safest method. You may want to wear thin latex gloves or hold the cut ends with paper towels. Immediately place the peeled circles in the vinegar water to keep them from turning color (brown, gray, and purple are all possible shades of discoloration) and to limit the viscosity of the cut surfaces. Soak for at least 2 minutes or up to 30 minutes, then drain and pat dry on paper towels.

Line a cutting board with paper towels to prevent slipping, and lay the *yama imo* circles in a single layer on the paper towels. Do not stack the slices; they will be too slippery. With the tip of a knife, cut each slice into matchsticks; use your knife as though it is a pencil, drawing lines. Gather the sticks into 4 piles, coaxing each pile into a tepeelike mound. Place 1 mound in the center of each portion of *soba* noodles.

Place a spoonful of the plum sauce on the top of each mound of *yama imo* sticks. Scatter with the *shiso* shreds and serve. Diners toss together their noodles and toppings in much the same way as one tosses a chef's salad just before eating.

SOBA NOODLE SOUP WITH
MOUNTAIN VEGETABLES

SANSAI SOBA

The Shinshu district (current-day Nagano Prefecture, where the 1998 Winter Olympics were held) boasts many regional delicacies, among them *soba* noodles and *sansai* (mountain vegetables). They combine here in soup noodles that have found an appreciative international audience in addition to die-hard local fans.

In their native land, the appearance of *sansai* on menus heralds springtime. If you can source fresh fiddleheads or other ferns such as *warabi* or *zenmai* (see box, page 71) in your local market, use them. You will be well rewarded for your efforts. If fresh *sansai* are not available, I provide instructions for using packaged, parboiled Asian ferns sold at many Japanese, Korean, and Chinese groceries outside Japan. If you have Fresh Bamboo Shoots (page 92) on hand, feel free to add them to the other springtime vegetables.

SERVES 4

6 to 7 ounces fiddlehead ferns (page 255) or 3 ounces packaged parboiled warabi and/or zenmai

2 dried shiitaké mushrooms

2 cups water

3 ounces thick stem from 1 head broccoli, peeled or scraped, cut into thin rounds

2 sheets thin fried tōfu (page 282)

1 teaspoon aromatic sesame oil

$^1/_2$ teaspoon sugar

1 tablespoon saké

3 ounces naméko mushrooms (page 273)

1 tablespoon Vegan Seasoned Soy Concentrate (page 131) or soy sauce

Cooked soba noodles, for serving hot (page 56), with soba yu reserved

2 to 3 tablespoons white sesame seeds, freshly dry-roasted (page 245)

If using fiddlehead ferns, prepare them as directed in Fiddlehead Ferns Steeped in Soy-Tinged Broth (page 123), then drain and reserve. If using packaged ferns, drain them, blanch them in boiling water for 1 minute, and drain again. Cut into 1-inch lengths and reserve.

Extract a stock from the dried shiitaké mushrooms: Break off the stems and set them aside for making stock on another occasion. Here you are using only the dried shiitaké caps to make a stock (and to cook later with the other vegetables). Soak the caps in the water in a bowl for at least 30 minutes and preferably for 1 hour or more. Remove the caps from the water and rinse them to remove any gritty material, then squeeze gently. Pour the soaking water through a fine-mesh strainer (or disposable coffee filter) into a clean bowl to remove unwanted bits that may have settled at the bottom of the bowl. Set the stock aside. Slice the dried shiitaké caps into very narrow strips.

Bring a small saucepan filled with water to a boil. Blanch the broccoli slices for 45 seconds or until they turn bright green. With a skimmer, scoop them from the pot and set aside. Blanch the tōfu slices in the same pot for 1 minute or until oil swirls on the water's surface. Drain and when cool enough to handle, cut each slice lengthwise in half, then cut each half crosswise into short, narrow strips. Blot away excess oil from the strips.

Heat the sesame oil in a skillet over medium-high heat. Add the shiitaké mushroom strips and fried tōfu strips and stir-fry for about 1 minute, or until the tōfu browns slightly. Sprinkle with the sugar and toss to distribute. Add the saké and deglaze the pan, stirring to dislodge any browned bits. Add the reserved mushroom stock and cook at a steady simmer for about 5 minutes, skimming away any large clouds of froth with a fine-mesh skimmer.

Add the *naméko* mushrooms, fiddlehead ferns, and broccoli slices. Simmer just until heated through. Season with the soy concentrate and simmer for about 1 minute to meld the flavors. If the amount of liquid seems too little, add some of the *soba yu* to compensate.

Divide the noodles among 4 warmed bowls, then divide the soup evenly among the bowls. Garnish with the sesame seeds and slurp away!

VARIETIES OF SANSAI AVAILABLE IN JAPAN

Nature's bounty takes many delicious forms, among them *sansai*. In Japan's mountainous woodlands, a host of edible treasures reward diligent forgers.

fuki: butterbur; *Petasites japonicus*
fuki no to: unopened butterbur bud
kogomi: fiddlehead of the ostrich fern; *Matteuccia struthiopteris*
tara no me: shoot of the angelica tree; *Aralia elata*
tsukushi: spore-bearing shoot of field horsetail; *Equisetum arvense*
udo: wild udo; *Aralia cordata*
warabi: bracken; *Pteridium aquilinum*
yomogi: mugwort; *Artemisia princeps*
zenmai: royal fern, Osmond fern; *Osmunda japonica*

STOCKS AND SOUPS

MANY THINGS STRUCK ME AS ODD when I first arrived in Japan. None were what could be considered of great importance, of course. But all were nonetheless baffling, even those in the everyday world of soups. Take the idea that clear broths with just a few morsels nestled at the bottom of a bowl were considered elegant. To me, they seemed rather stingy. Or, even more puzzling was that a creamy potage served with an inch-thick slice of toast (cut into two trapezoidal slabs set at jaunty angles!) constituted a "Western-style" breakfast. I expected that sort of soup to be served at lunchtime with a sandwich. As a child in the United States, I had always enjoyed stick-to-your-ribs oatmeal when it was served to me, but I was brought up in a household where the day began with orange juice (for everyone) and cold cereal (for children) or coffee and doughnuts (for grown-ups).

I quickly learned (though did not immediately appreciate) that *shirumono* (literally, "liquid foods" or, in other words, soups) were an essential part of all meals, even breakfast—especially breakfast— where miso-enriched soup is traditionally paired with rice and *tsukémono* (pickles). In thinking about which soups to include here, I wanted to make sure that all tastes and habits could be comfortably accommodated. To that end, I have provided chunky chowders, smooth purées, and clear broths, along with an old-fashioned home-style *miso shiru*. You can start your day with these soups, or you can wait until midday or evening to enjoy them. I also hope that these recipes will inspire you to create some of your own original soups from whatever you have on hand.

MAKING STOCKS

Making flavorful and nutrient-rich stock—what the Japanese refer to as dashi—is the key to producing not only flavorful soups in the Japanese vegan kitchen but countless other dishes as well.

The word *dashi*, used to describe a wide variety of flavorful liquids in the Japanese kitchen, derives from the verb *hiki dasu*, "to draw out" or "extract." Indeed, all dashi are extracted essences, many made by soaking sun-dried ingredients in cold water and others by applying heat. Depending on the specific items used, the timing and degree of heat varies.

In the vegetarian kitchen, it is useful to have several lidded glass jars or beakers, each for a different-flavored essence. Assemble the stocks at night before retiring, to simplify and speed food preparation the following day. Or, if you work outside the home, assemble them in the morning for use in dishes for that evening's supper.

If your tap water is hard (rich in minerals such as calcium and magnesium), you may find vegan stocks in which kelp is used taste faintly metallic. Using soft water or filtered water produces superior-tasting stocks. (Not sure about whether your water is hard or soft? Wash your hands with soap. The soap will lather richly in soft water.)

Unless you live in a particularly hot or humid climate in which food spoilage might be a problem, the extracts are best made and stored at room temperature and used within 12 to 15 hours. Most stocks can be made in 30 minutes at room temperature, though allowing the ingredients to steep for an hour does produce more intense flavors. If made in the refrigerator, most stocks require a minimum of 6 to 8 hours to develop flavor.

If making stocks at room temperature concerns you, assemble them and place them in the refrigerator from the start to extract the flavor. Stocks made at room temperature can be refrigerated for extended storage once the flavor has been extracted. In general, most stocks can be held for several days in the refrigerator; each recipe will guide you with specifics. Freezing does not work well for delicate vegetable stocks, especially those in which kelp has been used to enhance the flavor. The crystallized kelp-enhanced extracts often smell unpleasantly of iodine after they are defrosted.

When purchasing products for making stocks, check labels carefully to make sure the items have been sun-dried or air-dried naturally. You must never use chemically dried or artificially preserved items for stock, because most of the chemicals are water-soluble and leach out into the rehydrating liquid that becomes the stock. Also, never reserve the liquid used to rehydrate *hijiki* for stock or other consumption (see box on page 264 for more information).

BASIC KELP STOCK

KOMBU DASHI

The master stock used in making traditional vegetarian Japanese cookery is made from just *kombu*, a sweet but sturdy kelp. Different varieties of *kombu*, harvested from different waterways, yield slightly different flavors. The two types most frequently used are *Hidaka kombu* and *ma kombu*; both are pictured on page 265. Descriptions of them in A Catalog of Ingredients will help you identify and select the most suitable type for the particular dish you will be making. All varieties of *kombu* are rich in glutamates (*umami seibun*), the essence of flavor enhancement. Unlike artificially produced MSG, the naturally occurring glutamates in kelp do not seem to cause unpleasant reactions when consumed.

The higher the percentage of glutamates, the more heat-sensitive the *kombu* will be. Cold-water extractions will yield the best results, with gentle heat applied, if at all, after a minimum of 30 minutes soaking at room temperature. Sometimes this cold-water stock is referred to as *kombu-jiru*, literally "the liquid from soaking kelp."

Use a glass jar for best results. You can keep the *kombu* in the liquid in the jar for up to 2 days, or remove it (and use it in other dishes) soon after its flavor has been extracted. Early signs of spoilage are filament-like clouding and thickening sediment at the bottom of the container. Most cold-water extracts can be kept for 4 or 5 days in the refrigerator.

MAKES 4 CUPS

1 piece kombu (page 266), about 1^1/$_2$ by 4 inches if using Hidaka kombu or a 3-inch square if using ma kombu

4 cups water, preferably soft tap or filtered

Place the *kombu* in a large glass jar. Pour in the water, and cover with a lid or plastic wrap. Covering the jar prevents surrounding odors from entering the stock and helps trap the good seashore aromas.

To extract the most flavor, allow the *kombu* to sit submerged in the water at room temperature for at least 30 minutes or up to 12 hours before using the stock. If you prefer to refrigerate the stock from the start, allow the *kombu* to soak for at least 8 hours or up to 48 hours before using the stock.

Remove the softened *kombu* from the jar after the flavor has been extracted from it (at least 30 minutes if at room temperature or at least 8 hours if refrigerated), or after 2 days. The stock can be kept, refrigerated, for 4 to 5 days before using.

Many recipes in *Kansha* call for *kombu* that has been used in stock making. After removing, slip the *kombu* into a small, lidded container or resealable plastic bag, then store in the vegetable bin of your refrigerator for several days. If a sticky, pasty white film forms on the surface of the kelp, it has spoiled and must be discarded. Do not attempt to freeze the softened kelp. The texture becomes more fibrous and/or pulpy and an unpleasant iodine smell often develops.

VEGETARIAN STOCKS MADE FROM SUN-DRIED VEGETABLES

SHŌJIN DASHI-JIRU, KAMBUTSU HEN

Dried foods, known collectively as *kambutsu*, must be softened before cooking with them. The liquids that result from this softening procedure can be used alone or with other stocks. Sun-dried vegetables such as shredded radish (*kiriboshi daikon*), gourd ribbons (*kampyō*), and shiitaké mushrooms produce intensely flavored stocks and play an important role in the *shōjin* (Buddhist or temple vegetarian) kitchen. The simplest and most flavorful sun-dried vegetable stocks are made as cold-water infusions enhanced and enriched by the addition of *kombu*.

It is a good idea to have one or more of the following stocks in your kitchen at all times. The softened vegetables that are strained from the stock can be kept in sealed containers or bags in the refrigerator for up to 2 days. (Note that if a sticky, white paste forms on the *kombu* before using, discard it.)

EACH RECIPE MAKES 4 CUPS

SUN-DRIED RADISH STOCK (KIRIBOSHI DAIKON DASHI)

> ½ cup kiriboshi daikon (page 263)
>
> 1 piece kombu (page 266), about 2 by 1½ inches if using Hidaka kombu or 3 by 1½ inches if using ma kombu
>
> 4 cups water, preferably soft tap or filtered

SUN-DRIED GOURD RIBBON STOCK (KAMPYŌ DASHI)

> 2 or 3 pieces kampyō (page 262), about 15 feet total
>
> 1 piece kombu (page 266), about 2 by 1½ inches if using Hidaka kombu or 3 by 1½ inches if using ma kombu
>
> 4 cups water, preferably soft tap or filtered

SUN-DRIED SHIITAKÉ MUSHROOM STOCK (HOSHI SHIITAKÉ DASHI)

> 5 or 6 large or 8 to 10 small dried shiitaké mushrooms
>
> 1 piece kombu (page 266), about 2 by 1½ inches if using Hidaka kombu or 3 by 1½ inches if using ma kombu
>
> 4 cups water, preferably soft tap or filtered

Decide which stock (or stocks) you wish to make, then place the dried vegetable and *kombu* in a glass jar. Pour in the water, and cover with a lid or plastic wrap. Covering the jar prevents surrounding odors from entering the stock.

To extract the most flavor from the ingredients, allow them to sit submerged in the water at room temperature for at least 30 minutes before using the stock. If you prefer to refrigerate the stock from the start, allow the ingredients to soak for at least 4 hours before using. If you are rushed and want to speed up the flavor extraction, use warm (but not boiling or very hot) water and let the ingredients soak for at least 30 minutes. The stock can be kept, refrigerated, for up to several days before using.

When ready to use, strain the stock through a fine-woven cloth-lined or fine-mesh strainer (or disposable coffee filter) to remove any foreign matter. Set aside the softened vegetables and *kombu* for use in other recipes.

The softened radish shreds will yield a deep gold, faintly sweet liquid. The gourd will yield a pale amber, mild-flavored liquid (with a hint of dried apricots). Softened mushrooms will yield an earthy, reddish brown liquid (with woodsy overtones). Each stock can used in any recipe calling for stock.

SPARKLING BROTH

SAWANI WAN

The word *sawayaka*, the root of this soup's name, is used to describe many things in Japanese: the weather, personalities, and food and drink. When used in a culinary context, it suggests refreshing foods that are light on the palate or beverages that sparkle. The classic version of this soup is made with thread-thin slivers of vegetables and shreds of pork in a delicate soy-tinged broth; the vegan version substitutes thin strips of fried tōfu for the meat. Freshly cracked black pepper adds a spicy and sparkling finish.

SERVES 4

2 dried shiitaké mushrooms, soaked in 1 cup water for 30 minutes

1 sheet thin fried tōfu (page 282)

Splash of saké

3 cups stock, preferably Basic Kelp Stock (page 75)

1 generous teaspoon light-colored soy sauce

1/4 teaspoon salt

1/2 ounce boiled fresh bamboo shoot (page 92), preferably the bottom section, cut into thread-thin sen-giri strips (page 244), about 1 tablespoon

1/2-inch segment carrot, scraped and cut into thread-thin sen-giri strips, about 1 tablespoon

2 or 3 snow peas, strings and stems removed, blanched for 1 minute, and cut into thread-thin strips on the diagonal

1/2 teaspoon freshly ground black pepper

Drain the mushrooms, reserving the soaking liquid. Trim off the stems, rinse the caps to remove any gritty material, and squeeze out the excess liquid. Slice the caps into thread-thin strips and set aside.

Bring a small saucepan filled with water to a boil (this can be the same water that was used to blanch the snow peas). Add the tōfu and blanch for 30 seconds to remove excess oil, or until beads of oil float on the water's surface. Drain the tōfu, and when cool enough to handle, use paper towels to press out and blot away excess water and oil. Cut the tōfu lengthwise into 3 or 4 strips, and then cut crosswise into short, thin strips. Blot the strips again with paper towels.

Place a 3-quart pot over medium-high heat. Add the fried tōfu and sauté with the oil that still clings to it (even after pressing and blotting, there will be some oil remaining). When the tōfu is slightly browned and aromatic, add the shiitaké strips and sauté for 1 minute. Add the saké and deglaze the pot, stirring to dislodge any browned bits.

Add the mushroom liquid and the stock and bring to a boil. Skim away any clouds of froth with a fine-mesh skimmer, then adjust the heat to maintain a gentle simmer. Season the broth with the soy sauce and salt. Add the bamboo shoot strips and simmer for 1 minute. Add the carrot strips and simmer for 30 seconds more. Skim away any froth.

Remove the pot from the heat, add the snow peas, and immediately ladle into bowls. If possible, use 4 deep, lidded Japanese-style soup bowls, which will ensure the soup is served piping hot and will trap the aromas. Grind the pepper over the soup, lid the bowls, and serve immediately.

LOTUS ROOT DUMPLING SOUP

RENKON MOCHI-JIRU

Lotus root changes character with its method of preparation. When thinly sliced and barely blanched or stir-fried, it is crisp and crunchy. Cut into chunks and simmered, it remains firm while becoming tender. Grated and fried, as it is in this recipe, the texture changes to soft yet dense, and a bit chewy. Floated with *wakamé* in a *sanshō* pepper–flecked broth, the lotus root dumplings make a distinctive soup.

Fresh lotus root is increasingly available in Asian markets outside Japan and I urge you to seek out a source for it in your community.

SERVES 4

DUMPLINGS

    7 ounces lotus root

    1/4 teaspoon salt

    2 tablespoons cornstarch

    Vegetable oil for frying

    1 to 2 teaspoons aromatic sesame oil (optional)

    3 cups stock, preferably Basic Kelp Stock (page 75)

    Splash of saké

    1 generous teaspoon light-colored soy sauce

    1/4 teaspoon salt

    2 tablespoons dried wakamé (page 267)

    1/2 teaspoon kona-zanshō (page 258)

Make the lotus root dumplings: Scrub the lotus root to remove any residual earth or thinly peel, then finely grate the root (a ceramic grater, page 246, is especially effective).

Line a strainer with *sarashi* (page 250) or a double layer of cheesecloth. Gather up the edges of the cloth and, holding it over the sink, gently twist and squeeze to remove excess moisture. Ideally, the grated lotus root will have the texture of very moist sand.

Transfer the drained lotus root to a clean bowl and season with the salt. Sift 2 teaspoons of the cornstarch over the lotus root and stir to combine. It will be a soft, somewhat sticky mixture. It should be cohesive enough, however, to form into small balls with your hands. The lotus root is naturally viscous, and the cornstarch acts as a "glue" to hold the mixture together.

Put the remaining 4 teaspoons cornstarch in a small bowl. Divide the lotus root mixture into 12 equal portions, each about a scant teaspoon. Lightly roll each portion between your palms into a small sphere. One at a time, place each dumpling in the bowl of cornstarch and tap the sides of the bowl to help roll the dumpling in the cornstarch, dusting it lightly and evenly. As each dumpling is coated, transfer to a paper towel–lined rack.

Pour the vegetable oil to a depth of 1 1/2 inches in a small wok or other heavy skillet with sloped sides, add the sesame oil, and heat to about 350°F. Check the temperature with an unvarnished long wooden chopstick (or a bamboo skewer). Small bubbles will form around the tip when the oil is about 350°F. Or, test the oil with a pinch of the lotus root mixture: if it sinks slightly, rises to the surface, and puffs a bit but does not color immediately, the oil is ready.

Gently lower the dumplings, one at a time, into the hot oil, being careful not to crowd the pan. (If necessary, fry in batches.) They should sizzle immediately. Fry undisturbed for 2 minutes. Do not flip the dumplings back and forth;

they are delicate and can easily fall apart. After 2 minutes, flip the dumplings once and continue to fry for another minute, or until golden brown in spots (the dumplings do not color evenly). Using a fine-mesh skimmer, scoop out the dumplings and transfer to a paper towel–lined rack to drain and cool. The dumplings can be made in advance and refrigerated for 2 days. Zap them for 30 to 40 seconds in a microwave when you are ready to use them.

Serve the soup: Place the stock in a small saucepan, season it with the saké and soy sauce, and place over medium heat until it comes to a very gentle simmer. Add the dumplings, adjust the heat until the stock is barely simmering, and heat for about 2 minutes, or until the dumplings are heated through.

If possible, use 4 deep, lidded Japanese-style soup bowls, which will ensure the soup is served piping hot and will trap the aromas. Place an equal amount of the *wakamé* in each bowl. Scoop the dumplings out of the stock and place 3 dumplings in each bowl. Ladle the hot stock into the bowls and lid them (or cover with foil) for 1 minute; this will soften the *wakamé*. Remove the lids, garnish each serving with a generous pinch of *kona-zanshō*, and then re-lid the bowls. Serve immediately.

BURDOCK AND WHEAT STRIPS IN DARK MISO BROTH

AKA DASHI

Aka dashi soups made with smoky, pure bean Hatchō miso are often served in elegant establishments at the conclusion of a *kaiseki*-style banquet. This *aka dashi*, however, boasts a more plebeian profile, attributable to the fact that the burdock root is *not* soaked first. Because *aku-nuki*, or "bitterness removal," is not performed, some "froth" might need to be removed as you simmer the soup, but the intensely woodsy overtones that the untreated burdock contributes will provide character. The slivers of dried *ita-bu* (wheat gluten) absorb the flavors of the burdock and miso nicely and provide volume as well.

SERVES 4

¹/₂ teaspoon aromatic sesame oil

1 small burdock root, about 4 ounces, scraped and cut sasagaki style (page 244)

Pinch of sugar

1 tablespoon saké

3 cups stock, preferably Basic Kelp Stock (page 75)

3 tablespoons Hatchō miso (page 271)

1 sheet ita-bu, about 5¹/₂ by 8 inches, softened (page 268), cut with scissors in half lengthwise, and then crosswise into very thin strips

¹/₄ teaspoon kona-zanshō (page 258), optional

Heat the sesame oil in a sturdy 2-quart pot over high heat. Add the burdock root and sauté for about 1 minute, or until aromatic and wilted. Sprinkle with the sugar and sauté for about 30 seconds, or until a few edges appear caramelized. Add the saké and deglaze the pot, stirring to dislodge any browned bits. Add the stock, bring to a simmer, and then adjust the heat to maintain a gentle simmer. Cook for 2 minutes. If large clouds of froth appear, skim with a fine-mesh skimmer.

Place the miso in a *miso koshi* (page 250) and stir to dissolve directly in the pot. Or, place the miso in a small bowl and ladle in some of the hot stock from the pot. Stir to dissolve, then strain this mixture through a fine-mesh strainer into the pot if there are bits or lumps. Do not allow the soup to boil once the miso has been added. This traditional wisdom should be heeded for two reasons: boiling the soup diminishes the nutritional value of miso and compromises its aroma. Toss in the strips of *ita-bu* and stir. The strips will swell and open into thin ribbons.

If possible, use 4 deep, lidded Japanese-style soup bowls, which will ensure the soup is served piping hot and will trap the aromas. Ladle the soup into the bowls. Garnish each serving with a pinch of *kona-zanshō*, if you like a bit of spice. Lid the bowls and serve immediately.

RED AND WHITE MISO SOUP

KŌHAKU-JIRU

The color combination of red and white is used on happy occasions in Japan; foods named *kō* (red) *haku* (white) have an aura of festivity about them. In a desire to gussy up this simple but satisfying soup made from frankly mundane ingredients—daikon peels and carrots—I have decided to call it *kōhaku-jiru.*

SERVES 4

1 teaspoon aromatic sesame oil

Several strips of daikon peel, cut into thick julienne strips (about ¹/₂ cup)

1¹/₂ ounces carrot, cut into thick julienne strips (about ¹/₄ cup)

Pinch of salt

Splash of saké

3¹/₂ cups stock, preferably Sun-Dried Radish Stock (page 76), or equal parts radish stock and Sun-Dried Shiitaké Mushroom Stock (page 76)

1¹/₂ tablespoons red miso, preferably Sendai miso (page 271)

1 tablespoon white miso, preferably Saikyō miso (page 271)

A few daikon leaves, barely blanched and coarsely chopped (about 2 tablespoons)

1 or 2 scallions, thinly sliced on the diagonal (optional)

Heat the oil in a pot over medium heat. Add the daikon peel and carrot strips and sauté for about 1 minute, or until slightly translucent. Sprinkle with the salt, then add the saké and jiggle the pot to deglaze any browned bits. Add the stock, bring to a boil, and then adjust the heat to maintain a bare simmer. Cook for about 5 minutes, or until the vegetables are tender but still firm. If large clouds of froth appear, skim them away with a fine-mesh skimmer.

Place the miso in the *miso koshi* (page 250) and stir to dissolve directly in the pot. Or, place the miso in a small bowl and ladle in some of the hot stock from the pot. Stir to dissolve, then strain this mixture through a fine-mesh strainer into the pot. Do not allow the soup to boil once the miso has been added. This traditional wisdom should be heeded for two reasons: boiling the soup diminishes the nutritional value of miso and compromises its aroma.

If possible, use 4 deep, lidded Japanese-style soup bowls, which will ensure the soup is served piping hot and will trap the aromas. Place an equal amount of the daikon leaves in each bowl; add scallions for a more complex flavor. Ladle the hot soup over the greens. Lid the bowls and serve immediately.

KITCHEN CULTURE: AWASÉ MISO

Mixing different kinds of miso, what is known as *awasé* (combining) *miso*, is a common practice in the Japanese kitchen. No hard-and-fast rules exist regarding percentages, though most households prefer saltier miso soup in hot weather and sweeter in the cold months. This recipe blends robust red miso and milder, sweeter white miso for a mellow flavor and a rich burnished brown color. Feel free to adjust according to your preferences.

CREAMY JAPANESE LEEK SOUP WITH MISO

NEGI-JIRU

The harvesting of long, slender *naga negi* (Japanese leeks) begins when the soil in the fields crackles underfoot with morning frost. In and around Kyoto, the local heirloom variety, known as *Kujō negi*, has tender, green tufted tops and is both sweet and spicy. Residents enjoy them in simmered or braised dishes, but also raw, thinly sliced.

On those early winter mornings when it's hard to crawl out from under cozy futon, this soup is warm and comforting. If you prefer to wait until noon, you can enjoy this creamy leek soup at lunchtime, and even add croutons of toasted French bread.

SERVES 4

2 naga negi (page 273) or leeks, each about 6 ounces

1 teaspoon aromatic sesame oil

Pinch of salt

Splash of saké

3½ cups stock, preferably a combination of Sun-Dried Radish Stock (page 76) and Sun-Dried Shiitaké Mushroom Stock (page 76)

3 tablespoons Saikyō miso (page 271)

Trim the *naga negi*, and then cut the green tops off the white portion. Cut the white portion into very thin slices on the diagonal. Rinse the slices briefly in ice-cold water to rid them of any soil that might be trapped between the layers, then drain.

Cut the green *naga negi* tops into very thin slices on the diagonal. Don't be concerned if a slippery substance appears. This enzyme, known as allicin, is responsible for the distinctive aroma associated with onions and garlic, and it will help suspend the miso in the stock, thickening the soup.

Heat the oil in a saucepan over medium heat. If you are using a leek variety common in North America or Europe, the green tops may be a bit tough and require longer cooking than the slices from the white section. Add them to the pan and sauté for about 3 minutes, or until wilted and aromatic. Then add the white slices and continue to sauté for another 2 minutes, or until the white slices are wilted. If the green tops are not tough, add the green and white slices together and sauté for about 2 minutes, or until wilted and aromatic. Sprinkle with the salt, then add the saké and jiggle the pan to deglaze any browned bits. Add the stock and simmer for 3 or 4 minutes, or until the *naga negi* or leeks are very tender. Skim away any large clouds of froth with a fine-mesh skimmer.

Because Saikyō miso is creamy, no special strainer is needed to mix it with the stock. Place the miso in a small bowl and ladle in some of the hot stock from the pan. Stir to dissolve the miso, then add the mixture to the pan. Do not allow the soup to boil once the miso has been added. This traditional wisdom should be heeded for two reasons: boiling the soup diminishes the nutritional value of miso and compromises its aroma.

Divide the soup among bowls and serve piping hot.

CREAMY KABOCHA SOUP

KABOCHA NO SURINAGASHI

I encourage you to use *kabocha* in its entirety. The skin of this squash is tough but delicious and nutritious. In most preparations, it is left intact and cooked along (and eaten) with the flesh. In this soup, however, the bright, sunny color would be compromised by the green markings of the skin. Remove the skin in thick slabs with some of the bright orange-yellow flesh clinging to it. Refrigerate for up to 3 days and add to the Heaven-and-Earth Tempura Pancakes (page 109). Or, marinate the peels in soy sauce and fry them into chips along with Crispy Gourd Chips (page 145). *Kabocha* seeds can also be roasted and enjoyed as a snack, or finely minced and added to Rice Friends (page 152) in lieu of sesame seeds.

This puréed soup, equally tasty served chilled or piping hot, celebrates the bounty of late summer in Japan.

Pictured on page 86

SERVES 4

12 to 14 ounces kabocha squash (about 1 large wedge), seeded, peeled, and cut into small pieces

3 cups stock, preferably Basic Kelp Stock (page 75)

2 tablespoons saké

1/2 teaspoon sugar

1 teaspoon light-colored soy sauce

1 1/2 tablespoons white miso, preferably Saikyō miso (page 271)

1 cup soy milk, freshly extracted (page 156) or purchased

1 heaping tablespoon snipped fresh chives

Put the *kabocha* in a saucepan and add 2 cups of the stock, the saké, and the sugar. Place over medium heat, bring to a simmer, and cook for about 5 minutes after the stock begins to simmer, or until the *kabocha* is just tender.

Transfer the contents of the pan to a blender and purée until smooth. If necessary, add a few drops of water to engage the blades of the blender fully. Return the purée to the saucepan, add the remaining 1 cup stock, and heat gently over low heat, stirring, until heated through.

In a small bowl, combine the soy sauce, miso, and soy milk. Stir to dissolve the miso, then add the mixture to the pan. Cook the soup, stirring, for 1 minute to meld flavors. Do not allow the soup to boil.

Divide the soup among 4 bowls and serve piping hot. Or, allow the soup to cool completely, then cover and chill for at least 6 hours or up to several days, then serve chilled.

For color contrast, and a savory accent, garnish individual portions of the hot or chilled soup with chives.

EXTRACTING FLAVOR

When making chunky soups and chowders, adding vegetables to already simmering stock will preserve their flavor and shape. When making puréed soups, however, starting with cold liquid helps draw flavor from vegetables into the stock. If the vegetables crumble, it isn't a problem because they will be puréed later.

SPRINGTIME IN A BOWL

HARU NO SURINAGASHI WAN

Puréed soups, called *surinagashi* (literally, "grind" and "pour"), showcase seasonal vegetables on a Japanese menu. This elegant, celadon-colored soup captures the nutty, sweet essence of fava beans and sugar snap peas, a sure sign that springtime has arrived at table.

SERVES 4

   1 generous cup shelled fresh fava beans, steamed until tender and tough skins removed

   3 ounces sugar snap peas, strings and stems removed and steamed until tender

   1/2 cup soy milk, freshly extracted (page 156) or purchased

   1 teaspoon white miso, preferably Saikyō miso (page 271)

   1 1/2 cups stock, preferably Basic Kelp Stock (page 75)

   Pinch of salt (optional)

   About 6 ounces silken tōfu (page 282), drained of packing liquid and cut into 4 small squares

   1/2 teaspoon Japanese spicy mustard (page 257)

   Fresh mint leaves, snipped fresh chives, minced fresh parsley, or shreds of shiso leaves (page 258)

Place the fava beans, sugar snap peas, and soy milk in a food processor and pulse until the mixture is creamy and smooth. Scrape down the sides of the bowl as needed. Add the miso and 1/2 cup of the stock. Pulse until completely smooth. The sweetness of light miso various tremendously, so taste a bit and adjust with salt if necessary.

CLOCKWISE FROM TOP: *Creamy Kabocha Soup (page 85), Springtime in a Bowl, and Chilled Eggplant Soup with Myōga (page 89)*

There are two methods you can use to heat the tōfu: in a shallow saucepan or in the microwave. In both cases, have your soup bowls ready, preferably 4 deep, lidded Japanese soup bowls.

To heat the tōfu in a saucepan: Place the remaining 1 cup stock in a shallow saucepan just large enough to hold the 4 tōfu squares in a single layer. Cover the pan and heat slowly over low heat; it will take about 3 minutes for the tōfu to heat through to the center. Jiggle the saucepan several times to make sure the tōfu is not sticking. Use a broad, flexible spatula (a silicone spatula is especially good for this task) to lift the squares, placing 1 square in the bottom of each soup bowl. Cover to keep the tōfu hot while you finish the soup. Reserve the stock in the pan.

To heat the tōfu in the microwave: Place the 4 tōfu squares on a microwave-safe plate lined with paper towels. Zap for 10 to 20 seconds 2 to 4 times (this is more effective than heating for a continuous 30 or 40 seconds). Using the paper towels or a flexible broad spatula, lift the squares, placing 1 square in the bottom of each soup bowl. Cover to keep the tōfu hot while you finish the soup.

Pour the fava bean–snap pea purée into a small saucepan and add the stock remaining in the saucepan from heating the tōfu, or the remaining 1 cup stock if the tōfu was heated in the microwave. Place over medium-low heat and heat through, stirring constantly.

To serve, uncover the bowls and carefully pour the hot purée around the squares of tōfu. The tōfu will be higher

(continued)

STOCKS AND SOUPS

than the level of purée. Place a dab of mustard at the center of each tōfu square, then garnish with your herb of choice. Serve immediately.

The Japanese will use their chopsticks to stir the herb and mustard into the soup and to spear mouthfuls of tōfu; they will sip the purée directly from the bowl. I suspect that many will find using a spoon less challenging for all three tasks. Think of the tōfu as being sauced with purée and eat accordingly.

KITCHEN CULTURE: SERVING SOUP

The Japanese have special bowls for serving soup. Called *wan*, they come in a variety of shapes—slender and deep, squat and chubby, some straight-sided and others with curved or bulging sides. Most *wan* include lids that trap aromas and keep the soup hot. Lidded bowls are ideal for serving broths and arranged purées such as this soup, but they can be difficult to source outside of Japan. If you will be serving your soup in shallow Western-style soup bowls, preheat the bowls in a steamer or the oven. In addition, since most soups served in lidded Japanese bowls include a substantial preheated item surrounded by a pool of warm broth or purée, you will need to improvise a temporary lid from aluminum foil, plastic wrap, or pot lids to retain the heat of those items—in this instance, small squares of silken tōfu.

CHILLED EGGPLANT SOUP WITH MYŌGA

NASU NO HIYA-JIRU

Those who tend a garden or who have access to local farmers' markets know that crop yields can vary from wildly abundant to disappointingly sparse throughout the summer months and into early autumn. If "profuse" describes the quantity of eggplants in your garden, or coming to market in your community, this puréed soup will be a welcome addition to your repertoire. The recipe can be doubled or tripled and the purée frozen for several months.

If "meager" availability describes your eggplant situation, you will want to make the most of the little you have: cook the flesh and peels separately, getting two dishes to savor, rather than just one.

This soup can be made with any variety of eggplant because the skins are peeled (they can be prepared as in Eggplant Two Ways, page 125). And because the flesh is puréed, the shape is unimportant, too (here is a chance to use those bulbous, bulging, or oddly twisted crops).

Pictured on page 86

SERVES 4

$^1/_2$ teaspoon salt

2 cups water

1 pound eggplant, preferably Japanese variety, peeled and cut into small chunks

1 cup soy milk, freshly extracted (page 156) or purchased

4 cups stock, preferably Basic Kelp Stock (page 75)

2 teaspoons white miso, preferably Saikyō miso (page 271)

$^1/_2$ teaspoon light-colored soy sauce (optional)

1 bulb myōga (page 257), finely shredded

In a bowl, stir the salt into the water to make a brine. Add the eggplant and let soak for 10 minutes. To make sure the pieces are fully submerged, cover them with a dampened paper towel and/or an *otoshi-buta* (page 243).

Drain but do not rinse the eggplant pieces. Place them in a microwave-safe container and cover partially. Zap on high for 2 minutes. Allow the eggplant to cool, partially covered, to room temperature.

Transfer the eggplant with whatever liquid has accumulated in the container to a blender or food processor. Add the soy milk and 2 cups of the stock and pulse until smooth. Add the miso and the remaining 2 cups stock and process until smooth and creamy. Taste and adjust the seasoning with the soy sauce, if need be.

Transfer to a lidded container and chill for at least 2 hours or up to 24 hours. (The purée can be frozen for up to 3 weeks; defrost it slowly in the refrigerator, and then process it briefly to ensure a creamy texture.)

Divide the chilled soup among 4 bowls, garnish with *myōga* shreds, and serve.

FRESH FROM THE MARKET

B ORN AND RAISED IN A BIG CITY, I was not particularly attuned to nature's rhythms when I first went to Japan. The rapid turnover in produce at the market seemed almost like a vindictive trick was being played on me: just as I discovered the pleasures of *udo* (mountain celery) or *tara no mé* (a shrub with an asparagus-like flavor), they vanished from the stores. When I bemoaned the need to wait a full year before indulging in them again, a Japanese friend taught me three words: *hashiri*, *shun*, and *nagori*.

Hashiri are those eagerly awaited foods you finally find at market: the early spring peas, small and tender (but not yet fully sweet), or autumn's first wild mushrooms that hint of the woods (but are far from robust). Despite the high price, you buy them, indulging yourself. You just can't wait.

Shun describes that magic moment when a food is at its peak of flavor and abundant. It is biting into sugary-sweet corn, bought from a roadside stand on a blazing hot summer's day, or taking pleasure in firm, succulent leeks and spicy-crisp daikon on a wintry evening.

Nagori is culinary regret. With the first warm days of spring, the vendor selling roasted sweet potatoes no longer waits at the train station for hungry commuters to return home from work. It is also not being able to let go: buying eggplants one more time, late in autumn, knowing they can't be as tasty as the ones stewed with young ginger during the summer rains.

I urge you to savor the culinary moments nature provides: scour Asian markets early in spring to find fresh bamboo shoots; seek out sources for burdock roots that have moist earth still clinging to them, and for bunches of leafy, verdant *komatsuna* with their roots attached.

Recipes in this chapter will help you enjoy nature's bounty. In addition to recipes using classic Asian vegetables, I have included dishes featuring vegetables such as parsnips and kale that are less common in Japan but available in abundance in many countries at urban farmers' markets or suburban seasonal roadside stands. I have also selected recipes that will enable you to prepare your meals without waste, using the same ingredients in different ways so you will never tire of them.

FRESH BAMBOO SHOOTS

TAKÉNOKO

If you have access to Asian grocery stores selling fresh produce, I urge you to seek out fresh *takénoko* in the spring, sold with soil still clinging to them. Prepare the shoots according to the instructions provided here and forget any and all taste memory of the canned stuff. Indulge in a *takénoko-zukushi* menu (page 94), or savor the eating pleasure over several days, preparing one or two dishes per meal.

If you cannot find fresh shoots, purchase vacuum-sealed parboiled shoots in see-through packages, stocked in the refrigerated section of Asian stores. You can use them straight from the package, drained, in place of the home-boiled shoots prepared here.

MAKES 2¹/₂ POUNDS

> 2 or 3 small fresh bamboo shoots, 2¹/₂ pounds total weight
>
> ¹/₃ cup nuka (page 274)
>
> 2 small tōgarashi (page 259)

With a kitchen brush, scrub away any earth that may still be clinging to the shoots. Peel away and discard a few of the tough, darker, outer leaves, rinsing away any soil that may be trapped between the layers. Cut off a sliver on the diagonal from the very top of each shoot, exposing an elliptical pattern of concentric rings. Trim the base with a straight cut, removing a circular slice about ¹/₈ inch thick (all these scraps and other trimmings can be composted). Lay the shoot on the board upright, with the tip at top and the base at bottom. Holding the shoot securely to keep it from rolling about, make a shallow slash lengthwise, from the narrow tip to the wider base. Do not cut the shoot in half. You want to slash it only, which will permit better cir-

culation of moist heat during cooking (and make peeling easier later on).

Place the bamboo shoots in a deep pot and add the *nuka*, *tōgarashi*, and water to cover. (The starchy oils in *nuka* neutralize hydrocyanic acid, a toxin found in most bamboo shoots; the *tōgarashi* discourage spoilage and add a spicy "kick.") Ideally the shoots will fit snugly in the bottom of the pot. You need to leave plenty of headroom, however, as the messy *nuka* mixture easily bubbles over. Top with an *otoshi-buta* (page 243), if you have one. Or, use a colander that fits inside the pot, turned upside down; the weight will keep the bamboo shoots from bobbing about and the perforations or mesh weave will allow the bubbling liquid to penetrate the bamboo shoots.

Place the pot over medium heat, bring the water to a boil, and adjust the heat to maintain a steady simmer. Do not let it boil vigorously. Cook the shoots for 45 to 50 minutes, or until a skewer or wooden toothpick meets no resistance as it passes through the core. Remove from the heat and allow the shoots to cool, lidded, in the cooking liquid.

When the shoots are cool enough to handle, lift them from the cooking liquid. They may have a vague artichoke aroma. Rinse away the excess *nuka* under cold running water. Discard the *nuka* liquid in the pot, and soak the pot in sudsy warm water for 30 minutes or more to make cleaning it easier.

The exceptional aroma and exquisite taste of these shoots are best enjoyed the day they are boiled. However, if necessary, you can place shoots in a lidded container, cover them with cold water, and refrigerate them for up to 5 days, changing the water once a day. The appearance of a sticky, white film on the surface of the water is a sign of spoilage. If the shoots have a sweet odor as well, discard them. If the shoots have no odor, you can salvage them by reboiling them for 2 to 3 minutes. Let the reboiled shoots cool naturally, then use immediately.

Separate each shoot into segments: Begin by peeling away the dark brownish outer layers of the conical tip; these are not eaten (though sometimes they are used to line or decorate a platter, lending a slight bamboo aroma to the foods placed on them). The pale champagne–colored layers just beneath, however, are tender and delicious. You will want to save this delicacy, called *himé kawa*, or "princess skin," which will keep covered in water in a sealed glass jar or other container in the refrigerator for up to 3 days; change the water daily. Its aroma and texture may remind you a bit of hearts of palm, or perhaps of artichokes.

Next, shave off any large, pebbly bumps from the outer surface of the shoot's broad base. Stand the shoot upright, measure about 3/4 inch from the bottom, and slice it off horizontally. Cut this base section in half vertically to expose a pattern of horizontal ledges and hollows inside. Remove any white, chalky material caught in the hollows between the ledges. This calcification (plaque) is natural, and random in placement. Some deposits can be rather gritty (easiest to remove with a toothpick), and some can be almost creamy, like cottage cheese (use the curved edge of a spoon handle to scrape this out). Sometimes this calcified material appears as streaks in the bamboo shoot flesh (this cannot be removed, but no harm is incurred by eating it). This bottom segment tends to be a bit tough and fibrous.

Now, turn your attention to the tapered portion of the shoot that remains. Separate it into the tip (the top 1/2 inch or so) and the midsection. See Takénoko-Zukushi (page 94) for ideas on how to cut and use the various segments to their fullest advantage. To help you assemble a mini meal from those suggestions and place it properly on a serving tray, see One Soup (Ichi-jū), One Side (Issai) (below). Enjoy!

ONE SOUP (ICHI-JŪ), ONE SIDE (ISSAI)

Assemble a simple *washoku* menu on a small tray or placemat. The inclusion of *gohan* (cooked rice) on your tray makes it officially "a meal." When setting up your tray, create a triangular pattern. Place the rice at the lower left (this position is referred to as the *kami za*, or "place of honor and respect"), place the soup to the right of the rice, and put your third dish at the back, in the center. Set the chopsticks, parallel to each other, at the front of the tray, positioning them horizontally and with the tapered end that will enter your mouth pointing left, even if you are left-handed. (Western table settings remain constant, too, independent of hand preference.)

TAKÉNOKO-ZUKUSHI (BAMBOO SHOOTS IN THEIR ENTIRETY)

Once you have divided a bamboo shoot into three segments, you can allocate the segments to different dishes, cutting the segments into pieces according to what you are making.

The broad base segment is cut in two ways, julienne threads or small chunks. To make julienne threads, cut the base horizontally (with the grain) into half-moon slices, then stack the slices and cut across the grain. These threads are especially well suited to making Sparkling Broth (page 77), or you can prepare them as you would the daikon peels in Spicy Stir-Fry (page 122).

To make small chunks, cut the base vertically into 6 or 8 wedges, then cut each wedge in half horizontally to make shorter, stubbier pieces that retain a distinctive comb shape. Bamboo shoots cut in this manner make a nice addition to Mixed Vegetables Braised with Thick Fried Tōfu (page 176).

The tougher bits of the base can be simmered in any of the vegetable stocks (see page 76) and then puréed in a blender. The purée can be made into a soup similar to Creamy Kabocha Soup (page 85) or a pudding similar to Carrot Pudding (page 112).

The midsection is typically cut in only one way: thin, comblike slices. Stand the segment upright on a cutting board and cut it vertically into quarters. Then cut each quarter into comblike slices, or thin wedges. The thickness of the pieces can vary from gossamer thin to about $1/8$ inch thick, depending on how they will be used. Use the base of your knife as a compass, with the knife tip pointing toward the rounded edge of the bamboo segment. Once the cuts are made, remove any calcified material caught in the "teeth" of the "combs." You may find the easiest way to do this is to rinse the pieces in a shallow bowl of water. Thicker wedgelike slices are fine when making Rice with Fresh Bamboo Shoots (page 20). Thinner ones are better for the springtime version of Steamed Soy Milk Custard (page 162) or for Spring Breeze Aspic (page 95). These same dishes could also be prepared with the conical tip and/or the delicate *himé kawa*.

The *himé kawa* is especially suited to making Spring Breeze Aspic, but it can also be dressed in the sour plum sauce in Eggplant Two Ways (page 125). Or, you can slice the *himé kawa* into thin strips with the grain and toss them in a bit of peppery, *kona-zanshō*-flecked creamy Nutty Tōfu Sauce (page 99).

SPRING BREEZE ASPIC

SHUNPŪ YOSÉ

When spring breezes start to blow across the Kanto plains, tender, young *takénoko* (bamboo shoots) appear in Tokyo markets. Specially tended forests in Kyushu and Kyoto are the source of early-to-market crops. In America, bundles of fresh asparagus appear at local farmers' markets as winter weather dissipates. Here, I have combined the two in a savory aspic appetizer that celebrates springtime.

At elegant restaurants in Japan, this appetizer would likely be garnished with fresh *ki no mé*, the spicy leaves of the *sanshō* pepper tree, another spring delicacy that even in Japan must be purchased for a premium price at specialty shops. When found in Asian markets outside Japan, *ki no mé* leaves are usually very expensive. If you are looking for a less costly way to sharpen the delicate flavors of spring, you can sprinkle each serving with a pinch of *kona-zanshō* (dried *sanshō* pepper), or garnish with a dab of wasabi paste. This aspic makes a refreshing appetizer—a good match for a bone-dry saké or white wine.

MAKES 6, 9, OR 12 SMALL PORTIONS

   1 stick kanten (page 264), about 6 inches, or about 2 teaspoons powdered kanten

   3 or 4 slender asparagus spears

   2 to 2^1/$_2$ cups Basic Kelp Stock (page 75)

   1^1/$_2$ tablespoons mirin

   2 teaspoons light-colored soy sauce

   2 to 3 ounces boiled fresh bamboo shoot (page 92), preferably himé kawa, finely shredded, or the tip section, thinly cut into comb-shaped slices

   1 teaspoon wasabi paste (optional)

   ^{1}/$_2$ teaspoon kona-zanshō (page 258), optional

Soften and then dissolve the stick *kanten* or dissolve the powdered *kanten* as directed on page 264 and reserve.

Break off the tough stem ends of the asparagus spears, place the ends in a small saucepan, and add the stock. Bring to a boil over high heat and cook for 5 or 6 minutes, to infuse the broth with asparagus flavor. If the boiled stem pieces are very fibrous, discard them; if not, purée them and use in a soup. Cut the asparagus spears on a slight diagonal into thin slivers, add them to the boiling stock, and blanch for about 1 minute. Drain the asparagus slivers, reserving the stock. Let the asparagus slivers cool naturally. Return the stock to the pan.

Season the asparagus-infused stock with the mirin and soy sauce and bring to a simmer. Add the bamboo shoot, cover with an *otoshi-buta* (page 243) or circle of parchment paper, and simmer for 3 minutes. Remove from the heat and allow the bamboo shoot to cool in the stock for 5 minutes.

Drain the bamboo shoot, capturing the stock in a measuring cup. Set the bamboo shoot aside. If you have less than 1^3/$_4$ cups stock, add water or more stock as needed to reach the full measure.

In a small saucepan, combine the dissolved *kanten* with the seasoned stock. Stir to combine and heat gently to keep the mixture liquid as you set up your molds. If you own a *nagashi kan* (page 249), your aspic can look exactly like the delicate squares that are pictured on page 96. Individual portions of aspic can also be made in silicone muffin cups or in foil muffin-cup liners set in ramekins.

(continued)

If using silicone cups or foil liners, set them on a tray that will fit in the refrigerator.

Arrange the bamboo slices and asparagus slivers in the bottom of your molds. Pour in the warm liquid *kanten* mixture. If bubbles form as you pour, lance them or drag them up the sides of the mold or cup with the point of a toothpick.

Let the *kanten* mixture cool down and set before covering the molds with plastic wrap. Although *kanten* will set without refrigeration, chilling it for at least 30 minutes or up to 2 hours improves flavor and texture (any leftover aspic can be stored, covered and refrigerated, for up to 2 days). Cover the molds once the mixture has set to prevent the odors from other foods from being absorbed by the aspic.

When ready to serve, unmold. If using a *nagashi kan*, lift up and remove the inner tray. Spread the flanged sides of the inner tray slightly to help loosen the aspic, then slide out the block and cut as desired. If you have used the dividers, which eliminates cutting, lift them up before removing the aspics.

If using silicone muffin cups, press gently around the outer edges to release the aspics, then invert onto serving plates. If using foil liners, invert the aspics in the liners onto plates, and then peel the liners away. Garnish each aspic with a dab of wasabi or pinch of *kona-zanshō*.

VARIATION: In Japan, fresh salted *wakamé* (page 267) comes to market early in March. If you can find some in your Asian market (look in the refrigerator case) you can enjoy it in this aspic lieu of, or in addition to, asparagus. Use 2 to 3 fronds, about 2 tablespoons, salted *wakamé*, soaked and rinsed according to the directions on page 267. Dried *wakamé* can easily be substituted for salted *wakamé*. Soak 1 tablespoon dried *wakamé* in tap water to cover for 3 to 5 minutes, or until softened. Remove the softened *wakamé*, squeeze gently to remove the excess liquid, and chop coarsely. You should have about 3 tablespoons.

SKILLET-SEARED DAIKON WITH YUZU

DAIKON NO YŪAN YAKI

The Japanese prepare daikon in a wide variety of ways. Here, hefty circles are seared to produce juicy, tender yet firm slices. Finished with a savory soy glaze and a touch of citrusy peel, this dish makes a satisfying main course.

Pictured on the front cover

SERVES 4

8 slices daikon, each ¼ inch thick and about 2 inches in diameter (preferably from the neck portion), 8 to 10 ounces total weight

2 teaspoons cornstarch

1 teaspoon sesame oil

Scant 1 tablespoon sugar

1 tablepoon saké

3 tablespoons vegetarian stock (page 76) or cold water

2 to 3 teaspoons soy sauce, preferably light-colored soy sauce

1 strip yuzu peel (page 284), 2 inches long and 1 inch wide, pith removed and cut crosswise into thin slivers

Remove the peel from each daikon slice and set the peels aside for use in other recipes. Pat the slices dry with paper towels, then dust all exposed surfaces with the cornstarch. I find that using a pastry brush is best for applying the cornstarch in a thin, even coating.

Select a skillet large enough to hold the daikon slices in a single layer and heat over medium-high heat. Add the oil, let it warm for a moment, then place the daikon slices in the skillet. Sear, uncovered, for 3 minutes, then check on progress by lifting a slice. It should be golden brown in those places where it came into contact with the hot skillet. Flip the slices and sear the other side, uncovered, for 3 minutes, or until similarly browned. As the daikon cooks and becomes tender, it will begin to appear translucent.

Sprinkle the sugar over the daikon slices. Mix together the saké and 2 tablespoons of the stock and add it to the pan, drizzling the mixture in along the rim. Jiggle the pan to keep the slices from sticking and to deglaze the pan of any crusty bits. Lower the heat, cover with an *otoshi-buta* (page 243) or a circle of parchment paper, and cook for about 2 minutes, or until barely tender. A toothpick inserted into the center should meet little resistance.

Mix the remaining 1 tablespoon stock with 2 teaspoons of the soy sauce and again add along the rim of the pan. Jiggle the skillet to distribute the liquid, then raise the heat. Cook for about 1 minute and taste the sauce; if overly sweet, adjust with additional soy sauce. Cook an additional minute, or until the slices are well glazed. The pan juices will thicken (because the daikon was dusted in cornstarch at the start), creating a sauce that lightly cloaks each slice.

If serving hot, scatter the *yuzu* peel over the top and serve immediately. Or, let the daikon cool in the skillet and serve at room temperature, adding the *yuzu* just before bringing to table. As you serve, drizzle slices with any remaining glaze.

VARIATION: If you have some *yama imo* on hand, either can be prepared in the same manner as the daikon. Tips on preparing and handling these slightly slippery tubers can be found on page 276.

CHRYSANTHEMUM GREENS IN NUTTY TŌFU SAUCE

SHUNGIKU NO SHIRA AÉ

Shira aé is a classic tōfu sauce found on menus in elegant restaurants and as part of home-style meals. The version that I offer here is both creamy and nutty, enhanced by the addition of dry-roasted sesame paste. It is particularly well suited to dressing barely blanched greens—I especially like to pair it with slightly bitter chrysanthemum greens—though it also works well as a dip for crunchy raw vegetables.

Shira aé can be made with almost any type of tōfu, but I prefer the extra body and slightly rougher texture that results from using *momen*, or firm tōfu. It is especially delicious made with homemade tōfu (see page 158).

Prepare the sauce and blanched greens separately—each can be readied ahead and refrigerated—and combine them just before serving.

SERVES 4 TO 6

1 large bunch (about 12 ounces) chrysanthemum greens (page 269)

NUTTY TŌFU SAUCE

4 ounces firm tōfu, well drained

Pinch of salt

1 teaspoon white sesame paste

1/2 teaspoon Saikyō miso (page 271), optional

1 tablespoon Basic Kelp Stock (page 75), or water

1 tablespoon white sesame seeds, freshly dry-roasted (page 245), optional

Soak the greens in a large tub of fresh, cold water. Swish to loosen any soil that may be clinging to them, especially if the roots are attached. Trim the roots by shaving off just a bit (they are delicious and packed with nutrients). Drain away the sandy water and soak again in fresh water.

Bring a pot of water to a rolling boil and add the greens, briefly pushing them below the surface of the water with kitchen tongs or long cooking chopsticks. Allow the water to return to a boil, stir to make sure the greens are completely submerged, and cook for 30 to 40 seconds. Lift the greens from the pot and transfer them to a bowl of cold water to cool down. Then lift the greens from the cold water and gently press out the excess moisture. Cover until ready to use. If you will be holding the greens for several hours (or up to a day), refrigerate them. (You can also bundle the greens to cook them and then serve them in bunches, if you like, as described on page 100.)

Make the sauce: In the old-fashioned kitchen, the sauce was made in a *suribachi* (grooved mortar) using a *surikōgi* (wooden pestle) to mash the tōfu. The blanched greens were then tossed into the mortar where the sauce clung to the sides. In many homes, the mortar doubled as a serving bowl, placed on the table. If you wish to follow suit, see page 246.

In the modern Japanese kitchen, the tōfu sauce can be made quickly and simply with a mini food processor. Place the drained tōfu in the processor and pulse, using several short spurts. Scrape down the sides of the bowl as needed to mash the tōfu evenly. Add the salt and continue to pulse. Add the sesame paste and continue to pulse

(continued)

until completely incorporated and the sauce is creamy. If you have some white miso on hand, adding it will give the sauce a richer, more complex flavor. If the sauce seems too stiff, add a few drops of stock and pulse again to blend. The sauce can be kept for up to 3 days in a covered glass jar in the refrigerator. If white liquid puddles around the edges, pour it off before stirring the sauce.

Just before serving, coarsely chop the blanched greens and toss them in the tōfu sauce. Or, if you prefer, make neat bundles from the greens and top each with a dollop of the sauce. Garnish with the roasted sesame seeds for a crunchy accent.

BLANCHING BUNDLES OF GREENS

This tie-and-blanch technique can be applied to any leafy vegetable with an inch or longer stalk or stem. It is particularly well suited to bunches of greens such as chrysanthemum or *komatsuna* (page 269), a leafy green in the turnip family, with roots still attached. By tying the greens into clusters, aligning tender leafy tops in one direction with thicker, tougher stems in the other, you can cook the stem end longer without overcooking the leaves. When it comes time to plate the greens, you can make neat bundles and spoon sauce over them or you can chop the greens and toss them in a sauce.

Begin by soaking the greens in a large tub of fresh, cold water. Swish to loosen any soil that may be clinging to them; drain away the sandy water and soak the greens again in fresh water.

Lay out several 6-inch lengths of kitchen twine on your counter; each will be used to tie a bunch. Lift the greens from the tub of water and trim clusters or individual stalks, paring away as little as possible. The red roots of spinach (and white roots of *komatsuna*) are especially sweet and delicious. If the clusters, or individual stalks, are more than 1/4 inch thick, make a shallow X lengthwise through the thickest section. This allows the blanching water to circulate better, reducing cooking time and the loss of nutrients.

Lay your washed, slit greens with stems aligned (either right or left) and tie snugly into several bundles. Bring a pot of water to a rolling boil; add a pinch of salt to improve color and flavor. Holding a bunch of tied greens by their leafy tops, allow the stem end to cook in the boiling water. If your hands are sensitive to heat, using kitchen tongs or long chopsticks will make this easier and more comfortable.

Allow the water to return to a boil and cook for 30 to 40 seconds. Gently release the leafy tops, allowing them to enter the boiling water, too. Stir to make sure the tops are completely submerged, wait for the water to return to a boil, and cook for another 20 to 30 seconds. Lift the leafy greens from the pot and transfer them to a bowl of cold water. Repeat this blanching procedure with the remaining bunches.

Lift the blanched greens from the bowl of cold water and gently press out the excess moisture. Remove the strings (you can reuse them), keeping the clusters of greens aligned until ready to serve. Transfer the blanched greens to a container and drizzle a few drops of stock and/or soy sauce over them just to moisten. Cover until ready to use. If you will be holding the greens for several hours (or up to a day), refrigerate them.

BROTH-STEEPED KALE ROLLS

KEIRU NO NI-BITASHI

Several Japanese plants in the cabbage and turnip families are cultivated for their green leafy tops. Vegetables such as *komatsuna* (related to turnips) are often prepared *ohitashi* style, blanched and steeped in seasoned broth. Spinach is similarly prepared.

Other sturdier leafy greens, such as *fudansō* (a kind of chard), are blanched and tied into rolls, sometimes, as in this recipe, encircling other vegetables and strips of fried tōfu. These stuffed rolls are most often added to *nabémono* (casseroles) that are cooked at table (see Miso Oden, page 171), but they could be enjoyed on their own, too. Here, I tie the rolls with *kampyō* (gourd ribbons), softening the ribbons in water and then using the water as a stock to cook the rolls. But the rolls can be held together with toothpicks if you have another stock available.

Outside Japan, I suggest you use kale and chard, since both will hold up to this sort of cooking. Avoid any red-stemmed greens from the beet family in a *nabémono*, because they sometimes "bleed" and stain other foods in the pot.

MAKES 6 TO 8 ROLLS

6 to 8 large kale or chard leaves, trimmed

2 to 3 feet kampyō (page 262)

1 piece kombu (page 266), about 1 by 1½ inches if using Hidaka kombu or 2 by 1½ inches if using ma kombu

1½ cups cold water

Pinch of salt

1 or 2 sheets thin fried tōfu (page 282)

2-inch piece carrot, about 1 ounce, scraped, trimmed, and cut into matchsticks

2- to 3-inch piece burdock root, scraped and cut into matchsticks

1 teaspoon sugar

1 teaspoon saké

1 tablespoon soy sauce

Make a V cut to remove the core from each kale leaf. Shred the core pieces and reserve.

Bring a large pot of water to a rolling boil, add the leaves, and blanch for about 1 minute or until just wilted and flexible. Remove the leaves and reserve the hot water for rinsing away excess oil from the fried tōfu. Rinse the leaves briefly under cold running water and let drain in a colander.

Soak the *kampyō* and *kombu* in the cold water for at least 30 minutes. Remove the *kampyō* and *kombu*. The liquid is now a flavorful stock, and the gourd ribbons are ready to be used as edible ties. Apply the salt to the softened *kampyō*, rubbing as though you are trying to remove a spot from clothing. The gourd ribbons will become much softer and somewhat velvety to the touch. Rinse off the salt and squeeze out the excess moisture. Set aside. Cut the *kombu* into thread-thin strips and set aside.

With kitchen tongs or long chopsticks, submerge the fried tōfu sheets in the hot water saved from blanching the kale. This "rinsing" will help remove oil on the surface of the tōfu. Drain, and when cool enough to handle, use paper towels to press out and blot away excess water and oil. Slice the tōfu into thin strips.

(continued)

In a bowl, combine the fried tōfu, carrot, burdock root, and *kombu* strips. Add the shredded kale cores and toss to mix. Divide the mixture into 6 or 8 portions.

Cut the *kampyō* into as many ties as you have leaves and portions. Spread a single leaf of kale on your cutting board, with the open end of the V closest to you and the leaves spreading out fanlike away from you. Arrange 1 portion of the filling horizontally across the center of the leaf just beyond where the V narrows to a point. Fold in the flaps, right and left, meeting in the center. They should completely cover the filling. Bring the bottom section of the kale leaf up and over the filling and flaps. Roll away from you to enclose all snugly. Secure each bundle with a *kampyō* ribbon; use a double knot to tie.

Place the rolled kale packages, knotted ties down, in a skillet just large enough to hold them in a snug single layer. Add 1 cup of the reserved *kampyō* liquid, the sugar, and the saké. Swirl the skillet to distribute the seasonings and liquid evenly, and place the skillet over high heat. When the liquid begins to boil, lower the heat to maintain a simmer and cook for 5 to 6 minutes. It is best to use an *otoshi-buta* (page 243), though a standard lid, slightly askew, is fine, especially if you place a circle of parchment paper directly on the kale rolls to keep them moist.

Turn the kale packages so that the knotted ties face up, replace the *otoshi-buta* or the parchment and lid, and continue to cook for another 2 to 3 minutes. Season with the soy sauce and simmer for a final minute. Allow the rolled kale to cool, lidded, in the skillet. It is during this cooling down that flavors both meld and intensify. If you prefer to serve the rolls piping hot, reheat just before serving, adding a bit more *kampyō* liquid to the skillet, if necessary.

Arrange 2 or 3 rolls, horizontally and with knots facing up, in a shallow bowl. Pour a bit of what remains of the simmering broth over the rolls and serve.

NOTE: When using these rolls in *nabémono*, such as Miso Oden (page 171), you don't need to simmer them after you assemble them. They will be fully cooked in whatever broth you use for your *nabémono*.

BURDOCK ROOT, AUTUMNAL RAIN STYLE

GOBŌ NO SHIGURÉ NI

When the word *shiguré* appears on a Japanese menu, brace yourself for an intensely flavored ginger-and-soy-stewed food—a taste sensation that mimics the chilly showers after which the dish is named. The ginger flavor is thought to be like the stop-and-start autumnal rain—stimulating the appetite in spurts, but not drenching the palate. Although most *shiguré* dishes feature fish or meat, there are delightful vegetarian versions as well. This one, highlighting earthy burdock root, is my favorite. The addition of *shirataki* adds a satisfying texture to the dish without extra calories.

SERVES 4 TO 6

1 or 2 burdock roots, about 10 ounces total weight, scraped and sliced sasagaki style (page 244)

1 cup shirataki noodles (page 268), about 6 ounces, drained and cut into 1-inch lengths

1/2 teaspoon aromatic sesame oil

1 tablespoon saké

1/3 cup stock, preferably Basic Kelp Stock (page 75)

1/2 teaspoon sugar

1 tablespoon ginger juice (page 246)

2 tablespoons soy sauce

Some Japanese insist that sliced burdock root must be soaked in water to remove *aku*, or "bitterness"; others abhor the practice. If you choose to soak your sliced burdock root, do so in cold water for only 2 to 3 minutes to preserve nutrients and aroma. Drain and pat dry.

Place the *shirataki* noodles in a nonstick skillet and set it over medium-high heat. Jiggle the skillet to make sure all the noodles get a chance to throw off their excess moisture. As the noodles dry, they will emit a squeaking sound when pressed against the bottom of the skillet. This is your cue to drizzle in the sesame oil. Toss the noodles to coat them lightly in the oil.

Raise the heat to high, add the burdock, and sauté for 1 minute, or until aromatic and slightly wilted. Add the saké, stock, and sugar and lower the heat to maintain a steady but not especially vigorous simmer. Cook for about 3 minutes, or until the burdock is tender (a toothpick inserted into the thickest part meets with little or no resistance). Add half the ginger juice, stir to mix, and then add the soy sauce. Continue to simmer for about 1 minute, or until the liquid is nearly gone and the burdock is well glazed. Add the remaining ginger juice and toss to distribute well.

Serve in a large bowl, family style, or in individual dishes, coaxed into mounds.

MISO-GLAZED BITTER MELON WITH KABOCHA AND TŌFU

GOYA NO MISO CHAMPURU

Natives of semitropical Okinawa enjoy dishes with bitter melon in hot weather, believing it restores energy and nutrient balance to the heat-weary body. One of the most common ways of preparing bitter melon (the locals call it *goya*) is *champuru* ("mix" or "hodgepodge" in the local dialect), essentially a stir-fry that includes some kind of tōfu and possibly other vegetables. In this version, the miso glaze not only enhances the nutritional value of the dish but also softens the bitter aftertaste of the *goya*.

Increasingly, bitter melon is available in Asian markets outside Japan. When summer brings hot, muggy weather to your part of the world, I urge you to give this dish a try.

SERVES 4 TO 6

MISO SAUCE

1½ tablespoons mugi miso (page 271)

1 teaspoon sugar

⅓ to ½ cup stock, preferably Basic Kelp Stock (page 75)

1 teaspoon aromatic sesame oil

1 bitter melon, about 10 ounces, seeds removed, thinly sliced, salted with 1 teaspoon kosher salt, and drained (see box)

1 yellow onion, about 5 ounces, thinly cut kushi-gata style (page 244) through the stem

Scant 1 tablespoon saké

5 ounces kabocha squash, about 1 small wedge, unpeeled, seeded, and cut into ¼-inch-thick pieces, each with dark peel at one end

About 60 Tōfu Chunks (page 164)

Make the miso sauce: Place the miso and sugar in a small saucepan and stir to combine. Add the stock and stir to mix well. Place over low heat and cook, stirring, for about 1½ minutes, or until the sugar is dissolved and the mixture is bubbly and slightly thickened. Remove from the heat and set aside.

Heat a wok or heavy skillet over high heat and drizzle in the sesame oil. When the oil is aromatic, add the bitter

(continued)

PREPARING BITTER MELON

Cut the bitter melon in half lengthwise. Use a soupspoon to scrape out the center spongy, white section containing seeds. Place the cut edge of each half flat against the cutting board (to keep it steady) and slice thinly. Place the slices in a large bowl and toss them with the amount of salt specified in individual recipes; this aids in reducing bitterness. Set aside for 10 minutes, or until the bitter melon "sweats." Rinse with cold water (the water will become quite foamy) and drain. Rinse a second time in fresh cold water and drain again, then pat away surface moisture.

melon and stir-fry, tossing vigorously, for 1 minute. Add the onion and continue to stir-fry for 1 minute longer, or until the onion is wilted and slightly caramelized.

Add the saké and deglaze the pan of any crusty bits. Lower the heat to medium, add the *kabocha*, and continue to stir-fry, tossing occasionally, for about 1 minute, or until tender. A toothpick inserted into a piece of *kabocha* should meet little resistance. Pour in the miso sauce in a clockwise swirl, starting at the rim of the pan and jiggling the pan to distribute the sauce well. Add the tōfu chunks and jiggle the pan again.

Raise the heat to high and stir vigorously. The sauce will thicken quickly. The tōfu chunks may crumble a bit. When the miso has glazed all the ingredients, after about 45 seconds, remove the pan from the heat. Allow the contents to sit, undisturbed and uncovered, in the skillet for about 1 minute before serving. In these final moments, the miso sauce mellows the flavor of the bitter melon and the tōfu chunks absorb skillet juices, adding a richness and complexity to the dish.

Serve hot or at room temperature, family style in a deep serving bowl.

BITTER, SWEET, AND FRUITY SALAD

GOYA NO REMON MISO AÉ

Outside Japan, most people know miso as a seasoning for soup, though it is also used extensively in making sauces for tossed saladlike *aémono*. One of the oldest written recipes for *su miso*, a classic sauce made with sweet, light Saikyō miso and rice vinegar, appears in a sixteenth-century document. I offer a modern version, enhanced with fruity lemon juice and zest. I pair the sauce with barely blanched slices of bitter melon—a restorative salad to enjoy on sultry summer days. The sauce is also a fine dip for vegetables and crisp apple slices, so you may want to double the amount so you'll have extra for serving this way.

SERVES 2 TO 4

> 1 bitter melon, 10 to 12 ounces, seeds removed, sliced tissue-thin, salted with 1 teaspoon kosher salt, and drained (see box, page 104)

LEMON-MISO SAUCE

> 3 tablespoons Saikyō miso (page 271)
>
> 1¹/₂ teaspoons sugar
>
> 1 tablespoon fresh lemon juice
>
> ¹/₄ teaspoon lemon zest grated on a rasp-style grater
>
> 1 tablespoon rice vinegar, preferably brown rice vinegar (page 284)
>
> 1 tablespoon white sesame seeds, freshly dry-roasted (page 245)

Bring water to a rolling boil in a saucepan. Add the bitter melon slices and blanch only until the water returns to a boil, about 1 minute, then drain. Fan the bitter melon to cool it; do not "refresh" it in ice water, which will make the vegetable taste watery. When cool enough to handle comfortably, squeeze to wilt and drain off excess moisture. Pat the bitter melon slices dry with paper towels, cover, and refrigerate for at least 30 minutes or up to 24 hours.

Make the miso sauce: Place the miso and sugar in a small saucepan and stir to combine. Add the lemon juice and stir to mix well. Place over low heat and cook, stirring, for about 1 minute, or until the sugar is dissolved and the mixture is bubbly. Set aside to cool to room temperature. Stir in the lemon zest and rice vinegar. Transfer to a glass jar with a tightly sealed lid and refrigerate until needed, up to 3 days.

Just before serving, mix together the bitter melon and half of the miso sauce in a bowl. Toss to make sure each slice is lightly coated with sauce.

Divide the mixture into 2 to 4 portions, coaxing each into a small mountain. Place each mountain in a small, deep bowl and spoon a bit of the remaining sauce over the top. Garnish with the sesame seeds.

If it is an especially hot and muggy day, serve in clear glass bowls that have been chilled in the refrigerator for an hour or more before serving.

HEAVEN-AND-EARTH TEMPURA PANCAKES

TEN CHI KAKI AGÉ

The name of this dish, Heaven and Earth, is a euphemism for kitchen scraps, namely the tops (heaven) and bottoms (earth) of produce: tender, leafy celery tops; tougher leek tops; mushroom stems; carrot and daikon peels; stubby ends of lotus and burdock root, parsnips, rutabagas, and bitter melon. All sorts of neglected or remaindered vegetable bits can be transformed into lovely, lacy-crisp, colorful tempura pancakes.

The key to making tasty pancakes from disparate ingredients is to select items that cook at approximately the same temperature and time. Cutting your vegetables so that most are long and thin and a few are in crescents or rounds will make it easier to form a cohesive mass. Dusting ingredients with cornstarch before adding them to the batter will also help the pancakes hold together.

When you are ready to form the pancakes, use a large, flat stainless-steel spoon or ladle to help shape them. Dipping the spoon or ladle into hot oil first will ensure easy release of the pancake as you slip it into the oil.

Another bit of advice: *gaman*, which translates as "reticence" or "reluctance." Refraining from taking action is often considered a virtue in both the Japanese kitchen and Japanese society at large. My recipe instructs you not to take certain actions, though you may find it tough to follow such advice.

I provide two assorted-vegetable examples below, one using wintertime produce, the other showcasing summer's bounty. At any time of year, use this recipe to guide you in creating your own heavenly pancake with earthy flavors. Serve with lemon or lime wedges and the three-pepper salt.

MAKES 8 PANCAKES

WINTER PANCAKES

1/2 red onion, cut into thin slices through the stem end to make crescent shapes (about 1/3 cup)

1 tablespoon cornstarch

Scant 1/3 cup julienne-cut carrot peels (1-inch strips; about 3 ounces)

Scant 1/3 cup julienne-cut Japanese-style sweet potato (page 276) or other sweet potato peels (1-inch strips; about 2 1/2 ounces)

SUMMER PANCAKES

3-ounce chunk bitter melon, cut in half lengthwise, seeds removed, very thinly sliced, salted with 1/4 teaspoon salt, and drained (page 104), about 1/4 cup

1 tablespoon cornstarch

2 small zucchini, about 4 ounces total weight, tops trimmed, cut in half lengthwise, and then cut on the diagonal into thin slices, about 2/3 cup

Scant 1/3 cup julienne-cut kabocha squash peels (3/4-inch strips; about 3 ounces)

2 tablespoons finely shredded summer herbs such as fresh shiso leaves (page 258)

4 or 5 fresh chives, cut into 1/2-inch lengths

BATTER

Several ice cubes

1/3 cup cold water

1/4 cup self-rising cake flour

(continued)

Vegetable oil for deep-frying

1 to 2 teaspoons aromatic sesame oil (optional)

CONDIMENTS

¼ teaspoon kosher salt

Generous pinch of kona-zanshō (page 258)

Generous pinch of tōgarashi (page 258)

Generous pinch of freshly ground black pepper

Lemon or lime wedges

Depending upon seasonal availability, choose to make either the winter pancakes or the summer pancakes: To make the winter pancakes, place the red onion in a bowl. With a pastry brush, dust the slices thoroughly with some of the cornstarch. Pull gently to separate the crescent shapes, dusting again with a bit more cornstarch. Add the carrot and sweet potato peels to the bowl and dust with the remaining cornstarch. Toss to distribute the vegetables evenly.

To make the summer pancakes, with a pastry brush, dust the bitter melon slices thoroughly with some of the cornstarch, then place them in a bowl. Dust the zucchini slices and *kabocha* peels in a similar manner and add them to the bowl; toss to distribute evenly. Dust the shredded *shiso* leaves and chives with cornstarch and add them to the bowl; toss again to distribute evenly.

Make the batter just before frying: Place the ice cubes in a small bowl with half of the water. Sift the cake flour over the water and stir to mix slightly; there should still be lumps. If needed, add water, a few drops at a time, until the batter is the consistency of a thin pancake batter.

Pour the vegetable oil to a depth of 1½ inches into a small wok or small, deep skillet. Add the sesame oil and heat slowly. Check the temperature with an unvarnished long wooden chopstick (or a bamboo skewer). Small bubbles will form around the tip when the oil is about 350°F.

Wait for about 45 seconds longer to allow the temperature to rise a bit more—to about 370°F—and then test the oil temperature with a few drops of batter. If they sink slightly, then rise to the surface and puff quickly but do not color, the oil is ready. You may need to fry the pancakes in batches to avoid crowding them in the pan. Preheat the oven to 200°F for keeping the cooked pancakes warm.

Spoon a bit of the batter over the cornstarch-dusted vegetables and toss lightly to coat the vegetables with the batter. Dip a large spoon or ladle into the hot oil. Place one-eighth of the vegetable mixture in the bowl of the oil-dipped spoon. Carefully tilt the spoon to slide the pancake into the hot oil, aiming to make a disk about 2 inches in diameter. The batter and cornstarch act as "glue" to keep the vegetable slivers together. Repeat to make more pancakes, being careful not to crowd the pan.

Most important, refrain from touching the pancakes for a full 30 seconds after you place them in the oil. It will seem like an eternity, but *gaman* will yield the best results. If wayward bits are strewn at the edges of your pan, carefully pick them up and place them on top of the still-moist pancake batter in the center. (Skill with long chopsticks will be well rewarded, though a long-handled fine-mesh skimmer can scoop beneath as well.) If the center of the pancake is very dry, dip the wayward bits in some fresh batter before "gluing" them in place. When the batter in the center of the disk seems barely moist, carefully invert the pancake.

After flipping, allow the pancakes to fry undisturbed for about 1 minute, or until crisp. Using cooking chopsticks or a skimmer, remove the pancakes from the oil and place them on a rack set over a baking sheet to drain. If frying in batches, place the baking sheet in the oven to keep the fried pancakes warm. Use the skimmer to clear the oil of batter bits between batches.

When all of the pancakes are fried, transfer them to paper towels to absorb any additional surface oil.

To serve, line a plate or shallow bamboo basket with folded paper (the Japanese use ones called *shikigami* or *kai-shi* that are oil-absorbent on one side and oil-repellant on the other). Paper doilies make an attractive alternative. Mix together the salt and 3 peppers in a small bowl. Arrange the pancakes on the folded paper and put the lemon wedges and the pepper mixture on the side.

FREEZING AND REHEATING TEMPURA PANCAKES

Deep-frying small quantities of food may seem wasteful to home cooks because of the large quantity of oil needed to fry foods well. And many who work outside the home, pressed for time to put dinner on the table, want to pull something from the freezer, rather than start from scratch. I encourage you to double, even triple, the quantities listed here when you have the time to cook at leisure, freezing extra pancakes.

Be sure to drain and blot the pancakes well as they come out of the hot oil. Let them cool completely before stacking them with a fresh piece of paper towel between the layers. Place the stack in a resealable plastic bag, gently pressing out the air before sealing the bag. Refrigerate for 1 or 2 days or freeze for up to 1 month.

To reheat the tempura pancakes, use either a toaster oven or a conventional oven. In either case, take the pancakes directly from the refrigerator or freezer, unwrapping them just before placing in the oven.

If using a toaster oven, place the pancakes on the tray and adjust the rack so that the tray sits about 2 inches below the toaster coils. "Toast" the pancakes for 1$\frac{1}{2}$ minutes on a medium-high setting, then flip them over and repeat for 1 more minute. Blot away any moisture with paper towels and let the pancakes sit for 3 or 4 minutes before retoasting them for another minute on each side. If you are reheating refrigerated pancakes, 1 minute of toasting per side should suffice. If necessary to prevent edges from scorching, cover the pancakes lightly with aluminum foil after flipping them over.

If using a conventional oven, preheat to 250°F. Place the frozen pancakes on a rack set over an aluminum foil–lined baking pan. Bake them for 7 or 8 minutes, or until warm and dry. If you are reheating refrigerated pancakes, 4 or 5 minutes should suffice. If necessary, cover the pancakes lightly with foil after 2 or 3 minutes, to prevent edges from scorching.

CARROT PUDDING

NINJIN-DŌFU

This recipe takes the common carrot and transforms it into a savory-sweet pudding. In a classic Japanese context, small bright orange blocks of it would be served as an appetizer garnished with a dab of wasabi or a small mound of freshly grated ginger and served with a drizzle of soy sauce. Similar to *goma-dōfu*, the nutty rich sesame pudding that is included in classic temple vegetarian fare (see page 134 for my version), this pudding uses fresh vegetable purée. As a result, the preparation is less labor-intensive and the timing is a bit different.

If you are able to source carrots with their green tops attached, use those tufts in lieu of the chrysanthemum greens that are tossed in Nutty Tōfu Sauce (page 99) and serve them in a small mound alongside the pudding.

SERVES 6 TO 8

6 to 7 ounces carrots, scraped and diced

1¹⁄₃ cups stock, preferably Basic Kelp Stock (page 75)

¹⁄₂ teaspoon sugar

¹⁄₈ teaspoon salt

3¹⁄₂ tablespoons crushed kudzu (page 255), about 1 ounce

1 teaspoon grated fresh ginger

2 tablespoons Vegan Seasoned Soy Concentrate (page 131) or soy sauce

Place a 5 by 3-inch glass or metal mini loaf pan or in the refrigerator. Chilling the pan will make it easier to unmold the pudding for serving. The Japanese use a metal *nagashi kan* (page 249) to shape the mixture.

Place the carrots and ²⁄₃ cup of the stock, sugar, and salt in a small, deep saucepan and bring to a boil. Adjust the heat to a gentle simmer and cook the carrots for about 10 minutes, or until tender. A toothpick inserted at the thickest point of a chunk should meet no resistance. There is no need to skim away any froth should it appear. Once the carrots are tender, remove from the heat and let the carrots cool in the pan with whatever liquid remains. Transfer to a blender and pulse until you have a completely smooth, orange-colored purée.

In a small bowl, mix the remaining ²⁄₃ cup stock with the kudzu; stir until the powder dissolves. Add this mixture to the blender and pulse to thoroughly combine. The mixture may look pale and a bit chalky rather than bright orange.

Pour the mixture into the saucepan you used to cook the carrots and set over very low heat (to prevent scorching). Heat the mixture until it is barely simmering, stirring constantly. I recommend using a long-handled, broad-paddled wooden spoon or a sturdy silicone spatula for stirring. Alternate stirring clockwise and counterclockwise, and occasionally stir in a figure eight. Scrape down the sides frequently. After 2 or 3 minutes, the mixture will begin to thicken. It will be a bit lumpy at first, but diligent stirring will make it smooth. Large bubbles looking somewhat like molten lava may form as the mixture continues to thicken (the long-handled stirring tool will protect your hands from splatters as the bubbles burst). After about 4 minutes, you should be able to draw a line with your spoon or spatula along the bottom of the pan that remains visible for several seconds before it fills.

Cook, continuing to stir in a slow and steady manner, for 5 more minutes, or until the mixture becomes very thick. When the mixture is somewhat translucent and brighter in color, lift the spatula or spoon. If the mixture is so thick it does not immediately drop, you are ready to transfer it to your mold. If not, continue to stir until the mixture thickens sufficiently.

Spoon the pudding mixture into the chilled loaf pan. Although not traditional, foil liners for mini-muffin cups are handy and can be used instead; once the pudding has set, the foil liners can be peeled off.

Immediately after pouring the mixture into the mold, smooth the surface with a spatula dipped in cold water and cover to prevent an unpleasant "skin" from forming. Professional chefs place a sheet of glass dipped in water directly on the pudding. Plastic wrap pressed against the pudding with a piece of cardboard will also work well. Once the pudding has cooled and firmed, remove the glass or plastic wrap.

The pudding will set at room temperature within 5 minutes. If you wish to serve the pudding chilled, refrigerate it for no more than 30 minutes. If you wish to store the pudding, it will keep, covered and refrigerated, for up to 3 days. For optimal eating pleasure, remove the pudding from the refrigerator about 30 minutes before serving.

To unmold the pudding, place a cutting board over the top of the pan and invert the board and pan together. Lift off the pan. Slice the pudding in half lengthwise, then cut crosswise two or three times to yield 6 or 8 blocks. Transfer the blocks to individual serving dishes and garnish each serving with a small mound of grated ginger. Serve the soy concentrate in a small pitcher and let diners drizzle their own, or serve it in individual dipping dishes.

If using foil muffin liners, peel away the liners, invert the puddings onto individual serving dishes, and place a small mound of grated ginger on top of each serving.

GREEN AND GREEN ON GREENS

KYUURI NO OROSHI RAIMU AÉ

Salads of tossed greens, lightly dressed with rice vinegar, soy sauce, and sesame oil, began appearing on menus at Japanese restaurants outside Japan about twenty-five years ago. At the start, it was intended to appeal to locals in lieu of *tsukémono* (pickles), which were thought to be challenging to the uninitiated. In time, ex-pat Japanese customers developed a liking for these salads, too. In a reverse culinary exchange, the salads have since become enormously popular within Japan, so much so that supermarket shelves are filled with bottles of *wa fu* (Japanese-flavored) salad dressing.

What I offer here combines a classic Japanese *oroshi aé*, or grated vegetable sauce, with a Continental-style oil-and-vinegar dressing. In addition to rice vinegar, I use some lime juice. To keep the dressing a vibrant hue, combine it just before serving.

Pictured on page 168

SERVES 4

  1 small head Romaine lettuce, about 6 ounces

  2 to 3 ounces mizuna (page 271), washed, spun dry, and torn into bite-size pieces

  2 or 3 small red radishes, cut into tissue-thin slices

  1 small package radish sprouts (page 258), about 2 ounces, trimmed and rinsed and/or other micro greens (optional)

DRESSING

  2 tablespoons rice vinegar

  2 teaspoons sugar

  2 tablespoons fresh lime juice

  1 tablespoon aromatic sesame oil

  1 teaspoon soy sauce, preferably light-colored soy sauce

  2 Japanese or other cucumbers with untreated skins, about 3 1/2 ounces each

  Pinch of salt

Pull the leaves from the head of lettuce and rinse them well to remove any soil that might have been trapped between them. Tear the leafy portions into small pieces. Stack the thicker stems and cut them crosswise into paper-thin slices. Place all the torn and cut pieces in a salad spinner with the *mizuna*. Rinse and spin dry once more.

Divide the lettuces among 4 individual serving bowls and chill if you prefer your salads cold (the Japanese typically serve them at room temperature). Garnish with the radishes and sprouts.

Make the dressing: Combine the vinegar and sugar in a small saucepan, place over low heat, and cook, stirring, just to dissolve the sugar. Remove from the heat and let cool. Pour into a small glass jar and add the lime juice, sesame oil, and soy sauce. Cap with a tight-fitting lid and shake to mix.

Rub the cucumbers, one at a time, with the salt using the *ita-zuri* technique (page 215). Rinse the cucumbers (a greenish foam typically forms on the palms) and pat dry. Slice off the stem end and grate each cucumber, preferably on a ceramic grater (page 246) to avoid a metallic taste. Line a small strainer with paper towels and allow the grated cucumber to drain a bit, saving the liquid to adjust (mellow the tartness of) your dressing, if need be.

Add half the grated cucumber to the dressing, stir to mix, and pour over the salads. Garnish with a small mound of the remaining grated cucumber.

SCALLIONS AND LEEK IN TART MISO SAUCE

NEGI NUTA

Gunma Prefecture, not far from Tokyo, is known for several agricultural products, among them the enigmatic tuber called *konnyaku* (page 268) and *Shimonita negi*, a variety of leek with tender, herbaceous green tops. They come together here to make *nuta*, a category of miso-sauced dishes that typically combine some form of onion or leek with tart miso. In Japan, this would likely be served as an appetizer, with a very dry saké to balance the sweet and tart flavors.

When unable to source *Shimonita negi*, I use a combination of leeks and scallions; together they simulate qualities of the Gunma specialty. *Konnyaku*, however, has no simple substitute; its texture is unique: a satisfying chewiness (with no calories) and a foil for the yummy miso sauce. For this dish, the translucent white *konnyaku*, rather than a speckled variety, is best.

SERVES 2 TO 4

1 naga negi (page 273) or other leek, about 6 ounces

3 or 4 scallions, about 3 ounces

4 to 5 ounces konnyaku (page 268), about ½ small loaf, drained of packing liquid

TART MISO SAUCE

3 tablespoons white miso, preferably Saikyō miso (page 271)

1 to 1½ tablespoons sugar

1½ tablespoons brown rice vinegar (page 284)

Dab of Japanese spicy mustard (page 257), optional

Trim your leek and scallions, cutting edible portions into 1-inch lengths. Bring a pot of water to a boil and blanch the leek and scallions, allowing the tougher tops to cook slightly longer than the tender bottoms. When they are wilted, after about 1 minute for the leek and 30 seconds for the scallions, remove them, reserving the water in the pot, and allow them to cool naturally in a colander. Do not refresh in cold water. The leek and scallions are now ready to absorb the next flavor they come into contact with, and you want that to be the miso sauce, not plain water. When cool, press the leek and scallions gently to rid them of excess moisture.

Bring the same blanching water back to a boil. Add the *konnyaku* and cook for about 1 minute, then drain and allow to cool naturally in a colander. Do not refresh in cold water. It is during the cooling process that the unpleasant *aku* (astringency and odor) evaporates and makes the *konnyaku* porous, waiting to absorb the flavors of the miso sauce.

Make the miso sauce: In a small saucepan, combine the miso and 1 tablespoon of the sugar and stir to mix. Place over low heat and cook, stirring, for about 1 minute, or until the sugar has dissolved and the sauce looks glossy. Remove from the heat and stir in the vinegar. If you wish to add a bit of zip, mix the vinegar with the mustard, then add the mixture to the saucepan. Taste the sauce and add up to ½ tablespoon more sugar as needed to temper the saltiness of the miso.

Combine the cooled leek, scallions, and *konnyaku* in a bowl, add half the miso sauce, and toss to mix. Divide among individual bowls and chill if you like (the Japanese typically serve this at room temperature). Just before serving, drizzle the remaining sauce over the servings.

WARM AND SPICY CABBAGE AND PEPPER SLAW

HARU KYABETSU TO SHISHITŌ NO MISO AÉ

Cabbage, both briefly cooked and raw (finely shredded), is found on menus year-round in Japan, though springtime brings sweet, crisp yet tender-leaved heads of vitamin-packed *haru kyabetsu* to market. They are fabulous, and even the most skeptical eaters may rethink their opinion of cabbage. Outside Japan, I would substitute with crinkly leaved Savoy cabbages or tender, young Brussels sprouts.

Fresh capsicums are a late spring through summer plant in most regions of Japan. They pair well with warm-weather cabbages. Miniature, thin-skinned, sweet-and-spicy Japanese *shishitō* peppers are especially aromatic and increasingly available in Asian markets outside Japan. *Shishitō* are also fairly easy to grow from seed, even on a windowsill, if you have the inclination. The closest in heat and flavor are Anaheim or poblano chiles. If you want to notch up the heat, try serrano chiles.

SERVES 4

1 small head haru kyabetsu (page 253) or Savoy cabbage, about 1 pound, or 10 ounces small, young Brussels sprouts

2 teaspoons miso, preferably mugi miso (page 271)

1 tablespoon stock, preferably Basic Kelp Stock (page 75), or water

1 teaspoon aromatic sesame oil

1 small yellow onion, thinly cut kushi-gata style (page 244) through the stem

12 to 15 shishitō peppers or 5 or 6 Anaheim or poblano chiles, stemmed, seeded, and cut lengthwise into thin julienne strips

Pinch of salt

Splash of saké

Cut the cabbage in half, remove the core segment, and slice the core into paper-thin shreds. Set the slices aside. Cut the leafy portion of the cabbage into $1/4$-inch-wide strips. Keep the two shapes in separate piles. If using Brussels sprouts, trim and then quarter them through their stems.

In a small bowl, mix the miso with the stock and set aside.

Heat the oil in a skillet or wok over medium heat. Begin by stir-frying the shredded core of the cabbage or the Brussels sprouts, for about 1 minute, or until the pieces go limp. Then add the onion and continue stir-frying for about 2 minutes, or until the onion wilts, begins to color slightly, and becomes very aromatic. Add the leafy cabbage strips and the peppers and continue to stir-fry for 40 to 50 seconds, or until fragrant and slightly wilted.

Sprinkle with the salt, then add the saké. Stir-fry vigorously for 10 to 15 seconds, then pour in the miso mixture around the outer rim of the pan. Raise the heat to high and stir-fry vigorously for 30 seconds, or until the vegetables are slightly glazed.

Serve immediately, slightly mounded, in small individual bowls, or serve family style from a large bowl. Or, let cool, chill, and serve chilled. The slaw will keep in the refrigerator, tightly covered, for up to 4 days.

SKILLET-SEARED MANGANJI PEPPERS AND SHIITAKÉ MUSHROOMS IN SLEET SAUCE

MANGANJI TO SHIITAKÉ NO MIZORÉ AÉ

Keen awareness of the change in seasons is an integral part of Japanese cuisine. Market availability of produce and the weather report often come together to determine the day's menu. *Mizoré aé*, or "sleet sauce," is a tasty example of this seasonal sensitivity at table. As fall turns to winter, plump and juicy daikon radishes, perfect for grating and shredding, come to market. And with the plunge in temperature, precipitation changes from bone-chilling rain to icy sleet. At table, an edible ode to this end of autumn appears: spicy grated radish (picture wind-driven sleet) clings to skillet-seared peppers (envisage pine boughs) and earthy shiitaké mushrooms (imagine bare oak tree branches).

SERVES 3 OR 4

¹/₂ teaspoon aromatic sesame oil

6 to 8 Manganji peppers (page 271) or 3 or 4 small poblano chiles, about 12 ounces total weight, stemmed, seeded, and sliced into ¹/₂-inch-wide strips

10 to 12 fresh shiitaké mushrooms, about 12 ounces, stems removed and saved for stock, caps cut into ¹/₄-inch-wide strips or into 4 to 6 wedges

Pinch of kosher salt

Splash of saké

4- to 5-inch segment daikon (preferably the tapered end), about 10 ounces, peels removed thickly and set aside for use in other dishes

Lemon or lime wedges (optional)

Heat a skillet over high heat, drizzle in the sesame oil, and sear the peppers, skin side down. If you have an *otoshi-buta* (page 243), use it to press on the peppers. Or, press on the peppers with a broad flexible spatula. The pressing helps sear the surface, making the skin blister slightly but also trapping moisture in the skillet. This method of simultaneously searing with heat and trapping in moisture is called *mushi yaki* (steam-searing), a flavorful treatment for many foods.

When the skin has blistered, push the peppers to the outer edge of the skillet and add the mushrooms to the center. Sear the mushrooms, pressing with the *otoshi-buta* or broad spatula, for 30 seconds, or until they are barely wilted and slightly fragrant. Remove the *otoshi-buta* or spatula; droplets of moisture should be visible on the peppers and mushrooms and in the skillet. If not, flick a few drops of water over the mushrooms.

Jiggle the skillet, sprinkle with the salt, and sauté for 30 seconds. Add the saké and sauté for about 20 seconds, or until the alcohol evaporates. Toss the mushrooms and peppers, picking up any crusty bits from the skillet. Remove from the heat and let cool, uncovered in the skillet, to room temperature.

Meanwhile, grate and drain the daikon (page 247). Transfer the seared peppers and mushrooms to a bowl and toss with half the daikon. Divide the mixture among individual dishes, and top each serving with a small mound of grated daikon. Serve with lemon or lime wedges; diners squeeze a bit of the juice over their portion as they eat.

CRISPY AND CREAMY KABOCHA CROQUETTES

KOROKKÉ

Food halls in the basement level of Japan's leading department stores carry an incredible array of fresh foods, packaged grocery items, and prepared take-out items. Collectively known as *depachika* (literally "department store under ground"), these subterranean markets are justly famous for their extensive, high-end comestibles. Although the "sweets" section consistently produces the greatest profits—confectionary is a popular gift item and an affordable self-indulgence—the savory items at the deli-like *osōzai* counters do a high-volume, lucrative business.

Across the board in every store at every location, the most popular *osōzai* item is *korokké*, crispy-on-the-outside, creamy-on-the-inside croquettes. The Japanese eat these, and other fried foods, at room temperature—they are a favorite item in *obentō* lunchboxes. The shardlike slivers of the bread crumbs known as *panko* keep the exterior crunchy and crisp long after foods have cooled down.

In home kitchens, *korokké* are a fine way to use odd, forgotten, and forlorn chunks of root vegetables or gourds. These *kabocha* croquettes are my personal favorite, but the basic technique for mashing and making remains the same for most vegetables, and I offer several variations on page 120. Here, I toss *adzuki* or red kidney beans into the mashed mixture to pump up the nutrition and add visual interest.

SERVES 4

10 ounces kabocha squash

6 ounces potato, any variety

1/4 cup cooked dried adzuki beans (page 260) or red kidney beans

1/8 teaspoon salt

2 tablespoons cornstarch

2 to 3 tablespoons soy milk, freshly extracted (page 156) or purchased

1 cup panko

Vegetable oil for deep-frying

Lemon wedges

Kosher salt

Kona-zanshō (page 258)

Scrub the *kabocha* and potato and thickly remove the peels if you want to use them in other cookery such as Heaven-and-Earth Tempura Pancakes (page 109). Or, thinly peel unscrubbed, if you will be adding the peels to your compost heap. To simplify timing, cut the potatoes and the *kabocha* into fairly uniform 1 1/2-inch chunks. Steam them for 5 minutes, or until tender. A toothpick inserted into a thick chunk should meet no resistance. Transfer to a bowl, and while the vegetables are still warm, mash coarsely with a potato masher or fork.

Fold the red beans into the mashed mixture, distributing them evenly. Season with the salt and gently mix to distribute. Divide the mixture into 8 equal portions; each should be a mosaic of coarsely mashed vegetable chunks and whole beans held together by a purée made of the more thoroughly mashed vegetables. Dust your hands with half of the cornstarch and form each portion into a log. Roll the logs in the remaining cornstarch, tapping both ends to remove the excess and to make sure a light coating covers all the surfaces.

(continued)

Place the soy milk in a bowl and put the *panko* in another bowl. Have a paper towel–lined plate or tray nearby on which to place the breaded croquettes. Designate one hand to do the "wet" work (dipping in soy milk) and the other to do the "dry" work (rolling in bread crumbs) to avoid unnecessary washing of your hands. One at a time, dip the cornstarch-dusted croquettes in soy milk, then roll in the bread crumbs to coat. Use your wet hand to remove the croquette from the bread crumbs and redip in the soy milk. Place the croquette back in the bread crumbs and, with your dry hand, lightly press additional bread crumbs to all surfaces. Set the double-dipped croquette on the prepared tray. Repeat to double-dip the remaining 7 croquettes the same way. This can be done up to 8 hours before frying; cover and refrigerate if you want to hold for more than 30 minutes.

When frying these and other coated foods, the depth of the oil is critically important: a minimum of 1 inch is required, but 1¹/₂ inches is preferable. If you use a small wok or other skillet with sides sloping outward, you will need less oil to achieve depth. Pour the oil into the skillet and heat it slowly. Check the temperature with an unvarnished long wooden chopstick (or bamboo skewer). Small bubbles will form around the tip when the oil reaches 350°F. Wait for about 45 seconds longer to allow the temperature to rise a bit more—to about 370°F—and then test the oil temperature by dropping a few of the soy milk–coated crumbs that have fallen off the croquettes into the oil. They should sink immediately, then rise slowly and begin to sizzle slightly on the surface. If they start to color ever so lightly within 5 seconds, the oil is ready. If they never sink and begin to sizzle and color on the surface right away, the oil temperature is too hot. Stir the oil and reduce the heat slightly. If your sample sinks and takes more than 7 or 8 seconds to rise to the surface, the oil is not hot enough. Raise the heat slightly, stir, and wait for a minute before testing again.

When the oil temperature is ready, working in batches to avoid crowding, gently slip the croquettes into the oil. Allow them to fry undisturbed for 1¹/₂ minutes. Be patient; poking and excessive turning will cause the croquettes to fall apart. Flip them and fry for another 45 seconds, or until they are golden on all surfaces. Using a fine-mesh skimmer, remove the croquettes to a paper towel–lined rack to drain. Fry the remaining croquettes the same way. Use the skimmer to clear the oil of bits of bread crumb between batches.

Serve at room temperature with lemon wedges. Set out the salt and *kona-zanshō* in small mounds for sprinkling or dipping.

VARIATIONS: Try sweet potatoes and rutabagas, peeled, steamed, and coarsely mashed, then mixed with raisins and/or dried cranberries; serve with cinnamon sugar for sprinkling or dipping.

Also good are new red potatoes, steamed in their skins and coarsely mashed, then mixed with cooked corn and blanched peas; serve with freshly ground black pepper.

STEAMED TURNIP AND TŌFU IN SILVER SAUCE

KABURA MUSHI NO GIN AN KAKÉ

Japan's food elite will judge a meal by its *mushimono*, or steamed course. A skilled kitchen can coax out exciting yet subtle flavors in the steaming process, while a less-talented one leaves the diner disappointed. This particular steamed dish requires attention to timing more than skill.

Deep *chawan mushi* cups—the kind used for egg custards in the classic Japanese kitchen that can be lidded as they come out of the steamer—make especially attractive and practical serving dishes (they trap in heat and aroma). Deep $^3/_4$-cup ramekins, the kind used to make individual soufflés, or even teacups (best without handles) can also be used.

SERVES 4

8 to 10 ounces turnips and/or rutabaga with unwaxed skin

About 7 ounces grilled tōfu (page 282), about $^1/_2$ block cut into 12 cubes, or 12 Tōfu Chunks (page 164)

Pinch of salt

Splash of saké

2 tablespoons finely minced leafy greens from turnips or daikon or other greens

SILVER SAUCE

$^1/_2$ cup stock, preferably Sun-Dried Shiitaké Mushroom Stock (page 76)

$^1/_2$ teaspoon mirin

1 teaspoon light-colored soy sauce

$1^1/_2$ teaspoons crushed kudzu (page 255) or cornstarch

$1^1/_2$ teaspoons wasabi paste

Line a small strainer with *sarashi* (page 250) or other finely woven cloth and set the strainer in a small bowl. Scrub but do not peel the turnips, then grate them into the cloth-lined strainer. Lift the edges of the cloth and squeeze gently over the bowl. You should have about 1 cup grated turnip and about 2 tablespoons liquid. Save separately; both will be used.

Toss the tōfu with the salt and saké in a bowl; let sit for a few minutes, then blot up excess moisture. Divide the tōfu pieces, greens, and grated turnip among individual heatproof cups, lightly mounding the turnip on top.

Place the filled cups in a steamer fitted with a cloth-protected lid (page 251) and set over high heat. Once steam begins to flow, lower the heat and cook for 8 to 10 minutes.

While the cups are steaming, make the sauce: Pour the stock into a small saucepan and add the mirin and soy sauce. Place over low heat and gently cook for about 2 minutes, or until small bubbles appear at the edge of the pan.

Mix the reserved turnip liquid with the kudzu in a small bowl, and stir to dissolve the kudzu. Drizzle this cloudy mixture into the saucepan and continue to cook, stirring constantly, for about $1^1/_2$ minutes, or until the sauce begins to thicken. Toss the remaining chopped greens into the sauce and continue to cook, stirring, for about 45 seconds, or until the sauce begins to clear.

Protecting your hands from the heat, carefully remove the cups from the steamer. Spoon a generous amount of piping-hot sauce over each portion and top with a dab of wasabi. If you have lids, cover the cups immediately.

Serve piping hot, with small spoons. Diners stir the wasabi into the sauce as they eat. Any broth left at the bottom can be drunk directly from the cup.

SPICY STIR-FRY

KIMPIRA

Kimpira, a quickly assembled, skillet-stirred mélange of vegetables finished with a fiery blend of seven spices, frequently appears on the menu at casual eateries. Commonly made with whittled shreds of burdock root and slivers of carrot, *kimpira* in the *kansha* kitchen is an easy way to utilize kitchen scraps that accumulate. Daikon and carrot peels are especially well suited to this treatment. Slivers of bamboo shoot are a special springtime treat; finish them off with *kona-zanshō* (page 258) instead of the 7-spice blend. Cutting scraps into thin shreds makes the dish more attractive and cuts down on cooking time.

I find that something green brightens the dish visually and balances nutrients. Broccoli stems or the tougher bottom segment of asparagus cut into slender matchsticks, parboiled, and then tossed into the stir-fry at the last minute work well. When I have lemon, grapefruit, or orange peels on hand, I find they add a nice mildly bitter, pleasingly tart flavor accent. If you decide to use citrus, be sure the skins have not been treated post-harvest with any chemicals. Whatever combination I use, I find the spicy blend of peppers used to garnish this dish does a fine job of bringing different textures and flavors into harmony with one another.

Pictured on the front cover

SERVES 2 TO 4

½ teaspoon aromatic sesame oil

⅔ cup matchstick-cut daikon peels, about 2 ounces

⅓ cup matchstick-cut carrot peels, about 1 ounce

1 teaspoon sugar

1 tablespoon saké

2 tablespoons stock, preferably Basic Kelp Stock (page 75), or water, if needed

1 tablespoon soy sauce

¼ cup matchstick-cut peeled broccoli stems, about 1 ounce, parboiled (optional)

1 tablespoon pith removed and very finely shredded lemon, grapefruit, or orange peel (optional)

Pinch of shichimi tōgarashi (page 259)

Heat the sesame oil in a wok or skillet over high heat. Add the daikon and stir-fry for 1 minute, tossing constantly. Add the carrot and continue to stir-fry for another minute. The strips may brown slightly; the sesame oil should be very aromatic but not smoking.

Sprinkle the sugar over the vegetables and toss to distribute. Add the saké to deglaze the pan of any crusty bits, then stir-fry for 1½ more minutes. Add the stock if the vegetables look in danger of scorching.

Drizzle in the soy sauce, starting at the rim of the pan and working toward the center. Continue to stir and toss for about 30 seconds, or until the liquid is nearly gone and the vegetables are just tender and well glazed.

Add the broccoli and toss to meld the flavors. If you are adding the citrus peel, add it last, tossing to distribute. Finally, sprinkle with the *shichimi tōgarashi* and toss to distribute well.

Remove from the heat and let cool to room temperature. *Kimpira* is usually presented in small mounds, sometimes topped with an extra pinch of pepper.

FIDDLEHEAD FERNS STEEPED IN SOY-TINGED BROTH

KOGOMI NO NI-BITASHI

Sansai, literally "mountain vegetables," are foraged from woodland areas as winter snows begin to melt. When they appear at table in Japan, it signals the start of culinary spring fever—a craving for earthy-sweet flavors, tinged with a slightly bitter edge.

I am fond of *kogomi*, or fiddlehead ferns, prepared *ni-bitashi* style: briefly blanched, then steeped in a subtly seasoned broth. I find that freshly roasted sesame seeds, minced or cracked just enough to release their nutty aroma, are the perfect garnish for the ferns.

This same *ni-bitashi* treatment also works well with ramps (found in and around the Appalachian Mountains), wild leeks (the Great Lakes region), and broccoli rabe (throughout the U.S. and Europe). Thanks to the proliferation of farmers' markets in many urban communities, these harbingers of spring can be enjoyed by city folk.

SERVES 4

STEEPING BROTH

   1 cup Sun-Dried Gourd Ribbon Stock (page 76)

   1 tablespoon Vegan Seasoned Soy Concentrate (page 131) or 1 teaspoon each mirin, light-colored soy sauce, and soy sauce

   6 to 7 ounces fiddlehead ferns, submerged for 10 minutes in water to which a pinch of yaki myōban (page 284) or baking soda has been added

   ¼ teaspoon salt

   2 tablespoons white sesame seeds, freshly dry-roasted (page 245) and minced or cracked in a suribachi (page 246) or spice mill

Assemble the broth: Combine the stock and soy concentrate in a small saucepan and bring to a simmer over medium-high heat. Transfer to a small glass or ceramic baking dish or other nonreactive container. Avoid metal and plastic containers, as they contribute unwanted (metallic and chemical, respectively) overtones to the hot broth.

Drain the soaking fiddleheads and trim away any dark, discolored stems. Rinse the fiddleheads in fresh cold water and drain again. If the stalks are longer than 1 inch, cut them in half, making two piles: tender tops and tougher stems. Bring a small pot of water to a rolling boil, add the fiddlehead stems, and blanch for 2 minutes. Toss in the tops and blanch for 1 minute after the water returns to a boil. The water may turn dark, but this is of no concern.

Drain the fiddleheads but do not "refresh" them in cold water. Instead, immediately transfer them to the steeping broth, allowing them to cool there to room temperature. During this cooling-down period, they will absorb the flavors of the broth and continue to cook a bit, becoming tender yet remaining slightly crisp.

After about 10 minutes, when steam is no longer rising and the container does not feel especially warm to the touch, cover and refrigerate for at least 30 minutes or up to 3 days.

You can serve the fiddleheads chilled, brought back to room temperature (most typical in Japan), or briefly warmed (reboil the broth and steep again for a few minutes). When the fiddleheads are at the temperature you wish to serve them, remove them from the broth and mound in small, deep dishes. Garnish with the sesame seeds.

EGGPLANT TWO WAYS

MARUGOTO NASU

A recurring theme in Japanese cooking is the creative—and thrifty—use of the entire ingredient: *ichi motsu, zen shoku.* In vegetarian kitchens that inevitably means using peels and leaves or other edible but often discarded portions of the plant.

In this recipe, a single eggplant is peeled and then prepared in two utterly different ways: a small mound each of spicy, firm, strips of dark peel and tart, salty, sweet chunks of pale flesh are served together. The contrast makes for a refreshing appetizer that works especially well with a chilled very dry saké. To transform this dish into a wonderful hot-weather lunch, place a small mound of each element on a bed of soft lettuces and serve with crisp toasts or crusty baguette slices and iced tea.

I include a subrecipe for making a fabulous, immensely versatile sour plum sauce that can be used as a spread for sandwiches, served as a dip for chips or cold noodles, or sweetened with a bit more syrup to make a sauce for waffles or frozen desserts. You may want to double the recipe, especially since it stores well in a glass jar in the refrigerator for up to a month.

SERVES 4 AS AN APPETIZER OR 2 AS A LUNCHEON SALAD

SOUR PLUM SAUCE

1 tablespoon mashed pitted uméboshi (page 283) or plum paste (page 283)

1 teaspoon Saikyō miso (page 271)

1 to 2 teaspoons mizu amé (page 281) or maple syrup

1 teaspoon vegetarian stock (page 76) or cold water

3 or 4 firm Japanese eggplants, about 10 ounces total weight

TO COOK THE FLESH

1 tablespoon fresh lemon juice (reserve the spent fruit shell)

1 tablespoon saké

1 tablespoon vegetarian stock (page 76) or cold water

1 piece kombu (page 266) left from stock making (optional)

TO COOK THE PEELS

1/2 teaspoon aromatic sesame oil

1 teaspoon sugar

1 teaspoon saké

Scant 1 tablespoon soy sauce

1/8 teaspoon kona-zanshō (page 258)

Make the plum sauce: There is tremendous variation in sweetness, sourness, and softness among *uméboshi* plums. For this sauce, soft, squishy plums will be easier to mash. In a small glass or ceramic cup, mix the mashed plum paste, the miso, and 1 teaspoon of the *mizu amé.* I find using a small, flexible spatula to be the most effective tool for blending. Taste and adjust with more *mizu amé* if too sour or salty. Drizzle in a bit of stock, stirring to thin the sauce to a pourable consistency. Cover the sauce and chill until ready to serve.

Trim away the very top of the stem end from each eggplant. As you do so, the sepals should fall away (if not, pull them off and discard). Peel the eggplants from stem to flower end with 4 or 5 wide strokes of your knife. The

(continued)

pieces of peel should be about ¹/₈ inch thick, ³/₄ inch wide, and 4 or 5 inches long. Cut these into matchsticks 1 or 1¹/₂ inches long and set aside.

Prepare the flesh: In a small skillet or shallow saucepan, combine the lemon juice and spent shell, saké, and stock. Cut the eggplant flesh into ¹/₂-inch chunks, add to the pan, and toss in the lemon liquid as you arrange the pieces in a single layer. If you have a piece of *kombu* left over from making stock, lay it over the eggplant pieces, using it as an inner lid and flavor enhancer. Or, place an *otoshi-buta* (page 243) or a circle of parchment paper on the eggplant to keep it moist as it cooks.

Set the pan over medium-high heat and cook until the liquid begins to bubble. Reduce the heat, cover the pan with a regular lid, and steam the eggplant for 2 to 3 minutes. The chunks will become slightly translucent and turn a pale gold-celadon color. Remove the pan from the heat, lid intact, and let the eggplant cool naturally. Remove to a covered container and refrigerate until ready to serve.

Prepare the peels: Drizzle the sesame oil into a skillet and heat over medium heat. Add the peels and stir-fry vigorously for about 1 minute, or until slightly wilted and very aromatic. Sprinkle the sugar over the peels, toss to distribute, and then add the saké to deglaze the pan, stirring to dislodge any browned bits. Continue to stir-fry, jiggling the pan to keep the pieces moving, for about 1 minute, or until the saké has evaporated. Drizzle in the soy sauce and toss to distribute well. Remove the pan from the heat and let the peels cool in the pan. Sprinkle half of the *kona-zanshō* over the peels and toss to distribute well. The peels can be served at room temperature, or chilled.

To serve, arrange small mounds of the flesh and the peels next to each other in a bowl or on a plate. Garnish the chunks with a spoonful of plum sauce and the peels with the remaining *kona-zanshō*.

GINGERY ENOKI MUSHROOMS WITH CARROTS

ENOKI TO NINJIN NO SHŌGA ITAMÉ

Delightful to nibble on its own with a chilled dry saké, this mushroom and carrot combo can also be tossed into rice dishes, such as Temple Scattered-Style Sushi (page 31), or used as a topping for noodles, such as Slithery Sōmen Noodles (page 59).

SERVES 6 TO 8 AS AN APPETIZER OR TOSSED INTO SUSHI RICE, 4 AS A TOPPING FOR NOODLES

1 small carrot, about 3 ounces

$1/2$-ounce knob tender new ginger or 1 tablespoon ginger juice (page 246)

2 packages enoki mushrooms (page 272), about $3^1/_2$ ounces each

1 teaspoon aromatic sesame oil

1 teaspoon sugar

Scant 1 tablespoon saké

1 tablespoon soy sauce

1 teaspoon white sesame seeds, freshly dry-roasted (page 245), optional

Scrape the carrot and cut into 1-inch segments. Use a broad-bladed knife to first shave off a lengthwise sliver from each segment. Position a segment so the cut edge is flat on your cutting board, then shave off tissue-thin slices. Or, use a mandoline to produce the thin slices. Stack the slices, only slightly overlapping them, on the board and cut into thread-thin strips. Repeat with the remaining carrot segments. Scrape the skin from the knob of new ginger and slice in the same manner.

Trim the enoki mushrooms, discarding the spongy bottom section. Cut the stalks in half, then separate the halves into two piles, one with caps, one without.

Heat a cast-iron skillet over high heat and drizzle in the sesame oil. When aromatic, add the carrot and ginger threads and sauté, tossing vigorously, for 1 minute. (If using ginger juice, reserve for adding later.) Add the bottom section (without the caps) of the enoki stalks and sauté for 1 minute longer.

Sprinkle the sugar over the vegetables in the skillet and toss vigorously. Add the saké and enoki caps. Toss for 30 seconds, then drizzle in the soy sauce. Toss and stir to distribute the seasonings. If you are using ginger juice, add it now and toss again. Remove from the heat.

Allow the wilted vegetables to cool to room temperature in the skillet, then transfer them to a glass jar or other lidded container, cover tightly, and refrigerate. They will keep for up to 1 week.

When ready to serve, gently mound the vegetables and garnish with the sesame seeds.

THE WELL-STOCKED PANTRY

BEFORE REFRIGERATION BECAME WIDELY AVAILABLE, all premodern societies struggled to keep foods from spoiling. A variety of ingenious techniques were developed, including drying fresh produce in well-ventilated shade or in bright sunshine. In Japan, these dried foods are known collectively as *kambutsu* (literally "dried things") and are an important category of comestibles in both home and professional pantries. Although *kambutsu* were originally conceived of in archaic circumstances, they can become the modern, too-busy-to-get-to-the-grocery-store cook's best friend. Waiting patiently on your pantry shelf to be used on their own or in combination with small quantities of fresh produce already on hand, such as carrots, green beans, or salvaged broccoli or cauliflower stems, *kambutsu* can come to your rescue when you want to put another dish on the dinner table.

In the process of drying fresh produce, nutrients and flavor are concentrated. Many *kambutsu*, such as dried shiitaké mushrooms and sun-dried *kampyō* (gourd ribbons), play a double role in the Japanese *kansha* kitchen: the rehydrating liquid becomes flavorful stock or broth and the softened vegetable is used to prepare a variety of dishes.

Kaisō, a subgroup of *kambutsu*, is comprised of sea vegetables, such as nori, *wakamé*, and *kombu*. It is a welcome source of minerals, especially calcium (for those who choose not to eat dairy products) and iron (for those who choose not to eat red meat). For example, one tablespoon of dried *hijiki*, a dark, threadlike sea vegetable with an aroma vaguely reminiscent of anise, has the calcium equivalent of a glass of milk and fifteen times more iron than an average portion of spinach. All *kaisō* are rich in dietary fiber, too. Many people not brought up in a Japanese household may have limited familiarity with sea vegetables and little or no experience in preparing them. If that is the case for you, the recipes I have provided will hopefully start you on a happy journey of discovery.

Several fresh soy foods are dehydrated to extend their shelf life, yielding a second subgroup of *kambutsu*. Fresh firm tōfu, for example, is transformed into *kōya-dōfu* (freeze-dried tōfu), and fresh sheets of *yuba*, which have been skimmed from the surface of warmed soy milk, are changed into *hoshi yuba* (dried sheets of soy milk).

Dried beans, yet another type of *kambutsu*, are an excellent source of nonanimal protein. *Daizu*, dried soybeans from which fresh *tōfu* is made, are especially nutritious. I offer recipes for stewing the beige soybeans, the most common, as well as *kuro mamé* (black soybeans) and maroon *adzuki*.

Beans lend themselves to both sweet and savory preparations. I have placed sweet-cooked beans in the dessert chapter, even though sweet beans can be paired with savory tidbits, or served as a palate cleanser (not unlike sorbets in classic French cuisine), in a classic Japanese menu.

As is the case in the Western kitchen, fresh and dried products are rarely interchangeable. Think about the difference between fresh and dried tomatoes, for example, or fresh and dried apricots. Fresh daikon and sun-dried *kiriboshi daikon* are both delicious, but utterly different. Each recipe will guide you in choosing the most appropriate product.

SOFTENING DRIED INGREDIENTS

Kambutsu need to be softened before they can be consumed, and most, though not all, must be cooked. Because not all *kambutsu* are handled in the same manner, each recipe in this chapter will direct you to the page in the A Catalog of Ingredients for instruction about how to soften the ingredient or ingredients you will be using.

The liquid that results from soaking certain, but not all, *kambutsu* becomes flavorful stock. Information on softening *kombu* (kelp), dried shiitaké mushrooms, *kampyō* (gourd ribbons), and *kiriboshi daikon* can be found in the Stocks and Soups chapter (see Vegetarian Stocks Made from Sun-Dried Vegetables, page 76).

Each recipe calling for dried beans in this chapter describes the most suitable soaking and cooking process for making that particular dish.

VEGAN SEASONED SOY CONCENTRATE

SHŌJIN TSUYU NO MOTO

If you find a bottle of soy sauce crammed in the back of your pantry, long forgotten and with little aroma left, you can revitalize it by making this enriched soy sauce concentrate. Intense, sweet yet salty, and slightly syrupy, a few drops of it can enliven any simmered dish. In fact, you may become so enamored of this simple make-ahead seasoning, you won't want to wait for your soy sauce to "age" on a back shelf. It is fine to make it with sauce from a newly opened bottle, too. Drizzled over blanched or roasted vegetables, the enriched soy sauce imbues them with deep flavor. Diluted with a few drops of water, the concentrate makes a quick dipping sauce, or with a greater amount of water, a broth for noodles.

MAKES ABOUT 1/4 CUP

10 to 12 square inches kombu (page 266), preferably high-glutamate variety such as ma kombu

4 or 5 stems dried shiitaké mushrooms

1/3 to 1/2 cup soy sauce

2 1/2 to 3 tablespoons sugar

1 1/2 to 2 tablespoons saké

1 tablespoon mirin, mizu amé, or maple syrup (optional)

Put the *kombu*, mushroom stems, and soy sauce in a small, deep saucepan, cover, and let stand at room temperature for at least 1 hour or up to 12 hours.

Add the sugar and saké to the pan and place over low heat. Cook, stirring occasionally, until the liquid begins to simmer. Taste, and if very salty, add the mirin to mellow the flavor. Adjust the heat to maintain a slow, steady simmer. The sauce becomes quite foamy (that's why you want to use a deep pan). Simmer for 3 to 4 minutes, or until reduced by nearly half and the sauce becomes a bit syrupy. Remove from the heat and let the sauce cool naturally to room temperature.

Pour the cooled concentrate into a small glass jar, leaving the *kombu* and mushroom stems behind in the pan. Cover the jar with a tight-fitting lid and store in the refrigerator for up to 1 month.

SECONDARY STOCK (NIBAN DASHI)

Nothing goes to waste in the *kansha* kitchen. The bits of kelp and dried mushroom remaining in the pan after making the soy concentrate can be coaxed into a fine secondary stock. Pour 2 to 3 cups cold water over the bits and let stand for 10 minutes. Then place the pan over gentle heat and heat slowly, adjusting as necessary to maintain a very gentle simmer. Cook for at least 10 minutes or up to 30 minutes. Let cool to room temperature, strain through a fine-mesh strainer into a clean jar, cover tightly, and refrigerate for up to 3 days. The kelp and the mushroom bits will now have little flavor, though the kelp can be used to make the rice friends relish on page 152, or it can be added to your compost heap with the mushroom bits.

ROBUST MISO

TEKKA MISO

Long before the advent of refrigeration, miso, a naturally fermented product, was stored for long periods in the pantry, at (naturally) cool room temperatures. In other words, it does not spoil easily, but it does lose its aroma fairly quickly. Refrigerating miso after opening will slow this process. But if a package has been open for more than about six weeks, it will have lost its verve, even in the refrigerator. Fortunately, miso can be revitalized—given a boost of flavor and nutritionally enriched—by cooking it with other ingredients to make a condiment.

The classic version, popularized by the modern macrobiotic movement, is a slow-cooked affair called *tekka miso*. It uses fudge-colored Hatchō miso as its base and includes such root vegetables as lotus and burdock. Because these ingredients may be difficult to find in ordinary markets outside Japan, my version of *tekka miso* calls for easy-to-source carrots and ginger and any type of miso, or a combination of types: dark (*aka* or "red" miso), light (*shiro* or "white" miso), or enriched with rice or barley in addition to soybeans. (Of course, if you can find Hatchō miso, burdock, and/or lotus root easily, by all means use them.) I also grate the ingredients, rather than chop them, which reduces cooking time to less than 20 minutes.

The consistency and saltiness of miso vary dramatically from type to type and from brand to brand, so I have given you a range for quantities for the seasonings. Begin with the smallest amount, then adjust as needed to achieve the proper consistency (imagine thick jam, or tomato paste) and a sweet-salty balance you find pleasing.

MAKES ABOUT $1/2$ CUP

$1/3$ cup miso, any type or a combination

2 to 3 tablespoons stock, preferably Basic Kelp Stock (page 75), or cold water

2 to 3 tablespoons saké

1 to 2 tablespoons sugar

1 teaspoon aromatic sesame oil

$1/3$ cup grated scrubbed unpeeled carrot, with any accumulated juice reserved

2 to 3 tablespoons grated fresh ginger (if outer layer seems tough, peel first, otherwise just scrub), with any accumulated juice reserved

OPTIONAL

2 ounces burdock root, scraped and grated, with any accumulated juice reserved

2 ounces lotus root, scrubbed, unpeeled, and grated, with any accumulated juice reserved

You can use just a single type of miso or a combination of types. Combine the miso, 2 tablespoons each stock and saké, and 1 tablespoon sugar in a small saucepan and stir until thoroughly mixed. You should have a fairly smooth consistency similar to a thin purée (some types of miso include crushed soybeans, rice, and/or barley; this texture is fine). Place over medium-high heat and cook, stirring constantly, for about 2 minutes, or until the mixture is glossy and has the consistency of tomato ketchup. The mixture can sputter and splatter, so use a long-handled wooden spoon or silicone spatula to stir to prevent burns.

Using a small spoon, scoop out a tiny sample, let cool, and then taste. Adjust the balance of sweet and salty flavors as needed with additional stock, saké, and sugar. Set aside.

Heat the sesame oil in a skillet over medium heat until aromatic but not smoking. Add the carrot and its accumulated juice. If using the burdock or and/or lotus root and juice, add it now as well. Sauté, stirring constantly, for 2 to 3 minutes, or until only a little liquid remains. If the mixture threatens to scorch, lower the heat. Add half of the grated ginger, holding back on any juice, and continue to sauté, stirring constantly, for 1 minute longer.

Add the miso mixture to the skillet and stir to mix. Continue to cook, stirring occasionally, for 2 minutes, or until thick, glossy, and aromatic. Add the remaining gin-ger and the ginger juice, stir, and cook for 1 more minute. Remove from the heat and allow the mixture to cool naturally to room temperature. The sauce will stiffen as it cools. If you wish to store the miso sauce before using it, rinse a clean jar with a tight-fitting lid with boiling water and let drip-dry on a clean towel. Transfer the miso sauce to the jar, filling it no more than three-fourths full, then place a piece of plastic wrap or parchment paper directly on the surface of the sauce to minimize contact with air. Seal tightly, then label and date the jar. Refrigerate for up to 6 months; once opened, use within 2 weeks.

When ready to enjoy, be sure to use a clean spoon each time you take some miso from the jar to prevent unwanted bacteria from entering and spoiling the whole batch.

ROBUST MISO WITH VEGETABLE STICKS

Stir in a few drops of stock or water to thin the Robust Miso to dipping consistency. It is especially good with sticks of celery, cucumber, and daikon, served in the style of crudités. In the Rice chapter, this thick miso becomes a filling for rice "sandwiches" (page 45).

CREAMY SESAME PUDDING

GOMA-DŌFU

Although *shōjin ryōri*, shunning the consumption of all animal foods, became well established in Japan during the twelfth century, *goma-dōfu* is historically associated with a Chinese-style of temple vegetarian cookery called *fucha ryōri* that arrived in Japan a bit later, during the Edo period (1603–1868). Today, the creamy sesame pudding is considered the quintessential *shōjin* dish. The very act of preparing it exemplifies one of the prime virtues extolled in Buddhist practice (and Japanese society, at large): *dōryoku* (diligence). Making the pudding from scratch takes several hours. It requires carefully roasting sesame seeds, grinding them by hand until oily and smooth, mixing the resulting paste with water or broth and an arrowroot-like starch called kudzu, and then slowly, patiently cooking the mixture while stirring constantly. It is often a task assigned to acolytes as part of their spiritual training.

No disrespect intended, but there is a (slightly) easier way to make this yummy pudding using commercially prepared sesame paste (instead of roasting and crushing the sesame yourself) and employing an electric blender (instead of a hand-powered *suribachi*). When using such shortcuts, *kansha* could be expressed as gratitude for artisanal products and appreciation for modern technology. If, however, you wish to try the classic method, see the box on page 105.

SERVES 6 TO 8

1¼ cups stock, preferably Basic Kelp Stock (page 75)

3½ tablespoons crushed kudzu (page 255), about 1 ounce

1½ teaspoons powdered sugar

⅛ teaspoon salt

6 tablespoons white sesame paste

½ teaspoon wasabi paste

2 tablespoons Vegan Seasoned Soy Concentrate (page 131) or soy sauce

Place a 5 by 3-inch glass or metal mini loaf pan in the refrigerator. Chilling the pan will make it easier to unmold the pudding for serving. The Japanese use a metal *nagashi kan* (page 249) to shape the mixture.

Mix a scant ½ cup of the stock with the kudzu in a small bowl. Stir the mixture thoroughly, dissolving the crushed powder, then transfer to a blender or food processor. Add the powdered sugar, salt, and half of the sesame paste and pulse until blended. Add the remaining sesame paste and pulse again until the mixture is completely smooth. Pour the mixture into a small saucepan and place over low heat.

Bring the mixture to a very gentle simmer, stirring constantly with a long-handled wooden spoon or a sturdy silicone spatula. Alternate stirring clockwise and counterclockwise, and occasionally stir in a figure eight. Scrape down the sides frequently. After 2 to 3 minutes, the mixture will begin to thicken. As it does, it will be lumpy at first, but if you continue to stir with diligence for another 2 minutes or so, the mixture will become smooth again. This is your cue to add the remaining stock, stirring constantly as you drizzle it in. Cook, stirring constantly, for 2 to 3 more minutes; the mixture will become very thick. When you can draw a line with your spoon or spatula along the bottom of the pan that remains visible for several seconds before it fills, set your kitchen timer for 5 minutes.

Cook, continuing to stir in a slow and steady manner for the full 5 minutes; it is this final determined effort that ensures a rich, nutty-flavored, creamy-textured pudding. After a few minutes, you will notice the mixture beginning to form a single smooth mass with a slightly oily film on its surface and on the bottom and sides of your pot (depending upon the oil content of the sesame paste you are using, the amount could be barely noticeable to rather considerable—either is fine).

Spoon the pudding mixture into the chilled loaf pan. Although not traditional, small ceramic ramekins can be used to form and serve individual portions that won't need to be unmolded.

Immediately after pouring the mixture into the mold, tap it down to make sure no large air bubbles are trapped inside and smooth the surface with a spatula dipped in cold water. Cover the pudding to prevent an unpleasant "skin" from forming. Professional chefs place a sheet of glass dipped in water directly on the pudding. Plastic wrap pressed against the pudding with a piece of cardboard will also work well. Once the pudding has cooled and firmed, remove the glass or plastic wrap.

The pudding will set at room temperature within 15 to 20 minutes. If you wish to serve the pudding chilled, refrigerate it for no more than 30 minutes. If you wish to store the pudding, cover and refrigerate for up to 3 days. For optimal eating pleasure, remove the pudding from the refrigerator about 30 minutes before serving.

To unmold the pudding, place a cutting board over the top of the pan and invert the board and pan together. Lift off the pan. Slice the pudding in half lengthwise, then cut crosswise two or three times to yield 6 or 8 blocks. Transfer the blocks to individual serving dishes and garnish each serving with a dab of wasabi. Serve the soy concentrate in a small pitcher on the side and let diners drizzle their own, or serve the sauce in individual dipping dishes.

If you have used ramekins, garnish each serving with wasabi and serve the soy concentrate on the side.

GOMA-DŌFU THE SHŌJIN WAY

To make *goma-dōfu* in the classic *shōjin* manner, you will need patience, stamina, and a *suribachi* (page 246).

Dry-roast ²/₃ cup white sesame seeds (page 246) until aromatic, about 5 minutes. While the seeds are still warm, transfer them to the *suribachi* and grind them well. Once all the seeds are thoroughly crushed and a bit oily in appearance, season with ¹/₂ teaspoon sugar and a generous pinch of salt. Crushing granulated sugar will require dilligence—the true meaning of *shōjin*. Continue to grind until the mixture becomes very smooth and oily (this could take 30 or more minutes). Drizzle in 1 tablespoon of the stock or water and grind to make a thick paste (the addition of liquid will cause the color to go milky white at first). Scrape down the paste, collecting it in the bottom of the *suribachi* (be sure to scrape in the same direction as the grooves).

Dissolve the kudzu in the scant ¹/₂ cup stock as directed, then add to the paste and grind to blend. Gradually drizzle in the remaining stock, grinding to blend. If the mixture seems grainy, strain it through a fine-mesh strainer into a small saucepan. Place the pan over low heat and cook, mold, and serve the pudding as directed in the recipe.

SLOW-SIMMERED SOYBEANS AND MUSHROOMS

NI MAMÉ

Slow-simmered beans are a mainstay of many frugal Japanese households, a nutrition-packed boon to limited budgets. Although not particularly difficult, dried-bean cookery does require time—in some instances, several days from beginning to end—though most of it passes with only minimal attention of the cook. During both the soaking and the cooking steps, the beans undergo a transformation in several distinct stages, changing from a shelf-stable pantry item to a richly seasoned, fully cooked food.

Note that you will be simmering the beans for an extended time with only saké and sugar, both tenderizing agents. Soy sauce is added at the very end of the cooking. This kind of simmering is often described as "alphabetical," referring to the Japanese vocabulary for the various seasonings and the order in which they are used (see page 243).

This deeply flavored mélange can be tucked into an *obentō* lunch box, tossed in a green salad, or even nibbled with a cold beer or saké. If you have some Nutty Tōfu Sauce (page 99) on hand, it is terrific folded into it. The simmered beans will keep for a week in the refrigerator, but I would add fresh broccoli (or another green) just before serving.

SERVES 4 TO 6

1/2 cup dried soybeans

4 cups water

4 tablespoons saké

1 1/2 tablespoons sugar

3 dried shiitaké mushrooms

About 6 ounces konnyaku, white, black speckled, or a mixture (page 268), diced, blanched for 1 minute, and drained

3 tablespoons soy sauce

1/4 cup diced broccoli or cauliflower stems (diced to match the size of cooked beans), blanched for 1 minute

Rinse the dried soybeans, then place them in a saucepan with 2 cups of the water. Place over medium-high heat and bring to a boil. When a few beans begin to float to the surface, remove the pan from the heat, cover it, and let the beans cool to room temperature in the pan. Leave the beans in the pan or transfer them and their liquid to a glass jar with a tight-fitting lid and refrigerate overnight. Either way, the beans should swell to nearly twice their original size.

If necessary, return the beans to the saucepan. Place over medium heat and bring to a boil. Skim away any froth with a fine-mesh skimmer and reduce the heat to maintain a gentle simmer. Add 2 tablespoons of the saké and 1 tablespoon of the sugar. Cook the beans for at least 1 hour, though 1 1/2 hours would be better. Add boiling water as needed to prevent the beans from sticking or burning, always maintaining a simmer as you do. Skim away froth and any skins that float to the surface. Check the beans for tenderness: you should be able to spear them easily with a toothpick and find no resistance when you bite into one. Drain the beans and rinse out the saucepan.

While the beans are simmering, extract a stock from the mushrooms: Break off the stems and set them aside

(continued)

TOP: *Slow-Simmered Soybeans and Mushrooms*
BOTTOM: *Granny's Sun-Dried Radish (page 142)*

for making stock on another occasion. Here you are using only the caps to make the stock. Soak the caps in the remaining 2 cups water in a bowl for at least 30 minutes and preferably for 1 hour or more. Remove the caps from the liquid. Rinse the caps to remove any gritty material, squeeze, and dice. Pour the soaking water through a fine-mesh strainer (or disposable coffee filter) into a clean bowl to remove unwanted bits that may have settled at the bottom of the bowl.

Add the diced mushrooms, the *konnyaku*, the reserved mushroom stock, the remaining 2 tablespoons saké, and the remaining ½ tablespoon sugar to the clean saucepan. Reintroduce the beans to the pan and bring to a simmer over medium heat. Cover with an *otoshi-buta* (page 243), or with a circle of parchment paper and a flat metal lid slightly smaller in diameter than the rim of the pan. Cook, skimming away froth as necessary, for 15 to 20 minutes, or until the simmering liquid is reduced by about half. Add 2 tablespoons of the soy sauce and simmer for 10 more minutes. Remove from the heat and allow the contents of the pan to cool naturally, with the *otoshi-buta* in place. It is during this cooling-down period that flavors develop and meld.

Set the pan over medium heat again and bring to a simmer. Add the remaining 1 tablespoon soy sauce and cook for 5 minutes, or until nearly all the liquid is gone. Just before serving, add the broccoli stems and toss to mix. Serve family style from a large bowl, or divide among individual bowls.

SOY-BRAISED KABOCHA AND WHEAT WHEELS

KABOCHA TO KURUMA-BU NO NITSUKÉ

An important source of protein in the vegetarian diet, wheat gluten takes many forms in the Japanese kitchen. Shelf-stable *kuruma-bu*, literally "wheels of wheat gluten," are often used in braised dishes because they readily absorb the flavors of the foods with which they are cooked. *Kuruma-bu* has added gustatory benefits in mimicking the appearance and texture of meat.

Here, I have paired *kuruma-bu* with *kabocha* squash, used naturally sweet radish stock (to reduce the amount of sugar needed), and seasoned with soy sauce. The result is a richly braised vegetarian stew with a satisfying chewiness.

SERVES 4

1 teaspoon aromatic sesame oil

4 or 5 wheels kuruma-bu, softened (page 268) and cut into quarters

10 to 12 ounces kabocha squash, unpeeled, seeded, and cut into 1½-inch pieces

2 cups Sun-Dried Radish Stock (page 76)

2 tablespoons saké

½ teaspoon sugar

1 tablespoon soy sauce

12 green beans, stems trimmed, blanched for 1½ minutes, and cut into 1-inch pieces

Choose a skillet that can hold the pieces of *kuruma-bu* comfortably in a single layer. Heat 1/2 teaspoon of the sesame oil in the skillet over medium heat. Add the gluten pieces, and sear for 1 minute. Flip the pieces over and continue to sear. If you have an *otoshi-buta* (page 243), use it to press on the pieces. Or, press on the pieces with a broad flexible spatula or a small, flat lid. The pressing helps ensure that all surfaces will be evenly seared while trapping moisture in the skillet. This method of simultaneously searing with heat and trapping in moisture is called *mushi yaki* (steam-searing). When the pieces are lightly colored, after about 2 minutes, remove them from the skillet.

Add the remaining 1/2 teaspoon oil to the skillet over medium heat. Add the *kabocha*, flesh side down, and sear for 1 minute, or until lightly colored (the natural sugars in the *kabocha* will cause it to caramelize a bit). Add 1 cup of the stock and the saké, lower the heat to maintain a gentle simmer, cover with the *otoshi-buta* or a circle of parchment paper, and cook for about 2 minutes, or until tender. Because cooking times will vary with the variety of *kabocha*, test progress by inserting a toothpick through the skin of a chunk at the thickest point. It should meet with little resistance when tender.

Turn the pieces of *kabocha* over, skin side down, and cluster the pieces at the center of the skillet. Return the pieces of *kuruma-bu* to the skillet, fitting them around the outer edges of the *kabocha*. Add the remaining 1 cup stock and the sugar. Re-cover with the *otoshi-buta* or parchment, adjust the heat to maintain a gentle simmer, and cook for 1 minute. Flip the pieces of *kuruma-bu* and rearrange, if necessary, to make sure they are all coming into contact with the skillet surface. Drizzle in the soy sauce along the rim of the pan, and swirl the pan to make sure the soy sauce mixes well with the skillet juices. Re-cover and cook for about 45 seconds, or until all the liquid has been absorbed. Be on the alert in these final few moments to prevent pieces from scorching.

Toss the green beans into the skillet, then jiggle the skillet so they come into contact with the pan surface. Re-cover the skillet, remove from the heat, and allow the contents of the pan to cool naturally, with the *otoshi-buta* in place. It is during this cooling-down period that flavors develop and meld.

Serve at room temperature family style in a shallow bowl or deeply flanged plate, or in individual portions. If you would like to serve the dish warm, partially cover with plastic wrap and reheat by zapping in the microwave.

SUCCESSIVELY SIMMERED KŌYA-DŌFU AND VEGETABLES

KŌYA-DŌFU NO TAKI AWASÉ

Foods simmered *taki awasé* style are a mainstay of Japanese cookery. On vegetarian menus, broth-absorbing *kōya-dōfu* is commonly simmered with dried shiitaké mushrooms, then root vegetables, successively, allowing woodsy and earthy flavors to mingle and gradually intensify. The household version typically uses the same pot, allowing flavors to blend, while chefs in elegant restaurants will take care to have each item distinct. The final assortment is artistically arranged, landscape style, with taller foods at the back (these are the "mountains") and smaller items in the foreground.

SERVES 4

2 dried shiitaké mushrooms

1 piece kombu (page 266), about 1 by 2 inches

2 cups water

1¹/₂ tablespoons saké

Scant 1 tablespoon sugar

1 cup Basic Kelp Stock (page 75), with the kombu

1 slender carrot, about 2 ounces, scraped and cut ran-giri style (page 244) into 8 small chunks

2 ounces burdock root, scraped and cut sasagaki style (page 244), or 4 ounces boiled fresh bamboo shoot (page 92), cut kushi-gata style (page 244) into 8 or 12 thin slices

2 pieces kōya-dōfu, preferably old-fashioned style, softened (page 261) and each piece cut in half on the diagonal to produce 4 triangular pieces total

1 tablespoon mirin

1¹/₂ tablespoons light-colored soy sauce

2 teaspoons soy sauce

4 snow peas, strings and stems removed, blanched for 1 minute, and cut in half on the diagonal

Extract a stock from the mushrooms: Break off the stems and set them aside for making stock on another occasion. Here you are using only the caps to make the stock. Soak the caps and *kombu* in the water in a bowl for at least 30 minutes and preferably for 1 hour or more. Remove the *kombu* from the water and set aside. Remove the caps from the water and rinse the caps to remove any gritty material, then squeeze gently. Pour the soaking water through a fine-mesh strainer (or disposable coffee filter) into a clean bowl to remove unwanted bits that may have settled at the bottom of the bowl. Set the stock aside.

Slice the softened mushrooms in half on an angle, holding your knife nearly parallel to the cutting board, *sogi-giri* style (page 244). Cut each half in half again, using the same *sogi-giri* technique to yield a total of 8 flat-surfaced wedgelike pieces.

Combine the mushroom stock, saké, and sugar in a wide, shallow pot. Place over medium heat and bring to a simmer, skimming away any large clouds of froth with a fine-mesh skimmer. Cover with both pieces of *kombu* (from the mushroom stock and the kelp stock) and adjust the heat to maintain a steady gentle simmer. Cover with an *otoshi-buta* (page 243) or a circle of parchment paper and cook for about 10 minutes. If at any point the mushrooms (and later the other vegetables) look in danger of scorching, add a bit more water.

Add the carrot and burdock root, replace the *kombu*, cover, and cook for 7 to 8 minutes. Remove the pot from the heat and allow the vegetables to cool slightly in what remains of the simmering liquid (probably less than ¹/₄ cup). It is during this cooling-down period that flavors develop and meld.

Remove the mushrooms, carrot, and burdock and set them aside. Slice the *kombu* into 12 small squares and set aside. Do not worry if the *kombu* has developed blisters; in fact, they are a sign of tenderness.

Add the *kōya-dōfu* to the liquid remaining in the pot, then the kelp stock and the mirin. If using modern *kōya-dōfu*, add the light-colored soy sauce now *before* you begin the simmering process and add the regular soy sauce at the end. If using old-fashioned *kōya-dōfu*, add both of the soy sauces later. Cover with the *otoshi-buta* or parchment paper.

Bring the liquid to a simmer and cook the *kōya-dōfu* for 4 to 5 minutes, flipping the pieces halfway through if it looks like the simmering liquid is not circulating well in the pot. Remove from the heat and allow the *kōya-dōfu* to cool naturally to room temperature. It will soak up the cooking broth as it cools.

Arrange the pieces of *kōya-dōfu* around the edges of the pot to make room at the center for the mushrooms, carrot, burdock root, and simmered *kombu* that were set aside earlier. Cover with the *otoshi-buta* or parchment and bring the liquid to a simmer over low heat.

If using old-fashioned *kōya-dōfu*, now is the time to season with the light-colored soy sauce; swirl to distribute and simmer for 1 minute. Then add the regular soy sauce, flip the pieces of *kōya-dōfu*, and cook for a final minute or two longer. If using modern *kōya-dōfu*, add the regular soy sauce, flip the pieces, and cook for a final minute or two. There should be little or no liquid remaining in the pot.

Remove from the heat and let the contents of the pot cool naturally, with the *otoshi-buta* or parchment in place. This will probably take 20 minutes, or possibly longer. It is during this cooling-down period that flavors develop and meld.

If not serving within 30 to 40 minutes, refrigerate the cooled foods for up to 2 days. When ready to serve, bring back to room temperature (which is how foods are often served in Japan) or reheat gently in a pot. There will be little or no liquid, so you will need to add water or stock. You can use kelp broth, or make a stock from the dried shiitaké mushroom stems set aside at the start of the recipe. Drain off excess liquid from the *koya-dōfu* just before plating, applying gentle pressure to the pieces if you prefer them merely moist rather than juicy.

Arrange 1 triangular piece of *kōya-dōfu* (point up to suggest a mountain) at the back of each of 4 small, shallow bowls. Lean the mushroom slices against the *kōya-dōfu* to suggest rolling hills. The carrots become boulders and the burdock shreds and simmered *kombu* appear as foreground terrain. Finally, stand the snow peas on end (pointed tufts up), leaning against the vegetables and mushrooms, to suggest shrubs or trees.

MAKING MORE

I think foods prepared in this style taste even better after a few days, so I often double the recipe just to have more later in the week. Should you have any leftovers, they will keep for several days in the refrigerator. All of the various ingredients—*kōya-dōfu*, shiitaké mushrooms, kelp, carrot, and burdock root—can be chopped or minced and tossed with plain rice or sushi rice to make a wonderful pilaf that packs easily into a picnic lunch box. Just be sure to press out any excess liquid from the *kōya-dōfu* before packing it, to avoid leakage in transit.

GRANNY'S SUN-DRIED RADISH

GOMOKU KIRIBOSHI DAIKON, SOBO-FU

In many rural parts of Japan, the autumn landscape is dotted with farmhouses preparing for the cold months to come. Daikon radishes, their green tops drooping in the late-afternoon sun, are hung to dry on racks and under thatched eaves. Here and there, piles of shredded daikon can be seen spread out to dry on straw mats. These bits and pieces salvaged from bruised or malformed roots are transformed into *kiriboshi daikon*, a tasty, nutritious food. The ancient no-waste practice of *kansha* is alive and well with Japan's frugal farming grannies.

In this home-style recipe, the golden strips of radish are combined with bright slivers of orange carrot, green beans, and black threads of *hijiki*, a calcium-rich sea vegetable, to make a colorful and nutritionally balanced mélange.

Pictured on page 137

SERVES 6 TO 8

1 cup kiriboshi daikon (page 263), about 2¹/₂ ounces

2¹/₂ cups water

6 ounces shirataki noodles (page 268), drained and cut into 1-inch lengths

About ¹/₄ cup naga hijiki, mé hijiki, or aramé, ¹/₃ ounce, softened (page 263) and cut into 1-inch lengths if long strands

1 teaspoon aromatic sesame oil

1 tablespoon sugar

1 small carrot, about 2 ounces, scraped and cut into thin matchsticks

3 tablespoons soy sauce

8 to 10 slender green beans, stems trimmed, blanched for 1 minute, and cut into slivers on the diagonal

¹/₄ teaspoon shichimi tōgarashi (page 259)

Place the *kiriboshi daikon* in a bowl, add the water, and let stand for 20 minutes, or until softened. Drain, reserving the soaking water to use as stock for the dish. Squeeze the strips to release any excess moisture into the reserved liquid, then cut the strips into 1-inch lengths if long. Set the strips and stock aside separately.

Place the *shirataki* noodles in an 8- to 10-inch nonstick skillet and set it over medium-high heat. Jiggle the pan and stir the noodles for about 1 minute, or until you hear a squeaking sound (a sign that the noodles have thrown off their excess moisture). Add the *hijiki* and continue to stir and jiggle for 1 minute, or until a pleasant seashore aroma is released. Drizzle in the sesame oil, then toss and stir to coat the noodles and *hijiki*.

Add the *kiriboshi daikon* and continue to toss and stir over high heat for another minute. Add 1¹/₂ cups of the stock and the sugar and bring to a gentle boil, stirring to dissolve the sugar. Adjust the heat to maintain a steady, gentle simmer. Cover with an *otoshi-buta* (page 243) or a circle of parchment paper to keep the foods moist and cook for 5 minutes.

Test a piece of *hijiki* for tenderness; it should give easily when lightly pinched. If it is still stiff, add more stock or water and simmer for an additional 3 or 4 minutes. The *hijiki* must be completely tender before adding other ingredients or seasonings. Modern science confirms what

Granny experience has observed for generations: saké and sugar soften simmering foods, but once soy sauce is added, foods will no longer become tender (see page 243 for information about cooking in "alphabetical" order).

Add the carrots and continue to cook, covered with the *otoshi-buta* or parchment, for another 2 minutes. Add more stock or water if necessary to keep the vegetables from scorching.

When the vegetables are tender and only a bit of liquid remains in the skillet, drizzle in the soy sauce along the rim of the pan and swirl the skillet to distribute evenly. Re-cover and continue to simmer for 3 to 4 minutes, or until aromatic, well colored, and nearly all the liquid has been absorbed. Remove from the heat and allow the mixture to cool naturally in the skillet, with the *otoshi-buta* in place. It is during this cooling-down process that flavors develop and meld. This dish is typically served at room temperature.

Just before serving, add the green beans and toss to distribute well, then sprinkle with the *shichimi tōgarashi*. Transfer to individual small bowls or mound, family style, in a larger bowl. The finished dish will keep well in the refrigerator for 3 or 4 days.

CRISPY GOURD CHIPS

KARI KARI KAMPYŌ

This is a wonderful way to enjoy the gourd ribbons that remain after stock making. The chips are crisp yet tender, fully flavored (marinated in soy sauce, they require no further seasoning), and as addictive as potato chips—maybe more so. This recipe can easily be doubled or tripled.

MAKES ABOUT 180 PIECES (1 INCH LONG);
NIBBLES FOR ABOUT 10 PEOPLE

2 or 3 pieces kampyō (page 262), about 15 feet total

1 teaspoon salt, preferably kosher salt

MARINADE

1 teaspoon saké

1 tablespoon soy sauce

3 tablespoons cornstarch

Vegetable oil for deep-frying

Few drops of aromatic sesame oil

Put the *kampyō* ribbons in a glass jar, add water to cover, and let soak for at least 30 minutes or up to several hours at room temperature. Remove the *kampyō* from the water. Reserve the soaking water to use as a flavorful stock in other recipes; it will keep in a lidded glass jar in the refrigerator for up to 3 days. Apply the salt to the softened *kampyō*, rubbing as though you were trying to remove a spot from clothing. The gourd ribbons will become much softer and somewhat velvety to the touch. Rinse off the salt, squeeze out the excess moisture, and blot with paper towels. Using scissors or a knife, cut the ribbons into 1-inch lengths.

Make the marinade: In a bowl large enough to accommodate the ribbons, mix together the saké and soy sauce. Add the ribbons, turn to coat with the marinade, and then allow to sit for at least 20 minutes at room temperature or up to several hours in the refrigerator. Remove the strips from the soy mixture and blot up excess marinade.

Toss the soy-drenched strips in the cornstarch to dust them lightly. Set aside for 10 minutes. The reddish brown color of the soy will seep through. Shake the strips lightly to remove the excess cornstarch.

Pour the vegetable oil to a depth of at least $1^1/_2$ inches into a small wok or other pan with deeply sloping sides. Add the sesame oil and heat to 350°F. Check the temperature with an unvarnished long wooden chopstick (or a bamboo skewer). Small bubbles will form around the tip when the oil is about 350°F. Or, test the oil temperature by flicking a bit of the cornstarch you shook off of the gourd strips into the oil. If it sizzles immediately on the surface, drop in a strip of the dusted gourd; if it sinks slightly, surfaces immediately, and then begins slowly to turn golden, the oil is ready.

Fry the gourd strips in several batches. At first the oil will be quite foamy. When the bubbles calm, stir to ensure that all surfaces are frying evenly. Once the chips have turned golden, after about $1^1/_2$ minutes, remove them with a fine-mesh skimmer or a slotted spoon to a paper towel–lined rack. Allow the chips to drain until they no longer have an oily appearance. Indeed, some pieces will look lacy or chalky.

Eat the chips immediately. Or, let them cool completely and store them in a zippered plastic bag or lidded container at room temperature for up to 2 days.

THE WELL-STOCKED PANTRY

HIJIKI WITH THICK FRIED TŌFU

HIJIKI NO NIMONO

A classic combo, especially popular on cafeteria menus and in children's lunch boxes, this dish combines the bounty of the field—soy in the form of meaty chunks of fried tōfu—with the bounty of the ocean—*hijiki*, a mineral-rich sea vegetable. This surf-and-turf notion of balancing the source of foodstuffs in menu planning is typical of Japan's indigenous food culture, *washoku*.

You can make the soy-simmered *hijiki* without the fried tōfu and serve it on its own as a side dish or toss it into rice. I call for it in Temple Scattered-Style Sushi (page 31) and Toasted Hand-Pressed Brown Rice with Hijiki (page 48).

SERVES 4 TO 6

About 7 ounces thick fried tōfu (page 282)

¹/₄ teaspoon aromatic sesame oil

¹/₂ cup naga hijiki, mé hijiki, or aramé, about ²/₃ ounce, softened (page 263)

1 tablespoon saké

Scant 1 tablespoon sugar

³/₄ to 1 cup stock, preferably Basic Kelp Stock (page 75)

2 tablespoons soy sauce

2 teaspoons white sesame seeds, freshly dry-roasted (page 245)

Bring a small pot of water to a rolling boil. Add the fried tōfu and blanch for 30 seconds to remove the excess surface oil. Drain and blot with paper towels, then cut into bite-size pieces.

Heat the sesame oil in a nonstick skillet over high heat. Add the *hijiki* and stir-fry, as though lightly tossing a salad, for about 1 minute. Each piece of *hijiki* will become glossy with the oil and begin to exude a seashore aroma.

Drizzle in the saké and toss the contents of the skillet until the saké has evaporated.

Add the tōfu pieces to the skillet and let the edges sear a bit. Sprinkle the sugar over all and continue to sear, letting the edges caramelize slightly. Be careful not to let the tōfu scorch. Add ³/₄ cup of the stock and lower the heat to maintain a steady, vigorous simmer. Cover with an *otoshi-buta* (page 243) or a circle of parchment paper to keep the foods moist and cook for 6 to 7 minutes, or until nearly all the liquid is gone.

Test a piece of *hijiki*; it should give easily when pinched. If it does not, add a few spoonfuls of stock and continue to simmer until tender, possibly 4 to 5 minutes longer for thicker, longer pieces. Do not add any soy sauce until the *hijiki* is completely tender.

Drizzle in 1 tablespoon of the soy sauce along the rim of the pan and swirl the skillet to distribute evenly. Cook for 1 to 2 minutes, or until the liquid is nearly gone. Drizzle in a bit more soy sauce, stir, and taste. Balance any unwanted sweetness with additional soy sauce. Remove from the heat and allow the contents of the skillet to cool naturally, with the *otoshi-buta* in place. It is during this cooling-down period that flavors develop and meld.

If you wish to serve this dish hot, you can reheat it briefly just before eating. Or, the cooled dish, including any liquid remaining in the skillet, can be transferred to a lidded container and refrigerated for up to 3 days.

Just before serving, drain off any excess liquid. To assemble each serving, cluster or stack pieces of fried tōfu to one side of the dish, and place a mound of the *hijiki* in front. Garnish each portion with the sesame seeds.

WAKAMÉ WITH TART GINGER DRESSING

WAKAMÉ NO SUNOMONO

The Japanese will often combine sea and land vegetables in the same dish. This salad featuring *wakamé* pairs the briny sea fronds with slightly bitter field greens. Dressing them in a spritely ginger-infused vinaigrette makes this dish especially inviting.

Although a small amount of newly harvested *wakamé* makes its way fresh to some markets in Japan, most of the spring crop is salted and/or air-dried to extend shelf life and ensure availability throughout the year. The dried product is reliable and easy to use.

SERVES 4 TO 6

1/4 cup dried wakamé, softened (page 267)

TART GINGER DRESSING

2 tablespoons rice vinegar, preferably brown rice vinegar (page 284)

2 teaspoons sugar

Pinch of salt

1/2 teaspoon ginger juice (page 246)

4 to 6 ounces mizuna (page 270) and/or frisée, torn into bite-size pieces, washed, and spun dry

If the rehydrated *wakamé* pieces seem awkwardly large, coarsely chop them. Set aside.

Make the dressing: Place the vinegar, sugar, and salt in a small saucepan and stir to combine. Set over low heat and cook, stirring, for about 1 minute, or until the sugar and salt have dissolved. Set aside to cool to room temperature. Stir in the ginger juice (if your juice was extracted from young ginger, the color might turn pink—a natural and visually pleasing chemical reaction). Transfer to a glass jar and refrigerate until needed, or for up to 1 week.

Dress the salad just before serving to prevent the green *wakamé* from turning brown (extended contact with vinegar will cause this). Toss together the *wakamé* and salad greens in a bowl. Drizzle the dressing over the mixture and toss again to lightly and evenly dress the salad.

Divide the salad among 4 to 6 bowls, coaxing each into a mini-tower shape. On a hot day, place the salad in clear glass bowls that have been chilled in the refrigerator for an hour or more before serving.

MISO-SLATHERED NAMA FU

NAMA FU DENGAKU

A staple of the Japanese temple vegetarian kitchen, *nama fu* (fresh wheat gluten) boasts a satisfyingly chewy texture and easily absorbs the flavors of other foods with which it is cooked. In Japan, it appears in many guises on many menus, both vegetarian and not.

At elegant *kaiseki* establishments, you will find thin slices shaped and tinted to resemble foliage (green maple leaves in summertime, turning yellow then red as autumn deepens) or flowers (pink plum blossoms for New Year, cherry blossoms in the spring) and floated in broths or simmered dishes. Home cooks will sometimes add a few fancy-shaped slices to "dress up" an otherwise ordinary dish. At *izakaya* (pubs), however, *nama fu* is typically cut into slabs or disks, slathered with aromatic miso, and broiled *dengaku* style. (You could add slabs of grilled tōfu, briefly drained, to the disks of *nama fu* if you wanted to make this a more substantial dish.)

Nama fu is not readily available outside Japan, so I have provided the directions for making it from scratch. The original *shōjin* recipe required earnest temple acolytes to knead the dough for hours to develop the gluten, then rinse away the starch (this starchy water was then evaporated to produce *ukiko*, a fine, silky powder used in making confectionary). My recipe, which calls for vital wheat gluten and *mochiko* (sticky rice flour), is less time-consuming and physically less demanding.

MAKES TWO 4-INCH ROLLS (36 SMALL DISKS); SERVES 6

NAMA FU DOUGH

1/2 cup vital wheat gluten (page 256), tapped down and leveled, about 3 1/2 ounces

2 tablespoons mochiko (page 256), about 1/2 ounce

1/2 teaspoon ao nori (page 256)

1/2 teaspoon ground turmeric

1/4 cup warm water

MUGI MISO DENGAKU SAUCE

2 tablespoons mugi miso (page 271)

Scant 1 tablespoon sugar

1 tablespoon saké

2 tablespoons stock, preferably Basic Kelp Stock (page 75), or cold water

1/2 teaspoon aromatic sesame oil (optional)

1 teaspoon each white and black sesame seeds, freshly dry-roasted (page 245)

Make the dough: Combine the vital wheat gluten and *mochiko* in a bowl and stir to mix thoroughly. Divide the mixture evenly among 2 bowls. Add the *ao nori* to 1 bowl and add the turmeric to the other bowl. Stir the contents of each bowl to mix thoroughly. Then add 2 tablespoons of water to each bowl a spoonful at a time, stirring to mix. Gather the contents of each bowl into a smooth, soft ball of dough, and place each ball in a small, sturdy resealable

(continued)

plastic bag. Seal the bags and let both doughs rest for at least 2 hours or up to 8 hours at cool room temperature. During this resting time, the dough will become soft, stretchy, and slightly sticky. If you want to keep the doughs longer, you can refrigerate them for up to 2 days but bring them back to room temperature before continuing.

Meanwhile, make the *dengaku* sauce: Combine the miso, sugar, saké, and stock in a small saucepan and stir well to combine. Place over low heat and cook, stirring frequently, for about 5 minutes, or until glossy, aromatic, and the consistency of tomato paste. The sauce can sputter and splatter, so use a long-handled wooden spoon or silicone spatula to stir to prevent burns. Remove from the heat and allow the sauce to cool naturally to room temperature. The sauce will stiffen as it cools. (The sauce can be made up to 2 weeks in advance, then refrigerated in a glass jar with a tight-fitting lid.)

Remove the rested balls of dough from the plastic bags. They will be slightly sticky. Gently roll each ball between your palms to form a cylinder about 5 inches long and 1 inch in diameter. Set each roll on a damp 8-inch square of *sarashi* (page 250) or other finely woven cloth. (The cloths will become tinted yellow and green, respectively, but they can be reused several times, rinsing and drying after each use.) Roll up to enclose, and secure the ends with rubber bands.

Ready a steamer. When the steam is flowing freely, place the rolls in the steamer and steam for 10 to 12 minutes. They will be become slightly aromatic and very firm. Remove the steamer from the stove top, but keep it lidded. Allow the rolls to rest for 20 to 30 minutes. Remove the rolls from the steamer and rinse them briefly under cold running water. Shake off the excess moisture, then remove the cloth from each roll. The *ao nori* roll will have become quite green and the turmeric roll a golden yellow. Place the rolls in a sealed container and refrigerate until ready to serve. They will keep for up to 5 days. Or, wrap snugly in plastic wrap and freeze for up to 3 weeks; thaw them slowly in the refrigerator. Once they are thawed, use them within 24 hours.

SAME AS SEITAN?

I am often asked if *nama fu* is the same as *seitan*, and if *seitan* can be substituted for *nama fu* in recipes. The answer is yes, both are wheat gluten, but no, you cannot easily substitute one for the other. The word *seitan* came into being with the internationalization of the macrobiotic movement and continues to be used, especially in English-speaking countries. Few Japanese would recognize the word, unless they were familiar with macrobiotic cooking. Most of the *seitan* products I have seen (and that my volunteer recipe testers have told me about) are preseasoned (with pronounced garlicky-soy overtones) and not shaped as either blocks or logs. They do not lend themselves to being slathered with *dengaku* sauce and broiled.

In Japan, most of the *nama fu* produced is sold to the restaurant trade; it can sometimes be purchased at department-store food halls or specialty shops. If you do find it in an Asian grocery store outside Japan, it will be frozen. Once it thaws, it should be kept refrigerated and consumed within a few days and never refrozen.

When ready to serve, slice each roll into disks about ¼ inch thick. Arrange these flat on a piece of aluminum foil that will fit under your broiler or on the tray of a toaster oven. If you are concerned about the stickiness of the disks, lightly grease the foil with the sesame oil. Using a small spatula or knife, spread a bit of the *dengaku* sauce on each disk. Broil the disks for 2 minutes, or until the sauce becomes bubbly, aromatic, and slightly crusted. Allow the disks to cool for 1 minute, then peel them off the foil.

To make serving—and eating—simple, thread 2 or 3 disks onto a wooden skewer (the skewers will be easier to insert into disks that are still warm). You can mix colors (and flavors) on a single skewer or keep them separate. Continue until all disks are threaded onto skewers. Garnish with the sesame seeds and serve.

MAKING MORE DENGAKU SAUCE

This *dengaku* sauce is yummy slathered onto grilled vegetables, so you may want to make a double—or even triple—batch and set some aside. For long-term storage, I recommend Mason-type glass jars that seal well, or empty jam jars with tight-fitting lids.

Rinse the clean jars in boiling water and let them drip-dry naturally on a fresh towel. Fill each jar no more than three-fourths full with the sauce, then place a piece of plastic wrap or parchment paper directly on the surface of the sauce to minimize contact with air and seal tightly. Label and date the jars. Store the jars in the refrigerator for up to 6 months; once opened, use within 2 weeks.

When ready to enjoy, be sure to use a clean spoon each time you take some *dengaku* sauce from the jar to prevent unwanted bacteria from entering and spoiling the whole batch.

THE WELL-STOCKED PANTRY

RICE FRIENDS:
PEPPERY KELP SQUARES AND PLUMMY KELP SQUARES

GOHAN NO TOMO

If you make stocks daily, you will find that a great deal of *kombu* accumulates in your kitchen. There are many ways to recycle this by-product. Elsewhere I have suggested that you use it to line cooking pots to prevent other ingredients from sticking and to boost flavor. I have also suggested that after-stock *kombu* can be used as a lid when cooking or when storing food in a glass jar.

Here I provide you with a recipe for making the whimsically named *gohan no tomo*, or "rice friends." Indeed, the primary use of this condiment is as an accompaniment to steaming-hot rice; typically 5 or 6 pieces are eaten with a bowlful. You can place the relish directly on top of your rice, or serve it separately in a small dish. It can also be used as a stuffing for Hand-Pressed Rice Triangles with Fillings (page 45).

MAKES ABOUT 4 DOZEN PIECES OF EACH FLAVOR

About 10 pieces softened kombu (page 266) left over from making various kinds of stock

1¹/₂ cups water

Scant ¹/₄ cup vinegar

2 tablespoons sugar

1 tablespoon saké

6 tablespoons soy sauce

PEPPERY KELP

Generous pinch of kona-zanshō (page 258)

PLUMMY KELP

Generous pinch of yukari (page 259)

Cut the *kombu* into small squares, each about ¹/₂ inch; you will likely have a total of 100 or more squares. Bring the water to a rolling boil in a nonreactive pot and add the vinegar. The vinegar helps tenderize the *kombu* and eliminate any questionable bacteria, but it won't affect the final taste.

Reduce the heat to maintain a steady boil, add the *kombu* squares, and cook for 12 to 15 minutes. They should appear slightly blistered. To test their tenderness, remove a piece (use long chopsticks or tongs) and pinch it. It should

ANOTHER FRIEND

When making Fresh Soy Milk Sheets (page 160), or *yuba*, a residue always remains in the skillet. Stir to scramble it, then let it cool. Mix the bits with dry-roasted white sesame seeds (page 245) and serve it alongside one or both of these flavored *kombu*. The scrambled *yuba* becomes another good "friend."

be so soft that your thumbnail can easily cut through it. If necessary, continue to cook the *kombu* for several more minutes. You must not combine it with the soy sauce mixture until it is thoroughly tender, because the soy sauce will prevent it from becoming more tender. Drain the *kombu*, rinse briefly under running cold water, and drain again.

Rinse and dry the pot, and then add the sugar, saké, and soy sauce to it. Stir well, place over medium heat, and bring to a simmer. Add the *kombu* squares, reduce the heat to fairly low, and cover with an *otoshi-buta* (page 243) or a circle of parchment paper to keep the squares moist. Cook for 7 to 8 minutes, or until the *kombu* looks glazed and the liquid is nearly gone. Remove from the heat and let the *kombu* cool naturally, still covered, to room temperature.

Divide the soy-stewed *kombu* evenly between 2 bowls. To make the peppery kelp, sprinkle the *kombu* in 1 bowl with *kona-zanshō* and toss to distribute. To make the plummy kelp, sprinkle the *kombu* in the other bowl with the *yukari* and toss to distribute. You can eat the flavored *kombu* right away, still slightly warm, or cooled to room temperature. To store, place each flavor in its own glass jar and refrigerate for up to 1 month.

MOSTLY SOY

Soy foods are the main source of plant-based protein in the Japanese vegetarian diet. Although commercially prepared fresh soy foods are increasingly available in non-Asian markets throughout the world, being able to make soy milk and tōfu in your own kitchen will ensure that sometimes difficult-to-source perishable plant protein is yours when you want and need it. Making tōfu does require patience and diligence, but your efforts will be well rewarded with marvelous food. And, making tōfu is a fine way to experience *kansha*: an appreciation of nature's bounty (green soybeans growing in the field) and of human ingenuity (previous generations of clever—and perhaps somewhat desperate—people who dried fresh soybeans for long-term storage and then creatively coaxed them into myriad dishes).

This chapter begins with the basics of tōfu making. The master recipe explains how to extract soy milk from dried beans, a process that produces *okara* (soy lees) as a by-product. Then, I will show you how to prepare Firm Tōfu (and an herb-showered, soy-drizzled version), Fresh Soy Milk Sheets (known as *yuba*) and Steamed Soy Milk Custard (a vegan version of the classic egg dish *chawan mushi*) from the soy milk you have made. The soy lees will be transformed into a classic of the no-waste *kansha* kitchen: Pan-Toasted Okara with Leeks and Root Vegetables.

The other recipes in this chapter—everything from hearty amber-braised stews to fried tōfu pouches stuffed with good fortune (bits of dried and fresh produce)—will demonstrate the amazing versatility of soy foods. My somewhat eclectic collection of mostly soy recipes concludes with the playful Glazed Eel Look-Alike.

SOY MILK AND OKARA

TŌNYU, OKARA

Because the Japanese vocabulary for tōfu making does not easily translate to English, I have decided to explain the process using both languages, beginning with *daizu*, or dried soybeans, which are the basis for most soy foods. The beans are soaked in water until swollen and then mashed (stone-ground in the old days, puréed in a blender nowadays). The uncooked soy mash, which is called *nama go*, is boiled (it gets very foamy) and strained, yielding a liquid called *tōnyu* (soy milk) and fiber-rich solid lees called *okara*. This is the procedure described in detail in this recipe. Once you have completed it, you will have soy milk (*tōnyu*) and soy lees (*okara*) to use in various recipes throughout this book.

For some recipes using soy milk, a coagulant will be added. In Japan, the coagulant has traditionally been *nigari* (page 274).

MAKES ABOUT 3 CUPS SOY MILK AND ABOUT 1 CUP SOY LEES

$^1/_2$ cup dried soybeans, about 3 ounces

$3^1/_2$ cups cold water

$^1/_2$ cup boiling water

Place the dried beans in a large, deep bowl. Rinse them under cold running water for several seconds; a large cloud of froth will appear at first, gradually overflowing and leaving clear water covering the beans. Drain the beans, return them to the bowl, and pour 2 cups of the water over them. Let the beans soak at room temperature for at least 6 hours or preferably 8 to 12 hours. The beans will swell to twice their original size. If you want to soak them for longer than 6 hours, refrigerate them, especially on a hot summer day.

With a slotted spoon, scoop out the swollen beans and transfer them to a blender. Add about half the soaking water to the blender and pulse to begin breaking up the beans. Add the remaining soaking liquid from the bowl and process until smooth and very thick. (Be careful; the motor can become overheated.) At this stage, the mixture is called *nama* (uncooked) *go*.

Transfer the *nama go* to a deep stockpot. Add the remaining $1^1/_2$ cups water to the blender and pulse to "clean" the blades. Add this thinner mixture to the thicker *nama go* in the pot. Stir to mix thoroughly.

Place the pot over medium heat and cook, stirring occasionally to prevent scorching. Once the mixture reaches a temperature of about 185°F, the foamy mass will rapidly rise (that is why you need a deep pot!). Remove the pot from the heat and stir down the foam. Return the pot to the heat on the lowest possible setting, so that the liquid is barely simmering. Watch the pot closely and remove it from the heat if the liquid threatens to overflow the sides. Cook, stirring frequently, for 10 minutes. It is during this gentle cooking that the nutrients in soybeans become more digestible. The characteristic sweet aroma of soy will begin to fill your kitchen.

Prepare your workspace to accommodate the cooked *go*. You will need a fine-mesh strainer or colander lined with *sarashi* (page 250). Any similar colorfast and untreated sturdy cotton cloth that can withstand squeezing and wringing can be used instead; the weave must be fine enough to keep the *okara* solids behind, yet open enough to allow the soy milk to filter through. You will find it easier, I think, and more effective, if the cloth is fashioned into a bag. To make a bag, take a piece of cloth measuring approximately 12 by 18 inches and fold it in half to make a 9 by 12-inch rectangle. Stitch up both short sides (use a sewing machine set for regular running stitch, or if sewing by hand use a double running stitch). Place the cloth- or bag-lined strainer over a bowl to collect the soy milk.

Pour the cooked *go* into the lined strainer, gather the edges of the cloth (or the top of the bag), and twist closed, pressing with force to separate the liquid, *tōnyu* or soy milk, from the solids, *okara* or lees. Add the boiling water to the pot in which you cooked the *go* and swish it around to pick up any bits of crushed bean that may still be clinging to the sides or bottom. Untwist the top of the cloth or bag and pour the contents of the pot over the *okara*. Twist closed and press again. You should have about 3 cups soy milk and about 1 cup *okara* (see photo, page 159).

Fresh soy milk is divine: silky and rich, sweet and nutty. Consume it immediately while it is still warm, or cover it tightly and refrigerate it for up to 3 days. *Okara* is also yummy, but it needs further cooking to be digestible. The classic recipe for pan-toasted and simmered *okara* is on page 167. *Okara* is highly perishable, so if you will not be cooking it right away, cover it tightly and refrigerate it for no more than 3 days.

FIRM TŌFU

ZARU MOMEN-DŌFU

The key to making delicate, tender *momen*, or "firm," tōfu is to add the coagulant, traditionally *nigari*, to the warm soy milk at the perfect time. A candy thermometer is handy for this step, though keen observation is an equally sound tool for determining when the temperature is just right. If possible, use still-warm freshly extracted soy milk to make the tōfu, though commercial soy milk is fine.

Firm tōfu can be used in soups or stir-fried dishes, or can be drizzled with seasoned soy and showered with herbs (see box, page 159). It's delicious stuff, any way you serve it.

SERVES 2

3 cups soy milk, freshly extracted (page 156) or purchased

**1¹/₂ teaspoons nigari (page 274) diluted with
1 tablespoon water**

Pour the soy milk into a deep, straight-sided pot and place over medium-low heat to prevent scorching as the soy milk gradually heats. When the edges begin to thicken, the soy milk will be approaching 130°F. When fine bubbles form, the temperature will have risen to about 140°F. When you see a few bubbles break on the surface at the center of pot, the soy milk will be at 150°F. Remove the pot from the heat.

Using a *shamoji* (page 248) or flat spatula, stir the very warm soy milk seven or eight times in a clockwise direction, smoothly but with determination, to create a swirling vortex. Drizzle the *nigari* mixture over the flat surface of the spatula, aiming it so that it drips into the center of the vortex. Stir once or twice counterclockwise to stop the swirling, and gently remove the spatula from the pot. Always avoid jerky motions as you stir and add the coagu-

lant. Tightly cover the pot to keep the soy milk warm and let it sit for 8 to 10 minutes.

After about 5 minutes, slide the lid to one side and peek inside. If you see little indication that the soy milk has thickened (solidified) in the center and little or no liquid is forming around the edges, re-cover the pot tightly and gently reheat the soy milk on the lowest possible heat for about 2 minutes before removing from the heat and letting rest, tightly covered, for 5 minutes. If when you peeked inside, the soy milk had thickened at the center and a clear (or yellow-tinged) liquid was floating at the edges, you do not need to heat it further. Instead, just re-cover tightly and wait 5 more minutes.

As you wait, line 2 small strainers with finely woven cloth; traditionally, the Japanese use small, woven-bamboo *zaru* strainers and *sarashi* (page 250). Set the lined strainers over small bowls. When the soy milk has thickened properly, gently scoop out the softly formed curds into the lined strainers, dividing them equally (see photo, page 159). Flip the edges of the cloth over the curds.

To serve warm, allow the soft curds to drain for only 1 minute. Open the flaps of cloth to expose the tōfu, and place each strainer on its own attractive plate. (The plates will catch any continued dripping and will make serving easier.) Serve condiments and sauce in separate small bowls into which each person can spoon the tōfu just before each mouthful.

To serve chilled, slip the cloth-wrapped tōfu still in the strainers into the refrigerator for at least 1 hour. If you prefer a firm texture, place a small container filled with 1 cup water (this will weigh about 8 ounces) on top of the tōfu to compress it, then slip into the refrigerator.

SOY PUDDING SHOWERED WITH FRESH HERBS (ZARU-DŌFU)

Named after the woven-bamboo strainers in which it is made, *zaru-dōfu* is a rich soy pudding with a texture similar to thickly clotted cream. It can be enjoyed either freshly made and still warm or chilled for several hours. Either way, it is marvelous when paired with fresh herbs and a drizzle of seasoned soy sauce.

Classic Japanese summertime condiments include shredded *shiso* (page 258), a verdant, flat leaf with a hint of basil and mint and *myōga* (page 257), a pale pink bulbous rhizome related to ginger. These herbs, tossed with a drop of Vegan Seasoned Soy Concentrate (page 131), make a refreshing topping to ice-cold *zaru-dōfu* that has been transferred from its lined basket to a glass bowl. Use a soupspoon to scoop out large chunks, mounding them against each other. If you are looking to add fire, place a dab of wasabi on top.

When chilly weather arrives, serve *zaru-dōfu* warm, or even piping hot (you can zap it in the microwave for 30 seconds). Transfer the soy pudding to warmed ceramic bowls, sprinkle with finely minced scallions or leeks, and drizzle with Vegan Seasoned Soy Concentrate.

Western herbs that pair well with *zaru-dōfu* include dill, rosemary, and tarragon. Mint, lemon verbena, and lavender on chilled *zaru-dōfu* looks lovely and transforms the dish into dessert, especially if drizzled with Brown Sugar Syrup (page 224) or Sweet Black Sesame Syrup (page 227) in lieu of savory soy concentrate.

MOSTLY SOY

FRESH SOY MILK SHEETS

NAMA YUBA

Yuba, the pale yellow, wrinkled sheets that form on the surface of warm soy milk, resemble the skin of an old woman (*uba*). Indeed, this may well be the origin of the word *yuba*, though more elegant calligraphy—for "steam" and "leaves"—evolved in the fourteenth century to sound out the word. For most Japanese, the name *yuba* evokes a pleasantly poetic image.

SERVES 2 OR 3

> 2 cups soy milk, preferably rich (with a high soy-solid content) and freshly extracted (page 156)
>
> ½ teaspoon wasabi paste
>
> Soy sauce or Vegan Seasoned Soy Concentrate (page 131)

Ideally, your stove top provides a low but steady source of cooking heat. Place a 7- or 8-inch shallow skillet or pan, preferably nonstick, over low heat for about 1 minute. Slowly pour the soy milk into the warm pan. It should be about ¼ inch deep. Adjust the heat to the lowest possible setting and allow the soy milk to heat undisturbed.

After several minutes, you will notice the surface of the soy milk beginning to thicken. At this point, the temperature of the soy milk will probably be 140°F. Using an *uchiwa* (page 248) or a flat piece of cardboard (about 8 by 11 inches), gently fan the air above the pan to cause a drop in air temperature; this, in turn, will cool the surface of the warm soy milk. When the surface of the soy milk cools but

OTSUKURI AND SOBORO

In Japan, the fresh (untreated by heat) course in a formal meal or banquet is called *otsukuri*—written with calligraphy to suggest a creative transformation of the ingredients regardless of the application of heat. *Otsukuri* is an accurate, and appetizing, description of the creamy, slightly chewy, fresh soy milk sheets served as a part of many Japanese vegetarian menus.

Although soy milk sheets can be made in advance and refrigerated, eating them warm as they form on the surface of gently heated soy milk is a special treat. Many restaurants offer do-it-yourself *nama yuba* service. If you have a small, shallow skillet that can be set on a tabletop cooking unit, you can enjoy this at home.

After making *nama yuba*, you will have some soy milk left in the pan that is partially solidified but cannot easily be scooped up into sheets. I often scrape and scramble this directly in the skillet to form *soboro*, a mass that resembles loosely shirred eggs. I either nibble it on the spot (yum!) or refrigerate it to use later, minced and mixed with toasted sesame seeds as another rice "friend" (see Rice Friends, page 152).

the liquid beneath is still warm, wrinkles will form and the surface will thicken, making sheets of *nama yuba.*

Using a thick chopstick (or wooden knitting needle), scoop under and lift up the sheet and drape it across a small serving plate. Choose a dark or brightly colored plate for a dramatic presentation. Continue to fan, scoop, and lift sheets, arranging 2 or 3 of them slightly overlapping each other on each plate. You should be able to pull at least 8 sheets, and possibly 12 or more, from 2 cups soy milk. The sheets will be wrinkled, not smooth.

Set a small mound of the wasabi on, or near, the fresh *yuba.* Pour a small amount of soy sauce into individual dipping bowls. Each diner dissolves wasabi to taste in his or her soy sauce before grasping a *yuba* sheet, dipping it in the sauce, and enjoying.

STEAMED SOY MILK CUSTARD

SHŌJIN CHAWAN MUSHI

The classic version of *chawan mushi*, often part of a formal banquet menu, is made with eggs and fish-based dashi. But lightly seasoned soy milk can be transformed into a custardlike consistency reminiscent of the classic by adding the coagulant *nigari*, in a process similar to the making of tōfu. I have filled my vegan *chawan mushi* with seasonal tidbits: wild mushrooms in the fall and asparagus tips and fresh bamboo shoots in the spring.

The custard must be served in the same heatproof container in which it is steamed. The Japanese use special *chawan mushi* cups with lids that are placed on top only after steaming. Ramekins, custard cups, or teacups without handles can be used in their place.

SERVES 4 TO 6

2 cups cold soy milk, freshly extracted (page 156) or purchased

1¹/₂ teaspoons mirin

1¹/₂ teaspoons light-colored soy sauce

2 teaspoons nigari (page 274) diluted with scant 1 tablespoon water

STUDDED WITH MUSHROOMS (AUTUMN VERSION)
KINOKO CHAWAN MUSHI

1 cup mixed fresh mushrooms, such as matsutaké, maitaké, shiitaké, shiméji, and/or enoki, in any combination, trimmed and cut as directed on page 272 and 273

3 or 4 stalks mitsuba (page 257), roots trimmed, stalks and leaves cut into ¹/₂-inch lengths, or 2 teaspoons coarsely chopped flat-leaf parsley leaves

STUDDED WITH BAMBOO SHOOTS (SPRING VERSION)
TAKÉNOKO CHAWAN MUSHI

¹/₂ cup diced or thinly slivered fresh boiled bamboo shoot (page 92)

1 asparagus spear, tip sliced in half vertically and stalk thinly sliced on the diagonal, and then tip and stalk blanched for 30 or 40 seconds

Measure the cold soy milk in a quart-size pitcher and season it with the mirin and soy sauce. Add the *nigari* mixture and stir gently to combine. Try not to create any foam as you stir.

Choose between the autumn version and the spring version, then divide the mushrooms or the bamboo shoots and asparagus stalk among 4 to 6 heatproof 1-cup cups. Gently pour all but about 1 tablespoon of the soy-milk mixture into the cups, dividing it evenly. Leave the 1 tablespoon in the pitcher. Do not worry if some of the vegetables float to the surface, but do be careful not to incorporate air as you pour. Air bubbles will mar the final appearance of the dish, so bubbles on the surface of the soy milk should be lanced or dragged to the sides with the tip of a toothpick and removed.

Add the chopped *mitsuba* or sliced asparagus tip to the soy milk reserved in the measuring pitcher and set aside.

Place the filled cups in a flat-bottomed lidded steamer fitted with a cloth-protected lid (page 251). Set the steamer over medium heat. Once you hear the water boiling, turn down the heat to maintain a very fine flow of steam. Steam undisturbed for 8 to 12 minutes (the longer time for diced bamboo shoots or deeper cups). Carefully slide the lid to one side to check on progress. A bit of clear liquid should have formed at the edge of each cup. If there is none, insert a toothpick into the center of a custard. If the toothpick shows signs of loose soy milk residue, re-cover the steamer and cook for another 2 minutes. If it comes out clean, continue to the next step.

Carefully arrange the soy milk–drenched *mitsuba* leaves or asparagus tips on the top of each custard. If you are skilled in using long chopsticks, this step will be easy to do and you will limit your exposure to the burning steam. If not, use tongs held with a pot holder to avoid burning your hands. Re-cover the steamer and steam for 2 to 3 minutes longer.

Turn off the heat (if using an electric range, remove the steamer from the stove) and allow the custards to settle undisturbed for 2 to 3 minutes. Use caution when removing the lid of the steamer to avoid burns from trapped steam. Retrieve the custards with pot holders and/or tongs.

To serve hot: If you have lids for the individual cups, cover the custards as you remove them from the steamer. If you do not have lids and need to hold the custards hot for a few minutes, set a piece of parchment paper over each custard, being careful to balance it on the rim of the cup, and then anchor it with a saucer or other small, flat plate. Using foil to keep the cups warm is not recommended, because condensation easily forms on the underside and drips onto the custards, pockmarking them. Serve as quickly as possible, with spoons.

To serve chilled: As you remove the cups, set them on a rack to cool, uncovered. When steam is no longer visible, use strips of paper towel or cotton-tipped sticks to blot up any liquid that may have pooled on the surface. Cover the custards snugly with clear plastic wrap, place in the refrigerator, and chill for at least 2 hours or up to 24 hours. When ready to serve, remove the plastic wrap and serve with spoons.

TŌFU CHUNKS

SHIMI-DŌFU

Traditional kitchen wisdom cautions against freezing fresh tōfu, which can become unpleasantly spongy and tends to spoil rapidly after it is thawed. There are, however, certain circumstances under which tōfu can be successfully frozen, and, in the process, it is transformed into chewy meat-mimicking chunks that can be seared in a skillet and sauced. For the best results, choose silken, custardlike *kinugoshi tōfu*, rather than firm, rough-textured *momen-dōfu*, for freezing.

The simplest approach is to use commercially made silken tōfu, either aseptically packaged (stored on unrefrigerated shelves) or vacuum-packed in a plastic tub with water and sealed with a see-through top. The latter type can be found in the refrigerated section of Asian markets, health-food stores, and increasingly in large supermarkets in urban areas. If you have a choice between using two small loaves (about 6 ounces each) or a single large one (about 14 ounces), choose the smaller loaves, as they will be easier to work with at every step.

This recipe requires three actions; freezing, thawing, and pressing. The total elapsed time is at least 3 days, so plan accordingly. Always observe good kitchen hygiene when handling fresh tōfu: wash your hands before you handle the tōfu and avoid placing it on a cutting board or other surface where it could pick up bacteria or unwanted odors.

2 loaves silken tōfu (page 282), about 6 ounces each, in unopened packages or 1 loaf silken tōfu, about 14 ounces, in an unopened package

To freeze the tōfu: Leave the tōfu in its sealed packages. Place the packages in the freezer, and do not place other items on top of them until the tōfu is stiff. Because liquids expand as they freeze, the tops of the packages will swell; this is not cause for alarm.

Keep the tōfu undisturbed in the freezer for at least 24 hours and preferably for 2 or 3 days. (Extended freezing, such as more than 10 days, is not advised, however, because it can toughen the soy protein.) During this time the packaging liquid will thoroughly crystallize. If your packages have a see-through top, you will notice the tōfu and surrounding liquid darken to a deep golden ocher.

To thaw the frozen tōfu: Transfer the packages to a refrigerator shelf and leave for 36 to 48 hours, to ensure the tōfu thaws fully. If you are pressed for time, you can place the sealed tōfu on your kitchen counter and allow it to thaw at cool room temperature for 2 to 3 hours, then refrigerate it to complete the process (about 4 more hours).

Once the tōfu has thawed, open the packages and drain thoroughly. Freezing has changed the cellular structure of the tōfu, and it will appear sinewy and striated. With clean hands, wrap each loaf of tōfu in paper towels. (For hygienic reasons, paper towels are preferred over cloth.) Holding the thawed tōfu between your palms over a sink or bowl, gently press it. As you press, the tōfu will feel spongy and compress considerably, and excess moisture will drip away.

Spread fresh paper towels on a cutting board and lay the hand-pressed tōfu on the towels. If using 2 blocks, slice 1 loaf in half parallel to the board, keeping the 2 pieces stacked and aligned as a single block. Then, cut through the loaf lengthwise twice and crosswise 4 times, to yield a total of 30 small, uniform cubes. Repeat with the second loaf of tōfu. If you have used a single loaf, slice it in half parallel to the board, then cut it lengthwise 4 times and crosswise 5 times to yield 60 small, uniform cubes.

Use immediately, or transfer to a tightly covered container and refrigerate for up to 24 hours. As is the case with any fresh food, do not refreeze the tōfu. Bacteria can sometimes multiply with renewed vigor with repeated freezing and thawing.

SKILLET-SCRAMBLED TŌFU WITH LEAFY GREENS

KUDAKI-DŌFU

This dish, which calls for tōfu that is frozen, thawed, and then crumbled, is one of the "delicacies" included in the eighteenth-century cookbook *Tōfu Hyaku Chin*. Circulated among the merchants of Edo (the former name for Tokyo), the book featured one hundred tōfu recipes, displaying the ingredient's enormous versatility.

Long before modern refrigeration, unheated winter kitchens with naturally frigid temperatures would no doubt transform custardlike silken tōfu into a meaty texture. Although *Tōfu Hyaku Chin* did not specify that accidently frozen tōfu be used in making this dish, it is entirely possible that frugal cooks not wanting to create waste would have used it for this purpose.

Far from antiquated, this venerable recipe will be a boon to the modern cook pressed for time: from skillet to table, it takes less than 10 minutes to prepare. However, you will need to plan ahead, freezing and then thawing silken tōfu over at least 3 days.

Saving the leafy tops from daikon is the most practical green for this dish, but you can use any newly purchased leafy green, such as kale, chard, or beet greens.

SERVES 4

2 loaves silken tōfu, about 6 ounces each, frozen and thawed as directed in Tōfu Chunks (page 164)

1 teaspoon aromatic sesame oil

7 to 8 ounces daikon or radish tops or other leafy green, blanched for 30 to 40 seconds and chopped

1 teaspoon sugar

1½ tablespoons saké

1½ tablespoons stock, preferably Basic Kelp Stock (page 75)

1½ tablespoons soy sauce

¼ teaspoon kona-zanshō (page 258)

Once the frozen tōfu is fully thawed, wrap it in paper towels and press it between your palms as directed in the recipe. Then, using your hands, crumble the pressed tōfu into irregular-shaped pieces measuring roughly ¼ inch, capturing them in a bowl.

Heat the sesame oil in a skillet over medium heat. When the oil is aromatic, add the tōfu, spreading it out fairly evenly in the pan. Allow the tōfu to cook undisturbed for about 1 minute, or until it crusts a bit on the bottom. Stir-fry the tōfu for 1 minute, then add the greens to the skillet. Toss vigorously to mix the greens with the tōfu.

Sprinkle the sugar over the greens and tōfu and continue to stir-fry for 30 seconds. Add the saké and cook for about 10 seconds, or until the alcohol has evaporated. Add the stock and soy sauce and continue to cook, stirring frequently, for about 2 minutes, or until little or no liquid remains in the skillet.

Sprinkle with the *kona-zanshō*, toss to distribute, and serve family style in a large bowl or in shallow individual bowls.

PAN-TOASTED OKARA WITH LEEKS AND ROOT VEGETABLES

U NO HANA

Because the fluffy, pale ivory *okara* (soy lees) used in this stir-fry resembles the tail of a bunny rabbit, the finished dish is called *u no hana* (fluffy cottontail). This dish commonly appears on *izakaya* (pub) menus and is also a favorite in many homes, especially those with seniors in residence: *u no hana* is the kind of dish your frugal grandmother would make (if she were Japanese).

Okara is produced in abundance as a by-product of making tōfu. Highly perishable and requiring constant refrigeration, it is difficult to sell at a reasonable price in ordinary supermarkets. It is often sold to zoos, where it is mixed into feed for the animals (lucky creatures!). If you want to enjoy *okara* and do not have a local shop or merchant who makes tōfu, you may need to make it yourself (see Soy Milk and Okara, page 156). It is another reason to try your hand at making tōfu.

SERVES 4 TO 6

1 cup well-packed okara (page 274), about 3 ounces

1/2 thinly and diagonally sliced leek, preferably naga negi (page 273), white part only if greens are very tough (set the greens aside for another use)

1/3 cup coarsely chopped root vegetables such as peeled lotus root and/or scraped parsnip and carrot

1/3 cup trimmed and coarsely chopped shiméji or other fresh mushrooms (page 272)

1 tablespoon saké

1 cup vegetarian stock (page 76)

1 tablespoon mirin

1 1/2 tablespoons light-colored soy sauce

2 tablespoons shelled peas, lima beans, or green soybeans, blanched for about 2 minutes (optional)

Put a large, shallow skillet over high heat, add the *okara*, and dry-roast, stirring to break up lumps. After 4 or 5 minutes, the *okara* will be parched and quite fluffy; it will also be slightly aromatic and may have browned a bit. Add the leek and root vegetables and stir-fry for 1 to 2 minutes, or until the vegetables are wilted and slightly translucent. Add the mushrooms and toss to distribute well.

Add the saké and then the stock; the *okara* will become the consistency of wet sand. Reduce the heat to maintain a very gentle simmer. Cover with an *otoshi-buta* (page 243) or a circle of parchment paper to keep the surface moist, and cook for 5 minutes, or until most of the liquid is gone (it now resembles barely moist sand).

Add the mirin and continue to cook, uncovered, for 5 to 6 minutes more, or until the liquid is gone but the contents of the skillet are still somewhat moist. Stir frequently to prevent scorching (though brown crusting in spots is fine).

Add the soy sauce and toss. Cook for 1 to 2 minutes undisturbed. Break up whatever crusty bits have formed on the bottom of the skillet and toss to distribute them throughout the mixture. Taste and adjust, if necessary, by adding a few drops of either mirin or soy sauce.

Remove the skillet from the heat and let the mixture cool to room temperature. It is during this cooling-down period that flavors develop and meld.

Serve in small, mounded portions in individual dishes or from a large bowl. Add the peas just before serving for a brighter appearance. Transfer any leftovers to a lidded container and refrigerate for up to 2 days; drain off any excess liquid that might accumulate in the container and bring to room temperature before serving.

TŌFU-TŌFU BURGERS

TŌFU-TŌFU TSUKUNÉ

These protein-packed veggie burgers combine two forms of tōfu: freeze-dried *kōya-dōfu* and fresh firm (*momen*) tōfu. Flavor and texture are enhanced by the addition of bits of scallion, crushed *osembei* (rice crackers—ones that have gone soggy are fine), and softened broken pieces of dried shiitaké mushrooms (the liquid in which they are softened also supplies the broth for cooking the patties).

Care needs to be taken when cooking the soft tōfu mixture, especially when flipping the patties. Making the burgers small (about 2 inches in diameter) will yield more attractive results. The final soy glaze helps to cover any small cracks or crevices.

MAKES 6 SMALL BURGERS; SERVES 2 OR 3

1/3 cup finely crushed osembei (see box, page 170)

6 to 8 ounces firm tōfu (page 281), well drained and mashed, about 1/2 cup

1 block kōya-dōfu (page 261), grated into a fine powder, about 1/4 cup

1/2 teaspoon cornstarch

1 small dried shiitaké mushroom cap or 2 tablespoons small broken bits of dried shiitaké mushroom stem, soaked in 1/2 cup water for 30 minutes

1 scallion, trimmed and finely minced, about 1 tablespoon

1 ounce enoki mushrooms (page 272), trimmed and diced, about 2 tablespoons

1 teaspoon aromatic sesame oil

A CHILD'S ŌBENTO, OR LUNCH BOX (CLOCKWISE FROM TOP LEFT):
Jellied Grapefruit Wedges (page 232), Green and Green on Greens (page 114), Rice with Salted Cherry Blossoms (page 25), Tōfu-Tōfu Burgers

SOY GLAZE

1 1/2 teaspoons sugar

1 tablespoon saké

Generous 1 tablespoon soy sauce

Combine the *osembei*, firm tōfu, and *kōya-dōfu* in the bowl of a food processor. Pulse until well mixed and a mass forms. Sprinkle the cornstarch over the mixture and pulse again to blend. The mixture will be soft and sticky.

Remove the shiitaké cap or bits from the soaking water, reserving the soaking water. Squeeze the mushroom to press out the liquid, capturing the released liquid in the bowl. Set the liquid aside to use as stock. If using a softened cap or if the mushroom bits are awkwardly large or uneven, mince with a knife. Add the minced shiitaké to the tōfu mixture in the food processor and pulse to combine. Add the scallion and enoki mushrooms and pulse until the mixture is roughly textured but bits are evenly distributed throughout.

Off the stove, pour the sesame oil into a skillet just large enough to hold 6 patties, each about 2 inches in diameter, in a single layer. Divide the tōfu-mushroom mixture into 6 equal portions. Dip your fingertips into the oil and then tap your palms with your fingertips and thinly spread the oil on your palms. Pick up a single portion of the tōfu-mushroom mixture and, with lightly oiled palms, coax it into a patty about 2 inches in diameter and 1/2 inch thick. Press the center slightly to indent it (it will puff up

(continued)

MOSTLY SOY

when cooking, evening out the thickness) and set aside. Repeat to make 5 more patties.

Heat the oil in the skillet over medium heat. When the pan is hot, add the patties and sear for 1 minute, or until crusted and lightly browned on the first side. Carefully flip the patties: 2 flexible silicone spatulas—one wedged under the patty, the other lightly holding the top as you invert— works well. Cook for about 1 minute more, or until crusted on the second side. Lower the heat if the pan is smoking.

When both sides have been seared and crusted, add 1/3 cup of the reserved mushroom stock, reduce the heat to low, cover, and cook for 1 minute. Remove the lid, carefully flip the patties again, and add more mushroom stock (or water) if the patties look in danger of scorching or sticking. Cover and cook for 1 more minute. Remove the lid and continue to cook until the liquid is nearly gone.

Meanwhile, make the soy glaze: Stir together the sugar, saké, and soy sauce in a small bowl. Pour the glaze over the patties and jiggle the skillet to make sure it is well distributed. The mixture will become foamy and reduce rapidly, forming a glaze. Carefully flip the patties a final time to glaze evenly.

Remove the skillet from the heat and allow the patties to "rest" for at least 30 seconds or up to 1 minute or more before serving. It is in these final moments that the flavors meld and the shape settles. The patties will remain hot for quite some time. If you wish to serve them later at room temperature, wait until all steam has dissipated before covering them.

Serve 2 or 3 patties per person on individual plates, spooning any sauce from the pan over them.

OSEMBEI

I adore savory *osembei*, rice crackers that come in a wide variety of shapes, sizes, and flavors. I am especially fond of the kind that are toasted (rather than fried) and lightly glazed with soy sauce. I prefer to buy packages with individually wrapped crackers: this curbs the temptation to overindulge and it prevents the crackers from getting sticky or soggy in Japan's humid climate. In this recipe, however, it will not matter if your *osembei* are crisp and crunchy or not, because they are crushed and blended with tōfu.

Read the ingredients list on the cracker package carefully before buying. Many types of *osembei* will appear to be vegan but are in fact seasoned with bonito flakes and/or honey. Finally, I suggest you purchase crackers that are as plain as possible, so as not to overwhelm the other flavors in the dish.

MISO ODEN

On a sleet-slick winter day, the camaraderie of sharing a bubbling pot of *oden* is especially comforting. Most modern-day versions of this hodgepodge stew include various fish sausages, hard-boiled eggs, and sometimes meat, though historically the dish was made with tōfu. It originated in the Muromachi Period (1336–1573) with a dish called *dengaku*, in which skewered tōfu was slathered with a sweet-spicy miso paste and broiled. Written with calligraphy for "tilled field" and "enjoyment," *dengaku* was the term used for ancient harvest celebrations. These festivals featured dancing, and the skewered food looked a bit like robe-clad dancing figures. Although today *tōfu dengaku* is enjoyed essentially unchanged (see Miso-Slathered Nama Fu, page 148), the transformation of *oden* (the word is likely an abbreviated version of the word *dengaku*) into the mixed stew now enjoyed began in the nineteenth century.

I have returned to the stew's culinary roots to offer you a vegan version similar to what was prepared hundreds of years ago. Old-fashioned *miso oden* is still enjoyed today in many parts of Japan, including Kagawa Prefecture (Shikoku), where my husband was born and raised. It was in Shikoku in the late 1960s that I first tasted tōfu and root vegetables slowly simmered in a lightly seasoned broth, then dipped liberally in a pungent, sweet-and-salty miso sauce—and became an immediate and devoted fan of *miso oden*.

There are no rules about what does, or does not, get included in the pot, or how many different kinds of vegetables to include. I have provided you with lots of suggestions, including several items, such as Good Fortune Bags, that appear elsewhere in this book.

SERVES 6 TO 8

7 ounces daikon, cut into 6 or 8 half-circles, each about 1 inch thick

2 cups water, preferably togi-jiru (page 242), or a mixture of water and togi-jiru

6 to 8 ounces black-speckled konnyaku (page 268), about 1/2 large loaf

8 ounces grilled tōfu (page 282)

1 chubby carrot, about 3 ounces, scraped and cut ran-giri style (page 244) into 6 or 8 chunks

6 Good Fortune Bags (page 180), filled and tied but not simmered

6 or 8 Broth-Steeped Kale Rolls (page 101), assembled but not simmered

SIMMERING LIQUID

1 piece kombu (page 266), about 2 by 3 1/2 inches, preferably ma kombu

4 cups stock, a combination of Basic Kelp Stock (page 75) and the liquids that remain from softening dried shiitaké mushrooms and gourd ribbons when making Good Fortune Bags

1 tablespoon saké

1 tablespoon mirin

2 teaspoons light-colored soy sauce

Mugi Miso Dengaku Sauce (page 148)

Tender-prep the daikon: If you have *togi-jiru* liquid on hand, pour it into a small saucepan and add water as needed to make 2 cups. If you don't have any on hand,

(continued)

just use water. Place the daikon in the liquid and bring to a boil over medium heat. Simmer for 10 minutes, or until a skewer inserted into a piece of daikon meets little resistance. Drain, rinse briefly under cold running water to remove any rice-bran residue, and set aside.

Prepare the *konnyaku*: Drain the loaf and score the top and bottom surfaces on the diagonal with many shallow, parallel slits. Cut the loaf into 6 or 8 narrow rectangles. Skewer each piece with 2 slender bamboo skewers inserted parallel to each other. Bring a pot of water to a boil, add the skewered pieces, and blanch for 30 seconds, then remove from the water. Do not refresh in cold water. It is during this natural cooling process that the characteristic (and slightly unpleasant) smell dissipates. Blanching the *konnyaku* makes it porous, so it is ready to soak up the good flavors of the *oden* pot.

Prepare the grilled *tōfu*: Drain the loaf and cut it crosswise into 6 or 8 narrow, rectangular blocks. Insert 2 slender bamboo skewers parallel to each other in each block to steady the delicate *tōfu* and make it easier to pull from the pot later.

Set the carrot, Good Fortune Bags, and Kale Rolls aside with the other prepared ingredients.

Make the simmering liquid: Lay the *kombu* in a wide, shallow pot or other flameproof vessel and pour in 3 cups of the stock, the saké, the mirin, and the soy sauce. Place over high heat and bring to a rapid boil. Adjust to maintain a steady, gentle simmer.

Begin by adding the ingredients that need to cook for more than 30 minutes: daikon, *konnyaku*, and any of the optional ingredients listed in the box on page 173. Stand the *konnyaku* skewers on an angle so they are submerged in broth but the ends can easily be grasped and the skewers pulled from the pot. Skim away any froth (or *aku*) as it appears with a fine-mesh skimmer. Check frequently to make sure the heat is not too high, or the foods may scorch and stick.

After 10 to 15 minutes, add the ingredients that need to cook for about 15 minutes: Good Fortune Bags, Kale Rolls, grilled *tōfu*, and carrot chunks. Place the skewered *tōfu* as you did the *konnyaku*, submerged in broth but easy to remove. Continue to simmer gently for 15 minutes, skimming away any *aku* as it appears. Add some of the remaining 1 cup stock as needed to prevent scorching. Taste the broth and adjust the seasoning with soy sauce (if too sweet) and/or mirin (if too salty).

ODEN NABÉ

Some *oden* pots, called *oden nabé*, are square or rectangular, others round. They are fitted with removable dividers with a pattern of cutouts that allow the broth to flow from one section to another. These keep the food items separate but allow the broth to circulate throughout. Many of these pots, or casseroles, come with a wooden lid that rests on the rim (unlike an *otoshi-buta*, page 243, which rests directly on the simmering food). The lid is handy for extended service, as it keeps the foods moist and prevents unnecessary evaporation of the broth. Many pots come with a cup for the miso dipping sauce that fits in the center or a corner, making it easy to serve the dip warm.

Adjust the heat to maintain a very gentle simmer and begin serving the foods directly from the pot. Or, suggest that diners gather around the pot in anticipation that they can begin to help themselves. Each diner should have a shallow bowl or deep plate (called a *tori-zara* or "divvy-up dish") to hold the foods, including some of the simmering liquid to keep them moist. The *kombu* that lined the bottom of the pot will become tender and can be shared (it will shred easily) among those gathered at table. Ladle some of the miso sauce into a dipping saucer for each diner. Each item from the *oden* pot should be dipped in the miso sauce before eating.

OPTIONAL ODEN ITEMS

Any, or all, of the items listed below can be added to your *oden* pot. They require about 30 minutes of simmering, so add them early on.

- *Ganmodoki* are often sold at Asian groceries in the freezer or refrigerator case. They are made from a mixture of mashed tōfu, minced vegetables, and black sesame seeds formed into balls or patties and deep-fried. The name, literally "remembrance of wild goose," suggests these were one of many vegetarian foods intended to look like dishes made from animal flesh. Sometimes *ganmodoki* are served freshly fried with grated radish, but most often they are simmered with vegetables in a slightly sweet soy-seasoned broth or in *oden*. Before using, blanch *ganmodoki* to remove excess surface oil.
- *Nama kombu*, literally "fresh" kombu, is briefly blanched (turning it green) after harvesting and then heavily salted to extend its shelf life. It is pliable and usually sold in skeins. Look for it in the refrigerator case of Asian groceries (Korean cuisine also makes use of *nama kombu*). Rinse, then soak *nama kombu* in cold water for 10 to 15 minutes to wash away salt. Tear wide strips in half lengthwise, then tie each piece into a string of knots. Cut with scissors to separate into individual knots.
- *Chikuwa-bu* is a white, hollow, 6- or 7-inch-long cylinder of wheat paste with a distinctively ridged surface. These vegan "sausages" have been briefly steamed in the manufacturing process, but they must be slowly simmered in a broth—in this case, *oden* broth—to acquire flavor. They are sold in vacuum-sealed see-through packages in the refrigerator or freezer section of Asian groceries. Check the package carefully: *chikuwa-bu* are often displayed next to grilled *chikuwa* sausages that are processed from fish (*chiku* means "bamboo pole" and *wa* means "wheel" or "circle"). Cut on the diagonal into 1/4-inch-thick pieces.
- *Ito kon, musubi konnyaku* (page 268), drained of packing liquid, blanched for 30 seconds, drained, and set aside to cool naturally for about 5 minutes.
- Waxy potatoes, boiled until tender, peeled, and cut in half if larger than 2 inches.
- Burdock root, scraped, cut into thick batons or small chunks, and blanched for 30 seconds, preferably tender-prepped in *togi-jiru* as the daikon is, and then rinsed free of rice-bran residue.

MOSTLY SOY

TWO KINDS OF TŌFU, AMBER BRAISED WITH CARROTS

ATSU AGÉ, YAKI-DŌFU, TO NINJIN NO BEKKO NI

Bekko ni, literally "tortoise shell stewing," aptly describes the rich, amber color that foods acquire as they slowly braise in slightly sweet, thickened soy sauce. To illustrate just how hearty this sort of food can be, I have chosen the ubiquitous carrot and two kinds of meaty tōfu: fried *atsu agé* and grilled *yaki-dōfu*. I have finished the dish with a sprinkle of tongue-tingling *sanshō* pepper. If you have bamboo shoots, especially the thicker base segment, slice it into thin wedges and add it to the pot with, or instead of, the carrots.

SERVES 4 TO 6

> 1 loaf grilled tōfu (page 282), about 10 ounces, drained
>
> 1 loaf thick fried tōfu (page 282), about 10 ounces
>
> 2 teaspoons cornstarch
>
> Scant 1 teaspoon aromatic sesame oil
>
> 3 slender carrots, each about 2 ounces, scraped, trimmed, and cut in halves or thirds on the diagonal
>
> 2 teaspoons sugar
>
> 2 tablespoons saké
>
> 1^1/$_2$ cups Basic Kelp Stock (page 75) or vegetarian stock (page 76)
>
> 1^1/$_2$ tablespoons soy sauce
>
> ^{1}/$_2$ teaspoon kona-zanshō (page 258)

Begin by preparing the grilled tōfu and thick fried tōfu for further cooking. Each of these typically comes to supermarkets prepackaged in liquid and/or oil that must be removed. The simplest, and least wasteful, way to do this is in a single small pot of water. Place the pot on the stove and as you wait for it to come to a rolling boil, drain and blot the grilled tōfu and fried tōfu dry.

Grilled tōfu is typically sold in rectangular or square blocks about 1 inch thick. Thick fried tōfu is sometimes in squares or rectangles and other times precut into triangles (in the Kansai—Osaka and Kyoto—this shape is preferred). This dish looks best, and absorbs more of the tasty sauce, when all pieces are triangular in shape, and the cooking time is easier to calculate when all pieces are more or less uniformly sized. Slice each loaf of tōfu accordingly into 8 or 12 pieces.

Blanch the grilled tōfu first, then the fried tōfu, each for 1 minute after the water returns to a vigorous boil, then remove the pieces with a slotted spoon and let them drain. Do *not* refresh them in cold water. By blanching the foods in this order, you will be discarding only a single batch of greasy water.

Pat the pieces dry with paper towels. Using a pastry brush, lightly dust all the cut surfaces of the grilled tōfu and thick fried tōfu with the cornstarch. The cornstarch blots up excess moisture, which will ensure a richly colored, seared surface. It will also help the final sauce cling to and glaze the pieces. I have found that a pastry brush is the best way to apply the cornstarch in a thin, even coating.

Select a nonstick skillet that is just large enough to hold all the pieces in a single, snug layer and place over high heat. Drizzle in the sesame oil. When the oil is hot, add the grilled tōfu and thick fried tōfu and sear for about 2 minutes, or until aromatic and lightly colored. Flip the pieces and press with an *otoshi-buta* (page 243) or a broad flexible spatula for another 2 minutes, or until lightly colored. The pressing will help blister the surface and trap moisture in the skillet. This method of simultaneously searing with heat and trapping in moisture is called *mushi yaki* (steam-searing), a flavorful treatment for many foods. Flip the tōfu pieces again and add the carrot pieces to the outer rim of the skillet.

Sprinkle in the sugar, jiggle the skillet to distribute, and drizzle in the saké along the rim of the pan to deglaze. Pour in 1 cup of the stock. Swirl the skillet gently to mix, and then lower the heat. Cover with the *otoshi-buta*, or with a circle of parchment paper and a flat metal lid slightly smaller in diameter than the rim of the pan. Simmer for about 2 minutes, or until the carrot pieces are tender. A toothpick inserted into a piece should meet with little resistance. Add the remaining 1/2 cup stock if longer cooking is needed. Do not worry if the surface of the various pieces appear a bit sticky or tacky. This is a good sign that the cornstarch will continue to cling and later thicken the sauce.

When the carrots are fully tender, drizzle in the soy sauce along the rim of the pan, swirl the pan to mix well, re-cover, and cook for 1 1/2 to 2 minutes, or until well glazed. Remove from the heat and allow the carrots, grilled tōfu and thick fried tōfu to cool in the skillet with the *otoshi-buta* in place. It is during this cooling-down period that flavors meld, making for a better balance of savory and sweet.

If you wish to serve hot, reheat gently. Just before serving, sprinkle with the *kona-zanshō*. This sort of stewed dish is often served family style, with the pieces mounded in a single deep bowl from which diners help themselves. Or, divvy up among shallow individual bowls.

KITCHEN CULTURE: TRIANGLES VERSUS RECTANGLES

In the Kansai, thick fried tōfu is cut into triangles, rather than the squares, flat strips, or rectangular blocks commonly seen in other parts of Japan. I suspect the preference for triangles in and around Kyoto is linked to foxes (the shape is meant to conjure the image of fox ears) and to a famous shrine near the city. In Japanese legends, foxes are portrayed as being especially fond of fried tōfu; the burnished gold of fried tōfu is referred to as *kitsune iro*, or "fox colored." Foxes are thought to be messengers for Inari, the Shinto god of rice, which explains why fox statues stand guard at Inari shrines throughout Japan. The most famous of the Inari shrines, though, is in Fushimi, just outside of Kyoto, where, not surprisingly, fox-ear shapes for fried tōfu prevail.

MIXED VEGETABLES BRAISED WITH THICK FRIED TŌFU

CHIKUZEN NI

This dish is an adaptation of a popular standby in many Japanese households, where chicken or pork commonly replaces, or is combined with, the chunks of thick fried tōfu. Don't hesitate to increase the amount of vegetables or fried tōfu in the recipe (maintaining the relative proportions of sugar and soy sauce). Any refrigerated leftovers are wonderful reheated and served *domburi* style (over rice) within a few days. Because the flavors develop during the cooling-down process, *chikuzen ni* is actually tastier served the second time.

SERVES 2 OR 3

> 3 small dried shiitaké mushrooms
>
> 2 cups water
>
> 1 loaf konnyaku preferably black speckled (page 268), about 10 ounces, drained of packing liquid
>
> 1 loaf thick fried tōfu (page 282), about 10 ounces, blotted on paper towels to remove excess oil and cut into 1/2-inch cubes
>
> 1 slender burdock root or parsnip, about 3 ounces, scraped and cut ran-giri style (page 244)
>
> 2 teaspoons sugar
>
> 1 tablespoon saké
>
> 2 slender carrots, about 4 ounces total, scraped or peeled and cut ran-giri style (page 244)
>
> 2 tablespoons soy sauce
>
> 4 ounces fresh édamamé, blanched for 1 1/2 minutes and shelled, or flash-frozen shelled (about 1/4 cup), blanched just until water returns to the boil

Break off the stems of the mushrooms and set them aside for making stock on another occasion. Here you are using only the caps to make the stock. Soak the caps in the water in a bowl for at least 30 minutes and preferably for 1 hour or more. Remove the caps from the liquid. Rinse the caps to remove any gritty material, squeeze, and cut into quarters. Pour the soaking water through a fine-mesh strainer (or disposable coffee filter) to remove unwanted bits that may have settled at the bottom of the bowl. Place the mushroom pieces in the stock again until ready to use.

With the tip of your knife, score the surface of the *konnyaku* on the diagonal with many shallow, parallel slits. Flip the loaf over and repeat. These slits will make it easier for the *konnyaku* to absorb the flavorful braising liquid. Cut the loaf lengthwise into 4 equal strips, then cut crosswise into 1/2-inch cubes.

Place the *konnyaku* in a heated skillet or wok and place over high heat. Cook, jiggling the pan occasionally, for about 2 minutes, or until you hear a squeaking sound. This indicates that the *konnyaku* has thrown off its excess moisture and is ready to absorb new flavors.

Add the thick fried tōfu and stir-fry for 1 minute. Even though the pieces were blotted to remove excess oil, there should be enough still clinging to the tōfu to keep the cubes from sticking. Stir-frying with oil-repelling *konnyaku* helps, too. Unlike spongy foods such as eggplant that seem to soak up oil from the pan in which they are cooking, *konnyaku* does just the opposite: it throws oil back to the pan to circulate.

Remove the shiitaké mushrooms from the stock and press them over the bowl to capture any excess moisture. Add the mushrooms to the skillet and stir-fry for 1 minute, tossing them with the *konnyaku* and fried tōfu. Add the burdock root and stir-fry for 1 more minute, or until it exudes a woodsy aroma.

Sprinkle the sugar over the contents of the skillet, toss to distribute, and add the saké. Add 1 cup of the mushroom stock and lower the heat. Cover with an *otoshi-buta* (page 243), or with a circle of parchment paper and a flat metal lid slightly smaller in diameter than the rim of the pan. Simmer for about 10 minutes, or until the burdock becomes quite tender. A toothpick inserted into the thickest piece should meet little resistance. Add more mushroom stock or water as needed to keep the vegetables barely covered.

Once the burdock is tender, add the carrots, re-cover, and cook for 2 minutes. Lift the lid and season with 1 tablespoon of the soy sauce, swirling the pan to make sure the flavors meld. Re-cover and cook for another minute or two, or until nearly all the liquid is gone.

Lift the lid, add the remaining 1 tablespoon soy sauce, and stir the contents and jiggle the pan to blend the flavors. Scatter in the *édamamé* and cook for 1 minute, allowing them to absorb all the flavors in the skillet. Remove the skillet from the heat and let the mélange cool to room temperature with the *otoshi-buta* in place. It is during this cooling-down period that flavors develop and meld.

This dish is traditionally served at room temperature. It makes terrific picnic fare and is often packed into *obentō* (boxed lunches). If you wish to serve the dish hot, reheat it briefly just before serving. If the liquid is so reduced it looks in danger of scorching, add a few spoonfuls of mushroom stock or water before reheating.

CRISPY-CREAMY TŌFU, SOUTHERN BARBARIAN STYLE

AGÉ-DASHI NANBAN

A crispy kudzu coating on creamy cubes of tōfu gives this dish textural interest, and the spicy grated radish with fiery pepper topping offers flavor impact—two good reasons why this dish is a favorite at pubs and casual eateries.

When *nanban* (literally, "southern barbarian") dishes appear on a menu, Japanese diners are ready to enjoy spicy fried foods with a hint of citrus. The origins of this are traced to the *nanban jin*, the "barbarians who came from the south"—the Portuguese—and their penchant for spicy, tartly marinated fried foods such as *escabeche*. This dish, along with battered-and-fried tempura, is evidence that the Portuguese-Japanese culinary interchange during the sixteenth century had a lasting influence on Japan's food scene.

SERVES 4 AS A SIDE DISH, 8 AS AN APPETIZER

1 block silken tōfu (page 282), about 14 ounces, drained and lightly pressed (about 12 ounces after pressing)

COATING

2 teaspoons soy milk, freshly extracted (page 156) or purchased

2 tablespoons crushed kudzu (page 255)

Vegetable oil for deep-frying

SAUCE

1/4 cup stock, preferably Sun-Dried Shiitaké Mushroom Stock (page 76)

1 tablespoon soy sauce

1 teaspoon sugar

TOPPING

7 ounces daikon, preferably 3 to 4 inches from the tapered end, peel thickly removed and set aside for use in other dishes

1/4 teaspoon shichimi tōgarashi (page 259)

Lime or lemon wedges

Slice the tōfu into 8 pieces, each about 1 1/2 inches square and 3/4 inch thick. Gently pat dry all exposed surfaces.

Coat the tōfu: Put the soy milk in a small, shallow bowl. Put the kudzu in a second small bowl. Briefly dip each piece of tōfu in the soy milk, then lay the pieces, one at a time, in the kudzu and flip to coat all surfaces evenly. If necessary, use a spoon to scoop the kudzu powder over the top of each piece and press lightly to encourage the coating to stick. Flip to coat all surfaces evenly. Or, use a pastry brush to apply the kudzu to the surfaces. Set the coated tōfu aside on a dry paper towel.

Pour the vegetable oil to a depth of at least 1 1/2 inches into a small, deep skillet or small wok and heat to about 350°F. Check the temperature with an unvarnished long wooden chopstick (or a bamboo skewer). Small bubbles will form around the tip when the oil is about 350°F. Or, test the oil temperature by dropping a pinch of the kudzu (preferably with a bit of the soy milk clinging to it) into the oil: if it sinks ever so slightly, surfaces immediately and sizzles, and then begins to lightly color within 30 seconds, the oil is ready.

Lower the coated tōfu, 2 or 3 pieces at a time, into the hot oil and fry undisturbed for about 1 minute, or until well crusted and lightly colored. Flip the pieces over and fry undisturbed for another minute. Avoid flipping the pieces more than once or the tōfu will be unnecessarily greasy and the coating will scatter in the oil. Tōfu is a precooked food,

(continued)

so you don't have to be concerned with "cooking" it again by frying, only with crisping the coating on it. Using a fine-mesh skimmer, transfer the tōfu cubes to paper towels to drain, turning them once after about 30 seconds to blot up excess oil from all surfaces. Skim your oil between batches to clear away wayward bits of coating. Fry the remaining cubes in the same way.

When you begin to fry the final batch of tōfu cubes, make the sauce: Combine the stock, soy sauce, and sugar in a small saucepan over medium heat and bring just to a simmer, stirring to dissolve the sugar. Remove from the heat and keep very warm while you assemble the dish.

Place 1 or 2 chunks of tōfu in each of 4 or 8 small shallow bowls or flanged plates. Grate and strain the daikon (page 247) just before using to preserve its nutrients (especially vitamin C) and pleasantly sharp "bite." Garnish each tōfu portion with a dollop of grated daikon and a pinch of *shichimi tōgarashi*. Warm sauce can be spooned into the bowl or onto the plate and tōfu placed on top, or the warm sauce can be ladled over each tōfu portion. Serve immediately. Provide lime or lemon wedges for a light, fruity accent.

GOOD FORTUNE BAGS

FUKU-BUKURO

When tōfu is pressed, thinly sliced, and deep-fried, a pocket of air is trapped in the center of the slice. The slices can be slit and pried open to make small pouches. In the *kansha* kitchen, they are stuffed with bits and pieces of vegetables it is your "good fortune" to have on hand.

Not knowing what may be in your refrigerator at the moment, I have selected several commonly used items; stock for simmering these pouches is a by-product of softening some of the ingredients. In prepping, the same boiling water can be used in succession to blanch and soften gourd ribbons and to remove unwanted odor from *shirataki* and excess oil from fried tōfu sheets. Blanching the fried tōfu sheets will make it easier to pry them open, too.

MAKES 6 TO 10 POUCHES; SERVES 2 OR 3 AS A FEATURED DISH OR 6 TO 10 AS AN APPETIZER

2 small dried shiitaké mushrooms

1 cup water

About 6 feet kampyō (page 262), soaked in 1 cup water for at least 30 minutes

1 tablespoon saké

2 teaspoons sugar

1/4 teaspoon salt

1/2 cup shirataki noodles (page 268), drained, about 2 ounces

3 to 5 sheets thin fried tōfu (page 282)

1 package enoki mushrooms (page 272), about 3 1/2 ounces, trimmed and cut into 1-inch lengths

2 tablespoons soy sauce

Break off the stems of the dried mushrooms and set them aside for making stock on another occasion. Here you are using only the caps to make the stock. Soak the caps in the water in a bowl for at least 30 minutes or preferably for several hours. Remove the caps from the liquid. Rinse the caps to remove any gritty material, squeeze gently, and cut into thin slivers. Pour the soaking water through a fine-mesh strainer (or disposable coffee filter) into a clean bowl to remove unwanted bits that may have settled at the bottom of the bowl. If the mushroom slivers are not fully rehydrated, return them to the stock for 10 minutes. Then remove the mushrooms slivers to a separate bowl and pour the stock into a shallow pot or deep skillet wide enough to hold all the pouches in a single layer.

Remove the softened gourd ribbons from their soaking water and set the ribbons aside. Add the gourd stock to the mushroom stock in the skillet, then add the saké and sugar. Set the pan aside.

Apply the salt to the softened *kampyō*, rubbing as though you were trying to remove a spot from clothing. The gourd ribbons will become much softer and somewhat velvety to the touch. Rinse off the salt completely. Bring a small pot of water to a rolling boil, add the gourd ribbons, and blanch for about 45 seconds. Remove the gourd ribbons from the water and set aside to cool.

Add the *shirataki* to the same pot of boiling water and blanch for 1 minute. Using a fine-mesh skimmer or slotted spoon, scoop them out of the water and set aside to cool to room temperature naturally. Once they are cool, use scissors to cut them into short (about 1-inch) lengths.

Add the fried tōfu sheets to the same pot of boiling water and blanch until they puff and oil swirls on the water's surface, about 1 minute. With chopsticks or tongs, transfer the sheets to a cutting board. Cut each sheet in half crosswise. Pry each half open to make a square-shaped pouch. Japanese cooks use a single chopstick to do this, rolling-pin style, with the fried tōfu pouch set on a cutting board and rolling from the closed end toward the cut edge. Or, you can lay a slice on the open palm of one hand and slap down on it with the other palm, so the air trapped inside the slice will escape from the cut edge. Then gently pry the pouch open with your fingertips. Repeat the roll-and-pry or slap-and-pry procedure to make 6, 8, or 10 pouches in all. Either method can get a bit messy; so it's best to do this near or over the sink.

In a bowl, combine the shiitaké slivers, *shirataki*, and enoki mushrooms and mix well. Stuff the pouches with the mixture, dividing it evenly and pressing down slightly to fill the bottom half only. Gather the open end of each pouch, scrunching it slightly. Take one end of the gourd ribbon, circle the gathered top once (or twice if your ribbon is long enough), and tie a knot. Snip the gourd with scissors to leave at least 1/2-inch-long tufts on both sides of the knot. Each pouch will probably require 4 to 5 inches of gourd to close properly. Repeat with the gourd ribbon to tie all the pouches.

Arrange the stuffed pouches, knots facing up, in a single layer in the skillet with the stock. (They should fit snugly.) Set the skillet over medium-high heat and bring the stock to a boil. Adjust the heat to maintain a steady simmer and cover with an *otoshi-buta* (page 243) or a circle of parchment paper to keep the pouches moist, and cook for 8 minutes, skimming away any froth as it appears. (If you don't have a cover, check the pan often and add water if needed to prevent scorching.) Add the soy sauce at the rim of the pan, swirl, and jiggle the skillet to distribute, and simmer for another 2 minutes. When finished, there should be several spoonfuls of broth remaining in the pot.

Serve immediately in a bowl or deeply flanged plate, spooning the remaining cooking broth over and around the pouches. Or, let cool to room temperature, then cover and refrigerate for up to 2 days. To serve, reheat in a covered skillet over gentle heat, adding just enough stock or water to keep the pouches from scorching.

NOTE: If you are making these pouches to add to Miso Oden (page 171), assemble them, but do not cook. Use the shiitaké mushroom and *kampyō* stocks to cook your *oden*.

TRICOLORED VEGETABLES ROLLED IN FRIED TŌFU

SANSHOKU SHINODA MAKI

Japanese culinary culture is filled with references to foxes and their fondness for fried tōfu, and the names of dishes made with fried tōfu will often allude to this fox connection. *Shinoda maki* takes its name from the Shinoda Forest (near present-day Osaka), home to many legendary foxes, including one female fox that changed to human form and married a hunter (foxy lady!).

The most frequently encountered version of *Shinoda maki* uses *fuki (Petasites japonicus)*, a rhubarblike stalk that heralds springtime throughout most of Japan's main island of Honshu. Here, I have made use of asparagus (readily available outside Japan, and also a sign of spring) and two root vegetables (the *sanshoku* in the dish's name refers to its being tricolored). Each of the vegetables is wound in its own sheet of fried tōfu and secured with a tie made from *kampyō*. The technique remains the same regardless of what vegetable you use. But how long each roll cooks in the broth does depend on the type of vegetable.

MAKES 6 PIECES; SERVES 2

3 sheets thin fried tōfu (page 282)

1 teaspoon cornstarch

5-inch piece burdock root or parsnip, scraped and cut lengthwise into 4 to 6 strips

5-inch piece carrot, scraped and cut lengthwise into quarters

2 asparagus spears, tough ends trimmed

1/4 teaspoon salt

1 1/2 to 2 yards kampyō (page 262) and 1 small piece kombu (page 266), soaked in 1 1/2 cups water for at least 30 minutes

SIMMERING BROTH

1 1/2 cups stock from soaking kampyō and kombu

1 1/2 tablespoons saké

1 1/2 tablespoons sugar

1 tablespoon light-colored soy sauce

Bring a small pot of water to a rolling boil. Add the sheets of fried tōfu and blanch for about 1 minute, or until they puff up and oil swirls on the water's surface. Remove the pot from the heat. With chopsticks or tongs, transfer one sheet to a cutting board, leaving the other sheets in the water. With a sharp knife, trim off one of the narrow ends and set aside (this piece will be added to the filling later). Place a single chopstick at the untrimmed end and use it, rolling-pin style, to press air out from the cut end. You will also be pressing out greasy water, so position your cutting board accordingly.

With your fingers, pry the pouch open. With either the tip of a sharp knife or scissors, cut open the pouch along one long side and the other short side. When finished, you will have a flat, rectangular sheet measuring about 5 by 6 inches. One side will be golden and smooth (and still a bit greasy); the other side will be rough and webbed with white. Repeat with the remaining 2 sheets of fried tōfu.

When all the sheets are open and flat, press each one between your palms to rid it of excess moisture. Blot away additional moisture (and oil) with paper towels.

Lay the fried tōfu slices, rough side up and shorter ends left and right, on the cutting board. Lightly dust the surface with the cornstarch. I have found that a pastry brush is the best way to apply the cornstarch in a thin, even coating.

On 1 sheet, lay the strips of burdock root, and on another sheet, the carrot strips. On the remaining sheet, arrange the asparagus spears so tips face out at either end. Lay the 3 reserved strips of fried tōfu on top of the vegetables, 1 per roll. Starting at the long side nearest you, roll up each sheet to enclose the filling tightly. Place the roll seam down on the board.

Apply the salt to the softened *kampyō*, rubbing as though you were trying to remove a spot from clothing. The gourd ribbons will become much softer and somewhat velvety to the touch. Rinse off the salt completely.

Starting at one end, wind the gourd ribbon twice around the center of one of the rolls, then secure it with a double knot. Although it should be a snug fit, take care not to be overly energetic; you don't want the gourd ribbon to fray or tear. Snip the gourd with scissors to leave $^1/_2$-inch-long tufts on the roll. Gently push the knot toward one end of the roll, and make another knot at the other end, trimming it in a similar fashion. Place the knots about one-third of the way from each end, so that once the rolls are cooked, you can cut each roll in half between the knots to create 2 tied scrolls, each the same length.

Make the simmering broth: Select a shallow pot or deep skillet just barely wide enough to hold the rolls in a single layer. Combine 1 cup of the stock, the saké, and the sugar in the pot. Bring to a boil over medium heat and adjust the heat to maintain a steady, gentle simmer. Do not be concerned if some froth appears; you can either remove it with a fine-mesh skimmer or leave it as is.

Place the burdock root roll in the liquid (if using parsnip, add the roll with the carrot roll). Cover with an *otoshi-buta* (page 243) or a circle of parchment paper to keep the roll moist as it cooks, and simmer for 10 minutes, adding more water or stock, if needed, to keep from scorching. Add the carrot roll (add the parsnip roll, if using), re-cover, and continue to simmer for 4 minutes. Finally, add the asparagus roll, re-cover, and simmer for another 2 minutes. If at any point the rolls look in danger of scorching, add more stock.

Test the rolls to determine if the vegetable fillings are tender: a toothpick should meet little resistance when passed through the center. When they are done, add the soy sauce at the rim and swirl the pan to distribute evenly. Add a few drops of stock or water if needed to prevent scorching. Simmer for a final 2 minutes; there will be little or no liquid remaining in the pan.

Remove from the heat and let cool to room temperature in the covered pan. It is during this cooling-down process that flavors develop and meld. (If you will not be serving the rolls within 30 to 40 minutes of their cooling, cover tightly and refrigerate for up to 2 days.)

When ready to serve, reheat gently, adding a few drops of water or stock to prevent scorching. Cut each roll in half, exposing the filling at the center. To assemble each serving, stack *tawara mori*, literally "rice sheaf" style (the bundles look like rice sheaves in the fields at harvesttime), with 2 pieces at the bottom and 1 piece centered on top.

NATTŌ SPRING ROLLS

NATTŌ HARUMAKI

The Japanese love to engage in wordplay, especially homonyms (words pronounced the same way but written with different calligraphy). Although the word for fermented sticky beans, *nattō*, has its own distinctive "spelling" (calligraphy), the sound *na* can be written as the number seven, and the sound *tō* can be written as the number ten. July 10 (the tenth day of the seventh month) becomes Nattō Day, and many grocery stores will do special promotions. One summer, my local Tokyo supermarket had a *nattō* promotion that included samples of mini spring rolls. The sticky beans enclosed in crispy wrappers were yummy.

Here is my adaptation. I have added *wakamé* and scallions to the filling, and serve the rolls with a tart mustard-infused soy sauce dip. You don't have to wait until July 10 to enjoy them. Serve them as an appetizer any time of year!

MAKES 20 MINI ROLLS; SERVES 8 TO 10 AS AN APPETIZER

FILLING

  2 packages nattō (page 273), about 1½ ounces each

  1 tablespoon dried wakamé, softened (page 267) and chopped, about ¼ cup

  2 slender scallions, trimmed and finely minced, about 2 tablespoons

  10 Chinese-style spring-roll wrappers, each about 7 by 8 inches

  1 teaspoon cornstarch mixed with ½ teaspoon cold water to make a thick paste

DIPPING SAUCE

  ¼ teaspoon Japanese spicy mustard (page 257)

  2 tablespoons rice vinegar or fresh lemon juice

  1 tablespoon soy sauce

  Vegetable oil for deep-frying

  1 to 2 teaspoons aromatic sesame oil (optional)

Make the filling: Open the *nattō* packages. If there is a plastic film covering the top, peel it back and discard; you can also discard the sauce and mustard that is usually packaged with the sticky beans; typically they are filled with preservatives.

Place the *nattō* in a bowl, add the *wakamé* and scallions, and stir to distribute the beans well. Long chopsticks are the preferred tool: draw a figure eight through the mixture several times, rotating the bowl slowly as you draw. The *nattō* will string and be rather gooey. Do not worry. That is how *nattō* behaves.

Assemble the rolls: Cut the stack of spring-roll wrappers in half lengthwise. Carefully peel to separate into 20 strips, each about 4 by 7 inches. Have a rack ready to hold the rolls as you make them; place the cornstarch paste within easy reach.

Place 1 wrapper strip on a dry work surface, shorter ends on top and bottom. Place a spoonful of the *nattō* mixture about 1 inch from the edge nearest you, centering it right and left. Dip your finger into the cornstarch paste and draw a vertical stripe down both the right and the left edges of the wrapper.

Lift the wrapper edge nearest you and fold it over to cover the filling, pulling back slightly to make the roll snug. Do not apply excessive pressure as you roll the wrapper over, or you will push the filling out the narrow sides. Press lightly on the right and left edges of the wrapper to make them adhere. Now, roll again, flipping over and away just once to fully enclose the filling. Fold the right and left edges in toward the center and, keeping the edges tucked in, continue to roll away from you until just 1/2 inch from the far end of the wrapper. Dip your finger into the paste again and draw a horizontal line along this edge. Flip the roll over to close, seam down. Continue to make rolls with the remaining wrappers and filling. Let them sit for a few minutes before frying; the weight of the filling will settle, and the paste used to seal the edges will adhere.

Make the dipping sauce: In a small bowl, mix the mustard and vinegar, then add the soy sauce, stirring to combine well. If the sauce seems too intense, thin it with water (or stock, if you have some on hand), drop by drop.

Fry the rolls: Pour the vegetable oil to a depth of 1^1/$_2$ inches into a wok or deep pan and heat to about 350°F. Add the sesame oil. Check the temperature with an unvarnished long wooden chopstick (or a bamboo skewer). Small bubbles will form around the tip when the oil is about 350°F. Or, test the oil temperature by holding a corner of one of the rolls in it. If the wrapper edge sizzles slightly upon contact, the oil is ready. If it begins to color immediately, the oil is too hot. Stir the oil several times to lower the heat. If the wrapper does not sizzle at all, the oil is not hot enough. Wait for several seconds and test again.

When the oil is ready, gently lower the rolls, seam side down, into the hot oil. Add only as many as will fit comfortably without crowding. Allow the rolls to fry undisturbed for 1 minute. Flip the rolls over and fry undisturbed for 1 minute longer. Avoid flipping the rolls more than once or they will unnecessarily absorb oil. The rolls are done when the end edges are a bit darker than the center and the rolls are golden and appear crispy with a few blisters. Using long chopsticks, tongs, or a fine-mesh skimmer, transfer the rolls to a paper towel–lined rack to drain.

Serve the spring rolls hot, or let cool naturally and serve at room temperature. If part of a buffet, stack them in layers on a colorful platter. For a dramatic effect, and ease of taking the rolls one at a time from the platter, place 5 rolls parallel to each other on the plattter, stack 3 rolls on top as the next layer, and then top with 2 more. This arrangement is called *tawara mori*—literally "rice sheaf" style—because of its resemblance to rice sheaves stacked in the fields at harvesttime. Place a small bowl of the dipping sauce nearby with a spoon.

NATTŌ PANCAKES

NATTŌ OYAKI

Classic *oyaki* are dumplinglike patties filled with vegetables, seared, and flattened on a griddle. The slightly chewy unleavened dough is typically a combination of wheat and buckwheat. A popular snack in the Shinshu region (present-day Nagano Prefecture), the dumplings are often filled with leftover pickled or soy-simmered vegetables.

The version of *oyaki* I offer here is different. It was inspired by recipes submitted to a cooking contest I saw on television a few years ago, in which contestants were challenged to create healthful after-school snacks that incorporated the fermented soybeans known as *nattō*. Several contestants from Nagano made *nattō*-stuffed *oyaki*, and my recipe incorporates elements from them all.

Nattō boasts a heady aroma (not unlike strong cheese) and a sticky texture (not unlike melted cheese when it strings). Although *nattō* has devoted fans in Japan, especially Tokyo and eastern districts such as Mito in Ibaragi Prefecture, Japanese living in the west and south tend to be far less enthusiastic about the pungent, sticky beans.

If you have been reluctant to sample *nattō*, I urge you to give this recipe a try. If you are already a *nattō* partisan, I am certain you will be glad to add this nutrient-packed recipe to your repertoire.

MAKES 2 SMALL DISKS; SERVES 4 TO 6 AS AN APPETIZER OR 2 AS A FEATURED DISH

1/2 cup finely minced scallions or leeks

2 tablespoons soba flour (page 256)

Scant 1 cup soy milk, freshly extracted (page 156) or purchased, or more if needed

3 packages nattō (page 273), about 1 1/2 ounces each

2 tablespoons aromatic sesame oil

1/2 cup coarsely shredded carrot and/or zucchini

SAUCE

1/2 teaspoon Japanese spicy mustard (page 257)

3 tablespoons brown rice vinegar (page 284)

2 tablespoons soy sauce

Place the scallions in a deep bowl, sprinkle in the flour, and toss until all the scallion pieces are well dusted. (This will ensure that the pieces will be evenly distributed in the batter later.) Stir in 3/4 cup of the soy milk, scraping down the sides of the bowl as needed to make a smooth batter. Try not to incorporate air or overwork the batter. If the batter seems very stiff (does not easily flow when you tilt the bowl), add a bit more soy milk.

Open the *nattō* packages. If there is a plastic film covering the top, peel it back and discard; you can also discard the sauce and mustard that is usually packaged with the sticky beans; typically they are filled with preservatives. Add the *nattō* to the batter and stir to distribute the beans evenly. Long chopsticks are the preferred tool: draw a figure eight through the mixture several times, rotating the bowl slowly as you draw. The *nattō* will make the batter gooey and quite a bit thicker than before. It should be of pouring consistency, however. If it isn't, stir in a few drops of soy milk.

Heat a small skillet (about 7 inches in diameter) over medium heat. Drizzle in 1 tablespoon of the sesame oil and swirl to coat the pan. When aromatic, pour in half the batter and tilt and swirl the pan so the batter covers the surface in an even circle. Lower the heat slightly, and when the outer edges begin to dry a bit but the center is still quite moist (usually in less than a minute), scatter half the carrot across the top of the batter. Continue to cook, undisturbed, for 2 minutes. Slip a flexible spatula under the pancake and confirm that it is crusted at the edges and pleasantly browned elsewhere. Using a second spatula or chopsticks held spread in a wide V, carefully flip to invert. Press gently to flatten the disk slightly. Cook the pancake, undisturbed, for 2 minutes, or until browned and highly aromatic. Shake the skillet to make sure it will release easily (drizzle in a bit more sesame oil near the rim if there seems to be a problem). Slide the pancake from the skillet onto a cutting board. Repeat to make a second *nattō*

pancake with the remaining batter and the remaining 1 tablespoon sesame oil. Using a sharp knife or pizza wheel, cut each pancake into 4 or 6 wedges.

The sauce can be combined with the pancake wedges two ways: You can stir the mustard into the vinegar and soy sauce, and then dip each wedge into the mixture, or you can spread a dab of mustard on top of each wedge and then dip the wedge into a mixture of the vinegar and soy sauce. Most Japanese enjoy this snack piping hot from the skillet, though some, like die-hard pizza fans and their favorite food, are happy to eat any leftovers cold for breakfast the next morning!

GLAZED EEL LOOK-ALIKE

UNAGI MODOKI

The vegan kitchen is a playful place where culinary trompe l'oeil transforms vegetable matter into mock seafood. In this recipe, mashed tōfu provides protein and substance and grated lotus root and burdock root add an earthy flavor and slightly fibrous texture that mimics the taste and mouthfeel of real *kabayaki*, or soy-glazed eel. If you have *okara* (soy lees) and/or sesame paste in your kitchen, adding either or both of these to the mock eel mixture will further enhance the overall effect and flavor.

Freshly fried and piping hot, these mock eel strips make wonderful hors d'oeuvres to serve with dry saké or a bubbly rosé. The strips can also be used to make a Mini Meal in a Bowl (page 29).

Pictured on page 28

MAKES 12 BITE-SIZE PIECES; SERVES 3 OR 4

1 ounce burdock root, scraped and grated, about 2 tablespoons

1 ounce lotus root, peeled and grated, about 2 tablespoons

1 tablespoon okara (page 274), optional

1 teaspoon white sesame paste (optional)

Pinch of salt

About 6 ounces firm tōfu (page 281), 1/2 loaf, drained, wrapped in fine-woven cloth, and pressed for 20 to 30 minutes (page 250)

1 teaspoon cornstarch

2 sheets yaki nori (page 267)

Vegetable oil for deep-frying

GLAZE

2 tablespoons mirin

3 tablespoons soy sauce

2 teaspoons sugar

1 teaspoon kona-zanshō (page 258)

Shape the tōfu mixture: Combine the burdock, lotus root, *okara*, sesame paste, and salt in a bowl. Mash or sieve the tōfu, then add to the bowl. Mix and set aside for 3 or 4 minutes; if any liquid appears, pour it off, or blot the surface with paper towels. Sift the cornstarch over the mixture in the bowl and stir with a spatula.

With scissors, cut each sheet of nori in half lengthwise. Stack these strips and cut crosswise into thirds to yield 12 strips. Each strip will be about 3 by 4 inches. Spread one-twelfth (about 1 tablespoon) of the tōfu mixture over the rough side of each nori strip.

Fry the "eel" strips: Pour the vegetable oil to a depth of at least 1/2 inch into a small, deep skillet and heat to between 360°F and 375°F. Check the temperature with an unvarnished long wooden chopstick (or a bamboo skewer). Small bubbles will form around the tip when the oil is about 350°F. Or, test the oil temperature by gently lowering a small bit of the tōfu mixture into the hot oil: if it sinks ever so slightly, surfaces immediately, sizzles, and begins to color within 30 seconds, the oil is ready.

Carefully place 2 or 3 tōfu-spread nori strips, with the tōfu mixture facing down, in the hot oil and fry undisturbed for 1 minute. Oil will pool at the nori-covered center of each strip; this is of no concern. Carefully flip the strips over and fry for 1 more minute. If necessary to ensure the nori remains submerged in the hot oil and the tōfu mixture colors to a golden brown, lightly hold down the strips at both ends. Long chopsticks or tongs are useful for this task. Transfer the fried strips, nori side up, to a paper towel–lined rack to drain. Repeat with the remaining tōfu-spread strips.

The eel strips are best when served piping hot. Plan to serve them immediately after frying, or let the strips cool completely and store, tightly covered, in the refrigerator for up to 2 days or freeze them for up to 1 month. If refrigerated, reheat the strips cold; if frozen, reheat them frozen. Directions for reheating are included in Mini Meal in a Bowl (page 29).

When you are ready to serve, make the glaze: Combine the mirin, soy sauce, and sugar in a small saucepan. Place over high heat and bring to a boil, stirring to dissolve the sugar. When the mixture becomes foamy, lower the heat and continue to cook for about 1 minute, or until slightly thickened.

One at a time, dip the freshly fried or reheated eel strips in the glaze. Or, spoon, drizzle, or paint (with a pastry brush) the glaze over the eel strips. Arrange the strips, nori side down, on a platter, sprinkle each with a pinch of *kona-zanshō*, and serve immediately.

TSUKÉMONO

THE JAPANESE CULINARY TERM *tsukémono* describes a vast variety of foods that undergo flavor and texture transformations, typically by salting and/or submersion in a liquid or a paste. In making *tsukémono*, pressure (weight) is often applied to speed or enhance change. The application of heat, in contrast, is rare, except when brief blanching is used to eliminate unwanted surface bacteria or to halt the work of certain deleterious enzymes. How long a food remains in contact with the pickling medium or marinade can be short (sometimes only a few minutes or a few hours) or quite extended (several months or even years). The results—the actual changes in flavor, color, texture, nutritional profile, and shelf life that fermentation causes—can be subtle or dramatic.

Although *tsukémono* foods are often called "pickles" in English-language texts, they are not synonymous with *hozon shoku* (preserved foods) and should not be confused with them. Most *tsukémono* would be considered "raw" or "fresh" foods; you may want to think of these dishes as deeply flavored "salads" that require no dressing. In a classic Japanese culinary context, however, *tsukémono* dishes accompany rice served toward the end of the meal, nearly always with soup. Indeed, the trio of soup, rice, and pickles is the cornerstone of traditional Japanese fare.

If you adhere to a strict vegan regimen and are eager to add healthful microorganisms to your diet, you will be pleased to know that plant-based lactic acid bacteria, typically sourced from dairy products in Western cuisines, are produced in the making of many kinds of *tsukémono*.

BASIC TSUKÉMONO TECHNIQUES

Here are some classic shelf life–extending (but not necessarily "preserving") *tsukémono* techniques—salting, pressuring, and marinating in a vinegar liquid or in a paste—for transforming fresh vegetables, fruits, and kitchen scraps into nutritious side dishes.

SALTING Salt is usually the first agent of change in the *tsukémono*-making process. After salting, items are often placed under pressure or in a pickling paste or vinegar-based marinade. The abrasive action of the initial salting both cleanses the surface and draws out excess liquids from fruits and vegetables, making them porous and more receptive to absorbing the flavors and nutrients of the later pickling mediums. The Japanese typically use an abrasive salt known as *ara-jio* when making *tsukémono*. Kosher salt is fairly easy to source outside Japan and has similar characteristics. Salting takes three different forms, described here.

SALT-SQUEEZING (SHIO MOMI) is a sprinkling, tossing, and squeezing action that is likely to take place in a bowl and be performed on finely diced, thinly sliced, shredded food, or on the green tops of radishes, turnips, or other root vegetables. Sometimes the resulting liquid (brine) is rinsed away, and sometimes the brine is saved as a marinade.

SALT-RUBBING (ITA-ZURI) is a rubbing-in-salt action that can take place on a cutting board or the palm of one hand while rotating or rolling the vegetable or fruit with the other hand. Whole cucumbers, radishes, and cylindrical items such as thick sticks of carrot or daikon are often treated to *ita-zuri*. Sometimes the natural "fuzz" on okra or *édamamé* pods is removed by performing *ita-zuri*. Rubbing abrasive salt up and down the vegetable creates friction that produces moist, gritty foam known as *aku*, a bitter substance that interferes with the enjoyment of the vegetable or fruit. The foam is wiped or rinsed away before the vegetable is submerged in a brine or marinade.

SALT-SWEATING (SHIO FURI) is a sprinkling-with-salt action followed by waiting (usually 5 to 6 minutes) for the food to "sweat" (wilt). Water is often added to this meager moisture to create brine that barely covers the food. Salt-sweating is typically used on sliced, diced, or shredded foods.

APPLYING PRESSURE The application of pressure to salted foods speeds the process of chemical and physical change. The addition of dried *kombu* to wilted or brined foods placed under pressure helps intensify their flavor. The use of softened leftover *kombu* as a lid on foods under pressure keeps the vegetables submerged in brine, which hastens the pickling action and yields more attractive results. The addition of *kombu* in either form is optional in many *tsukémono* recipes. It also causes the brine to become slightly sticky and the kelp itself to become a bit slippery. Both are a good sign—evidence that the natural glutamates in the kelp are doing their flavor-enhancing work.

In the traditional Japanese kitchen, stones (placed on a dropped lid set into a tub or vat) or presses (often made of flat stones) were used for weights. Such sizable equipment presumed the cook had access to a cool (but not freezing), well-ventilated room with lots of floor space, which was fairly common in rustic surroundings but less so in an urban setting. About fifty years ago, a clever device called a *shokutaku tsukémono ki* came on the market and into the homes of many metropolitan families with cramped kitchens. These screw-top devices, small enough to fit in tiny refrigerators on hot summer days, became very popular, especially with modern city cooks who had little time or patience for extended processes.

Shokutaku tsukémono ki (pictured on page 240) are for sale at many Asian groceries, and if you find yourself making quick-pickle dishes often, buying one will simplify your kitchen routine. Transfer the foods you are pickling (usually wilted vegetables, brine, and kelp) to the bowl of the *shokutaku tsukémono ki*, then close the screw-top, tightening it fully to apply maximum pressure. As you do so, the water level should rise. If it has risen $1/4$ inch or more after 30 minutes, loosen the screw device a few turns. Conversely, if the water level does not rise significantly in 20 or 30 minutes, loosen the lid and add water just to cover the vegetables, then snugly screw the lid in place again. After applying pressure, marinate for the time specified in the recipe (usually a minimum of 30 minutes at room temperature or up to 24 hours in the refrigerator).

If you cannot find a *shokutaku tsukémono ki* to purchase, you can set up a workable version using everyday kitchen equipment. Select a glass baking dish just large enough to accommodate all the pieces to be pickled in a single layer. They should fit snugly and rise to just below the rim of the dish. Place a cutting board or other flat-surfaced (washable) object directly on the food, then top the cutting board with unopened food cans or with cups or jars filled with water to weight it down. Start with five weights, one in each of the four corners and one in the center. The weights should total 5 to 6 pounds. (A gallon-size jar filled with water weighs about $1^1/2$ pounds.) The level of the liquid (brine) should rise within 5 to 10 minutes of applying the weights, and it should be high enough to ensure the vegetables will remain submerged in at least $1/4$ inch of liquid. If necessary, add a few drops of water and increase the weight.

An alternative setup calls for a heavy-duty, gallon-size resealable plastic bag, two flat trays (or small cutting boards or baking sheets), and some heavy objects for weights. Transfer the wilted vegetables, brine, and kelp to the bag and flatten it to distribute the contents evenly. Sandwich the bag between your two flat surfaces. Place evenly distributed weights on top and allow them to sit, undisturbed, for the time specified in the recipe. The bag should fill with liquid after several minutes; if the foods remain dry or seem just barely moist, open the bag, add a few drops of water, reseal, and reassemble the weights.

Allow the vegetables to marinate in the brine under pressure. Each recipe will indicate how long to maintain the pressure. In general, 8 hours of brining at cool room temperature is the equivalent of 24 hours in the refrigerator.

USING VINEGAR-BASED MARINADE Sweet-and-sour marinades, or *amazu* (literally "sweet-and-sour" sauce), are used to pickle many fruits, vegetables, and even tōfu on occasion. Sweetness is obtained from sugar, maple or corn syrup, or honey (if you do not adhere to a strict vegan diet). Sour flavors come from vinegar—sometimes (naturally very salty) plum, sometimes rice (brown or white), and sometimes a mixture of grains—and from citrus fruit. Recipes that call for *amazu* will instruct you as to proportion and timing.

USING KASU MARINADE AND NUKA MARINADE Here are two fine examples of never allowing anything to go to waste in the *kansha* kitchen, one a by-product of saké making and the other a by-product of rice processing. *Kasu*, the pasty rice lees left after saké has been drawn off, are sometimes used on their own and other times mixed with miso to make a pungent marinade (Pungent Pickles, page 209). *Nuka* (rice bran), the hard outer shell removed from rice grains during polishing, is used to make a paste in which vegetables are buried and left to ferment. During the process they also absorb many of the nutrients in the bran (Vegetables Pickled in Rice Bran, page 214).

QUICK-FIX PICKLES:
CRISP AND FIERY CHINESE CABBAGE AND CUCUMBERS

HAKUSAI TO KYUURI NO PIRIKARA-ZUKÉ

This quick-to-assemble dish is similar to a coleslaw—minus the mayo. Indeed, it could be served in lieu of a salad at a non-Japanese meal or even stuffed into a crusty roll for a tasty sandwich.

SERVES 4 TO 6

$^1/_4$ head hakusai (page 253), about 3$^1/_2$ ounces

1 teaspoon kosher salt

1 small cucumber with untreated skin, preferably Japanese or other seedless variety, about 2 ounces

1-inch square kombu (page 266)

1 teaspoon yuzu koshō (page 258)

1 teaspoon Saikyō miso (page 271) or other light, sweet miso

Trim away any yellowing or blackened areas from the cabbage wedge (add the trimmings to your compost heap), then rinse the cabbage to remove any soil trapped between layers of leaves. Blot the cabbage dry.

Lay the wedge flat against a cutting board and apply pressure to flatten it. Cutting across the grain, slice the cabbage into thin shreds. Place the shreds in a bowl, and sprinkle with a generous $^1/_2$ teaspoon of the salt. Toss lightly and set aside.

To bring out the natural sweetness in cucumbers, the Japanese often perform a circular rubbing technique to remove *aku* (astringency). Slice off a sliver from the stem (nonflowering) end of the cucumber, then, holding the trimmed piece in one hand and the cucumber in the other, rub the cut ends against each other in a circular motion.

Friction created by this circular rubbing will produce a white, foamy paste, which is the *aku*. Rinse well and pat the cucumber dry. Slice the cucumber into gossamer-thin circles. Place the circles in a bowl and sprinkle with the remaining salt. Toss lightly and set aside.

Return to the bowl of shredded cabbage. The salt will have leached out liquid from the cabbage and the moisture should be clearly visible. Salt-squeeze the cabbage *shio momi* style (page 192), applying pressure gently at first, until it is wilted and limp. Set aside with whatever liquid has accumulated in the bottom of the bowl.

Move on to the bowl holding the cucumbers and repeat the salt-squeezing process, then add the cucumber slices with any accumulated liquid to the bowl holding the cabbage. Add the piece of *kombu* and toss lightly.

Place the wilted vegetables and the accumulated liquid in a *shokutaku tsukémono ki*, glass baking dish, or sturdy resealable plastic bag as described on page 193, and allow them to sit, weighted and undisturbed, for at least 30 minutes at room temperature (refrigerate if you wish to hold them for longer than 4 hours) or for up to 24 hours in the refrigerator.

Just before serving, drain the vegetables, rinse briefly under cold running water, drain again, and squeeze lightly to press out all excess moisture. You will have about 1$^1/_2$ cups pickled vegetables.

Mix together the *yuzu koshō* and the miso in a small dish. Add this mixture to the pickled vegetables and toss to distribute. Arrange *ten mori* style (see box, page 205) in a large bowl or small individual bowls.

QUICK-FIX PICKLES:
FRUITY, SWEET-AND-SOUR DAIKON

DAIKON TO RINGO NO AMAZU-ZUKÉ

Many pickles require extended time to mature and are then put aside for long-term storage—delayed gratification. In contrast, these pickles take only 45 minutes or so to develop fully, though they could be saved for a day or two in the refrigerator—quick-fix satisfaction. This style of pickling is especially well suited to using up stubby ends, peels, and trimmings of fruit and vegetables that remain after making other dishes.

Although many possibilities exist when it comes to sweet-and-sour quick-fix pickling, I am giving you a classic example in which lemon peels infuse thin slices of daikon and apple with a delicate fruitiness. Make sure none of the produce is waxed or has been sprayed with chemicals, as these treatments are not easily removed. If in doubt, do not use.

SERVES 4 TO 6

SWEET-AND-SOUR MARINADE

3 tablespoons rice vinegar

$1/4$ cup stock, preferably Basic Kelp Stock (page 75), or water

Drop of light-colored soy sauce

1 tablespoon sugar

2 or 3 strips lemon peel, each about $1/4$ inch wide, or $1/4$ teaspoon finely grated lemon zest

1-inch square kombu (page 266)

1 small tart apple, about 6 ounces, quartered, cored, and thinly sliced, or $1/4$ cup $1/2$-inch-long matchstick-cut apple peels, about 4 ounces

1 teaspoon kosher salt

1 chunk daikon, about 8 ounces, unpeeled, cut in half lengthwise and then thinly sliced crosswise into half-moons, about 1 cup

1 tablespoon white sesame seeds, freshly dry-roasted (page 245) and cracked or minced

Make the marinade: Combine the vinegar, stock, soy sauce, sugar, lemon peel, and *kombu* in a small saucepan over low heat and heat slowly, stirring, just until the sugar dissolves. Remove from the heat and pour into a 1-pint glass jar and let cool naturally. The marinade can be made up to 1 week in advance and refrigerated. Bring to room temperature before using.

Place the apple slices in a small bowl, add $1/2$ teaspoon of the salt, and toss to coat evenly. Place the daikon slices in another small bowl and toss with the remaining $1/2$ teaspoon salt. Let the apple and daikon slices sit for 10 minutes; moisture will form. If your apple has red skin, the color may "bleed," tinting the brine. Lightly press and squeeze to encourage further wilting (this is a very light-handed variation on the *shio momi* technique, page 192). Drain the apple and daikon slices, then press out the excess liquid.

Transfer the wilted apple and daikon to the marinade. Place the *kombu* on top to keep the apple and daikon submerged in the marinade. Cover and marinate for at least 30 minutes at room temperature (refrigerate if you wish to hold them for longer than 4 hours) or for up to 24 hours in the refrigerator.

When ready to serve, use clean, dry chopsticks or a fork to remove pieces from the marinade. Press out the excess liquid, then mound tepee style and garnish with the sesame seeds.

NOTE: If you wish to make a second batch of Fruity, Sweet-and-Sour Daikon reusing the pickling medium, strain the liquid through a fine-mesh strainer into a small saucepan and discard (compost) all solids, including the *kombu*. Boil the pickling liquid for 1 full minute, skimming away any froth. To restore full flavor, add a few drops of fresh lemon juice before transferring the marinade to a clean, dry, heatproof glass jar and let cool naturally. Refrigerate and use within 1 week. Even with diligent kitchen hygiene, the marinade should not be used for more than two batches of pickles.

IN-THE-PINK PICKLES

HAJIKAMI SU-ZUKÉ

Many plant foods have natural coloration that can be heightened through pickling. These pickles are aptly called *hajikami* from the noun *hazukashii*, which means "embarrassment," and indeed these pickles blush deeply!

More challenging to source than new ginger, though absolutely worth the effort, is *myōga*, a rhizome related to ginger that turns a, vibrant fuchsia when properly pickled. Radicchio also turns a wonderful rosy color, and its bitterness subsides when pickled in a sweet-and-sour marinade.

Try these pickles minced and tossed with soft lettuces (no dressing needed for this salad) or in combination with other *tsukémono*, such as Quick-Fix Pickles: Crisp and Fiery Chinese Cabbage and Cucumbers (page 195) and Sweet, Spicy, and Tart Sun-Dried Radish (page 204). These pickles are also featured in Pom-Pom Sushi (page 43).

MAKES ABOUT 2 CUPS

SWEET-AND-SOUR MARINADE

    3 tablespoons sugar

    ³/₄ cup rice vinegar

    ¹/₂ teaspoon kosher salt

    Two 1-inch squares kombu (page 266)

    3 or 4 myōga bulbs (page 257)

    3 or 4 radicchio leaves, preferably large leaves from the outside of a head

Make the marinade: Place the sugar, vinegar, and salt in a small saucepan over medium heat and cook, stirring, just until the sugar dissolves. Divide the marinade evenly between 2 glass jars, and place a piece of *kombu* in each jar.

Bring a small pot of water to a rolling boil and add the *myōga*. The bulbs will turn pale at first; do not be alarmed. When the water returns to a boil, remove the bulbs with a slotted spoon and place them, still warm, in one of the jars holding the marinade. Do not lid until cooled.

Return the water in the pot to a rolling boil, skimming away any froth with a fine-mesh skimmer. Add the radicchio leaves, stir to submerge them, and immediately remove the pot from the heat. Allow the leaves to sit undisturbed for 20 to 30 seconds, then lift them from their scalding-water "bath." The leaves will appear faded; do not be alarmed. Place the barely blanched leaves in the second jar of marinade. Do not lid until cooled.

Within 20 minutes, the color of the *myōga* and radicchio will gradually brighten. Within 1 hour, the color will be dramatically vivid. When completely cooled, cover the jars, date them, and refrigerate for up to 2 weeks.

Remove the *myōga* and radicchio from their marinades with clean, dry chopsticks or a fork just before using.

NOTE: If you wish to make a second batch of In-the-Pink Pickles reusing the pickling medium, strain the liquid through a fine-mesh strainer into a small saucepan and discard (compost) all solids, including the *kombu*. Boil the pickling liquid for 1 full minute, skimming away any froth. Transfer the liquid to a clean, dry, heatproof glass jar and let cool naturally. Refrigerate and use within 10 days. Even with diligent kitchen hygiene, the pickling liquid should not be used for more than two batches of pickles.

LEFT: *In the Pink Pickles (radicchio leaves),* CENTER: *In the Pink Pickles (myōga),* RIGHT: *Home-Style Purple-Pickled Eggplant (page 202)*

SOUR SOY-PICKLED RAMPS

RAKKYŌ NO SHŌYU FUMI SU-ZUKÉ

Although this style of pickling requires patience—assembly in two stages a week apart, then several weeks for the flavor to develop—it is one that many Japanese cooks continue to practice at home. Early in the summer, even urban supermarkets set up a special section with all the essentials: large glass jars, vinegar, soy sauce, raw sugar, and mounds of fresh *rakkyō*, with soil still clinging to them.

Unlike Japanese *rakkyō*, which grow in clusters, the botanically related ramps I have seen in North American markets are single bulbs, each with its own stalk. Both are in the *Allium* genus, as are onions and garlic, which is part of the large lily family.

There are many Japanese variations on the theme of pickled *rakkyō*; sweet and sour, chile-spiked soy, and sour plum infuse three of the most popular kinds. The recipe I am sharing here, which combines a fruity-sour tang with a sweet soy base, is a bit different. In the 1970s, when I was living in Ogikubo, a community in the western sector of Tokyo, I had a neighbor who adored lemons, and whose husband had a connoisseur-level appreciation of artisanal soy sauce. She accommodated both their tastes with her version of pickled ramps, serving the finished product as a condiment with a wickedly hot curry stew and ice-cold beer.

MAKES ABOUT 1 QUART

- 1 pound Japanese rakkyō or ramps, or 3 large heads garlic
- 1-inch square kombu (page 266)
- 1 organic lemon, ends trimmed and sliced into paper-thin circles

STAGE ONE MARINADE

- 1/3 cup rice vinegar
- 1 cup cold water
- 1 teaspoon kosher salt

STAGE TWO MARINADE

- 1/4 cup soy sauce
- 1 tablespoon saké
- 1 tablespoon raw sugar or packed dark brown sugar
- 1-inch square kombu (page 266)

If you have sourced true Japanese *rakkyō*, separate the clusters into individual bulbs. If you have North American ramps, trim away the top stalks. If you are using heads of garlic, separate them into individual cloves. Using a dry cloth, rub to remove the thin outer skins of the *rakkyō*, ramps, or garlic cloves. Try not to bruise the surfaces as you rub. Use an old (dry) toothbrush to help dislodge any soil clinging to the roots of the ramps, then shave the roots away with a sharp paring knife. (Save the roots. They are delicious additions to Heaven-and-Earth Tempura Pancakes, page 109.) Rinse the bulbs in cold water and pat completely dry with a clean, soft-textured cloth. Arrange the cleaned bulbs snugly at the bottom of a clean, 1-quart glass jar with a tight-fitting lid. A canning jar with a gasket-fitted lid that clamps in place will make sealing the jar easy. If you want to keep this pickle for several months after it reaches maturity, sterilize the jar first.

Place the piece of *kombu* on top of the bulbs and arrange the lemon slices on top. The bulbs should be completely covered.

Make the stage one marinade: Combine the vinegar, water, and salt in a small saucepan over low heat and heat, stirring, until the salt dissolves. Pour the warm vinegar mixture over the *rakkyō* and lemon slices. Ideally, the liquid will barely cover the produce, depending on the shape of the jar and how snugly you have filled it. If you need more liquid, make additional marinade (1 part vinegar to 3 parts water, no extra salt needed). Let cool completely, then seal the jar closed, label and date, and refrigerate for 1 week. Do not be alarmed if the *rakkyō* bulbs turns a pale blue; it is just the vinegar changing their pH factor.

Make the stage two marinade: Combine the soy sauce, saké, sugar, and *kombu* in a small saucepan over low heat and heat, stirring, until the sugar dissolves. Do not allow the mixture to boil or its aroma will be diminished. Remove from the heat and let cool completely in the pot.

Drain off the stage one marinade in the jar (immediately combined with oil, it makes a good salad dressing; refrigerate and use within 3 days), then add the stage two marinade and the *kombu*. Let the *rakkyō* marinate at cool room temperature for 1 to 2 hours, then seal, label and date, and place the jar in the refrigerator.

Refrigerate for at least 1 week, or until the *rakkyō* bulbs and lemon slices begin to take on a burnished soy color. The color and flavor will intensify with time. When ready to serve, use a clean spoon to remove the amount you need. Blot on paper towels to remove excess liquid and serve the bulbs whole or sliced.

Do not reuse either marinade for pickling additional batches, and do not use the stage two marinade for salad dressings. You can, however, use it as a marinade for food that will be grilled or well seared within a few days, provided that you keep it refrigerated until you use it.

HOME-STYLE PURPLE-PICKLED EGGPLANT

JIKA SEI SHIBA-ZUKÉ

The classic version of this *tsukémono* is made by tossing salt-rubbed thinly sliced eggplant, *uri* (gourd), and *myōga* with brine-cured *aka-jiso* (broad leaves that bleed a bright pink-purple, salty-tart liquid). Placed under weights with glutamate-rich *kombu* that draws out the natural sweetness of the vegetables, the pickle takes several weeks to develop full flavor.

Because some of these ingredients may be difficult to source outside Japan, I have developed a home-style version—with several variations—that will enable you to enjoy these tart, salty-sweet pickles at home.

On a Japanese menu, they are typically served on their own, or in combination with other *tsukémono*, along with rice and soup. They also find their way into plump sushi rolls or are minced and tossed with seasoned sushi rice, in scattered-style *chirashi-zushi*.

Pictured on page 199

MAKES 1 SCANT CUP; ABOUT 12 SMALL PORTIONS

2 or more Japanese eggplants, about 8 ounces total weight

1¹/₂ cups plus 3 tablespoons water

1 teaspoon kosher salt

3 tablespoons plum vinegar (page 284)

¹/₄ cup sugar

5 or 6 aka-jiso leaves in brine (page 259), optional

2 or more myōga bulbs (page 257), ¹/₂-ounce knob tender new ginger, or ¹/₄ teaspoon ginger juice (page 246)

1-inch piece kombu (page 266), cut into 3 strips

Rice vinegar, if needed

Trim away the stem from each eggplant. As you do so, the sepals should fall away (if not, pull them off and discard). Cut the eggplants in half lengthwise, then cut crosswise into thin half-moons.

Make a brine: Combine the 1¹/₂ cups water and the salt in a small saucepan and heat through, stirring, just until the salt dissolves. Remove from the heat and transfer to a widemouthed glass bowl or other nonreactive container. Let cool.

Add the eggplant slices to the cooled brine and top with an *otoshi-buta* (page 243), or with a circle of parchment paper and a flat plate to keep the eggplants submerged (avoid a metal lid). Allow the eggplants to soak at room temperature in the brine for at least 30 minutes or up to several hours. The brine will turn brown, though the eggplant slices should not darken.

Drain the eggplant, rinse briefly under cold running water, drain, and squeeze lightly to remove excess moisture. The eggplant slices will have wilted somewhat and be more pliable.

Combine the plum vinegar, sugar, and remaining 3 tablespoons water in a small saucepan and heat over low heat, stirring, until the sugar dissolves. Add any *aka-jiso* leaves you might have on hand (they are often packed with *uméboshi*, or pickled plums) to deepen the color and enhance the aroma of the pickling medium.

If using *myōga*, cut the bulbs lengthwise into thin slices. If using fresh new ginger, scrape away the thin peel, then slice into tissue-thin threads. Add the *myōga* or ginger to the warm plum vinegar mixture. Set aside to cool to room temperature. If using ginger juice, add it to the plum vinegar mixture after it has cooled.

Choose a glass jar that will hold about 1¹/₂ pints. A squat, widemouthed jar will be easier to handle than a tall, narrow one. A Mason-type jar is especially good. Place 1 strip of the *kombu* at the bottom of the jar. Add half the wilted eggplant, another strip of *kombu*, and the remaining eggplant. Top with the third strip of *kombu*. Pour the cooled plum vinegar mixture (with the *myōga* or young ginger if you have used it) over the wilted eggplant and *kombu*. Press on the vegetables to make sure they are fully submerged in the liquid. If you have *kombu* left over from making stock, use it as an extra "lid" to keep the vegetables from being exposed to air. Depending on the dimensions of the jar, and the degree to which the eggplant slices have wilted, you may need more pickling liquid. If you do, add plain rice vinegar as needed to cover the eggplants, then stir or swirl to blend the plain and plum vinegars. Secure the lid, label and date the jar, and refrigerate it.

The pickle will mature in 5 to 7 days. Once matured, it can be enjoyed for several weeks. Keep it refrigerated throughout its storage.

When ready to serve, use clean, dry chopsticks or a fork to remove pieces of the vegetables and the *aka-jiso* leaves from the jar. Blot away excess pickling liquid with paper towels, then chop or mince and coax into small mounds *ten mori* style (see box, page 205) to serve. The *aka-jiso* leaf bleeds a vibrant natural colorfast pink-purple dye that can stain fingers, cutting boards, and clothing.

NOTE: If you wish to make a second batch of Home-Style Purple-Pickled Eggplant reusing the pickling medium, strain the liquid through a fine-mesh strainer into a small saucepan and discard (compost) any solids, including the *kombu* and *aka-jiso* leaves. Boil the pickling liquid for 1 full minute, skimming away any froth. Transfer the liquid to a clean, dry, heatproof glass jar and let cool naturally. Refrigerate and use within 2 weeks. Even with diligent kitchen hygiene, the pickling liquid should not be used for more than two batches of pickles.

SWEET, SPICY, AND TART SUN-DRIED RADISH

KIRIBOSHI DAIKON NO HARI HARI-ZUKÉ

Kiriboshi daikon, a tasty, nutritious example of kitchen *kan-sha,* cleverly puts to use what might otherwise go to waste— bits and pieces of bruised or malformed daikon radishes. This recipe calls for softened *kiriboshi daikon* left over from making stock. If you don't have leftovers, make the stock and reserve for another use and then use the softened daikon pieces to make this pickle. You can also use *kombu* reserved from stock making.

The bright yellow pickle is eaten in small quantities, most often paired with other pickled vegetables to create an assortment that contrasts in color, flavor, and texture. The same style of pickle can also be made with sun-dried gourd ribbons (*kampyō*), though the balance of sweet, sour, and spicy flavors in the marinade is quite different (see Sour and Spicy Gourd Pickles, page 212).

MAKES 20 TO 25 PORTIONS

½ **cup kiriboshi daikon left over from making Sun-Dried Radish Stock (page 76)**

1 small piece fresh ginger, about the size of a quarter, peeled and cut into fine threads

MARINADE

1 kuchinashi no mi (page 269), cracked, or 1 or 2 drops yellow food coloring

⅓ **cup rice vinegar**

2 tablespoons light-colored soy sauce

3 tablespoons mirin, corn syrup, or mizu amé (page 281)

1 tōgarashi (page 259), seeds removed

6 to 10 square inches kombu (page 266)

If the *kiriboshi daikon* pieces are awkwardly long, cut them into ½-inch lengths.

Bring a small pot of water to a rolling boil, add the radish and ginger, and blanch for 2 minutes, starting the clock from when the water returns to a boil. Drain immediately, reserving 3 tablespoons of the water.

Make the marinade: Combine the *kuchinashi no mi,* rice vinegar, soy sauce, mirin, *tōgarashi,* and the 3 tablespoons blanching water in a 1-pint jar and stir to distribute the flavors and color evenly. Add the still-warm blanched daikon and ginger pieces to the marinade, then, with scissors or a knife, cut the *kombu* into narrow strips and add them to the marinade.

Let the contents of the jar cool completely, then cover and let sit for at least 2 hours at room temperature or up to several weeks in the refrigerator. The color and flavor will intensify with time.

When ready to serve, use clean, dry chopsticks or a fork to remove the amount of the *kiriboshi daikon* you need from the jar. Blot away excess pickling liquid with paper towels, but be aware that *kuchinashi no mi* bleeds a vibrant, though entirely natural, colorfast neon-yellow dye that can stain fingers, cutting boards, and clothing. Coax the pickles into small, tall mounds *ten mori* style (see box, page 205) to serve.

NOTE: If you wish to make a second batch of Sweet, Spicy, and Tart Sun-Dried Radish reusing the pickling medium, strain the liquid through a fine-mesh strainer into a small saucepan and discard (compost) any solids, including the *kuchinashi no mi.* Boil the pickling liquid for 1 full minute, skimming away any froth. Transfer the liquid to a clean, dry, heatproof glass jar and let cool naturally. Refrigerate and use within 10 days. Even with diligent kitchen hygiene, the pickling liquid should not be used for more than two batches of pickles.

KITCHEN CULTURE: HEAVENLY ARRANGEMENT

Finely shredded vegetables are often coaxed into mounds that narrow at the top, like peaked mountains pointing toward the heavens. This plating style is called *ten mori* in Japanese, literally "heavenly arrange-ment." It makes an impressive presentation, allowing relatively small amounts of food to look quite substan-tial. If you would like to try this, use clean hands to gather a mass of finely shredded salt-wilted vegetables. Compress into a cylindrical shape in the palm of one hand by wrapping your fingers around the mass and squeezing. Place the cylinder upright in the center of a bowl (like a short, stubby tube standing on end). Hold the top of the cylinder between your fingertips and press down on the mass. This will form a mound with a broad, stable base.

GOOD FORTUNE PICKLES

FUKUJIN-ZUKÉ

Named after the Seven Gods of Good Fortune, Shichi Fuku-jin, this pickle combines assorted chopped vegetables with ginger and either dried red chiles (*tōgarashi*) or peppercorns. The pickling medium, a balanced blend of vinegar, sugar, and soy sauce, provides depth of flavor, and a bit of *kombu* heightens the overall effect.

As the name suggests, this pickle is typically made with seven ingredients, but in many frugal kitchens this pickle becomes a tasty vehicle for clearing out the vegetable bin. Most versions include radishes, eggplant, and gourds; I have added root vegetables and enoki mushrooms to the mix. It is the traditional accompaniment to curried rice dishes and would be the perfect companion to Skillet-Tossed Curried Rice (page 27). Finely minced and tossed into cooked rice, it becomes a tasty filling for rice "sandwiches" (see Hand-Pressed Rice with Fillings, page 45). Or, wrapped in crisp lettuce leaves it makes a delightful salad substitute.

MAKES ABOUT 3 CUPS

BRINE

3 cups water

2 teaspoons kosher salt

1 chunk daikon, about 3 ounces, peeled or unpeeled, cut into 1/4-inch dice

1/2 carrot, about 1 1/2 ounces, peeled or unpeeled, cut into 1/4-inch dice

2 small Kirby or other pickling cucumbers, each about 2 ounces, unpeeled, cut into 1/4-inch dice

2 ounces burdock root, scraped, cut into 1/4-inch dice, blanched for 1 minute, and drained (do not refresh in cold water)

1 small knob tender new ginger, about 1/2 ounce, scraped and finely minced

1 Japanese eggplant, about 3 ounces, trimmed and cut into 1/4-inch dice

1 package enoki mushrooms (page 272), about 3 1/2 ounces, trimmed and cut into 1/4-inch lengths

PICKLING MEDIUM

1/3 cup sugar

1/2 cup soy sauce

3-inch piece kombu (page 266), preferably high-glutamate variety such as ma kombu

1/4 cup saké

1 cup rice vinegar

1 tōgarashi (page 259), broken in half and most seeds removed, or 3 or 4 black, green, or pink peppercorns

Make the brine: Combine the water and salt in a small saucepan and heat through, stirring, just until the salt dissolves. Remove from the heat and transfer to a widemouthed glass bowl or other nonreactive container. Let cool.

Place the daikon, carrot, cucumber, burdock root, ginger, and eggplant in the cooled brine and let soak for at least 30 minutes or up to 3 hours at cool room temperature. Because the vegetables tend to bob to the surface, use an *otoshi-buta* (page 243) or a flat plate to keep the vegetables submerged in the brine.

Drain the vegetables, squeezing them gently to rid them of excess moisture. Add the enoki mushrooms to the mixture in the bowl and toss to distribute.

(continued)

Make the pickling medium: Combine the sugar, soy sauce, and *kombu* in a wide, shallow pot over medium heat and bring to a boil, stirring to dissolve the sugar. Lower the heat to maintain a steady, gentle simmer. Add the vegetables, stir once, and wait until bubbles form around the rim of the pot. Stir again and remove the pot from the heat. Allow the vegetables to cool in the liquid until there is no longer any steam rising.

Using a slotted spoon, transfer the vegetables to a widemouthed 1-quart Mason-type jar, arranging the *kombu* on top of the vegetables.

Add the saké, vinegar, and *tōgarashi* to the liquid remaining in the pot and bring to a boil over high heat. Lower the heat to maintain a steady, vigorous simmer and simmer for 3 to 4 minutes, or until reduced by half. Skim away any clouds of froth with a fine-mesh skimmer. Remove from the heat and let cool to room temperature.

Pour the cooled liquid over the vegetables. When the jar no longer feels warm to the touch, secure the lid, label and date the jar, and refrigerate it. The pickles will develop flavor slowly during the first week. After 4 or 5 days, open the jar and, with clean chopsticks or a fork, pull out a sample and taste. If the flavor is too intense, add 2 or 3 tablespoons cold water to the pickling liquid, re-cover, and refrigerate for about 2 more days.

The pickle will taste best 1 to 2 weeks after assembling, but it can be enjoyed for 4 to 5 weeks if kept refrigerated throughout. Flavors will continue to intensify, however, and you may wish to dilute the pickling liquid after a couple of weeks.

When ready to serve, select an assortment of chunks, draining only the amount you wish to use at that time. Briefly rinse the pieces under cold running water and squeeze out excess moisture. Mince the pickled vegetables, then gently squeeze the pile to form a low-rising mound.

Do not reuse either the brine or the pickling medium; assemble with fresh ingredients each time you wish to make a batch of Good Fortune Pickles.

KITCHEN CULTURE: SEVEN GODS OF GOOD FORTUNE

The Seven Gods of Good Fortune, or Shichi Fukujin, are often pictured on posters depicting mercantile trade. They also appear at table in the guise of foods with seven spices or flavors, such as *fukujin-zuké*. The seasoning called *shichimi tōgarashi* (page 259) is also associated with the seven good luck gods. Here are the gods:

- Ebisu, god of fishermen and merchants, often depicted carrying a sea bream
- Daikokuten (Daikoku), god of wealth, commerce, and trade (Ebisu and Daikoku are often paired and represented as carvings or masks on the walls of small retail shops)
- Bishamonten, god of warriors, demonstrates strength and prowess
- Benzaiten (Benten-sama), goddess of knowledge, beauty, art, and music
- Fukurokuju, god of happiness, wealth, and longevity
- Hotei, plump, happy god of abundance and good health
- Jurōjin, god of wisdom

PUNGENT PICKLES

NARA-ZUKÉ

Kasu, the pasty lees saved from saké making, are a popular pickling agent. Root vegetables, ginger, and gourds are slowly transformed into heady, amber-colored pickles by submerging them in a mixture of the lees, mirin, sugar, and salt. Sometimes citrus peels are added to the mix. One particular style of *kasu*-marinated food, called *Nara-zuké*, was developed and perfected by Buddhist monks during the Nara period (710–794).

Old-fashioned *Nara-zuké* is made in large quantities (several pounds of vegetables in each batch) and take from 1 to 3 years to mature. Once they are ready, they can be enjoyed for nearly a year. Because these old-style pickles gradually intensify in flavor over time, they are typically sliced very thin.

My version is suited to the home kitchen: it works well with smaller quantities, takes only a few weeks to develop a heady aroma (the addition of miso speeds things up), yet can be enjoyed for up to 2 months. Serve these home-style pickles minced, coarsely chopped, or thinly sliced; they are wonderful tossed into tartly seasoned sushi rice. They can also provide a pleasantly pungent accent to an assortment of other milder pickled vegetables.

Although difficult to source in markets outside Japan, *shira uri* (page 278) is the classic choice when making *Nara-zuké*; it is what you see pictured on page 210. Should you have the good fortune of obtaining it in an Asian market, follow the instructions I provide as an alternative to the easier-to-source daikon radish, carrot, and ginger.

MAKES SEVERAL DOZEN PORTIONS

> 3-inch segment daikon (preferably from the neck), 6 to 8 ounces, unpeeled, cut into quarters lengthwise
>
> 2 slender carrots, each 4 to 5 inches long and about 3 ounces, unpeeled, cut in half lengthwise if more than $3/4$ inch in diameter
>
> 2 small knobs tender new ginger, each about 1 inch square and 1 ounce, scraped, then cut in half lengthwise
>
> Generous 1 tablespoon kosher salt
>
> 1 shira uri gourd (page 278), about 8 ounces (optional)

BRINE

> 3- to 4-inch piece kombu (page 266)
>
> $1^1/2$ teaspoons salt
>
> $2/3$ cup water

PICKLING MEDIUM

> 14 to 16 ounces saké kasu (page 268)
>
> $1/4$ cup Saikyō miso (page 271) or other light, sweet miso
>
> $1/3$ cup packed light brown sugar
>
> $1/4$ cup saké
>
> 3 to 4 tablespoons stock, preferably Basic Kelp Stock (page 75)

Begin by salt-rubbing the daikon, carrots, and ginger *ita-zuri* style (page 192) with the salt, saving 1 teaspoon to use with the *shira uri*, if you have been able to obtain it. To prepare the *shira uri* for pickling, follow the instructions for preparing bitter melon on page 104, using the salt that you have reserved. Once moist foam appears, rinse the vegetables and arrange them in a *shokutaku tsukémono ki*, glass

(continued)

baking dish, or sturdy resealable plastic bag as described on page 193.

Make the brine: Combine the *kombu*, salt, and water in a small saucepan over low heat and heat, stirring, until the salt dissolves. Remove from the heat and let cool to room temperature.

Pour the cooled brine over the vegetables and lay the *kombu* on top as an inner lid. If using a *shokutaku tsukémono ki*, close it and screw the top snugly in place. If using an alternative setup, apply at least 5 pounds of evenly distributed weight. Allow the vegetables to sit, under pressure, for at least 4 hours at room temperature or 8 to 12 hours in the refrigerator.

Make the pickling medium: Place the *saké kasu* and miso in your pickle pot (see Pickle Pots, page 211) and sprinkle the brown sugar over them. Using a fork or whisk, mash until well mixed. Drizzle in the saké and stock and stir to combine. You will end up with a thick paste. Ideally, the volume of paste will fill about two-thirds of the con-

tainer. Using a spatula or wooden spoon, push half of the *kasu* paste to one side of the container, leaving a thin layer of paste on the bottom.

Add the vegetables to the pickling medium: Remove the vegetables from the brine, rinse lightly under cold running water, and blot away excess moisture with paper towels. If you are using *shira uri*, place it in the bottom of your pot and cover with a thin layer of the pickling paste you scraped aside. Next, lay the daikon and carrot strips on top of the *kasu* paste, pressing them slightly to submerge them partially in the paste. Cover the vegetables with the remaining paste you scraped aside and smooth the surface. Again, lay the *kombu* left from the brining stage on top as a cover. Close the container with a tight-fitting lid, or seal it with a layer of plastic wrap pressed flush against the pickling paste, then heavy-duty aluminum foil.

Label the container clearly with its contents (for example, 4 strips daikon, 2 strips carrot, 2 knobs ginger, 2 halves *shira uri*) and the date. Store the container in a cold, dark place. In most modern kitchens, the best place is on a back shelf of the refrigerator.

Allow the vegetables to pickle for at least 1 week, preferably 2 weeks, before checking progress. When mature, the pickled vegetables become somewhat translucent and golden and have a pleasant but heady aroma. The pickling medium and the vegetables submerged in it will darken considerably over time; an amber color is not unusual after several months. Drain off or blot away any accumulated liquid that pools on the surface.

When you extract a chunk to sample, do so with clean chopsticks or tongs, then slice off a sliver with a clean knife. Wipe away the paste clinging to the test sliver, rinse briefly under cold running water, and pat dry before nibbling. Personal preferences vary from mild to intense. I like my ginger and *shira uri* deeply pickled and usually keep it in the pot for 4 or 5 weeks. But I pull out my daikon and carrot after 10 days or so. Remove the chunks that seem sufficiently pickled to you and keep the others submerged in the paste until they test ready to serve, but at most, for 2 months. Pickled vegetables removed from the pot can be kept, refrigerated with a bit of their paste still clinging to them and covered, for up to 10 days before serving. Rinse away clinging paste, pat dry, and slice or chop before serving.

You can reuse the *kasu* paste for pickling future batches if you take care to use clean chopsticks or tongs when removing mature pickles and you continue to monitor the paste for unwanted organisms (see Monitoring the Pickle Pot for Freshness, page 220). If you want to add new pieces to the pickling medium before consuming everything in the first batch, arrange the older pieces in a cluster to one side, so they can be easily identified.

PICKLE POTS

Always use a nonreactive container for your pickle pot. Good choices include glass, enamel-lined metal, or glazed ceramic. Rectangular containers 5 to 6 inches long and 2 to 3 inches deep are the most convenient shape for pickling vegetable strips; deep containers are best for pickling vegetable chunks. Containers that have their own tight-fitting lids, such as Mason jars or Japanese crocks, or enamel-lined metal pots (what the Japanese call *horo* ware), are ideal, but it is also possible to seal lidless glass baking dishes with clear plastic wrap, then heavy-duty aluminum foil.

KITCHEN CULTURE: DREGS

The word *kasu* means "by-product" or "dregs." In a culinary context, it almost always refers to *saké kasu*, the pasty lees that remain after liquid saké has been drawn off from a fermenting rice mash. In nonculinary situations, though, the word *kasu* is a slur, similar to "the dregs of humanity."

SOUR AND SPICY GOURD PICKLES

KAMPYŌ NO HARI HARI-ZUKÉ

This golden pickle is eaten in small quantities, most often paired with other *tsukémono* to create an assortment that contrasts in color, flavor, and texture.

The Japanese name for this dish, *hari hari*, is one of many onomatopoeic terms used to describe the sound of eating. The closest English word would be crunchy, though *hari hari-zuké* is neither brittle nor crisp. Rather, this version, made with *kampyō*, is both tender and chewy. As with Sweet, Spicy, and Tart Sun-Dried Radish (page 204), this pickle is made from leftovers from stock making. If you don't have softened *kampyō* on hand, make the stock and reserve for another use, and then use the softened gourd ribbons to make this pickle. You can also use *kombu* reserved from stock making.

MAKES 20 TO 25 PORTIONS

1/4 teaspoon kosher salt

2 or 3 pieces kampyō, about 15 feet total, left over from making Sun-Dried Gourd Ribbon Stock (page 76)

MARINADE

1 kuchinashi no mi (page 269), cracked, or 1 or 2 drops yellow food coloring

1/2 cup rice vinegar

2 tablespoons light-colored soy sauce

2 tablespoons mirin, corn syrup, or mizu amé (page 281)

1 teaspoon ginger juice (page 246)

1 tōgarashi (page 259), seeds removed

6 to 10 square inches kombu (page 266)

Apply the salt to the softened *kampyō*, rubbing as though you were trying to remove a spot from clothing. The gourd ribbons will become much softer and somewhat velvety to the touch. Rinse off the salt, squeeze out the excess moisture, and blot with paper towels. Using scissors or a knife, cut the ribbons into 1/2-inch lengths.

Bring a small pot of water to a rolling boil. Add the gourd pieces and blanch for 1 minute, starting the clock after the water returns to a boil. Drain immediately but do *not* refresh in cold water.

Make the marinade: Combine the *kuchinashi no mi*, rice vinegar, soy sauce, mirin, ginger juice, and *tōgarashi* in a 1-pint jar and stir to distribute the flavors and colors evenly. Add the still-warm blanched gourd pieces to the marinade, then, with scissors or a knife, cut the *kombu* into narrow strips and add them to the marinade.

Let the contents of the jar cool completely, then cover and let sit for at least 2 hours at room temperature or up to several weeks in the refrigerator. The color and flavor will intensify with time.

When ready to serve, use clean, dry chopsticks or a fork to remove pieces of the vegetables from the jar. Blot away excess pickling liquid with paper towels, but be aware that *kuchinashi no mi* bleeds a vibrant, though entirely natural, colorfast neon-yellow dye that can stain fingers, cutting boards, and clothing. Cluster 6 or 7 pieces on a small plate alone or with other pickled vegetables. (These pickles pair especially well with Home-Style Purple-Pickled Eggplant, page 202.)

NOTE: If you wish to make a second batch of Sour and Spicy Gourd Pickles reusing the pickling medium, strain the liquid through a fine-mesh strainer into a small saucepan and discard (compost) any solids, including the *kuchinashi no mi*. Boil the pickling liquid for 1 full minute, skimming away any froth. To restore full flavor, add a few drops of fresh ginger juice (page 246). Transfer the liquid to a clean, dry, heatproof glass jar and let cool naturally. Refrigerate and use within 10 days. Even with diligent kitchen hygiene, the pickling liquid should not be used for more than two batches of pickles.

VEGETABLES PICKLED IN RICE BRAN

NUKA-ZUKÉ

Like miso soup, *nuka-zuké* is quintessentially Japanese. When I first arrived in Japan in the mid-1960s, most home kitchens boasted a well-tended *nuka* pot, from which tender yet crisp vegetables, deeply flavored and with a bracing aroma, were pulled daily. Avoiding waste while enriching the diet, *nuka-zuké* pickles exemplify the *kansha* kitchen.

Making and maintaining a *nuka* pot, however, requires patience and care, not unlike growing vegetables from seed: both activities are demanding yet rewarding. Because the *nuka* paste contains live (plant-generated) lactic acid bacillus, it must be stirred and mixed by hand at least once a day.

What follows is a detailed description of how to set up and maintain a *nuka* pot that I hope will encourage you to start tending your own *nuka* pickle pot.

NUKA PICKLING PASTE

8 cups nuka (page 274), preferably dry-roasted iri nuka

3 tablespoons kosher salt

2 tablespoons Japanese spicy mustard powder (page 257)

1 cup beer

1½ cups water

INITIAL SEASONINGS FOR PICKLE PASTE

2-inch piece kombu (page 266), cut into thin strips

3 or 4 dried shiitaké mushroom stems or 1 or 2 broken dried caps

1 clove garlic, peeled but left whole

1 small knob fresh ginger, peeled and cut in half or in thirds

2 tōgarashi (page 259), stems and seeds discarded and each pod broken into 4 or 5 pieces

BEGINNING BATCH

1 cup vegetable scraps such as ginger peels; daikon, turnip, and carrot peels and tops; and/or celery leaves (do not use potatoes or onions)

1 teaspoon kosher salt

SECOND AND THIRD BATCHES

2 small cucumbers, each about 2 ounces, with untreated skin

2 chunks daikon, each about 2 ounces, or 6 or more strips of daikon peel

1 teaspoon kosher salt

SUBSEQUENT BATCHES

Vegetables, salted as directed (page 215)

Make the pickling paste: Select a pickle pot (see Pickle Pots, page 211) that will comfortably hold 3 or 4 quarts of pickling paste, with several inches headroom to spare. Place the *nuka*, salt, and mustard powder in the pot and stir to mix well. Pour in the beer and then the water and mix with well-washed hands to make a stiff paste. The warmth of your hands will hasten the maturation of the paste, but a clean spoon could be used instead. Next, season the paste with initial seasonings, adding the *kombu*, shiitaké, garlic, ginger, and *tōgarashi*. Mix to distribute evenly. Do not pack down the paste. You want it to fill the pot loosely. Cover the pot and store it undisturbed in a cool, dark spot for 36 to 48 hours.

(continued on page 216)

VEGETABLES FOR THE NUKA PICKLE POT

Each of the following vegetables is either salt-rubbed (*ita-zuri*) or salt-squeezed (*shio momi*) before it goes into the pickle paste. See page 192 for information on both techniques.

CARROTS: Peel carrots. If they are stocky, cut them in half or into quarters lengthwise. If they are slender, leave them whole. Vigorously salt-rub (*ita-zuri*), then wipe off excess salt.

CELERY: Snap off the leaves, pulling down to remove any stringy fibers from the stalk. Compost tough fibers or add them to a soup stock. Vigorously salt-squeeze (*shio momi*) the leaves and salt-rub (*ita-zuri*) the stalk. Rinse lightly and pat dry.

CUCUMBERS: Salt-rub (*ita-zuri*) whole cucumbers, removing "thorns" or "fuzz" from skin. Use about $1/4$ teaspoon salt per cucumber. Wipe off excess salt, or quickly rinse if very foamy.

RED RADISHES (WITH LEAVES) AND JAPANESE EGGPLANTS: Both of these vegetables "bleed" when salted. This does not affect the taste, but it does make the pickles appear less vibrant. To ensure they hold their color, they are salt-rubbed with a mixture of *yaki myōban* (alum powder, page 284) and kosher salt in equal amounts, rather than salt alone. Many households and commercial makers of artisanal *nuka-zuké* maintain a separate batch of *nuka* paste for vegetables requiring this special treatment, because alum tends to make the pickling medium go musty after several weeks. If you find yourself pickling these vegetables often, it is a good idea to start a second pot just to accommodate them.

Rinse red radishes and their greens carefully to remove all traces of dirt. Cut off the greens and treat them as turnip greens (below). Cut fat radishes in half. Salt-rub (*ita-zuri*) with a mixture of equal parts alum and salt.

Rinse eggplants, pat dry, and trim away stem. Cut in half lengthwise. Rub mixture of equal parts alum and salt on the cut surfaces, place the surfaces together so they are no longer exposed to the air, and squeeze. Salt-rub (*ita-zuri*) outside surfaces.

TURNIPS (WITH LEAVES), DAIKON (WITH LEAVES), AND KALE OR OTHER STURDY GREEN LEAVES: Separate turnips and daikon from their leafy tops and set the roots aside. Rinse the leafy tops, discard any yellowing or black leaves, and tie each type in its own bundle with kitchen twine. Treat kale or other greens the same way. Use about $1/4$ teaspoon salt for each bundle of greens. Salt-squeeze (*shio momi*) the bundles until green liquid appears. Rinse off excess salt, then squeeze dry.

Peel turnips or daikon if waxy; otherwise, scrub surfaces with a coarse brush or sponge. Cut turnips in half or into quarters lengthwise and salt-rub (*ita-zuri*) cut surfaces. Use about $1/8$ teaspoon salt for each chunk. Wipe off excess salt. Cut daikon into $1/2$-inch-thick rounds, then cut rounds in half or into quarter wedges and lightly salt-rub (*ita-zuri*) cut surfaces. Wipe off excess salt.

Then, at least once a day for the next 3 days, but preferably 2 or 3 times a day at this early stage, remove the cover and dig, flip, and stir the paste with your hands.

Pickle the beginning batch: Before you try pickling fresh vegetables, pickle a batch of vegetable scraps. Salt-rub the scraps *ita-zuri* style with the salt as directed on page 192, rinse them lightly, place on a square of cheesecloth, bring up the edges to form a bag, and tie the top with kitchen twine. (This makes later removal from the pot easy.) Bury the bag in the pickle paste (leaving the twine visible), lightly pat down the paste to level it, and then cover the pot. Keep the bag submerged for at least 12 hours, but preferably 48 hours. If the room temperature is below 40°F, keep the bag submerged for at least 24 hours, but preferably 72 hours. Remove the bag of vegetable scraps. Although no harm will come to you if you eat these scraps, they will be harsh tasting and are usually discarded.

Pickle the second and third batches: The primary purpose of these batches, like the beginning batch, is to "condition" the paste for the fresh vegetables. Lapsed time is necessary for the paste to be ready, and rather than leave the pot empty, which would increase the time it takes to get the good bacteria going, you need to add something to it. Adding a few vegetables or vegetable scraps in several batches will be more effective than adding a lot of vegetables in a single batch. Most Japanese home cooks add cucumber and daikon because they are always on hand and neither one is so distinctive that it will give the paste an off taste or smell, as carrots or other carotene-rich vegetables sometimes do.

Salt-rub one each of the cucumbers and daikon chunks *ita-zuri* style with $^1/_2$ teaspoon of the salt, wrap in cheesecloth, tie with kitchen twine, and bury in the paste as you did the beginning batch; cover the pickle pot. Allow the vegetables to remain submerged for 12 to 48 hours, again depending on the room temperature. Repeat with the second cucumber, daikon chunk, and the remaining $^1/_2$ teaspoon salt.

Most people toss out these second and third batches as well, though not my mother-in-law. She would wipe them off, lightly rinse, and pat them dry. She would then slice them thinly, toss with a few dry-roasted sesame seeds, and serve them as *furu-zuké* (old pickles). I generally tell my students to taste pickles at all stages to familiarize themselves with the ways in which the pickles change, but that they should not feel compelled to consume them.

Pickle subsequent batches: Choose one or two types of vegetable for each batch of pickles. For the quantity of paste indicated here, do not try to pickle more than two types at one time. Cucumbers, turnips (and their tops), daikon (and their tops), and carrots (and their tops) are among the simplest vegetables to pickle, providing consistently good flavor and texture. Salt each vegetable as directed before burying the vegetable pieces in your pot. Cucumbers and other long, narrow vegetables are typically placed horizontally, while radishes and other round or squarish chunks are usually placed vertically on the surface. Apply light pressure to push the vegetables deeply into the paste. Cover completely by scraping surrounding paste over the buried vegetables. Cover the pot.

Reaching maturity: The *nuka* pickle pot has its own seasonal rhythm. In the spring and fall, an active pot ripens vegetables into flavorful pickles in 8 to 12 hours. I typically put vegetables in my pot after breakfast to enjoy for dinner the same night. When daytime temperatures rise above 80°F, the vegetables will take only 6 hours (often less) to reach maturity, which means I can put vegetables in the pot in early afternoon and still enjoy them for dinner. If I must be out of the house all day during warm weather, I put the vegetables in the pot the night before, remove them in the morning, and then refrigerate them with the paste still

(continued on page 218)

TROUBLESHOOTING THE NUKA PICKLE POT

Sometimes pickles develop an unwanted flavor or texture. But the problem is usually easily solved. Here are four common "troubles" and their solutions.

TOO SOUR: When pickles are too sour, sprinkle 1 teaspoon Japanese spicy mustard powder (page 257) over the paste, re-cover the pot, let sit for several hours, and then fold, knead, and flip the paste.

TOO SALTY: If your *nuka* pot is a fledgling (less than 6 months old) and your vegetables are consistently too salty, the problem may be that you oversalted the vegetables before they went into the pot. Go light on the salt, though vigorous on the rubbing—enough to produce a bit of moist, gritty foam—then rinse the vegetables well and pat them dry. If your *nuka* pot is mature (more than 6 months old) and your vegetables seem too salty, add fresh (dry) *nuka* moistened with beer (the hops will help adjust the salinity). Fold, knead, and flip to mix well.

TOO LOOSE OR WATERY: If you notice that moisture is pooling in spots in your paste or that the paste seems loose or watery, try blotting up the excess moisture with paper towels. If the problem persists, insert very small cups to collect and discard the excess liquid: Gently pat the surface of the paste to flatten it, then press a small cup (a saké cup is a good size) down into the center of the pot, so the rim is well below the surface of the paste. Liquid will pool in the cup after 6 or more hours. Remove the cup, discard the liquid, and sprinkle ¼ cup fresh (dry) *nuka* over the moist paste. Wait for at least 4 to 6 hours or up to overnight, then fold, knead, and flip to mix well.

TOO MILD: *Nuka* paste usually has a heady aroma, an indication that fermentation is actively producing lots of healthful microorganisms. If there is little smell and the vegetables are still rather tasteless after being submerged in the paste for 6 to 8 hours, you need to increase the "good bacteria" levels to speed up the fermentation. Add ½ cup well-packed fresh (dry) *nuka* mixed with ½ cup beer; 1 slice unseeded whole-grain bread, shredded into small bits (or crusts from 2 or 3 slices of whole-grain bread); 1 clove garlic, peeled but left whole; and 1 piece *kombu*, preferably *tororo* or *oboro kombu* (page 266). Mix well.

clinging to them. That night, I rinse off the paste and serve them. When temperatures drop below 45°F, it will take at least 15 hours, or possibly 20 or 24 hours, to achieve a ripe flavor. In the cold months, I add the vegetables to the pot at night after dinner to enjoy the following evening.

If vegetables remain in the *nuka* paste after they have reached maturity, they turn very sour. *Furu-zuké*, as these "old pickles" are known, have their fans (much like folks who like very sour dill pickles). Old pickles are still safe to consume if fewer than 24 "extra" hours have elapsed. Thinly slice them and toss them with dry-roasted sesame seeds (page 245) or with shredded *shiso* (page 258) or another herb.

Maintaining the pickling paste: Daily maintenance of the pickling paste is required, whether there are vegetables in it or not. Fold, knead, and flip the paste well at least once a day. Over time, the initial bits of *kombu*, shiitaké, ginger, garlic, and *tōgarashi* will disintegrate, enriching the paste. Wipe edges of your container after each "turning" session to remove any traces of clinging paste, and rinse and dry the lid each time you remove pickled vegetables. Throughout the year, the pot should be kept in a cool spot. If daytime temperatures rise above 75°F, you may want to transfer the paste to a container that can be refrigerated (if you do, use the cold-weather guidelines for gauging when the pickles are mature).

If you will be away for several days, transfer the *nuka* paste to several resealable heavy-duty plastic bags, pressing out the excess air as you seal them shut, and refrigerate. Never freeze the paste. Chilling slows fermentation, but freezing destroys the organisms needed for proper fermentation. Wash out the pickle pot and dry thoroughly. Then, when you are ready to restart your pickle pot, sprinkle fresh

(dry) *nuka* over the bottom of the pot. Add the refrigerated paste (do not pack it down), sprinkle the top with more fresh *nuka,* and cover the pot. Store on a cool shelf for at least 8 hours but preferably 24 hours. Fold, knead, and flip the paste, then resume pickling in the reactivated pot.

To serve: Remove the pickled vegetables from the pot with clean hands. Scrape off the excess paste, tossing it back into the pot, and set aside the pickles for a moment while you fold, knead, and flip the *nuka* paste. Do not flatten the surface of the paste until you have added your next batch of vegetables.

The pickles are usually consumed immediately after they are removed from the pot. They can, however, be covered and held for 6 to 8 hours (the cooler the weather, the longer the holding time). If the weather is warm (75°F), refrigerate them.

When ready to serve, rinse off any residual paste and pat dry. Cucumbers are typically cut on the diagonal into $1/4$-inch-thick slices. Turnips and small radishes are usually cut into slender wedges. Leafy greens are finely minced, rinsed, squeezed dry, and then coaxed into a mound. Daikon, whether in half-moon chunks or quarters (what the Japanese call *icho-giri* or "ginko leaf cut"), is most often cut into $1/8$-inch-thick slices. In Japan, carrots are stocky, so they are usually halved or quartered for pickling, and then thinly sliced, squeezed, and mounded for serving. If you have pickled whole carrots, slice them a scant $1/4$ inch thick. Eggplant are often cut into $1/2$-inch chunks or $1/4$-inch-thick slices on the diagonal. Celery is not traditionally eaten in Japan and is very expensive to buy. But my overseas recipe testers liked pickling celery, especially the leaves and heart, which they chopped, mounded, and sprinkled with dry-roasted sesame seeds.

SEASONAL ADJUSTMENTS TO THE NUKA PICKLE POT

Japanese cooks who maintain a *nuka* pickle pot are keenly aware of the seasonal temperature and humidity changes that can adversely affect the paste, and they treat them as they happen. For example, at the start of the rainy season in June, the pot can become unpleasantly musty. Look for bunches of tender young ginger at the market, remove the tender buds at the bottom of each stalk (the buds can be pickled in the same manner as the *myōga* bulbs on page 198), and place the stems and stalks in the *nuka* paste for 2 or 3 days days (if they turn pink, the pH balance is good), then remove and discard. If young ginger is unavailable, cut a small knob of unpeeled mature ginger into 1/4-inch-thick slices and bury the slices in the paste for 2 days, then remove and discard. Repeat the ginger-refreshing treatment as needed every few days for 1 month.

As autumn turns to winter (late October in most of Japan), the *nuka* paste starts to go both slightly sour and rather salty, possibly because it was regularly used for pickling zucchini-like gourds and squashes during late summer. If you decide to pickle zucchini (follow instructions for cucumbers; see box, page 215) and/or watermelon rinds (peel away any waxed outer skin and follow instructions for radishes), you will want to add dried persimmon peels to your pickle pot in early November.

If you drive through the Japanese countryside from late October through November, you will see pictureque strings of topaz-colored peeled *hoshi-gaki* (dried persimmons) hanging under farmhouse eaves. The peels, though not on display to the casual visitor, are also being dried. They are typically hung from laundry pins (the kind used to hang socks) and placed near a window for good ventilation, where they curl, shrivel, and are no longer sticky to the touch within 3 or 4 days. They are then added to the pickle pot and left to decompose eventually. Because city dwellers are less likely to engage in this frugal practice, some urban supermarkets sell bags of dried persimmon peels. If you want to save peels (after enjoying the fruit) for adding to your pickle pot, make sure the persimmons were raised organically. Then peel them as thinly as possible and hang the peels in a well-ventilated area to air-dry, or dry them in a dehydrator, following the directions for drying fruits.

KITCHEN CULTURE: ORUSUBAN

Orusuban, or asking others to "mind the store" in your absence, is a well-established practice in Japan. On your return, you typically present whoever helped you out with an *omiyagé* (souvenir) as a thank you. For several years, my husband's business has meant that we must maintain two homes, one in Tokyo and one in Osaka, and I have an *orusuban* relationship in both cities. And in both cases, my precious pickle pot is what needs watching. My neighbors were surprised at first (shocked, really) to discover that I kept pickle pots at all, but have since become willing and enthusiastic "babysitters." They like the daily reward of pulling pickles from the pot. When I must be away for longer than a week, I arrange for *orusuban* service: my refrigerated-in-bags method works for only 10 days at most, and then it is difficult to get the paste back to full flavor.

MONITORING THE PICKLE POT FOR FRESHNESS

Nyūsan kin lactic acid bacillus (which aids in digestion and enhances the inherent sweetness of certain vegetable sugars), *kōji kin* (*Aspergillus oryzae*, rice-mold spores), and *kōbo* (various edible yeasts) are some of the plant-based, active fermenting agents used in Japanese soy sauce, miso, vinegar, saké, and *tsukémono* production. Many fermented foods contain healthful microorganisms that are created by these agents.

Some fermentation agents, such as healthful yeasts, convert starch into sugar and break down proteins. They are typically white or pale yellow. If blue, green, or pink molds appear in fermented foods, they may be evidence of unwanted elements. Blue and green molds are distant relatives of penicillin and could be a problem for anyone with allergies to certain antibiotics. Reddish or pink fungi (often fusarium) are of greater concern, as they are widely toxic.

According to traditional Japanese home wisdom, any whitish growths that appear only on the surface of a pickling medium can be scraped away without risking illness. If visible organisms reappear within a day, or visible evidence of unwanted organisms is found elsewhere in the pickling medium, the entire batch should be discarded. The appearance of blue or green molds in a household with people allergic to penicillin would also be cause for disposal. And in all households, pink-tinted molds are held suspect and the medium is destroyed.

Monitoring of fermentation is done by smell as well as by sight. Although many fermented foods have a heady aroma, none should smell putrid: this would signal the presence of harmful *rakusan*, or butyric acid. The most effective way of preventing butyric acid from forming is to aerate the *nuka* paste frequently and thoroughly. That is why the paste needs to be gently flipped and stirred daily. If a strong smell makes you suspect the *nuka* paste has spoiled, don't hesitate to throw it out.

KTICHEN CULTURE: THE PLEASURES OF THE PICKLE POT

I first tried making *nuka-zuké* more than forty years ago. At the time, I was living with the Ohta family in Tokyo, and Eiko Ohta, who had herself been tutored in the fine art of pickle making by her mother and grandmother, promised to show me the basics: how to dry-roast the rice bran and then how to mix it in a large ceramic crock with coarse salt, scraps of kelp, and broken bits of dried shiitaké mushrooms.

That evening, I brought my newly purchased ceramic crock to her kitchen, where we toasted the start of my pickling career. After taking a sip of beer from my glass, she told me to pour the rest of it into the pot. Immediately, the powdery bran mixture began to bubble and hiss, as the hops in the beer brought the *nuka* to life. With great ceremony, Mrs. Ohta added some of her mature paste to my fledgling batch and demonstrated, with sheer delight, the ritual of daily care: digging, flipping, and kneading, scooping and stirring the paste.

I developed a satisfying rhythm of my own (dig, flip, squeeze, and knead; scoop, stir, and scrape), and within a few days, when I removed the lid of the crock, I was rewarded with a heady aroma. After a week of nurturing my *nuka* paste with buried radishes beyond their prime (retrieved and tossed in the compost heap the following day), I was ready to try a cucumber with my morning bowl of rice and miso soup. My first attempt was much too salty and harsh. In fact, it took nearly a month of constant monitoring and adjustment before I was able to produce a reasonably tasty pickle. Later I would learn that seasonal temperatures changed the timing and rhythm of pickling: In the cold months, radishes and turnips needed to be buried in the paste before going to bed to have them just right for dinner the following day. In the heat of summer, cucumbers placed in the pot as late as four in the afternoon were ready to enjoy by dinnertime.

Over the years, I have received lots of advice, and occasional transfusions of seasoned *nuka* paste, from many experts: neighbors, shopkeepers, and relatives. Indeed, cultivating a *nuka* pot has provided me with special access to the lives of many Japanese women—pickle bonding across an otherwise difficult cultural divide.

DESSERTS

I N THE PAST, mealtime in Japan did not conclude with something sweet. Nowadays, however, many Japanese restaurants offering classic fare add a dessertlike course to their menu. Sometimes it is as simple as fresh fruit in season, perhaps elaborately cut in high-end establishments. Or, on occasion, French-style pastries make an appearance on an otherwise traditional menu. But by and large, confectionary in Japan is consumed late afternoon as *oyattsu*, a sort of high tea.

For this book, I have selected sweets that can be enjoyed as a snack or dessert. To accommodate those who want to finish dinner with something that is sweet and also contributes positively to the nutritional profile of a meal, I have chosen sweets that are both good for you and good tasting.

To simplify instructions in the recipes that follow and to enable you to develop your own original vegan desserts, I have opened this chapter with with three basic recipes: Brown Sugar Syrup, Chunky Red Bean Jam, and Sweet Rice Dumplings. You will find each of them a valuable addition to your kitchen inventory.

BROWN SUGAR SYRUP

KURO MITSU

Made from *kuro-zatō*, literally "black sugar," this syrup is used in many traditional *washoku* sweet dishes, such as *an mitsu* (cubes of *kanten* with sweet beans) and *Abekawa mochi* (rice taffy with toasted soy flour). It is yummy drizzled over crisp apple slices, or spooned into cored whole apples for baking. Superior-quality *kuro-zatō* has a wonderful malted flavor; the best I have found comes from Okinawa.

MAKES ABOUT 1/2 CUP

2/3 **cup packed kuro-zatō (page 280) or brown sugar**

1/4 **cup boiling water**

Pinch of salt

Place the sugar and boiling water in a small, deep saucepan. Stir with a wooden spoon or a silicone spatula to dissolve the sugar as much as possible before putting the pan on the stove top. Put the saucepan over medium heat and bring to a boil, stirring constantly. Lower the heat slightly and cook the mixture, continuing to stir occasionally, for about 1 minute, or until it becomes very foamy. When the foam can no longer be stirred down, the mixture will rapidly thicken and become syrupy. As you lift the spoon or spatula, the syrup will cling to it, rather than drip from it.

Add the salt and stir it in; it will mellow the sweetness. Then immediately remove from the heat to prevent scorching. Pour the hot syrup into a heatproof glass jar and let cool completely. Cover with a tight-fitting lid, label and date, and store for up to 3 months on a dark, cool shelf or refrigerate for up to 6 months.

CHUNKY RED BEAN JAM

TSUBU AN

A Japanese classic, this chunky bean jam can be used in many ways: sandwiched between pancakes to make cymbal cakes (page 234), mixed with *kanten* to make jellies (page 229), or served as a side sauce with fresh or lightly poached fruit (summer peaches or fall persimmons are especially delicious). Although many commercially made bean jams are available in Asian groceries, most of them are too sweet. Making your own ensures that won't be the case. For extended storage, I recommend you divvy up the jam in a few small glass jars, rather than a single large one.

Although the instruction to throw off the first batch of cooking water may sound wasteful, it is necessary to ensure a bright color and to reduce the possibility of musty flavors. You can save the bean liquid and use it to water plants.

MAKES 2 CUPS

- ³/₄ cup dried adzuki beans (page 260)
- About 7 cups cold water
- 1 cup granulated sugar
- 2 tablespoons packed kuro-zatō (page 280) or brown sugar
- 1 teaspoon salt
- 1 teaspoon light-colored soy sauce

Rinse the dried beans, then place them in a 3-quart pot with 2¹/₂ cups of the water. Place over medium heat and bring to a boil. Reduce the heat to maintain a steady, not-too-vigorous simmer and cook for about 8 minutes, or until the water turns wine red. Drain the beans. Discarding this first batch of cooking water is called *shibumi kiri*, or "removing astringency." Rinse the pot to remove any *aku* (froth, scum, or film) that might be clinging to the sides.

Return the beans to the pot, add 3 cups of the water, and place over medium heat. When the water comes to a boil, adjust the heat to maintain a steady, gentle simmer. Cook, uncovered, for about 30 minutes, or until the water barely covers the beans. Add ¹/₂ cup of the water (this is called *bikkuri mizu*, or "surprise water") and continue to cook over medium heat, periodically skimming away any froth and loose skins with a fine-mesh skimmer.

Repeat the "surprise water" treatment every 15 to 20 minutes, or until the beans are very tender. This should take 35 to 40 minutes. To check for tenderness, take a bean from the pot, and when cool enough to handle comfortably, hold it between your thumb and pinkie and press gently. It should yield easily. (This pinch test is accurate because the pinkie is usually a "weak" finger and can exert less pressure in the pinch. If a simmered bean can yield to this weaker pressure, you can be sure it is tender.)

Add the granulated sugar, stir, and simmer for 20 minutes. The sauce will darken and appear less cloudy than before. Add the *kuro-zatō*, stir, and simmer for about 5 minutes, or until the sauce becomes glossy and very thick. If you draw a line on the bottom of the pan with a spoon or silicone spatula, the line should remain visible for several seconds before it fills.

Add the salt and soy sauce (these ingredients will mellow the intense sweetness of the jam and help "set" the consistency) and stir to mix well. Remove from the heat and set aside to cool to room temperature. Transfer to glass jars, cover tightly, label and date, and store in the refrigerator for up to 2 months. Once a jar has been opened, use the entire contents within 7 to 10 days.

SWEET RICE DUMPLINGS

SHIRATAMA DANGO

These sweet dumplings trace their roots to China, first appearing in Japan on ceremonial occasions in the eighth century. They are typically made with equal quantities of two types of rice flour, *mochiko*, which looks like crushed chalk, and *jōshinko*, which resembles a silky powder. The classic recipe for these chewy, marshmallow-like dumplings calls for water. Soy milk can be substituted for the water to boost their nutritional value. The dumplings are delicious dusted with cinnamon sugar enriched with toasted soy flour (see box, page 227).

MAKES 30 TO 40 MARBLE-SIZE DUMPLINGS

> ¹/₄ cup mochiko (page 256), loosely measured (scant 1 ounce)
>
> ¹/₄ cup jōshinko (page 256), loosely measured and lightly tapped down rather than leveled (about 1 ounce)
>
> About 2 tablespoons warm water or 2¹/₂ tablespoons soy milk, freshly extracted (page 156) or purchased, at room temperature

Empty the rice flours into a bowl and stir to combine them well. Lightly crush any large lumps of the *mochiko* between your fingertips, tossing to coat with the finer *jōshinko*. Do not be concerned by the inconsistency of the dry mixture.

Drizzle in 1 tablespoon of the warm water in a spiral pattern, starting at the rim of the bowl and working toward the center. Using your fingertips, stir to mix. Gradually add more water until the flour easily forms a mass that comes cleanly away from the sides of the bowl. Lift the mass and throw it back in the bowl, as though you are throwing a baseball into a catcher's mitt. Repeat this pitching action several times until the mass is smooth and uniform. The dough should be soft but firm, what the Japanese call *mimi tabu*, or "earlobe consistency." Lightly pinch your own earlobe, then the dough in the bowl. They should have a similar texture.

Divide the dough into 30 to 40 equal pieces. One at a time, roll the pieces between your palms to form marble-size spheres. Set aside on a flat plate or tray.

Bring a wide, shallow pot of water to a rolling boil. Gently drop the spheres into the boiling water and cook for about 4 minutes. The spheres will bob to the surface as they cook through; allow them to cook for at least 1 minute after they surface.

Using a fine-mesh skimmer, remove the dumplings from the pot and drop them briefly into a bowl of very cold water or ice water. Within 1 minute, drain them and let cool to room temperature.

These dumplings are at their chewy-tender best when eaten within 30 minutes of making them. If you need to hold them for longer, place in a single layer in a covered plastic container or resealable bag (laid flat on a plate or baking sheet) to keep them from drying out. Refrigerate in warm weather if holding or more than 30 minutes; in cool weather they can stay at room temperature for 2 hours.

KINAKO-CINNAMON SUGAR

The nutty flavor of *kinako* (toasted soy flour, page 255) marries well with sugar and cinnamon in a quick and easy topping for *shiratama dango* (opposite). Combine 2 tablespoons *kinako*, 1/2 teaspoon ground cinnamon, and 2 teaspoons granulated or crushed brown sugar in a small glass jar, cover tightly, and shake to mix well. When ready to use, pass the mixture through a fine-mesh strainer held over the cooled dumplings.

SWEET RICE DUMPLINGS IN BLACK SESAME SYRUP

KURO GOMA SHIRUKO

Many Asian cultures use black sesame when making sweet snacks, and Japan is no exception. In this dish, the intensely nutty and sweet sesame syrup is ebony, delivering a striking contrast to the pearly white rice taffy dumplings with which it is served.

SERVES 6

BLACK SESAME SYRUP

1/2 cup black sesame paste

3 tablespoons mizu amé (page 281) or corn syrup

1 to 2 tablespoons boiling water

Pinch of salt or drizzle of soy sauce

1 recipe Sweet Rice Dumplings (page 226)

Make the sesame syrup: Place the sesame paste and *mizu amé* in a blender or food processor and pulse to mix. Carefully drizzle in 1 tablespoon of the boiling water and pulse again. If the syrup seems too thick, add more boiling water, a few drops at a time, blending well after each addition. Ideally, the mixture will be lustrous and the consistency of thick maple syrup. Add the salt (it will mellow the intense sweetness) and blend a final time. The syrup is ready to enjoy. You should have about 1/2 cup. If not using immediately, transfer to a lidded glass jar and refrigerate for up to 2 weeks. Bring to room temperature before serving for better flavor and easier pouring.

Divide the dumplings evenly among 6 small individual bowls. Pour the syrup over them. For a more dramatic effect, pour the sauce on a white or brightly colored plate and arrange the dumplings on top of the sauce. Serve with a spoon or cocktail forks.

ROASTED RICE DUMPLINGS WITH STICKY-SWEET SOY SAUCE

MITARASHI DANGO

These dumplings are eaten like marshmallows cooked at a campfire: skewered and roasted. Because the savory-and-sweet soy sauce that is slathered on the rice dumplings can get a bit sticky, the Japanese often serve the skewers with *oshibori* (damp towels) within easy reach.

MAKES 12 SKEWERS, 3 DUMPLINGS ON EACH

Vegetable oil for greasing

1 recipe Sweet Rice Dumplings (page 226)

MITARASHI SAUCE

2 tablespoons soy sauce

2 tablespoons mirin

1 tablespoon sugar, preferably brown sugar

1 tablespoon cornstarch

2 tablespoons cold water

Preheat your broiler on high, then turn it down to the lowest broiler setting. If using a toaster oven, set on a medium setting.

Soak 12 slender bamboo skewers in cold water. If using a broiler, line a baking sheet with aluminum foil and lightly oil the foil with the vegetable oil; if using a toaster oven, use the tray that came with your appliance and line it in a similar manner.

Thread 3 dumplings onto each skewer, and arrange the skewers on the prepared baking sheet or tray (you may need to do this in batches). To keep the exposed parts of the skewers from scorching, wrap them in foil.

Make the sauce: Combine the soy sauce, mirin, and sugar in a small saucepan over low heat and heat, stirring constantly, to dissolve the sugar. Mix together the cornstarch and water in a small bowl. Add the cornstarch mixture to the soy mixture and stir over low heat for about 30 seconds, or until the sauce is thickened. Remove from the heat. (The sauce can be made ahead and refrigerated for up to 1 week—be sure to reheat before using.)

Broil or toast the dumplings for 2 minutes, or until lightly colored on top. Turn the skewers to expose the unbrowned surfaces and broil or toast those for about 1 minute, or until slightly blistered.

While the dumplings are still piping hot, using a pastry brush, paint them with the sauce. Serve hot.

MINI RED BEAN JAM JELLIES

MINI MIZU YŌKAN

Traditionally, *mizu yōkan* is made in an easy-to-unmold loaf pan called a *nagashi kan* (page 249), then sliced into small rectangular blocks. For those unable to source special Japanese cooking equipment, I have reconfigured this classic confection to make miniature jellies from the chunky red bean jam. Because the jam is made with *kanten*, a sea gelatin, they hold their shape at room temperature without "weeping," as regular gelatin would. They can be packed into a picnic lunch or can sit out on a dessert buffet for several hours.

MAKES 24 JELLIES

1 stick kanten (page 264), about 6 inches long, or about 2 teaspoons powdered kanten

1 or 1½ cups water, depending on type of kanten

1 cup Chunky Red Bean Jam (page 225)

1 teaspoon light-colored soy sauce

Set up a tray with 24 small foil cups, the kind used for making candies and truffles, and place in the refrigerator to chill while you cook the red bean mixture. Using cold molds or containers will help the *kanten* solidify more quickly, which will keep the jellies from spreading out from the weight of the beans.

If using stick *kanten*, soften as directed on page 264. When it is pliable, squeeze out and discard all the liquid. Shred the softened *kanten* into a nonreactive 1-quart saucepan, add the 1½ cups water, and place over low heat. Heat, stirring, until the *kanten* is fully dissolved.

If using powdered *kanten*, place it in the nonreactive saucepan, add the 1 cup water, and stir to mix well. Place over low heat and heat, stirring, until the *kanten* is fully dissolved.

Add the bean jam to the *kanten* mixture, stirring it in gently with a *shamoji* (page 248) or other broad wooden spatula. Use the spatula to draw figure eights in lazy, sweeping strokes. This will help distribute the crushed beans evenly throughout the mixture and avoid incorporating air that would create unwanted bubbles.

Add the soy sauce (it will mellow the intense sweetness of the jellies and help "set" the consistency), stirring as before to mix well. Continue to cook for about 3 minutes, or until the mixture starts to thicken and becomes slightly opaque. Remove from the heat.

Carefully spoon the bean mixture into the foil cups, trying not to create bubbles. If some do form inadvertently, lance them or drag them up the sides of the foil cup with the tip of a toothpick. Most of the solids (the larger beans) will sink to the bottom of the cups as the mixture cools. Because these cups will be inverted later, what appears to be at the bottom now will be on the top when served.

Allow the jellies to sit undisturbed on your kitchen counter for 7 to 8 minutes, or until solidly set. Then cover the jellies until serving to prevent them from absorbing unwanted odors from other foods. They will keep at cool room temperature for up to 4 hours.

When ready to serve, invert onto plates and peel away the foil liners.

BROWN SUGAR ICE

KURO MITSU AISU

This frozen dessert is a cross between a granita and a sherbet. *Ama-zaké*, or sweet saké mash, gives body to the ice and provides much of its sweetness (along with the brown sugar). The powdered *kanten* (a sea gelatin) mixed with a bit of soy milk acts as a stabilizer and makes the texture creamier than it might otherwise be. In lieu of a cookie, I like to serve this ice with Sweet Black Beans (page 238), threading 3 beans onto a toothpick for each serving.

SERVES 4

¹/₃ cup soy milk, freshly extracted (page 156) or purchased

1 teaspoon powdered kanten (page 264)

Scant 1 cup ama-zaké (page 280)

¹/₄ cup Brown Sugar Syrup (page 224)

¹/₄ teaspoon soy sauce

Pour the soy milk into a small bowl and sprinkle the *kanten* over it. Wait for a few minutes and then stir to combine. Set aside for another 5 minutes. The *kanten* will begin to absorb the soy milk and swell slightly.

Put the *ama-zaké* in a blender and pulse until creamy and smooth. Add the soy milk mixture and continue to pulse until thoroughly blended. Add the sugar syrup and soy sauce, and process until smooth.

Pour the mixture into a freezer-safe container, cover tightly, and place in the freezer for 1 to 2 hours, or until firm but not fully frozen.

Remove the mixture from the freezer. Using a handheld mixer, beat the partially frozen mixture until it is aerated and smooth. Beating the ice at this point ensures a fluffier, creamier finish. Tap down the mixture to force out any large air pockets, re-cover, and return to the freezer for at least 3 or 4 hours or up to 3 weeks (aroma dissipates beyond that point and the ice is less tasty). Because of the fairly high alcohol content of *ama-zaké*, the ice tends to be softer set than fruit juices or purées alone would produce.

When ready to serve, scoop as you would ice cream.

KURO KURO SUNDEI

A wonderful and dramatic dessert can be fashioned from scoops of Brown Sugar Ice drizzled with Black Sesame Syrup (page 227). I like to call the results *Kuro Kuro Sundei*, or "Black on Black Sundae." To add a bit of crunch, garnish with dry-roasted white sesame seeds (page 245) or slivered blanched almonds. Shredded coconut also makes a good topping.

JELLIED GRAPEFRUIT WEDGES

KANKITSU KAN

Both the juice and the shell of the grapefruit are used to make this refreshing dessert. The final configuration, many multifaceted wedgelike pieces, is intriguing to behold and practical when it comes to eating (just peel back the skin). If you are sure the grapefruit was organically grown, save the peel after serving to make marmalade (see box, page 235). Because the peel is boiled during jam making, any potentially dangerous bacteria is eliminated.

Pictured on page 168

MAKES 12 SEGMENTS

1 thick-skinned, unblemished grapefruit, preferably Ruby

1 stick kanten (page 264), about 6 inches long, or about 2 teaspoons powdered kanten

2 teaspoons sugar

1 or 1¹/₂ cups water

Cut the grapefruit in half through the stem end. Holding a grapefruit half over a bowl lined with *sarashi* (page 250) or a double thickness of cheesecloth, carefully scoop out the flesh, allowing it to drop into the bowl. Use your fingertips, rather than a knife, to prevent bruising the shell. Ideally, you will be able to remove much of the white pith along with the juicy flesh. Repeat with the remaining half.

Gather up the edges of the cloth and squeeze the flesh to release the juice into the bowl. You should have about 1 cup juice. If you have less, add water or fruit juice (grapefruit or orange) to make up the difference. If you have more than 1 cup, you will adjust the volume later.

Arrange the grapefruit shells on a tray or in individual cups or bowls so that they don't rock back and forth. These will be filled with liquid gelatin.

If using stick *kanten*, soften as directed on page 264. When it is pliable, squeeze out and discard all the liquid. Shred the softened *kanten* into a nonreactive 1-quart saucepan, add the sugar and the 1¹/₂ cups water, and place over low heat. Cook, stirring, for about 2 minutes, or until smooth and slightly thickened. If you have more than 1 cup grapefruit juice, cook the *kanten* mixture for about 1 more minute to reduce the volume. Remove from the heat.

If using powdered *kanten*, place it in the nonreactive saucepan, add the sugar and the 1 cup water, and stir to mix well. Place over low heat and cook, stirring, until the sugar and *kanten* are fully dissolved. Add the grapefruit juice, raise the heat to medium, and cook, stirring, for 2 minutes, or until slightly thickened. If you have more than 1 cup of juice, cook for about 1 more minute to reduce the volume. Remove from the heat.

Carefully spoon the *kanten* mixture into the grapefruit shells, dividing it evenly and trying not to create bubbles. Using a toothpick, drag any foam to the edges to remove it. Make sure the surface is entirely smooth. Let cool at room temperature for about 30 minutes, or until the mixture begins to set. Cover and refrigerate for at least 30 minutes or up to 24 hours.

Before serving, trim the edge of each shell so that the surface of the gelatin is flush with the edge. Slice each grapefruit half into 3 wedges, then cut each wedge on the diagonal to create smaller, multifaceted pieces. To eat, peel back the skin.

MATCHA MUFFINS

MATCHA MUSHI PAN

This moist and fluffy steamed green tea confection has a texture similar to that of chiffon cake. My favorite version includes sweet-simmered black beans randomly scattered throughout the batter. A dried fruit–studded *kinako* (toasted soy flour) version (see below) is also popular.

As with many Japanese confections that were adapted from European cuisines, the traditional recipe calls for eggs and cow's milk. I offer a vegan version using soy milk. The richer the soy milk is (higher percentage of soy solids), the better the texture will be. (See page 279 for how to check for richness on the label of purchased soy milk.)

MAKES 6 TO 8 MUFFINS

- ³/₄ cup cake flour, about 4 ounces
- 1 tablespoon baking powder
- 1 tablespoon matcha (page 271)
- 2 tablespoons powdered sugar
- ¹/₂ cup soy milk, freshly extracted (page 156) or purchased
- 1 tablespoon maple syrup
- Drop of soy sauce, preferably light-colored soy sauce
- ¹/₄ teaspoon vegetable oil (optional)
- 2 tablespoons drained Sweet Black Beans (page 238), optional

Sift together the cake flour, baking powder, *matcha*, and powdered sugar into a bowl. Set aside.

In a separate bowl, whisk the soy milk until foamy. Add the maple syrup and soy sauce and continue to whisk and incorporate air. Add the vegetable oil if your soy milk is not especially "rich."

Resift the flour mixture. Fold it into the soy milk mixture in two or three batches, stirring gently after each addition to combine. The resulting batter should be smooth, thick, and slightly foamy. Line individual freestanding cupcake forms, or a 6-muffin tin (if it will fit in your steamer), with paper or foil liners and pour in a scant ¹/₄ cup of the batter. Tap down to level the batter. If you are using the black beans, place 6 or 7 beans on top of the batter in each cup (the weight of the beans will cause them to sink).

Place the filled cups in a flat-bottomed, lidded steamer fitted with a cloth-protected lid (page 251). Set the steamer over high heat. Once you hear the water boiling, adjust the heat to maintain a steady flow of steam. Steam for 15 to 20 minutes, or until the tops of the muffins crack and split and a toothpick inserted into the center of a muffin

(continued)

DRIED FRUIT–STUDDED KINAKO MUSHI PAN

Follow the directions for Matcha Muffins (above), substituting 1 tablespoon *kinako* (page 255) for the *matcha* and 1 tablespoon brown sugar for the maple syrup. Toss 1 tablespoon minced dried fruit (cranberries and/or apricots are especially good) with ¹/₂ teaspoon cake flour, and fold the mixture into the batter just before dividing it among the lined cupcake forms; omit the black beans. Steam as directed.

comes out clean. Always remove the lid carefully to avoid the steam burning your hand.

Transfer the muffins to a rack to cool. Keep the paper or foil liners in place until ready to eat. The muffins will keep at room temperature for up to 6 hours; to keep them soft and moist, place them in a closed container or slip them into a resealable bag. To store longer, refrigerate for up to 2 days. To rewarm before serving, place the muffins in a microwave (remove foil liners first) and zap on high for 10 seconds.

CYMBAL CAKES WITH CHUNKY RED BEAN JAM

DORA YAKI

Usagiya, a confectionary that opened in Tokyo's Ueno district about a century ago, is generally credited with giving *dora yaki* its current configuration: a pair of small pancakes sandwiched together with sweet bean jam. Although the classic version calls for eggs and cow's milk in the pancake batter, I have developed a vegan version that makes use of soy milk. I add some *kinako* (toasted soy flour) to give the cymbals a richer color and more complex flavor—and an extra boost of protein. *Tsubu an*, a chunky red bean jam, is the most popular filling, though you could use any fruit-flavored jam or marmalade in its place, such as the grapefruit marmalade on page 235.

SERVES 6

½ cup sifted cake flour, 1½ ounces

1 tablespoon kinako (page 255)

2 tablespoons powdered sugar

2 teaspoons baking powder

⅓ cup soy milk, freshly extracted (page 156) or purchased

2 tablespoons mirin or maple syrup

¼ teaspoon soy sauce

Vegetable oil for greasing

½ cup Chunky Red Bean Jam (page 225)

Sift together the cake flour, *kinako*, powdered sugar, and baking powder into a bowl. Set aside. In a separate bowl, mix together the soy milk and mirin. Stir in the soy sauce (it will mellow the sweetness of the batter). Fold the flour mixture into the soy milk mixture and stir gently to make a smooth, thick, but pourable batter. If it is too thick, thin with a few extra drops of soy milk or with a few drops of water. Cover and let sit for 10 minutes.

Place a heavy skillet or griddle over medium heat. Lightly grease the pan with vegetable oil. (I find using a small wad of paper towel dipped in oil to be the easiest way to coat the pan thinly.) When the skillet is hot, lower the heat slightly and pour in the batter. For each pancake, pour a scant 2 tablespoons of the batter into the pan and let it spread naturally into a circle 2 to 2½ inches in diameter. Cook the pancakes undisturbed over medium-low heat for about 1 minute, or until bubbles appear on the top surface and burst. Flip and cook the other side until lightly browned and dry. The batter browns quickly. Using a flat metal spatula, transfer to a rack to cool completely. Repeat to make a total of 12 pancakes, each with a rough side (covered with small craters) and a smooth side (deep golden brown).

When the pancakes are cool, spread one-sixth of the bean jam on the rough side of 6 pancakes. Concentrate the bean jam at the center. Top each jam-spread pancake with a second pancake, rough side down, to make 6 "sandwiches." Press lightly to spread the jam to the edges.

Eat immediately, or wrap in plastic wrap to keep moist. If you will be keeping the stuffed cakes for more than 1 hour, refrigerate them. They will keep for up to 3 days. They will have a better texture if allowed to return to room temperature before serving.

HOMEMADE GRAPEFRUIT MARMALADE

Use the peels left over after the Jellied Grapefruit Wedges (page 232) have been eaten to make an easy marmalade that can be used in place of the bean jam in the cymbal cakes (above). Finely mince the peels to about the size of whole sesame seeds (or pulse in a food processor). You will have between $1/2$ and $3/4$ cup. Place the minced peel in a small, deep pot and add 2 to 3 tablespoons sugar and 1 tablespoon each water and saké. Place over high heat and bring to a rapid boil. Adjust the heat to maintain a very gentle simmer and cook, stirring occasionally, for about 3 minutes, or until very thick. Add a drop of light-colored soy sauce or a pinch of salt to mellow the sweetness. Remove from the heat and let cool completely. Transfer to a lidded glass jar and refrigerate for up to 1 month.

CANDIED SWEET POTATOES

DAIGAKU IMO

Hanamaru Market, a highly successful, long-running Japanese television talk show, opens with a short cooking segment every weekday morning. Finding ways to make impressive classic cuisine simpler and less technically demanding is the theme of many of the episodes. In the autumn of 2008, one of the broadcasts featured an innovative recipe for *daigaku imo* (candied sweet potatoes) that topped all previous viewer-rating charts. Indeed, as of this writing, nearly a year later, it remains the all-time favorite.

Syrup-glazed, black sesame–studded sweet potato first became a popular snack among university students at the turn of the twentieth century. Indeed, that is the origin of the name of the dish: *daigaku* means "university" and *imo* is "potato." Most recipes for *daigaku imo* instruct the cook to deep-fry sweet potato chunks first and glaze them afterward. Although delicious, the classic version results in a high-calorie snack that is messy both to make and to clean up. In contrast, the *Hanamaru Market* version offers a (relatively) healthful snack.

SERVES 6 TO 8

1/4 cup granulated or packed light brown sugar

1/4 cup vegetable oil

2 tablespoons water

1 teaspoon soy sauce

1 teaspoon rice vinegar

1/2 teaspoon salt

2 large Japanese-style sweet potatoes (page 276), about 1 pound total weight, unpeeled, cut ran-giri style (page 244) into chunks

1 to 1 1/2 tablespoons black sesame seeds, freshly dry-roasted (page 245)

Combine the sugar, vegetable oil, water, soy sauce, vinegar, and salt in a skillet just large enough to hold the sweet potato chunks in a single layer. Place over medium-high heat and bring to a simmer. Arrange the sweet potatoes in the pan in a single layer and cover with a circle of parchment paper to keep the surface moist. Lower the heat to maintain a very gentle simmer and cook for 2 minutes. Cover the skillet with a lid (keep the parchment in place) and cook for another 2 to 3 minutes, or until the potatoes are tender. A toothpick inserted into the thickest part of a piece should meet no resistance. If the chunks are not yet tender, add a bit more water and simmer for another minute or two. Check to make sure the sugar doesn't burn.

Once the potatoes are tender, remove the lid and parchment and jiggle the skillet to allow the potato chunks to roll around in the rapidly reducing glaze (the vinegar, by the way, will keep the sugar from seizing after the glaze has cooled). After 6 minutes or so, the water and oil in the skillet will have separated and most of the water will have evaporated, enabling you to remove the lightly glazed sweet potato chunks with little or no oil clinging to them.

Transfer the glazed chunks to a plate, spreading them out in a single layer. Sprinkle with the black sesame seeds. Let cool to room temperature before serving. They keep at cool room temperature for 6 to 8 hours. If you will be keeping them longer, place them in a covered container and refrigerate for up to 2 days. For optimal texture, bring the potatoes back to room temperature before serving.

SWEET BLACK BEANS

KURO MAMÉ

Many of the items served to celebrate New Year's in Japan have symbolic meaning, expressed as wordplay. Sweet black beans are a good example: the word *kuro* means "black," but the meaning shifts to "hard work" when the calligraphy changes and the final vowel is extended. Similarly, the word *mamé* means "bean," but when written with different calligraphy, *mamé* becomes "sincere" or "earnest." Eating black beans in syrup on New Year's ensure that those who work in earnest will have a sweet new year.

The traditional method of preparing *kuro mamé* is a long (3 days from start to finish) and rather tedious procedure, though one that results in utterly delicious plump, glossy, tender beans in a light sugar syrup that can be kept for months. Over the years, observing many Japanese home and professional cooks and experimenting in my own kitchen, I have developed a modified version of the classic technique that I am sharing here.

The key to preparing luscious, wrinkle-free sweet black soybeans is patience: the beans must be completely tender before sweetening them (adding the sugar too early will cause the beans to seize and toughen), and the pot must be frequently watched, adding more water as needed to keep the beans barely submerged through the lengthy cooking process so they don't wrinkle.

Pictured on page 231

MAKES 3 TO 3½ CUPS

- 1 cup dried kuro mamé (page 260)
- 3 cups water for soaking and cooking beans
- 1 teaspoon baking soda
- 2 cups sugar
- 1½ cups cold water for syrup
- 2 teaspoons soy sauce

Rinse the dried beans. In a deep bowl, mix the 3 cups water and baking soda, stirring to dissolve the baking soda. Add the beans and let them soak, completely submerged, at room temperature for at least 8 hours or preferably 10 to 12 hours (if it is very warm in your kitchen, soak the beans in the refrigerator for 24 hours). As the beans soak, they will swell to several times their original size. To make sure they remain moist throughout the soaking, dampen *sarashi* (page 250) or several layers of finely woven gauze or cheesecloth and place directly on the soaking beans.

Transfer the swollen beans and what remains of their soaking water to a deep 3-quart pot. If the beans are no longer covered with water, add water as needed to cover them. Place over medium-high heat and bring to a boil. Skim away any *aku* (froth, scum, or film) with a fine-mesh skimmer and add water as needed to cover the beans by about 1 inch. Adjust the heat to maintain a steady, not-too-vigorous simmer. Place the cloth you used when soaking the beans on top of the simmering beans. The cloth will become discolored, but if it is *sarashi* or other sturdy muslinlike cloth, it can be reused for the same purpose several times. If you have an *otoshi-buta* (page 243) or other flat lid slightly smaller in diameter than the rim of the pot, place it on top of the cloth.

Cook the beans for 2 hours, checking the intensity of the heat and the water level every 15 to 20 minutes. Ideally, the beans will gently simmer in water that barely covers them. Throughout, keep the surface of the beans moist with the cloth (and *otoshi-buta*).

As the beans cook, some skins may loosen and a few beans may split, but neither is a good indication of tenderness. To check for tenderness, take a bean from the pot, and when cool enough to handle comfortably, hold it between your thumb and pinkie and press gently. It should yield easily. (This pinch test is accurate because the pinkie is usually a "weak" finger and can exert less pressure in the pinch. If a simmered bean can yield to this weaker pressure, you can be sure it is tender.) Cooking times will vary tremendously with the age and variety of the soybean. On some occasions, I have had to cook beans for 4 or more hours. Continue to cook the beans, checking the water level frequently and adding water as needed to keep the beans barely covered, until they are completely tender. At this point, the beans and their cooking liquid can be immediately transferred to a glass jar, covered with the cloth, then with a tight-fitting lid, and refrigerated for up to 3 days. (Before closing the jar, make sure none of the beans is exposed to air.)

Make the syrup: Combine the sugar and 1$^1/_2$ cups water in a deep, heavy 2-quart saucepan over medium heat, stirring to dissolve the sugar. Reduce the heat slightly and continue to cook, stirring occasionally, until the liquid is syrupy and reduced to about 1 cup. This should take about 10 minutes. During this reduction process the bubbles will become quite frothy.

When ready to combine the syrup and beans, remove the *otoshi-buta* and cloth from the beans in the saucepan or open the jar and peel back the cloth and transfer to a heavy pot. Add the syrup, replace the cloth, and bring to a simmer over medium heat. Simmer for 10 minutes, or until the beans are barely covered with the syrup.

Remove from the heat and allow the beans to cool to room temperature in the syrup. During the cooling process, the sweetness of the syrup penetrates to the core of the beans. Make sure the beans are covered with the cloth as they cool to avoid excessive wrinkling of their skins.

Peel back the cloth, add the soy sauce to the cooled syrup (it will mellow the intense sweetness), and stir to distribute well. Replace the cloth and place the pot over low heat. Bring the syrup slowly to a boil and cook for 2 minutes, then remove the pot from the heat. Allow the cloth-covered beans and syrup to cool to room temperature again. It is in this final cooling process that the flavors develop and meld.

Set the beans aside to cool completely, then transfer them with their syrup to a clean glass jar. Seal with a tight-fitting lid and refrigerate for up to 10 days. If you wish to store the beans for an extended time, use heatproof canning jars and process in a boiling-water bath as you would a jam or jelly, then store the cooled jars in the refrigerator for up to 2 months.

shokutaku
tsukémono ki

otoshi-buta

maku no
uchi kata

nagashi kan

saibashi

miso koshi

A GUIDE TO THE KANSHA KITCHEN

A CATALOG OF TOOLS AND TECHNIQUES

Much of the equipment and many of the culinary practices found in the contemporary Japanese kitchen have been passed down from previous generations—established routines and time-tested tools that remain relevant to modern cooks who seek to run both a fuel-efficient and a personal-energy-efficient kitchen. I have incorporated details on many of these tools and techniques into the recipes and their accompanying text. As with the guide to ingredients, this catalog, with the entries arranged alphabetically, supplements that information.

Appliances

Integrating applied science and granny know-how to the tasks of daily living has produced several automated, thermostatically controlled appliances that can make your *kansha* kitchen run more efficiently. In particular, dehydrators, rice cookers, and soy milk makers can ease the process of meal preparation and greatly improve the flavor and quality of the food you cook.

DEHYDRATOR Dried foods, known collectively as *kambutsu*, play a dual role in the *kansha* kitchen: the rehydrating liquids become flavorful stocks and the softened vegetables are cooked and consumed. The drying process extends the shelf life and intensifies the flavor and nutrients of fruits and vegetables. Potential negatives exist, however.

Any chemicals or additives used in growing or processing dried foods become more potent, possibly rising to toxic levels, in the drying process. Because not all commercially available *kambutsu* are free of chemicals, sourcing organically grown crops and drying them yourself is a good idea.

Although it is possible to make *kambutsu* without special equipment if you live in a dry climate and can find a well-ventilated space in your kitchen, using a dehydrator will be a tremendous boon to busy people (especially urban dwellers) who prepare their meals daily in a warm, moist home kitchen. Following the instructions that came with your dehydrator, you can make your own dried leafy greens to use in Rice Tossed with Radish Greens (page 23) or your own *kiriboshi daikon* (page 263) from peels and thin slices of daikon. Thin slices of burdock root and thin slices and peels of lotus root are also good candidates for the dehydrator.

RICE COOKER Called *suihanki*, both gas-fueled (usually institutional size) and electric rice cookers (in all sizes) are available. If you will be cooking rice several times a week, you will find a rice cooker a tremendous boon to meal preparation. The models that run on "fuzzy logic" are especially sensitive to variables, such as moisture levels (new crop rice is moister than rice stored for half a year or longer), degree of bran removal (cooking whole-grain brown rice requires adjustment in rice-water ratio and in cooking time), and the addition of other grains, such as millet. Appliances with a timer feature permit you to wash the rice and then set it to cook hours later, and those with a "keep warm" feature hold the rice for many hours after the cooking cycle has finished. Fully automated, higher-end models often provide a countdown to eating readiness; some play music, others ring a bell and/or light up to summon you to the table. The modern approach to *kansha* is marveling at the clever human beings who invented and engineered these appliances!

Each rice cooker is typically sold with its own measuring cup that should be used with that particular appliance. These cups vary in size but typically hold 180 cc (cubic centimeters), which is the size of a *gō*, the traditional Japanese cup (modern Japanese cups hold 200 cc), and is roughly equivalent to the ³⁄₄-cup measure in the American kitchen. The lines marked on the rice-cooker bowl indicate the amount of water needed to cook rice that has been measured with that cup, so if you want to use these lines to guide you in measuring water, you must use that cup to measure the raw rice.

SOY MILK MAKER If you like fresh *yuba*, find yourself eating tōfu several times a week, and/or drink one or more glasses of soy milk a day, buying an automatic soy milk maker is a wise investment. Good ones are efficient (higher yield) and simple to operate and clean. (In this instance, *kansha* appreciation is for modern technology and inventive thinking.) Most soy milk makers will produce rich milk (about 10 percent soy solids) with a nutty, sweet flavor. (See the information on soy solids in the soy milk entry on page 279.) If you prefer, the richness can be thinned with filtered water. And if you make your own soy milk you get a bonus: *okara* (page 274).

Blanching and boiling

Blanching (submerging foods briefly in bubbling-hot liquid) and boiling are often performed to shorten cooking time later and/or to draw out, and be rid of, *aku* (the natural froth or scum that clings to foods and cooking vessels). Timing can vary from less than a minute (little more than dunking and swishing the item in the boiling liquid) to nearly an hour (boiling fresh bamboo shoots, for example). The liquid can be plain water, salted water, acidulated water (water to which vinegar has been added), *nuka-jiru* (water to which rice bran has been added), and *togi-jiru* (the cloudy first rinsing water from washing rice). When *nuka* is used with vegetables such as bamboo shoots, or *togi-jiru* is used with corn, daikon, burdock root, or asparagus, the rice oil and starch in the *nuka* and *togi-jiru* neutralize bitter enzymes, allowing the natural sugars in the vegetables to be more noticeable. When I use these rice oil–imbued liquids to blanch vegetables, I call the procedure "tender-prepping."

I urge you to save water, fuel, and personal energy by using the same pot of boiling water to blanch different foods in succession. When using tap water for blanching, put fresh items—leafy greens or carrots, for example—into the pot first (some chlorophyll or carotene may leach out, making the water green or orange, respectively, but that is fine). Then, blanch any fresh starchy root vegetables (daikon, burdock root, potatoes, lotus root). *Konnyaku* and *shirataki* (page 268) are next. Fried tōfu (page 282)—thick blocks or thin sheets—come last, and is left in the pot until you can see swirls of oil form on the surface (about 30 seconds). By blanching foods in this order, you will be discarding only one batch of greasy water, thus saving resources (fuel and water) and personal energy (no need to stop and wash the same pot three or four times) as you prepare a meal.

Use long cooking chopsticks, tongs, a slotted spoon, or a fine-mesh skimmer to remove foods from the blanching water. Leafy greens are often plunged into cold water (then squeezed to remove moisture), but most other blanched foods are allowed to cool naturally to room temperature. Tender-prepped vegetables (boiled with *nuka* or blanched in *togi-jiru*) are briefly rinsed to remove rice-bran residue. Each recipe will instruct you accordingly. The mechanics of blanching leafy greens are fully explained in Blanching Bundles of Greens, page 100.

Braising and simmering

Braised and simmered dishes, what the Japanese call *nimono*, are included in nearly every meal, most often served at room temperature, rather than piping hot or chilled. The type of stock used (plain kelp, or dried mushroom, radish, or gourd) and the length of the cooking time (a few minutes to an hour or longer) vary widely. Flavors also vary: some braised or simmered dishes emphasize sweet tastes, and others sour or salty tastes. Each recipe offers specific instructions, but here I want to point out two features shared among *nimono* dishes: the use of an *otoshi-buta* and the "alphabetical" order in which seasonings are added to the pot.

OTOSHI-BUTA Literally "dropped" lid, an *otoshi-buta* (pictured on page 240) is a circular lid that sits directly on braising food, rather than on the rim of the cooking vessel. It keeps food moist as it simmers, even in shallow liquid. Ideally, it is just slightly smaller in diameter (about 1 inch) than the pot with which it is paired, which allows the braising liquid to reduce and concentrate flavors slowly.

Otoshi-buta are traditionally made from wood, usually fragrant but sturdy *hinoki*, a type of cedar. In place of a knob, the lid is fitted with a short standing handle set in a groove that runs completely across its center. Most *otsohi-buta* are flat on the bottom—so they sit flush on the simmering food—but some have parallel ripplelike ridges. This textured surface is less likely to adhere to food. Moistening the lid with water just before setting it atop braising foods, or laying a piece of *kombu* left over from stock making between the braising food and the lid, also helps keep the wooden lid from sticking.

Today, some *otoshi-buta* are made from heat-resistant silicone. A play on the words for "pig" (*buta*) and "lid" (*futa* changes to *buta* when an adjective such as *otoshi* precedes it) accounts for the seemingly bizarre shape of these modern *otoshi-buta*: a pig face with a protruding snout.

COOKING IN "ALPHABETICAL" ORDER (SA, SHI, SU, SÉ, SO) Unlike *kanji* (calligraphy) that typically have several possible pronunciations, *hiragana* is a Japanese syllabary in which each symbol is always pronounced the same way. A combination of these two writing systems is used for most documents and literature (another syllabary, *katakana*, following the same order as *hiragana*, is used for emphasis and to write words of foreign origin). Japanese dictionaries and other reference works, however, will list words and topics in (constant) *hiragana* order, in much the same way that English-language reference books alphabetize word lists, beginning with A, then B, C, and so forth.

To maximize flavor and achieve tenderness with minimal cooking time (frugal use of fuel), the Japanese speak of cooking in "alphabetical" order: *Sa, Shi, Su, Sé, So*. What this refers to is the order in which various seasonings, such as saké, *satō* (sugar), *shio* (salt), *shōyu* (soy sauce), *su* (vinegar), and miso, should be added. If you are unfamiliar with *hiragana*, the order will seem arbitrary. It is worth remembering, however, especially when cooking with *kambutsu* (dried foods). I point out examples of this throughout *Kansha*, but *Sa, Shi, Su, Sé, So* is especially important when making Slow-Simmered Soybeans and Mushrooms (page 136) and Granny's Sun-Dried Radish (page 142).

Cutting and slicing

Although Japanese cooking is often associated with expensive knives, most home cooks will do very nicely with just one all-purpose knife, what the Japanese call a *bunka-bōchō* ("culture" blade) or *santoku-bōchō* ("three-feature" blade).

SANTOKU-BŌCHŌ The three features of a *santoku* knife (pictured on page 35) are a broad blade, a pointed tip, and hefty weight. This combination makes the knife suitable for a variety of cutting techniques, and it will be all you need when making the recipes in this book.

For basic slicing, grasp the knife in one of two ways: either place your thumb extended along the top (noncutting edge) of the blade with your index finger against the outside of the blade (your remaining fingers are curled around the handle), or position your thumb flat against the inside of the blade with your index finger stretched along the top. Fingers on your other hand should firmly grasp the item to be sliced. Most cooks will keep the thumb of this hand tucked under curled fingers that allow knuckles to barely touch the inside of the blade, retreating as the knife advances. Whenever possible, place vegetables flat against a cutting board to steady them.

SLICING AND SHREDDING Here are a few specialized cuts that I call for in the recipes.

SEN-GIRI To make thread-thin shreds, or *sen-giri* (one thousand slices), first slice several tissue-thin pieces from your vegetable. Unlike Western knife techniques that flex the wrist and bring the knife blade down to cut, Japanese slicing technique pushes the forearm forward while keeping the wrist steady. In other words, the cutting is accomplished with a pushing-away motion, rather than a bringing-down motion. Bring the blade back as needed to the starting position and repeat pushing away. Stack the slices in an overlapping pattern, much as you might spread a deck of playing cards. Repeat the slicing action, always pushing away, not down, while thinking "thin, thin, thin." Speed will come with practice. Aim for uniform pieces, maintaining a steady rhythm. Here are a few specialized cuts that I call for in the recipes.

KUSHI-GATA Literally "comb cut," *kushi-gata* produces thin crescents or half-moons, or wedges. The classic *kushi-gata* technique is used when cutting bamboo shoots lengthwise, which produces slices or wedges that indeed look like little combs with teeth. The blade of the knife is held perpendicular to the vegetable. Round onions, especially those that will be sautéed, are usually cut *kushi-gata* style to bring out their natural sweetness. When a chunky appearance is desired, the onion is cut into thick wedges; when matchstick strips are desired, the slices are cut paper-thin so the layers will separate when cooked.

RAN-GIRI This technique produces multifaceted pieces that absorb flavorful pan juices but do not crumble with long braising or stewing. The cut is especially good for cylindrical vegetables and tubers, such as carrots, parsnips, burdock root, sweet potatoes, and lotus root, that may be thicker at one end than the other. It ensures the pieces will be uniform in size, so they will cook more evenly. Begin at the thicker end and slice on the diagonal, starting $1/2$ inch from the edge. Keeping the knife pointing in the same diagonal direction, roll the vegetable toward you (about one-third turn) and slice again. Continue in this manner, adjusting the length and angle as needed to produce small, multifaceted, uniform chunks.

SASAGAKI Literally "young bamboo leaf cut," this technique produces slim, tapered, multisurfaced slices. It is used most frequently on burdock root, but it can also be used on carrots, parsnips, or celery. The knife is held, cutting edge facing away from you, as though whittling a pencil. When the vegetable is thicker than $1/2$ inch, it is often scored (with the tip of the knife drawing long, lengthwise strokes) before it is whittled. If you are working with even thicker root vegetables, you can cut the root in half lengthwise, then cut crosswise on the diagonal into thin half-moons.

SOGI-GIRI The name for this technique comes from the verb *sogu*, which describes a shaving motion performed with a blade. In a culinary context, the blade is a knife held at an angle that puts it nearly parallel to the food (placed on a board) it is cutting, producing slim, broad, flat slices. In the vegetarian kitchen, this technique is often used when preparing shiitaké mushrooms, as it evens out the thickness of the caps and at the same time exposes more surfaces (encouraging a transfer of flavors between the mushrooms and the broth in which they are simmering).

Dry-roasting

In the *kansha* kitchen, dry-roasting, which is done in a heavy skillet on the stove top, is primarily used to enhance the flavor, aroma, and texture of sesame seeds and *nuka* (rice bran). You can also dry-roast minced air-dried *kabocha* seeds for adding to freshly cooked rice. It is best to dry-roast foods just before using them; roasting releases oil that can go rancid.

NUKA A by-product of rice polishing, *nuka* has two important culinary roles: it is used to make a pickling medium and to extract *aku* (unwanted enzymes, naturally occurring chemicals) from certain foods, such as bamboo shoots. In performing both tasks, the *nuka* will be most effective if it is dry-roasted first. Sometimes you can purchase *nuka* that is already roasted; check the label on the bag. If it has not been roasted, here is what you need to do: Place a heavy skillet over low heat. Add the *nuka* and spread it with a wooden spatula to make a thin, even layer. Stir occasionally and gently shake or jiggle the skillet to keep the *nuka* in motion. After a minute or so, the *nuka* should begin to color ever so slightly. Dry-roast, watching carefully to avoid scorching, for 2 or 3 minutes, or until slightly aromatic. Remove the skillet from the heat and allow the retained heat to finish the roasting process. Let the dry-roasted *nuka* cool in the pan, or transfer to a dish to cool faster. If not using right away, store cooled dry-roasted *nuka* in a resealable plastic bag, tightly lidded jar, or other container. Store it in the refrigerator or on a cool, dark pantry shelf and use it within a few months.

SESAME SEEDS When sesame seeds are exposed to heat, their oil releases an appetizing aroma and rich flavor. But this oil can go rancid rather quickly if the roasted seeds are exposed to air. I recommend that you dry-roast only a few tablespoons of sesame seeds at a time to ensure their freshness.

Place the seeds—white or black—in a small, heavy skillet over medium-high heat. Stir occasionally with a wooden spatula or gently rotate the skillet in a circular motion. In about 1 minute, white sesame seeds will begin to darken to a golden color and black seeds may appear duller, that is, have a matte, rather than shiny, surface (when roasted black seeds are ground to a paste they become lustrous). A few seeds may pop as the warm air trapped between the kernel and hull expands. Stir the seeds for another 20 to 30 seconds. The skillet retains heat, so the seeds will continue to roast even after the pan is taken off the stove. If the seeds look in danger of scorching, transfer them to a dish to cool faster.

Let the roasted seeds cool to room temperature before transferring them to a lidded container. Store on a dark, dry, cool pantry shelf for no more than a week or so.

Frying

Properly fried foods are crisp and crunchy, not greasy. To ensure your efforts are effective, each recipe that calls for frying will have specific advice for you. In addition, here are two general points worth remembering: Monitoring and maintaining oil temperature when frying in deep oil (about $1^1/_2$ inches) is the key to greaseless fried foods (I find that a small Chinese wok, narrow at the base and wider at the top, helps me achieve this). Resisting the urge to poke, prod, and flip foods when they are in hot oil is the key to keeping batter and coating clinging to your morsels (a small, long-handled fine-mesh skimmer will enable you to keep the oil litter-free should bits of the coating fall off).

Most Japanese home cooks and professional chefs find long, unvarnished wooden chopsticks, called *saibashi* (pictured on page 240), indispensable for deep-frying. You can use them to check on the temperature of the oil: Place the tip of the chopstick in the hot oil. If small bubbles immediately form around it, the oil is about 350°F. You can test oil temperature with any unvarnished wood, such as a bamboo skewer, but long chopsticks are also handy for wielding the foods in and out of the pot, keeping the cook's hands safely away from the hot oil.

Grinding and grating

Grinding, mashing, crushing, puréeing, and grating vegetables, fruits, seeds, and nuts releases their full flavor and aroma while making them (and their nutrients) easier to digest.

GRINDING Most Japanese cooks use a combination of modern (electric-powered) kitchen tools, such as food processors and blenders, and old-fashioned (self-powered) implements, such as a mortar and a pestle, to grind, mash, and crush foods.

The *suribachi* (grooved ceramic mortar) used with a wooden *surikogi* (pestle) is an excellent tool for crushing, especially when small quantities of dry-roasted sesame seeds or tōfu are called for in making a sauce. Since the *suribachi* also serves as the vessel in which foods to be sauced will be tossed, none of the precious sauce is lost to the bowl.

To use a *suribachi* to best advantage, place it on a non-slip surface, such as a silicone pad or wrung-out dampened washcloth. It is also nice to have someone else hold the mortar steady for you as you grind. Hold the base of the *surikogi* firmly with one hand and cup the palm of your other hand over the top. Then, pressing down from the top, rotate the *surikogi* in a circular motion, scraping the bottom of it against the sides of the mortar and pulver-

izing and mashing the foods as you work. This motion will make a rough, grating noise. Indeed, the word *surikogi* is written with calligraphy for "thunder," "powder," and "wooden stick." (The best pestles are made of *sanshō*, the bumpy, rough wood of the peppercorn plant, though most commercial ones are made of cedar.)

When using a *suribachi*, alternate hands when they tire (hand on top pressing down and hand on bottom drawing circles), and alternate direction (clockwise and counter-clockwise) to improve effectiveness in crushing.

To clean a *suribachi*, soak it in warm, sudsy water for several minutes, then use a stiff-bristled brush to scrape down the sides in the same direction as the grooves. Rinse, invert, and let dry naturally. No special care is needed for the pestle; wash it as you would any wooden kitchen tool.

GRATING Performed both in the kitchen and at table, grating is done on thorn-spiked tools called *oroshi-gané*. *Kané* (or *gané* when an adjective such as *oroshi*, meaning "to grate," proceeds it) means metal, and indeed the original implements were made of tin and copper. Classic, professional graters are still made of layered metals; the thorns are notches that expose copper beneath a tin surface. But many foods, including daikon, ginger, and cucumber, can take on an unpleasant metallic taste and discolor when grated on metal tools. I recommend you use round ceramic graters, the kind that have a well, or moat, around the outer rim (pictured on page viii). Models with nonskid silicone or rubberized rings on the bottom are especially good.

GRATING GINGER AND EXTRACTING GINGER JUICE Peel or scrape away the skin from fresh ginger and rub it against the thornlike protrusions of the grater. Gather the gratings into mounds and serve as a garnish or condiment. If you require ginger juice, press the gratings with your fingertips to extract the juice. The skin, peel, and fibrous pulp can be steeped in boiling water to cover for 10 minutes, then strained and added to tea to spice it up.

GRATING DAIKON AND CUCUMBER Always grate daikon and cucumber as close as possible to the time when you will be consuming them. As already noted, I highly recommend a ceramic grater for this task. It will help preserve the spicy sweetness and air-volatile vitamin C of daikon and the vivid emerald color and sweet flavor of cucumber. Also, it will not bruise or shred either vegetable.

Daikon is usually peeled before grating. If you do peel daikon, get into the habit of thickly peeling it and setting the peels aside for use in other dishes, such as Spicy Stir-Fry (page 122) and Heaven-and-Earth Tempura Pancakes (page 109). Once you peel the radish, place the peels in a resealable bag or a lidded container to limit exposure to air that leads to a loss of nutrients and diminished flavor. The peels can be refrigerated for several days. Or, if you have a dehydrator, turn the peels into homemade *kiriboshi daikon.*

As you grate the radish or cucumber, collect it in a fine-mesh strainer set over a bowl. The professional Japanese kitchen will use *sarashi* (page 250) to line the strainer, but most home cooks will use a paper coffee filter. Gather up the edges of the cloth or filter and press lightly. The liquid that results can be used to make salad dressings or a spicy health tonic: sweeten with sugar or maple syrup and add a few drops of fresh lemon juice.

ZESTING CITRUS In the past few years, rasplike graters, imported originally from the United States, have become popular for removing the zest from citrus peels, while leaving behind the white pith.

Mixing and tossing

In the Japanese kitchen, many foods are lightly tossed in sauces. Making these saladlike dishes, requires no special tools or techniques. The dish that does necessitate both special instruction and equipment is Classic sushi rice (page 17).

HANDAI In preparing sushi rice, freshly cooked, still warm rice is seasoned with sweetened vinegar in much the same way a salad of delicate lettuces is tossed with a dressing. Ideally, the seasoning of the cooked rice is done using a *handai* (literally "rice tub") made from *kiso sawara*, a fine-textured, pale, sturdy wood that exudes a pleasant cedarlike aroma.

The tubs are about 2 1/2 inches deep, flat-bottomed, and wide (14 inches in diameter is the perfect size for seasoning 4 to 6 cups of cooked rice). The size allows the rice to be distributed over a larger area than most bowls would permit, and because *handai* are made of porous wood, condensation from the rapidly cooling rice does not puddle at the bottom the way it would in a metal, glass, or plastic bowl. *Handai* are available at most stores that cater to a serious Japanese cooking clientele. A tub banded in copper (the bands help it hold its shape) and reinforced with *aotaké* ("green" bamboo) is especially good.

Before you use a *handai* for the first time, set it in the sink, fill it with boiling water, and let it sit until the water is cool. Refill with boiling water, but this time add 1 cup vinegar (the more astringent the vinegar, the better) to the water. The vinegar will bleach, disinfect, and help "cure" the wood and remove the sticky *yani* (sap). Wash the tub with hot water and mild dishwashing detergent, scrubbing with the rough side of a sponge or a bottlebrush. Pay special attention to the circular edge where the side and bottom meet. Rinse thoroughly with hot water, and turn upside down to drain. When dry (still moist to the touch but light again in color), pour in 2 to 3 tablespoons vinegar and rub it over the inside of the tub with your hand. Turn the tub upside down again and let it dry thoroughly.

Wash the *handai* immediately after each use, soaking it in hot water with mild dishwashing detergent and scrubbing away any clinging rice grains with a brush. Rinse with hot water and drain; turn it upside down to dry. Rub 2 to 3 tablespoons vinegar over the inside of the tub. Store upside down in a large plastic bag. Depending on your climate, keep the bag tightly closed during dry or cold weather to seal in moisture—so the wood doesn't shrink, causing the copper bands to slip out of place—and leave it open during hot and/or humid months to increase air circulation—to prevent the growth of mold. A blue-green mold called *aokabi* in Japanese is the most commonly seen; it is related to penicillin, so those with allergies to antibiotics should take heed.

If mold appears on your *handai*, rinse it with scalding hot water and then rub it with spent green tea leaves (use leaves enclosed in a bag to make cleanup easier). Green tea kills most mold spores that grow on wood and discourages future development and growth of them. It also keeps mites from taking up residence in the grain of the wood. Do not be alarmed if, after several tea treatments, the wood assumes a mild tea aroma and pale green coloration.

SHAMOJI *Shamoji*, or rice paddles, are used to scoop up cooked rice from your pot or rice cooker. They come in various sizes and are made from various natural (bamboo and other woods) and manmade (plastic) materials. Electric rice cookers often come with a small plastic paddle. Wooden *shamoji* are also useful for sautéing and flipping. To extend the life of your wooden paddle, hand wash it (allow it to dry naturally), rather than put it in a dishwasher.

UCHIWA The Japanese fan away steam from freshly cooked rice before condensation can cause puddles to form (they also fan-cool most briefly blanched vegetables, rather than "refresh" them in cold water). A flat fan called *uchiwa*, is the best and most attractive tool, though a stiff, flat piece of cardboard will work, too.

Marinating

In the Japanese kitchen, many types of foods are placed in marinades—liquid or paste—that cause significant changes in their appearance, flavor, and texture. Two categories of dishes result: *ohitashi*, from the verb *hitasu*, or "to steep," and *tsukémono*, from the verb *tsukéru*, most often translated as "to pickle."

In the case of *ohitashi*, each recipe will instruct you in the best procedure and timing; no special equipment is needed, though glass, ceramic, or enamel-lined metal containers (the latter are called *horo* ware) are best because they are nonreactive. Foods set to steep in plastic containers sometimes pick up unwanted odors from previously stored foods, and the containers become easily discolored.

An entire chapter has been devoted to the subject of *tsukémono*. There you will find a full discussion of the various techniques involving salt, vinegar, miso, soy sauce, and other ingredients used in marinades. Special tools (and alternatives for them) for making *tsukémono* are described in the chapter, too, but the same general principle that applies to steeping is also good advice for making *tsukémono*: use containers made of nonreactive materials.

Rolling, shaping, and molding

The Japanese delight in configuring foods to decorative effect. Often it is a seasonal or festive motif that is chosen to focus the diner's attention on the time of year or the special occasion the meal celebrates. But the aesthetic pleasure derived from cleverly fashioning foods is not the only reward. Practical benefits also accrue: decorative pieces such as compact rolls, logs, and cubes are easier to serve and eat.

Specialty tools and gadgets such as *maku no uchi kata*, *nagashi kan*, and *sudaré* are used in this book to ease preparation and improve the appearance of certain dishes. Several recipes guide you in using your hands (page 45) and plastic wrap (page 43) to shape and mold rice. Comprehensive instructions on how to prepare each dish are provided in the recipes.

MAKU NO UCHI KATA Traditionally, *maku no uchi* (pictured on page 240) and other rice molds were made from carved wood. Most professional Japanese kitchens continue to use wooden molds, washing them by hand, letting them dry naturally, and monitoring them for warping or cracking. Most home cooks use plastic rice molds. These also need to be washed by hand, in hot, sudsy water. Because dishwashers are not standard kitchen equipment in Japanese homes, few household gadgets are designed to withstand the heat that would make them dishwasher-safe. Details on how to shape rice using this mold can be found in Rice with Salted Cherry Blossoms (page 25).

NAGASHI KAN These rectangular metal molds (pictured on page 240) with a removable inner tray make unmolding aspics easy. Some come with dividers so that 6 or 9 individual cubes can be made at one time, though most will form a single loaf, about 6 by 4 inches and 2 inches deep. The molds are made of thin sheets of metal that can tolerate high temperatures. Care needs to be taken to ensure they do not get bent out of shape, especially the inserts.

Fit the tray flat in the box (and the dividers, if using them) and pour in the liquid gelatin. When firm, unmold by lifting up and removing the inner tray. Spread the flanged sides of the inner tray slightly to help loosen the gelatin; slide out the block and cut as desired. If you have used dividers, lift them up to remove; no need to cut.

A glass or nonstick loaf pan can be used in place of a *nagashi kan*. Or, individual servings can be prepared in silicone muffin pans and inverted onto plates to unmold.

SUDARÉ Slatted bamboo mats called *sudaré* or *maki su* can vary widely in overall size, size of slats, and surface tex-

ture. A mat measuring about 8 by 10 inches, with 1/8-inch-wide slats that are smooth on one side and rounded on the other, offers the greatest flexibility. When using a mat, always place it on your work surface with the slats running horizontally; if only one edge is tasseled, position it farthest from you.

Rinse the mats immediately after use in warm, sudsy water. If necessary, use a toothpick to remove bits of food lodged between the slats. Rinse carefully and let dry naturally. If sticky rice grains are firmly trapped between the slats, soak the mat in warm, sudsy water to cover for about 10 minutes, then scrub gently (parallel to the slats) with a bottlebrush, rinse well, lean the mat against a wall or other straight surface with the slats running vertically, and let dry naturally.

Sudaré are used for rolling sushi and for shaping other foods into cylinders, such as bundles of blanched leafy greens. Outside the kitchen, the word *sudaré* refers to bamboo curtains hung in the summertime that allow cool breezes to pass into homes and afford privacy from passersby.

For directions on rolling sushi, see Festive Flower Sushi Rolls, page 33. To roll cylinders of blanched greens, arrange the greens horizontally (parallel with the slats) on the mat. Place them so that half the stem ends are on your right and the other half are on your left. This will help even out the thickness of the roll. Place your thumbs under the near corners of the slatted mat. Hold the edges by pinching with your index fingers. This will leave three fingers "free" on each hand to hold the greens in place as you lift and roll away from you. Lift up the edge of the mat and flip it over the greens, aiming to make contact just beyond the bundle. With one hand, hold the bottom of the mat flat on the work surface while tugging back slightly on the rolled portion. Continue to roll to enclose the greens completely. You should have a snug cylinder. Hold the mat-wrapped roll over the sink and squeeze gently to release excess moisture. Use rubber bands to secure both ends of the rolled mat, then place in a plasic bag in the refrigerator for at least 20 minutes or up to several hours.

When ready to serve, remove the rubber bands and unfurl the mat. Place the cylinder on your cutting board with the mat loosely draped over it. Using the edge of the mat to guide your knife, cut the cylinder into 4 to 6 bundles. Lay the bundles lengthwise or stand upright to serve.

Softening dried ingredients

Dried ingredients, known collectively as *kambutsu*, need to be softened before they can be consumed, and most, though not all, must be cooked. Because not all *kambutsu* are handled in the same manner, details are for provided with the description of each ingredient in A Catalog of Ingredients that begins on page 253.

The liquid that results from soaking certain, but not all, dried ingredients becomes flavorful stock. Information on softening *kombu* (kelp), dried shiitaké mushrooms, *kampyō* (gourd ribbons), and *kiriboshi daikon* can be found in the Stocks and Soups chapter (pages 72–89). Each recipe calling for dried beans describes the most suitable soaking and cooking process for making that particular dish.

Straining, draining, and pressing

Many recipes will instruct you to strain a liquid to remove unwanted matter; to line strainers with cloth or a coffee filter to easily separate solids from liquid; to drain unwanted liquid from packages; or to press foods such as tōfu, wrapped in cloth and sandwiched between two small cutting boards or other sturdy, flat surfaces to further remove moisture. If you will be making homemade tōfu, I highly recommend fashioning a cloth bag to strain the *go* (soybean mash).

Although ordinary colanders, strainers, and lint-free kitchen cloths will be fine in most cases, the traditional Japanese kitchen does use a few special items that are especially well suited to these tasks.

MISO KOSHI The Japanese have a special strainer for mixing miso into broth. Called a *miso koshi* (pictured on page 240), it has a vertical handle with a deep mesh cup. Many *miso koshi* are fitted with a hook that allows the strainer to sit on the rim of a pot. Some come with a matching ladle, though an ordinary soupspoon works well for scooping up miso from the package and pressing it through the mesh strainer. Many types of miso contain bits of rice, barley, and/or chunky beans. Although these bits do not need to be removed from miso-thickened broths, many Japanese prefer to do so, since soup is traditionally sipped directly from a bowl, not eaten with a spoon.

If you do not have a *miso koshi*, you can combine the miso and several spoonfuls of stock from the soup pot in a small bowl and whisk to dissolve the paste. Ladle in a bit more of the stock, stir to mix, and add the thinned miso directly to the pot, or through a strainer if you wish to remove textured bits.

SARASHI The Japanese use a muslinike cotton cloth called *sarashi* for all sorts of tasks, culinary and otherwise (until disposable diapers became available in Japan about twenty-five years ago, cloth diapers were made from *sarashi*; some undergarments and handkerchiefs are still made from it). In the kitchen, the fine-woven texture of *sarashi* is ideal for lining strainers, making condensation-catching caps for steamer lids, and (when moistened) wrapping delicate dried ingredients such as sheets of *yuba* or dried wheat gluten to be softened.

The cloth is sold in bolts about 10 yards long and 13 inches wide. In Japan, professional kitchen supply shops carry *sarashi*, as do the babywear sections (rather than housewares sections) of department stores (maybe there is a cloth diaper revival among today's young couples?).

Each recipe that calls for *sarashi* will suggest a suitable substitute. When using any cloth for culinary purposes, it is best to rinse it first in plain water without soap or detergents (it is hard to be rid of the soapy smell). If you are concerned about hygiene, boil the cloths briefly before wringing out and air-drying.

Steaming

Cooking food with steam (moist indirect heat) is fuel efficient and typically produces less-cloying and often healthier dishes than frying, grilling, or simmering. Having the right equipment will help you easily integrate steamed dishes into your menu plans.

Recipes for steamed foods in this book require a flat-bottomed steamer. Adjustable baskets or racks that are sloped or have a central pole or handle will not work. Neither will a double boiler, because the top pot must have a perforated bottom to allow steam to circulate throughout the vessel.

Professional kitchens in Japan use square metal steamers (they hold more for the same burner space); most home kitchens have round ones. Chinese woven-bamboo steamers that sit stacked above boiling water in a wok are also popular in Japan. Whatever type of steamer you use, make sure the water in the pan is at least 1/2 inch below the bottom of the rack holding the food.

If you don't already have a steamer (and don't wish to buy one), you can improvise with a deep, wide pot (one that has a tight-fitting lid) and a few empty tall cans of the same height (tops and bottoms removed). Fill your pot with several inches of water (your cans need to be at least 1/2 inch taller than the water level). Arrange your cans at intervals that will provide a steady base for a heatproof flat plate, then place the plate on top of them. Make sure the plate is 1/4 to 1/2 inch smaller in diameter than the pot so the steam can circulate well.

Always use a cloth cap on the steamer lid to prevent condensation from forming on the underside of the lid and dripping onto your steamed foods. "Dew-catcher" is the poetic name many old-fashioned Japanese cooks affectionately use for this highly practical piece of cloth. You can easily fashion a cap from a tea towel. Select one several inches larger than your lid. Lay the towel on a flat surface, and place the lid—knob facing up—in the center. Gather up the edges of the cloth and secure them with a rubber band around the knob. If you find yourself steaming foods frequently, you may want to make a more permanent cap by sewing a narrow track around the edge of the towel and threading elastic through it. This lid cover will look a bit like a shower cap.

True steamers have handles on the top layer that enable you to remove it to a cool surface easily with pot holders. To remove hot foods from your improvised steamer safely, you will need to use a sling in addition to pot holders. The sling needs to be a narrow piece of sturdy cloth, long enough to extend well beyond the rim of the pot. Place the sling beneath the plate before steaming. Set the item or items to be steamed on the plate. Place the lid on the pot, fold the end pieces of the sling over the top of the lid, and secure the ends with a clip. When finished steaming, move the pot away from the stove, remove the clip, and then remove the lid. Holding both ends of the sling with pot holder–protected hands, remove the plate.

kuruma-bu

ita-bu

kuro mamé

adzuki

daizu

millet

kudzu

kuchinashi no mi

Japanese-style
brown rice

Japanese-style
white rice

kampyō

aka-jiso

salted cherry blossoms

yukari

hoshi yuba

dried shiitaké
mushrooms

kiriboshi daikon

black rice

A CATALOG OF INGREDIENTS

Authentic Japanese vegan fare can be made with many of the same ingredients you already use, but one of my goals in writing *Kansha* was to introduce you to new foodstuffs that will expand your culinary horizons. As a result, many of the ingredients called for in the recipes may be unfamiliar to you. Whenever possible, I have included information about these items in the recipes themselves. When those explanations became cumbersome or repetitive, I placed additional information in this catalog. These entries, listed in alphabetical order, supplement the instructions and information included in the recipes and their accompanying text.

Glancing at this list, you may wonder whether you will be able to find some of the more exotic items. Although not every member of my advisory council (volunteers scattered around the world who helped me test recipes) was able to source every item, most of them could find nearly everything. And many of them were surprised at how readily available such seemingly foreign items were.

Rather than attempt to list vendors here—such information is too tied to specific locales and rapidly becomes outdated—I make the same suggestion to you that I made to my volunteer testers: begin your shopping expedition with an online search, using both the Japanese names and their English equivalents when I have provided both. English alone generally won't do, as English labels are invariably incomplete and confusing and are often incorrect. Also, search for stores in your community. First, look for stores that carry Asian foodstuffs and then contact them directly with requests for specific items. Next, try health-food stores or specialty supermarkets; they often carry large selections of Japanese food products. Finally, check farmers' markets and other independent vendors that carry local, sustainably farmed, fresh produce.

Bitter melon

Looking somewhat like a bumpy, chubby cucumber, bitter melon (*goya* or *nigauri* in Japanese) is a common ingredient in the cuisine of Okinawa. Other Asian food cultures also enjoy this subtropical "fruit," and you are likely to find it in the summertime in cities with a large Chinese population (it is a warm-weather crop). Look for firm, dark green, pebbly skin. Flabbiness, yellowing, and black spots are all signs of unwanted aging. Store loosely wrapped in newspaper in your vegetable bin for up to 5 days.

Cabbage

In most parts of Japan, compact heads of green cabbage are available throughout the year and find their way into a wide variety of dishes. Broad outer leaves are blanched and used as wrappers (think stuffed cabbage rolls), gossamer-thin shreds shaved from inner leaves are often mounded as a backdrop for breaded fried foods, while thin slivers from the stiff core are commonly made into quick-fix pickles.

HAKUSAI Literally "white leaves," *hakusai* is the Japanese name for what Americans call Chinese cabbage, a crinkly leafed, loosely packed, oblong head of cabbage that can be enjoyed cooked or raw. Typically, outer leaves are green. Napa cabbage and bok choy make fine substitutes.

HARU KYABETSU In Japan, *haru kyabetsu* comes to market in March and April—hence its name meaning "spring cabbage." The loose leafy heads of this incredibly sweet, tender cabbage are enjoyed raw or briefly steamed or skillet seared. Crinkly leaved Savoy cabbage or young, tender Brussels sprouts are good substitutes.

Daikon

Written with calligraphy for "big" or "important" and "root," daikon (*Raphanus sativus* var. *longipinnatus*), a type of white radish, can be both "big" (they average 12 inches long and 2½ inches in diameter and weigh 2 to 3 pounds each) and "important." As with many foods enjoyed in modern Japan, daikon likely traveled there by way of China. The earliest written mention of it is in the *Kojiki* and *Nihon Shoki*, eighth-century Japanese documents that contain myths and chronicle history. The variety known as Aokubi (literally "green necked") is easy to grow and stores well, making it the most readily available type.

If you will be grating daikon (page 247), always do it just before serving to preserve the rich amount of vitamin C that it naturally contains. All varieties have tasty, nutritious leaves, bursting with vitamin A and calcium. To extend postharvest quality of both the roots and the tufts of leaves, slice off the verdant tops just below where they attach to the firm, bulbous root. Wrap both the leaves and the root in damp paper towels, then in newspaper. Keep at very cool room temperature or refrigerate.

Daikon are shredded and dried to make *kiriboshi daikon* (page 263), an inexpensive pantry item that frugal Japanese households depend on to stretch the food budget and expand menus.

Édamamé

A favorite beer snack in Japan, *édamamé* (fresh green soybeans) come to market in their fuzzy pods still clinging to bundled branches. If a farmers' market near you sells the sweet, nutritious raw beans in the pod, grab them—but with gloved hands. The fresh pods are tapered with a sharp tip, and they are tough to pull off the branches. To avoid painful poking (or worse, piercing), wear gardening gloves when handling the pods. To benefit from their rich nutrients, and savor their naturally sweet and nutty flavor at its peak, cook them as soon as possible after purchase.

If you have cooked the beans and will be serving them later the same day, store them in their pods in the refrigerator, and then sprinkle them with kosher salt just before you set them out on the table. The Japanese eat them by placing a whole pod between their teeth and pressing gently to split it open, which pops the beans into their mouths (save the pods to add to your compost). To store freshly cooked soybeans for several days, shell them and refrigerate in a resealable bag, pressing out all the air as you close it. They can be frozen for longer storage, but most home freezers do not get them cold fast enough to prevent freezer burn. You may find that commercially processed frozen beans—buy them in their pods rather than shelled, if possible—are a better bet.

Eggplant

All "true" Japanese eggplants (*nasu*) have no visible seeds and dark (nearly black) purple skin and sepals (the petal-like pieces surrounding the stem). Many varieties of Japanese eggplant exist, but the ones most commonly seen in American markets (or grown from seeds available outside Japan) are about 3 inches long, 3 inches in diameter at their fattest point, and weigh about 3 ounces each. Also widely available are *naga nasu*, literally "long" eggplants that, as their name suggests, are slender and can be 6 inches or longer.

Other Asian eggplant varieties have pink or lavender skin, with the sepals the same color or green. The flesh of these varieties tends to be soft and a bit spongy. If they are the only kind you can find, dice them rather than thinly slice them. Large, bulbous European varieties tend to have green sepals, tough peels, and obvious seeds. They are not well suited to pickling, though they can be used in Eggplant Two Ways (page 125).

Fava bean

Fava beans (*sora mamé*) grow on slender stalks, with the bean-filled pods pointing toward the sky—their Japanese name, *sora mamé*, means "heaven bean" (could this be the magic beanstalk Jack climbed?). When fava beans are used, the finished dish is often called *hibari*, or "skylark."

Freshly picked pods are still fuzzy—almost velvety—and the beans inside will have green lines where they attach to the pod. If you can source such fresh produce, shell and blanch the beans as soon as you get back to your kitchen. Eat right away for a real treat. Or, if you must hold them, allow them to cool naturally, then place in a resealable bag and refrigerate for up to 3 days.

Fiddlehead fern

Fiddlehead ferns (*kogomi*) are foraged from woodland areas in many parts of the world as winter thaws into spring. Markets in some cities in America (Pacific Northwest and New England), Canada, Scotland, and Scandinavia often have fiddleheads for sale. In Japan, most of the commercially sold crop is sourced in Nagano Prefecture. Look for tightly wound tops and green stalks with few blemishes. As soon as you get them in your kitchen, soak them for 10 minutes or so in water to which a pinch of *yaki myōban* (page 284) or baking soda has been added. If you will not be cooking them right away, drain and wrap in paper towels. Place in a resealable bag and refrigerate for up to 2 days.

Flours and coatings

The Japanese use a variety of different flours, some derived from wheat, others from rice, and still others from buckwheat, beans, or starchy roots. Each recipe will guide you with specific recommendations, but here are a few guidelines on how to choose the most appropriate product for a particular purpose.

KINAKO Whole dried soybeans (*daizu*) are toasted and crushed to make *kinako*, a silky, powdery flour packed with protein and fiber. Soybeans are rich in unsaturated fat (the "good" kind of oil), and toasting the dried beans brings these oils to the surface, where they are more volatile. To keep *kinako* from turning rancid, store opened packages in the refrigerator (it usually comes in a resealable bag) and use by the expiration date printed on the package.

KUDZU Made from the root of a fast-growing vine called kudzu (pictured on page 252), this arrowrootlike starch is used as a thickener, mostly in traditional confections and puddings and as a coating for foods to be fried. In its native Japan, kudzu has been cultivated for culinary purposes since the seventh century. It was first introduced to the United States in 1876, at the Centennial International Exposition in Philadelphia, Pennsylvania, not as a food but as an ornamental plant. It was initially used to prevent soil erosion, but the climate in the southeastern United States, especially in and around the state of Georgia, was so ideal to its growth that the vine spread rapidly. Indeed, kudzu became so insidious that in 1972, the United States Department of Agriculture officially designated it a weed.

Kudzu is indispensable in the making of *goma-dōfu* (a sesame pudding that appears on Buddhist temple vegetarian menus) in the classic manner (see box, page 134). The most prized kudzu is processed from roots grown in Yoshino, near Nara. Sold in bags of about 100 grams (3 ounces), the chalky white starch is typically clumped in odd-shaped chunks. To measure it properly, crush it to a fine powder, or weigh it on a scale.

PANKO These coarse, irregular, shardlike bread crumbs are used to coat certain foods for frying, such as Crispy and Creamy Kabocha Croquettes (page 118). They produce a crunchy coating that remains crisp even when cooled to room temperature. Indeed, the Japanese penchant for including fried foods in *obentō* (lunch boxes) served at room temperature probably led to this culinary "invention." If you adhere to a strict vegan diet, check the package label to make sure that no egg, milk, or honey was part of the bread used to make the crumbs.

RICE FLOURS Rice flours—and the foods made from them—are typically well tolerated by those with allergies to wheat gluten. Flours that are labeled "glutinous rice" or "sticky rice" are made from *mochi-gomé*, a naturally sweet strain of rice that is usually steamed and pounded to make sticky (and deliciously gooey!) *omochi* (rice taffy). *Mochi-gomé* is washed, dried, and then pulverized to make *mochiko* (sticky rice flour). *Mochiko*, also known as *shirata-mako*, looks like crushed chalk. Fine, silky *jōshinko* (short-grain rice flour) is processed from *uruchi mai*, a strain that is typically boiled and eaten with other foods, what I often refer to as "table rice." *Dangoko*, or "dumpling flour," is a premixed combination of (sticky) *mochiko* and (nonsticky) *jōshinko*.

Japanese home kitchens typically have scales for weighing rice flour and other dry ingredients (metric measures are used). Most home cooks in America use volume measures—cups and spoons—for the same ingredients. I offer guidelines for both methods. Some rice flours are finely pulverized and others are quite lumpy and chalky. If you will be measuring by volume, it is important that you use the flour as is, and do not attempt to pulverize it before you measure it. My measures have taken into account the empty spaces that will surround clumps.

SOBA FLOUR Sold in many health food stores and nearly all Asian groceries, the primary use of *soba* flour (buck-wheat flour) is to make *soba* noodles. Buckwheat is gluten-free, though most commercially made *soba* noodles also contain wheat flour (check labels carefully if you have an intolerance to wheat gluten). In this book, I have used *soba* flour, mixed with soy milk, to make a savory pancake batter. I encourage you to try cooking with *soba* flour. Store it as you would any flour in a closed bag or lidded container on a cool, dark, dry shelf.

WHEAT FLOURS For tempura batter, low-gluten wheat flour is best. In most American markets, this flour is labeled "cake flour." Self-rising cake flour, which has baking soda and salt already added, is also readily available. If these products are not stocked in your local market, you can fashion your own. For cake flour, substitute an equal amount of unbleached all-purpose flour and add 1/4 teaspoon cornstarch for each 1/4 cup flour. For self-rising cake flour, add a pinch of baking soda and a pinch of table salt in addition to the cornstarch. For making *udon* noodles, a high-gluten flour yields better texture than all-purpose flour. In Japan, such flour is often called *udon ko*, and the label will indicate it is best to use for noodle making. In America, what is often sold as bread flour works well. Whole-wheat bread flour will provide greater nutrition than white wheat flour; it will also have more flavor.

Vital wheat gluten is concentrated gluten extracted from wheat. The elasticity of foods such as *nama fu* (fresh wheat gluten) depends on this gluten. If you wish to make Miso-Slathered Nama Fu (page 148), you will need to source this product. Many large supermarkets that carry health foods and foods for people with various food allergies will carry specialty flours, including vital wheat gluten.

Herbs, spices, and seasonings

Many of the distinctive herbs and spices used in the Japanese kitchen can enliven your cookery whether you choose to make classic Japanese fare or an eclectic mix of cross-cultural foods. A comprehensive list of such ingredients would be much too long to be accommodated here, so I have included only those seasonings called for in this book.

AO NORI A feathery, green aquatic plant, *ao nori* (pictured on page 265) is dried and then pulverized to make an herblike powder. It imparts a delightful seashore aroma to foods on which it is sprinkled, most often rice and noodles (though it is fabulous on potatoes—indeed, it is the favorite flavoring for potato chips in Japan). It is sometimes mixed with salt, and is sometimes added to the 7-spice blend known as *shichimi tōgarashi* (page 259). As with other herbs, rubbing it between your fingertips as you sprinkle it on food releases its full aroma.

GINGER A knobby rhizome that grows in large clusters in shallow earth, fresh ginger (*shōga*) is not interchangeable in the kitchen with other common forms, such as pickled or ground. Choose firm, shiny-skinned knobs; if possible, break off a piece to check the aroma. Some fresh ginger, especially if grown in volcanic soil (as in Hawaii), may have a bluish cast.

New ginger, sometimes labeled "young" or "stem" ginger, is pale gold with pink-tinged areas. Tender and juicy, it is ideal for pickling (briefly blanched, it will turn pink naturally when marinated in a sweet-and-sour sauce).

Mature ginger is darker and sometimes fibrous. If that is all you can find, and it seems very stringy, grate and then squeeze to extract the juice (page 246).

JAPANESE CURRY POWDER Dried blends of Indian spices, such as turmeric, coriander, cumin, fennel, and cloves, are labeled "curry powder" (*karéko* in Japanese) and have become a staple in Japanese grocery stores worldwide. S&B brand and House brand, two giants of the Japanese food industry, dominate the market. Avoid all Japanese curry roux mixtures or other moist curry products. These invariably contain large amounts of beef suet, lard, dairy, or other animal products.

Although the powder does not easily spoil, it can get musty once the tin or small glass jar is opened. To minimize deterioration, store curry powder on a cool, dry shelf, sealing it snugly after each use.

JAPANESE SPICY MUSTARD Like other mustards, Japanese spicy mustard (*karashi*) is made by crushing the dried seeds of *Brassica juncea* (mustard greens). It is sold in powdered form in small cans and as a paste in tubes. Powdered *karashi* is mixed with *iri nuka* (roasted rice bran) for making pickling pastes.

To make prepared mustard from powdered *karashi* to use as a condiment, mix it with cold water, a few drops at a time, stirring until a thick, smooth paste forms. The paste sold in tubes typically has vegetable oil added as an emulsifier. Check labels to make sure that no artificial coloring, preservatives, or animal fats have been added. Once a can of powdered mustard has been opened, store it in the refrigerator to maintain full aroma and spiciness.

MITSUBA Literally "three leaves," *mitsuba* (pictured on page 270), often called trefoil in English, is a cresslike herb. Both the leaves and the stalks are edible. It is used primarily as a garnish for soups: pouring hot broth over the chopped stalks and leaves releases the herb's fresh aroma, which is vaguely reminiscent of celery or watercress. Mitsuba is easy to grow in a pot.

MYŌGA This pale pink, bulb-shaped rhizome has a snappy, fresh gingerlike flavor. It can be eaten raw, thinly sliced lengthwise into shreds or crosswise into curling bits. On its own, or combined with finely shredded fresh green *shiso* (page 258), it makes a delightful topping for blocks of chilled tōfu drizzled with a few drops of soy sauce. Or, place shreds or curls at the bottom of a soup bowl and pour hot broth on top; the heat of the soup will release a marvelous aroma and change the flavor of the rhizome slightly (tone down the spiciness). When *myōga* is briefly blanched and marinated in a sweet-and-sour sauce, it turns vivid pink (page 198).

Myōga are usually displayed with other refrigerated produce and/or herbs at Asian groceries. Often two or three bulbs will be packaged together under clear plastic wrap. Look for firm, compact bulbs with a soft sheen. If you will be pickling them, make sure the bulbs have good, deep color, with just a hint of dark green at the base. These will have more *shikiso*, or pigmentation potential, and will turn a brighter pink color when pickled.

RADISH SPROUTS Daikon radish sprouts (pictured on page 270) are called *kaiwaré*, literally "split seashell," because they resemble shells that have opened. They have a delightful, crisp, and spicy bite and are loaded with vitamin C. You can use them as a garnish on their own or in combination with minced scallions, shredded *myōga*, and/or green *shiso*.

Increasingly, radish sprouts are grown hydroponically on spongelike material rather than in soil. Pull the sprouts from their spongy bed and rinse them in cold water to loosen the seedpods that inevitably get caught among the slender stalks. Shake off excess water and pinch, or cut, the stalks, leaving the roots behind in the sponge. Sprouts do not last for more than a day or two; blackened or yellowed leaves are evidence of deterioration. Some seed catalogs sell home-sprouting kits.

SANSHŌ Also known as Japanese prickly ash (*Zanthoxylum piperitum*), *sanshō* is a deciduous shrub. In early spring, tender, aromatic leaves called *ki no mé* appear. As spring turns to summer, female plants produce green *mi* (berries). These ripen in the fall, turning brown and then splitting to reveal shiny black seeds.

The green berries are plucked in late May or early June and either crushed and used fresh in season or preserved whole for future use. The fresh berries possess an extraordinary aroma and tongue-tingling spiciness: if there is any way to obtain *sanshō no mi*, I urge you to do so. The berries freeze well raw (no need to blanch them first). Preserved berries, both brined and soy stewed, are often available in overseas markets, packaged in glass jars and sometimes in vacuum-sealed packets (transfer the contents to a clean glass jar after opening and refrigerate).

Ki no mé sprigs have 7 or 8 tiny leaves attached to a central branch. The leaves are sometimes pulled from the branch and crushed with sweet, light miso to make a thick sauce for bamboo shoots, another springtime delicacy. When used as a garnish, the sprigs are kept whole. If you are able to source fresh *ki no mé* sprigs, rinse in cold water, then place several on the open palm of one hand. Slap them with your other hand to release the wonderful aroma. Store any extra sprigs (unslapped) in moist paper towels in a closed plastic bag in the refrigerator. Use within a day or two. They do not freeze well.

Kona-zanshō is the most commonly available form of aromatic, spicy *sanshō*. Made by cracking and crushing dried green berries, and/or grinding seeds taken from mature berries, most *kona-zanshō* is a mixture of both green and mature berries. It comes to market in small glass bottles (peek inside; you should see a coarse powder), though mills for cracking the dried berries yourself as you need them are now available.

SHISO An annual herb related to mint, *shiso* (pictured on page 270) boasts broad, flat leaves with saw-toothed edges. It comes in two colors, green and red. The green leaf is more common and is usually called simply *shiso*. But when it is necessary to distinguish it from *aka-jiso*, the red (purple, really) leaf, the green leaf is called *ao-jiso* (literally, "blue").

Green *shiso* has a flavor and aroma somewhat reminiscent of mint, with a hint of basil. In some English-language texts, you will see it referred to as beefsteak plant or perilla, though increasingly it goes by *shiso*. Green *shiso* is rich in beta-carotene, vitamin A, calcium, and iron. As a garnish, it often accompanies sashimi, spread under or near the slices of fish. In the vegan kitchen, it is served finely shredded or minced and added to dips and sauces, especially cold *sōmen* noodles and blocks of chilled *tōfu*.

Aka-jiso (pictured on page 252) that has been salted, squeezed, rinsed, and freshly brined is used in pickling. In Japan, packages of brined leaves in deeply colored liquid (this is a vinegar produced as a by-product of pickling plums) are sold in supermarkets from late May through July—the time of year for preserving *uméboshi* (pickled plums). Outside Japan, it may be difficult to obtain *aka-jiso* unless you grow your own. But brining the leaves is a frankly complicated and messy process. Instead, I suggest you purchase *uméboshi* plums that are packed along with the leaves and brine and use these by-products in your cooking.

If you are able to source the brined leaves, break the contents into several clean glass jars. Label and date the jars and refrigerate. They are best used within a year. The reason for making several smaller packets is that each time you open the jar to extract a few leaves you could be introducing unwanted bacteria. Be careful when you handle the leaves, not only to preserve good kitchen hygiene, but also because the dye stains fingers, cutting boards, and aprons.

Shiso no mi (*shiso* seedpods) and *ho-jiso* (flowering *shiso* stalks) can be harvested from the same *shiso* plant that produces green leaves—another good reason to seek out a source for seeds. You don't need a garden; several pots on an urban window ledge will do. The seedpods are used in pickling (also a wonderful accent when minced and tossed into salads), and the delicate purple flowers can be floated on soy sauce, so that they cling to foods dipped into it.

TŌGARASHI Compared to other Asian cuisines, such as Korean, Chinese, or Vietnamese, Japanese cookery may seem a bit bland. It does, however, have its moments of fire, many of them induced by the mildly incendiary *tōgarashi* (dried red chile). The small, slender, pointed green chiles turn fire engine red as they mature. As they dry, they begin to curl. Whole dried peppers are sometimes called *taka no tsumé*, literally "hawk claws," because of their appearance.

When the dried red chile is pounded into fine flakes and packaged alone, the label will read *ichimi*, or "single flavor." When the red pepper flakes are mixed with other spices, the blend is called *shichimi*, literally "seven flavors." I refer to it as 7-spice blend. (The addition of "sh" at the beginning of the word signifies the addition of 6 more spices.) Although no rigid rules exist on what other spices are added, they are likely to be *ao nori* (a mild, briny sea herb), *sanshō* (a tongue-tingling crushed peppercorn), *yuzu* peel (a type of citrus), *keshi no mi* (white poppy seeds), *kuro goma* (black sesame seeds), and *asa no mi* (hemp seeds).

WASABI This incendiary Japanese horseradish has been cultivated in its native Japan for more than a millennium. Its spiciness tends to clear nasal passages and induce tearing (it is nicknamed *namida*, or "tears," at the sushi bar). It is most likely that you will find wasabi as a paste in tubes or as a powder in tins. The tubes usually contain real *Wasabia japonica* (though sometimes mixed with seasonings, emulsifiers, and preservatives); the tins are usually green food coloring and ordinary horseradish. Check the label.

YUKARI This fruity-salty seasoning is made by drying and pulverizing salt-cured *aka-jiso* leaves. These leaves (pictured on page 252) are a by-product of pickling plums (see *uméboshi*, page 283) and another fine example that nothing goes to waste in the *kansha* kitchen. An added bonus is the antibacterial properties attributed to *yukari*; it is often sprinkled on rice to retard spoilage, especially in warm weather.

YUZU KOSHŌ Tubes of *yuzu koshō* are a recent addition to the spice and condiment section of Japanese grocery stores. This combination of citrus zest (taken from green-skinned *yuzu*) and minced green chiles (usually medium-hot, green *shishitō*) is served primarily in lieu of wasabi with *soba* noodles or *tōfu*. *Yuzu koshō* is also used as a seasoning for my quick-pickled cabbage and cucumber (see page 195).

Kabocha

Botanically a fruit and commonly labeled a squash, *kabocha* usually comes to market whole or in large wedges, giving you plenty of opportunity to try new ways to prepare it. The flesh (bright golden orange), seeds (fairly flat), and skin (dark green, often striated) are all edible.

In the spirit of nothing goes to waste, I offer the following suggestions: Peel *kabocha* thickly and use the peels when making a miso-enriched soup or tempura pancakes, or marinate the peels in soy sauce and fry them into chips (page 145).

Roast the kabocha seeds in a 250°F oven, turning and stirring them every 10 to 20 minutes, for about 1 hour, or until they are completely dried. Or, dry-roast using a dehydrator. Sprinkle with salt and let them cool. Alternatively, air-dry the seeds (this was the common method in traditional Japanese kitchens that did not have ovens) for several days before mincing them with a sharp knife. Dry-roast the minced seeds in a skillet as you would sesame seeds (page 245). Let the seeds cool completely before storing them in a glass jar or other lidded container. The whole seeds make a nice nibble with green tea; the minced seeds are good mixed with dry-roasted sesame seeds and tossed into rice.

Kambutsu

The calligraphy for *kambutsu* is written with two characters, "dried" and "thing." Because dried foods are lightweight and can be stored for extended periods of time at ordinary room temperature, they tend to be easy and inexpensive to ship long distances. You will find many *kambutsu* products for sale in groceries outside Japan. In the vegan kitchen, *kambutsu* are mostly vegetables (both land and sea), though legumes (such as *adzuki* beans), wheat gluten (such as *kuruma-bu*), and soy foods (such as freeze-dried tōfu) are also part of the family.

DRIED BEANS Dried beans are an important source of plant protein for those who choose not to eat animal products. In the traditional Japanese kitchen, *daizu* (dried soybeans) and *adzuki* appear in myriad preparations

ADZUKI Used in both sweet and savory dishes, these small, dark maroon beans (pictured on page 252) are rich in iron, fiber, and vitamin B_1. The *adzuki* beans grown in the Tokachi region of Hokkaido are well known, especially the small, shiny, brightly colored *sasagé mamé*.

DAIZU Written with the character *dai* (meaning "big" or "important") and the character *zu* (an alternate reading of *mamé*, or "bean"), *daizu* (pictured on page 252) are dried soybeans, the most important legumes in the Japanese pantry. Their prominence is due to the fact that all tōfu products, known collectively as *daizu seihin*, derive from them. In the Japanese vegan and vegetarian kitchen, *daizu* are the single most important source of plant protein. They contain a balanced quantity of complete protein (all the essential amino acids in the amounts needed for human health), carbohydrate, and fat. In addition, they provide vitamins (especially B vitamins) and minerals (including calcium and iron).

Although most *daizu* are beige, there are two botanical variants: the charmingly named *uguisu mamé* ("nightingale bean," for its pale green color resembling the songbird) and the *kuro mamé* ("black" bean). All *daizu* are rich in phytochemicals, but black beans, because of their deep coloration, have a greater concentration of polyphenols (which act as antioxidants) than other soybean varieties. Black soybeans are prepared in both sweet and savory ways. Tokachi (Hokkaidao) and Tamba (not far from Kyoto) are known for their fine black beans.

DRIED SOY FOODS Tōfu and other fresh soy foods, such as *nama yuba* (page 285), are highly perishable. It is not surprising, then, that previous generations of Asian cooks developed methods of extending shelf life, chiefly by drying, with either dry heat or naturally frigid conditions.

HOSHI YUBA Unlike fresh *yuba*, which is pliable, creamy, and somewhat chewy (and requires refrigeration), *hoshi yuba*, or dried yuba, is brittle (and shelf-stable). You will find dried *yuba* sold as flat, thin sheets (2 or 3 to a package) and as decorative small bundles (sometimes rolled or scrunched up and tied with *kombu* threads). The latter type is for use in clear broths: Place in a soup bowl, preferably one with a lid, and pour scalding hot, seasoned broth on top. The heat of the liquid is sufficient to "cook" the dried *yuba* within 1 minute.

In this book, I have called for sheets of dried *yuba*. Some recipes call for broken bits and pieces, since inevitably sheets do crack and shatter. When careful, though, you can keep sheets whole and soften them to use as wrappers to enclose other foods and to make thin omelet look-alikes. The sheets are naturally pale gold. To make them appear omeletlike, *kuchinashi no mi* (page 269), a natural food dye, is often used.

To soften sheets of dried *yuba*, the Japanese wrap them in damp *sarashi* (page 250); cheesecloth or another fine-woven cloth such as a thin kitchen towel could be used instead. Dip your cloth in warm water and carefully wring out excess moisture before wrapping a single sheet of dried *yuba* in the warm, moist cloth. Use a separate cloth for each sheet of dried *yuba*, and make sure that each sheet is entirely enclosed. Let the sheets sit, wrapped, for at least 30 minutes or up to 2 hours. To hasten the process, place the wrapped sheets in a resealable plastic bag and leave at room temperature. If you want to leave the sheets for a longer period of time, refrigerate the wrapped sheets in the plastic bag. They will keep for up to 2 days.

KŌYA-DŌFU This protein-rich, freeze-dried tōfu is featured in many Japanese temple vegetarian dishes. The name, which is written with the same calligraphy used to write Mount Kōya, refers to the Shingon Buddhist temple not far from Nara, founded by Kōbō Daishi in the ninth century. The monks at the temple developed (some say "perfected" an existing technology brought from China) a way of preserving fresh tōfu: they set it out at night in the cold mountain air to freeze, and then put it in the sun during the day to dry. The alternate name for this type of tōfu is *kōri-dōfu*, or "frozen tōfu," which indicates the method used to extend shelf life but does not assign credit for developing it. When simmered, the freeze-dried tōfu absorbs flavor from the broth.

There are two types of *kōya-dōfu* and the type you have purchased will affect the timing for adding other ingredients to the recipe. Each recipe will instruct you accordingly. Ideally, purchase *kōya-dōfu* that has been freeze-dried naturally, known as old-fashioned style. Some products are dried with baking soda (sodium bicarbonate), and these tend to crumble easily when simmered. If you are using *kōya-dōfu* dried with baking soda, follow instructions for modern *kōya-dōfu*. Avoid any product that lists ammonia or other chemicals as drying agents or preservatives. Also, check the label to make sure the product you are purchasing has not been preseasoned with soy sauce or sweeteners (many artificially dried types have).

Before cooking it, *kōya-dōfu* must be softened. Place blocks in a single layer in a wide, shallow container; the blocks will expand as they soften. Pour in very warm, but not boiling, water to barely cover. Let the blocks soak for about 5 minutes, or until swollen and a bit spongy. Flip the blocks, add a bit more very warm water, and continue to soak for another 5 minutes. Lift the *kōya-dōfu* from the container and press carefully but firmly between your palms to force the cloudy liquid out. Soak in fresh water (cool tap water is fine) for another 3 to 4 minutes; remove from the container and press out the cloudy liquid. Repeat this cool-water rinse-soak-press activity once or twice, or until the water is no longer very cloudy when you press on the softened blocks. Note: the water does not need to be crystal clear.

DRIED VEGETABLES FROM THE LAND The three dried land vegetables that I call for often are shiitaké mushrooms, *kampyō*, and *kiriboshi daikon*. Each plays a dual role in the vegan kitchen: the liquid that results from rehydrating them becomes flavorful stock, and the softened vegetables are cooked on their own, or paired with fresh produce, in numerous dishes.

Because you will want to use the rehydrated liquid, you must purchase products that have been naturally dried by the sun and/or air without chemicals. In Japanese, these natural products are marketed as either *ten nen* (natural), *muhyōhaku* (unbleached), or *mutenka* (no additives). The English equivalent varies, so check the labels carefully to see whether chemical drying agents have been employed. And make a point of mentioning to the store manager your insistence on chemical-free dried foods. The more consumers insist on naturally dried products, the more likely shopkeepers will be to seek out such products to sell to their customers.

DRIED SHIITAKÉ MUSHROOMS Throughout Asia, dark oak mushrooms are both foraged in the wild and cultivated on logs. *Donko*, with its thick, striated, bumpy caps, is the most prized variety and the most costly. When dried, shiitaké mushrooms (pictured on page 252) develop a rich, almost heady fermented aroma. Minerals become concentrated in the drying process, resulting in an earthy, deep-forest flavor. Dried mushrooms are not interchangeable with fresh ones (think about the difference between dried and fresh apricots or tomatoes).

Dried shiitaké have a depth of flavor that is desirable in slow-simmered dishes and as a garnish for cold noodle salads and scattered-style sushi. In the process of softening the dried mushrooms, an intensely flavorful liquid results, and this "broth" is often used in conjunction with, or in lieu of, traditional sea-based stock.

I snap off the stems of dried shiitaké mushrooms for use in stocks or, on occasion, to balance the flavor of pickles coming from my *nuka* pot. I reserve the caps for cooking in a variety of ways, always saving the soaking liquid. When soaked in water for at least 30 minutes (or preferably for several hours), dried shiitaké yield a flavorful liquid that forms the basis of many vegetarian stocks. If you are in a hurry, use warm (but not boiling or very hot) water when soaking the mushrooms. Depending on the recipe, the softened caps are thinly sliced, cut into wedges, or minced before cooking. You can prepare dried mushrooms in advance and refrigerate them for several days. Dried shiitaké will keep best if stored on a dark shelf in an airtight container with the antimoisture packet from the original bag.

KAMPYŌ Looking a bit like a spool of thread set on a large bobbin, pale green pumpkin-like gourds called *fukubé* are set spinning against a sharp blade. Coiled gourd ribbons form, which are then hung to dry in the sun. In the drying process, minerals and sugars are concentrated, yielding an aroma vaguely reminiscent of dried apricots. *Kampyō*, or sun-dried gourd ribbons (pictured on page 252), are used to tie up any number of edible packages, or are simmered in a sweet soy broth or plum-infused sauce and used as a filling for rolled sushi.

Kampyō is sold in cellophane bags containing very long (several yard) or short (6-inch) ribbons. I suggest you buy the uncut gourd ribbons, since they offer more options when cooking. Stored in a closed plastic bag on a cool, dark shelf, they will keep for months. The dried gourd is, like other sun-dried ingredients, quite lightweight; most packages will contain less than an ounce. To help tenderize the gourd ribbons, many of the recipes that call for them as an ingredient will instruct you to rub the ribbons with salt that is later rinsed off.

KIRIBOSHI DAIKON Readily available outside Japan in Asian groceries, look for cellophane-wrapped bags of straw-colored, dried-but-still-somewhat-pliable sun-dried shredded radish (pictured on page 252). *Kiriboshi daikon* will be stocked alongside other dried products such as *kampyō*. As with other sun-dried foods, flavor and nutrition are concentrated, especially the sweetness and vitamin C. The stock that results from softening sun-dried radish is quite sweet; when used to simmer vegetables that normally get cooked with sugar and soy, you can often reduce (even eliminate) the amount of sugar.

On opening the package, you will be aware of a distinctive almost sauerkrautlike aroma. This is perfectly normal. Transfer any unused *kiriboshi daikon* to a resealable bag, pressing out air as you close it to slow oxidation (and contain the aroma).

DRIED VEGETABLES FROM THE SEA The Japanese have been harvesting sea vegetables (*kaisō*) for millennia, both cultivated aquatic plants and what nature provides. It is unfortunate that the derogatory (and inaccurate) label of "seaweed" persists. Sea vegetation is highly nutritious (many aquatic plants are especially rich in calcium) and a source of flavor enhancement (naturally occurring glutamates abound in them).

Throughout the book, I have called for a number of very different sea vegetables. They are no more interchangeable than soil-grown mint would be in place of soil-grown Brussels sprouts. It is important that you understand the characteristics of each sea vegetable so that you can expand your dietary repertoire to include them. I have limited my discussion here to the vegetables I have called for in the recipes: *aramé, hijiki, kanten,* various kinds of *kombu* (including shavings of *oboro* and *tororo*), nori, and *wakamé*.

ARAMÉ Nutrient-rich *aramé* (pictured on page 265), a type of kelp, comes to market dried in long, thin, dark slivers that look very much like *hijiki*. Because of the unfortunate ban on *hijiki* in some markets (parts of Canada and the United Kingdom, at the time I am writing), I have provided instructions for using *aramé* as a substitute for *hijiki*. Although *aramé* has a similar flavor and texture, I personally prefer the aniselike flavor and tender texture of *hijiki*. *Aramé* is often sold at health-food stores.

To soften *aramé*, cover it with warm water and let soak for 20 to 30 minutes. It will not expand, but will become a bit softer to the touch and more pliable. Softened *aramé* does not yield to pressure, but your fingernail should easily leave a mark on the surface of a test piece. Drain off the deep brown liquid produced and rinse with cold water. Drain again. Blot up excess moisture with paper towels.

HIJIKI This dark, calcium- and iron-rich sea vegetable is sold dried in two forms (both pictured on page 265): short bits called *mé hijiki* (I call them "buds") and longer, slender pieces called *naga hijiki* ("long" stems). They can be used interchangeably, though the *naga hijiki* should be soaked for at least 30 minutes (*mé hijiki* needs only 10 minutes or so) and will take a few minutes longer to cook, especially if the pieces are fairly thick. In reality, they are harvested from the same plant: the longer pieces are the branches and the shorter pieces are the equivalent of leaves. They are put through a filter to separate buds from stems.

Nearly all *hijiki* comes to market in dried form (during a very short period in March, freshly harvested *hijiki* can sometimes be found in supermarkets in Japan). As with other dried foods, the flavors and nutrients are far more concentrated in dried *hijiki* than in fresh.

To soften *hijiki*, place pieces in a bowl and cover with several inches of cold water. *Hijiki* expands, so use a large bowl. Drain and rinse with fresh cold water. Drain again. Blot up excess moisture with paper towels. When fully rehydrated, you should be able to compress a piece of *hijiki*

SPECIAL NOTE ON HIJIKI

In 2004, the British Food Safety Agency (FSA) placed a ban on the sale of *hijiki* in the United Kingdom, explaining that the sea vegetable naturally contained high levels of inorganic arsenic that made it unsafe for human consumption. The FSA noted that levels were especially high in the liquid remaining after rehydrating, which is why the Japanese always discard this liquid and then rinse the rehydrated *hijiki* under cold running water before cooking it. Unlike other Japanese sun-dried vegetables, such as kelp, radish, mushrooms, or gourd, that produce fabulous stocks when they are rehydrated, the by-product of soaking *hijiki* must never be consumed.

The World Health Organization and other international organizations and governmental bodies have done considerable research on the potential dangers of consuming *hijiki*. On July 30, 2004, the Japanese Ministry of Health and Welfare, after conducting their own investigations and taking into consideration the work of others, issued the following statement: "There are no records of cases of arsenic poisoning as a result of the arsenic content of sea vegetables." As a result of this finding, the Japanese government recommends consuming *hijiki* once a week as part of a normal, healthy balanced diet.

Eden Foods, a company that sells *hijiki* and many other sea vegetables, has posted a detailed explanation of the extensive research done on *hijiki* on their website: www.edenfoods.com/articles/view.php?articles_id=79.

Because readers in Canada and the United Kingdom will likely find *hijiki* banned from their store shelves, I suggest using *aramé*, a variety of kelp with a similar flavor and appearance that has not been banned in any markets, in its place.

---

between your thumb and index finger with only slight pressure. Do not consume the liquid that results from soaking *hijiki*, or use it in lieu of stock (see box).

KANTEN Known in the West as agar-agar, *kanten* is processed from *tengusa*, or "heavenly grass," a red marine alga. The harvested *tengusa* is freeze-dried (alternating frigid nights and dry sunny days), which increases its ability to gel liquids. Indeed, its gelling properties are truly remarkable: it will solidify liquids without refrigeration. Although *tengusa* has been known and used in many Asian cuisines for centuries, the Japanese claim *kanten* as their contribution to the culinary world. In Japan, the clever monks at Manpukuji Temple, near Kyoto, are credited with naming

kanten (literally, "cold sky"). It is used in both sweet and savory dishes.

Kanten is traditionally sold as 2 sticks of what appear to be brittle cellophane wrapped in what is actually thin cellophane. To soften 1 stick, break it into 2 or 3 pieces and place the pieces in a bowl with cold water to cover. Allow the *kanten* to soak, soften, and swell for at least 10 minutes or up to 1 hour. To improve the texture, squeeze the pieces gently a few times at the start to make sure they are completely waterlogged. When the gelatin is pliable, squeeze out and discard all the liquid. Shred the moist *kanten* into a 1-quart saucepan, preferably nonreactive, add 1 cup water,

hoshi wakamé

aramé

oboro kombu

Hidaka kombu

Hidaka
kombu

ma kombu

tororo kombu

naga hijiki

ao nori

mé hijiki

stir well, then place the saucepan over low heat. Cook, stirring, to dissolve the *kanten*, which is then ready to use.

More recently, powdered *kanten* has come on the market, in small packets (in a larger box) or loose in a resealable pouch. One packet of powdered *kanten* contains 4 to 5 grams (about 2 teaspoons), which is not quite the equivalent of 1 stick. One stick can usually gel about 1³/₄ cups liquid; 1 packet of powder gels about 1²/₃ cups liquid. A great deal depends on the chemistry of the specific liquid; greater acidity usually requires more *kanten*. Individual recipes will provide you with instructions. Place powdered *kanten* in a nonreactive saucepan with 1 cup water and stir well. Set it aside for a minute (it will swell ever so slightly), then place over low heat and cook, stirring, to dissolve the *kanten*.

Store stick or powdered *kanten* in an airtight container on your shelf; it will keep indefinitely.

Kombu Perhaps the single most important sea vegetable in the Japanese pantry, *kombu* is used primarily to make stocks because of its abundant, naturally occurring glutamates. Several varieties of *kombu*, each with its own distinctive flavor and cooking properties, are worth knowing about, and I describe them briefly here. Outside Japan, it may be more difficult to source some of them. In the photograph on page 265, you will see the two kinds most commonly available, *Hidaka kombu* and *ma kombu*. I have called for simply *kombu* in the ingredients list of most recipes, though on occasion I will recommend a particular type, if you can source it.

There is no easy way to measure quantities of *kombu*. Some packages have long, narrow strips; others have wide, flat pieces, tapered tips, or broken shards. It is lightweight (I suspect that few of you will have an accurate kitchen scale, unless you do a lot of baking), and cups or tablespoons won't work, either. As a result, I indicate the amount in inches, sometimes in a range. As you will discover, *Hidaka kombu* is narrow and usually rippled; it has

relatively fewer glutamates, so you should err on the side of generous when doling it out. *Ma kombu* is broad, flat, often quite thick, and much higher in glutamates, so you can get away with using less.

Hidaka kombu is named after the place in Hokkaido where it is grown and harvested. It is typically thinner and narrower than other kelp varieties and has a mild (briny) flavor. Because it is relatively low in glutamates, heat can be applied with little or no previous soaking to extract full flavor. This type of kelp is sold as *dashi kombu* (literally "kelp for stock") in most supermarkets. It is sometimes labeled *Mitsuishi kombu* or by its botanical name, *Laminaria angustata*.

Ma kombu, or "true" kelp, is primarily harvested near Hakodate (Hokkaido). (*L. japonica* is the scientific name for this variety.) It is fairly thick and broad, usually slate black, and is typically packaged in 3- or 4-inch lengths. Throughout the Kansai area (southwest Honshu, including Osaka and Kyoto), it is sold as *dashi kombu* and is used for nearly all home-style preparations. *Ma kombu*, even lesser-grade products, is high in glutamates. For superior flavor extraction, let the kelp sit in water for at least 10 minutes (preferably 30 minutes) at room temperature before applying gentle heat.

Oboro kombu and *tororo kombu* are two types of shaved kelp (both pictured on page 265) made by marinating *ma kombu* in vinegar and then shaving it to produce melt-in-your-mouth-tender, slightly sour (but naturally sweet and salty, too), pale green, gauze-thin pieces. I use them to cover hand-pressed rice "sandwiches" (page 45) in place of nori.

Oboro kombu is made by shaving a single piece of *ma kombu*; the outer layers produce dark olive-green pieces and the center yields almost-white pieces. The remaining core, a chalky celadon color, is called *shirata kombu* and is marinated in a sweet-and-sour sauce. In the professional Japanese kitchen it is used to cover blocks of mackerel sushi. *Tororo kombu* is made by slicing across many pieces of vinegar-softened *ma kombu* that have been stacked and compressed. The resulting shavings are striated and primarily used as a garnish or to make a quick soup: place in the bottom of a bowl, add a few strips of softened *ita-bu* (see dried wheat gluten, page 268) and a few sprigs of *mitsuba* (page 257) and/or minced scallions, drizzle in hot water until the ingredients float, then stir and drink.

Two other specialty kelps worth mentioning are *Rishiri kombu* and *Rausu kombu*. *Rishiri kombu* (*L. ochotensis*) yields an exquisitely clear broth with a deep, rich flavor and silky mouthfeel. The very best grades are quite expensive (a single strip several yards long could cost as much as seventy-five dollars), and favored by chefs at elegant establishments. Broken and cut bits are often available at more reasonable prices. *Rausu kombu* (*L. diabolica*) is the kelp of choice in many vegan kitchens because it yields a rich, almost buttery broth reminiscent of meat-based stocks. Although highly flavorful, *Rausu kombu* typically produces a cloudy stock that is less attractive in clear soups and sauces.

Nori Also known as laver, nori is a cultivated alga that is briefly submerged in a cauldron of seawater, rinsed, chopped to a pasty consistency, and then spread on slatted bamboo mats to dry. Sketches documenting this process date back centuries. Today's production, mostly off the coast of Chiba (near Tokyo), has been streamlined and modernized.

Sheets of crisp nori are best known for their use in rolls at sushi bars. In Japanese home kitchens, they are used to wrap rice sandwiches known as *omusubi* or *onigiri*. Most sheets have been pretoasted and are labeled *yaki nori*, to distinguish them from preseasoned sheets, or *aji-tsuké nori*. Check the label carefully to make sure you are purchasing unseasoned sheets. Because the sheets quickly become soggy when exposed to damp air, be sure to store them in a sealed bag or container in a dry spot. They can be frozen (and refrozen), but care needs to be taken not to capture cold mist from the freezer in the package.

Wakamé This mineral-rich brown alga (its botanical name is *Undaria pinnatifida*) is sold in two forms: dry, brittle bits called *hoshi wakamé* (pictured on page 265) and salted fresh *wakamé*. It is available most of the year in dried form. In the springtime, freshly harvested *wakamé* is briefly blanched (it turns an emerald green) and then heavily salted to preserve it. It comes to market labeled as *nama*, or "fresh," to distinguish it from shelf-stable *hoshi*, or "dried," *wakamé*. Both types appear dark green in their respective packages. Each is softened slightly differently, though the soaking liquid in both cases is traditionally discarded (or used for watering plants).

To soften *hoshi wakamé* for salads, soak in cold water for 3 to 5 minutes. Rinse the pieces briefly under cold running water, then drain and gently squeeze out excess liquid. Avoid extended soaking of dried *wakamé*, which impairs flavor and depletes nutritional value.

When using for soups, small bits of *hoshi wakamé* can be placed, as is, at the bottom of lidded bowls. Pour hot soup over the dried bits, cover with the lid, and wait for 1 minute. This is usually sufficient to rehydrate the bits. When using in braised or simmered dishes, add unsoftened *hoshi wakamé* at the last minute, allowing the flavors of the cooking liquid to be absorbed.

To soften fresh salted *wakamé*, rinse thoroughly to remove the salt and then soak in fresh cold water to cover for 3 to 5 minutes. Drain and rinse under cold running water, then drain again.

Sometimes the fronds of softened dried or fresh *wakamé* have tough "ribs" or "veins." To remove them, use the tip of a knife like a pencil, drawing a line to trim them away. If *wakamé* pieces are awkwardly large, chop them into bite-size pieces.

DRIED WHEAT GLUTEN Known collectively as *hoshi-bu*, dried wheat gluten is a useful ingredient in the home kitchen. Shelf-stable, it waits in the cupboard, ready to provide extra volume and plant-based protein to a dish. The two most commonly encountered forms are *kuruma-bu* (wheels) and *ita-bu* (sheets). Both types (pictured on page 252) need to be softened before they can be added to stews and soups.

To soften: Soak a clean kitchen towel in warm water and wring it out well. Arrange the pieces of dried gluten flat on the cloth, preferably in a single layer, and wrap the cloth around them. This will help them retain their shape. Fit the wrapped pieces into a shallow container wide enough to hold them, allowing for them to swell a bit as they soften. Drizzle a few spoonfuls of very warm, but not boiling, water over the cloth to moisten it thoroughly. Do not submerge the pieces; they must not float in the liquid. Let the dried gluten rest in its moistened cloth for 7 or 8 minutes. Flip the wrapped pieces, drizzle in a few more spoonfuls of very warm water, and let rest for another 5 minutes. The *kuruma-bu* wheels will feel a bit springy when pressed; the *ita-bu* sheets will be somewhat pliable but not spongy. Lift them from the container, still wrapped in the cloth. Press *kuruma-bu* wheels firmly between your palms to force out unwanted liquid and unwrap. No pressing is needed for *ita-bu* sheets; merely unwrap.

Kasu

During saké production, a fermented rice mash is pressed and then liquid—the saké—is drawn off. The pasty lees that remain behind are called *kasu*, and in true nothing-goes-to-waste-in-the-*kansha*-kitchen fashion, they are used in making a heady pickling medium. Most saké producers will package and sell their lees as either sheets or chunks. You will find *saké kasu* in the refrigerated case of most Asian groceries.

The lees do not readily spoil, but some of the (pleasantly) heady aroma fades with time. It is best to assemble your pickling medium immediately after opening the package, though any unused portion can be stored in the refrigerator for several months.

Konnyaku and shirataki

Konnyaku is sold as a gelatinous loaf in varying sizes; when purchasing, check the weight and compare it to the quantity required for the recipe. *Konnyaku* also comes in noodle-like threads called *shirataki* (literally "white waterfall"); when bundled and tied, it is called *ito kon* ("thread" *konnyaku*) or *musubi* ("bundled") *konnyaku*. Both the loaf and the noodles are processed from a tuber called *konnyaku imo* that is rich in dietary fiber and low in calories, with no real taste of its own. *Konnyaku* and *shirataki* are inexpensive and absorb the flavor of foods with which they are cooked; they are often added to stewed or simmered dishes by dieters and those with tight budgets to create extra volume.

The speckled varieties of *konnyaku* and *shirataki* have *hijiki* (page 263), a calcium-rich sea vegetable, added for texture and nutrition. For those using *konnyaku* products for the first time, be reassured that the (frankly funky and rather unpleasant) smell on opening the package is entirely normal. It is not a sign of spoilage. If you will not be using the entire package, pour off the liquid and transfer the remaining loaf or noodles to a lidded container filled with fresh cold water. Refrigerate for up to 5 days, changing the water daily. Drain before using. You will notice a chalky residue develop on the inside of whatever container you use to store your *konnyaku* products. This is a natural mineral buildup from the lime (calcium oxide or calcium hydroxide) used to solidify the *konnyaku* tuber gel. It is a nuisance to remove (you may want to dedicate a container for this use and then just leave it be), but not a cause for concern.

Kuchinashi no mi

Used in the traditional Japanese kitchen to color fruits and vegetables, *kuchinashi no mi* (pictured on page 252) are dried gardenia pods (the scientific name for the flower is *Gardenia jasminoides*). Although they may be difficult to source outside Japan, I urge you to try and find them.

Several Japanese companies that sell spices also package 5 *kuchinashi no mi* to a small, resealable bag. In Japan, these bags come to supermarket shelves at the end of the year, since the most common use for the pods is to enhance the golden color of chestnuts and yams used in making a New Year's sweet called *kuri kinton*. If you cannot locate *kuchinashi no mi*, a few drops of yellow food coloring will produce a similar visual effect, though with none of the medicinal protectiveness of the pods. Indeed, in the mid-1960s, when I first went to Japan, the pods were only available in pharmacies, suggesting that the dye had significant antibacterial properties.

The gardenia pod dye is odorless and tasteless but intensely yellow. The dye easily stains cutting boards, aprons, dish towels, and fingertips. I suggest you wrap the dried pod in several paper towels before you place it on your cutting board. Crack the pod with the back (noncutting) edge of a knife, or crush it by placing the blade flat against the wrapped pod and pressing carefully but with determination. To ease removal of the pod from pickling liquids or cooking pots, place it on a 2- or 3-inch square of gauze or cheesecloth and bring the corners up to enclose the pod. Tie the package with kitchen twine.

Leafy greens

In the traditional Japanese kitchen, the leafy tops of turnips, radishes, and other root vegetables were regularly consumed in addition to leafy vegetables. It is an increasing challenge to find markets, especially in large urban areas, that sell vegetables with their greens attached. Yet several leafy greens that had at one time been nearly impossible to find outside Japan have become increasingly popular overseas. I call for three of them in this book: *komatsuna*, *mizuna*, and chrysanthemum greens. To store leafy greens, wrap them in moist paper towels, slip them into a loose-fitting plastic bag, and keep in the refrigerator. Wash greens just before using them.

CHRYSANTHEMUM GREENS These greens, called *shungiku* in Japanese, are pleasantly bitter, making them a wonderful foil for the nutty tōfu sauce known as *shira aé*. Sold in small bunches, hopefully with roots still attached because they are sweet and delicious, the greens (pictured on page 270) can be briefly blanched and used in a number of ways, such as nestling them at the bottom of clear soups (Lotus Root Dumpling Soup, page 78) or adding them to a dish just before saucing (Steamed Turnip and Tōfu in Silver Sauce, page 121).

KOMATSUNA Similar to spinach in its culinary application, the leaves of *komatsuna* (pictured on page 270) are curved (rather than pointed) and the roots are white (rather than tinged with red). The name is often attributed to the area of old Edo (former name for Tokyo) where the greens were commercially grown in abundance. The eighteenth-century shogun Tokugawa Yoshimune was said to be especially fond of *komatsuna*. It is rich in vitamins A and C and minerals such as iron and calcium.

komatsuna

radish sprouts

scallions

shiso

mizuna

mitsuba

chrysanthemum
greens

MIZUNA A member of the mustard family, *mizuna* (pictured on page 270) has been enjoyed in Japan since ancient times, though it has only recently become widely available overseas. It has an elusive flavor, sometimes reminding me of cress, and a celerylike crunch. It makes a wonderful salad, but it can also be used in soups (chop coarsely, place at the bottom of the bowl, and pour in the broth; the heat of the broth releases a lovely fresh-meadow aroma).

In Japan, *mizuna* is sold in plump clusters of pale stalks and verdant pointed leaves and needs to be soaked in a tub of cold water to flush out soil caught between stalks. When I have seen *mizuna* in American markets, it has been as loose leaves and torn stalks, piled high (and at very high prices) alongside other "specialty" greens such as arugula. It is fairly easy to grow if you have a small garden (it does not do well in windowsill pots).

Manganji peppers

Manganji tōgarashi, a specialty of Kyoto, are mild, tender capsicums with an earthy-rich aroma. They can be stocky or rather slender in appearance, but all have distinctive wrinkles or folds at the stem end. When buying, look for shiny, brightly colored skins and peppers that are light for their size (a sign that fewer seeds are contained within).

First cultivated in South America thousands of years ago, capsicums rapidly made their way around the globe and were probably introduced to Japan with the Portuguese missionaries in the sixteenth century. The oldest documented varietal in Japan, an annual called *Fushimi ama* (*ama* means "sweet"), was developed in the kitchen gardens of feudal lord Toyotomi Hideyoshi's Fushimi Momoyama castle. Manganji, a mild, tender capsicum with an earthy-rich aroma and a specialty of the Kyoto region, is a relative newcomer in the world of chile pepperdom: about eighty years ago, Japanese growers created this hybrid by marrying a slightly incendiary capsicum known as *Fushimi tōgarashi* with the California Wonder bell pepper.

Matcha

Tea plants produce tender buds in the late spring. The buds are gathered, steamed, chilled, and then air-dried before they are pulverized to make a jade-colored powder called *matcha*, which is whisked (with a special bamboo whisk) to make ceremonial green tea. It is what gives the distinctive color and flavor to many traditional confections. Long exposure to dry heat (Western-style ovens), or even brief exposure to excessively high temperatures, can cause the powdered tea to become bitter and an unappetizing brown. In *Kansha*, I use *matcha* to color and flavor sweet steamed muffins (page 233). If you are careful not to trap air in the storage tin or bag (trapped air contains mist that, when the tea is thawed, becomes unwanted moisture), green tea freezes well.

Miso

Unlike some foodstuffs that are difficult to find in Asian groceries, miso usually presents the shopper with a different dilemma: too many choices! For most Japanese, miso preferences will be a matter of regional upbringing in much the same way that wine or cheese preferences in Europe tend toward hometown tastes.

In this book, I have specified four types of miso that have strong regional identities. Light, sweet, creamy-textured Saikyō miso is preferred by those in the Kansai, especially Kyoto. Dark, stiff, and fudgelike in appearance, Hatchō miso is mellow and savory, with smoky overtones; it is the regional pride of Nagoya. Sendai miso, native son of Sendai (a port town on the Pacific coast, north of Tokyo), is a richly pungent, russet miso that comes in both smooth and chunky versions (I prefer chunky—peanut butter, too). Inhabitants of Kyushu and parts of Shikoku are fanatic in their adoration of *mugi miso*, a yeasty, rough-textured (with barley bits), golden paste.

A GUIDE TO THE KANSHA KITCHEN

RED MISO AND WHITE MISO In some recipes I have called for generic types: *aka*, or "red," miso would be any russet, brown, or other dark shade (and usually a robust and salty flavor); *shiro*, or "white," miso refers to pale beige, golden tones (and usually sweeter, milder flavors). In the examples above, Saikyō miso and *mugi miso* would be considered white, and Sendai miso and Hatchō miso would be red miso.

GENMAI MISO One other type of miso that you will readily find is *genmai miso*, which is enriched with whole grain (brown rice). There is no special regional identity; most parts of Japan enrich their fermented soybean pastes with *kome koji*, or rice bacillus. When brown rice is used, the miso tends to be saltier than when polished rice is used, because the tough rice bran needs relatively more salt to encourage fermentation.

That brings me to the subject of modern, consumer-driven miso products that have appeared on the market in the past decade or so. As with soy sauce, I question the value (and don't care for the taste) of reduced-sodium miso. I would prefer to use far less of the old-fashioned miso in cooking (thinning it, perhaps, with water or *kombu* stock), and choose to serve (and consume) dishes made with miso less often (savoring the full flavor and aroma when I do indulge). Miso made with reduced salt has a shorter shelf life; aroma, in particular, will be lost after a few weeks.

Unless you have a dark, very cool pantry shelf, it is best to store all types of miso in the refrigerator once they have been opened.

Mushrooms

Autumn is the season for foraging most wild fungi, though cultivated mushrooms, such as enoki, are readily available year-round. I have included the best-known mushrooms here, with instructions on preparing them for cooking. Wrapped in barely moistened paper towels or damp news-paper and kept in the vegetable bin of your refrigerator, most varieties of fresh mushrooms can be stored for several days or up to a week. Clean and slice as close as possible to cooking time to preserve aroma and texture.

ENOKI If you are using cultivated ivory-colored enoki mushrooms, sometimes sold as *énokidaké*, remove them from their plastic bag, rinse the heads under cold running water, and shake them dry. Remove and discard the spongy bottom (moldy-looking) section, and cut the remaining portion of the stems into 1/2-inch lengths or as directed in individual recipes.

MAITAKÉ If you are using beige-gray, ruffled *maitaké* (also called hen-of-the-woods), trim away any moldy parts of the white stems and, with your hands, separate the clusters lengthwise into thin strips. The irregular surface that results from hand-tearing mushrooms will make them more flavorful than knife-sliced ones.

MATSUTAKÉ As their name suggests (*matsu* means "pine" and *také* means "fungi"), these mushrooms grow in symbiotic bliss with red pine trees and boast an incredible woodsy aroma. They must be foraged (to date, no one has successfully cultivated them) and command a high price. The highest quality *matsutaké* come to market early in the autumn and can go for nearly $100 apiece. *Matsutaké* have tight, unopened, bulbous caps that top stocky 3- to 4-inch columns. The color varies from pale white (characteristic of those found in Japan, especially around Kyoto) to dark brown (typical of ones found in Canada and Korea).

Gently wipe *matsutaké* mushrooms with a dry cloth to remove any soil, but do not wash or peel. If you must, use a mushroom brush with soft bristles. Trim and discard the very bottom if wiping does not remove unwanted bits of the forest still clinging to the mushroom. Cut the mushroom in half so the cap and stem are separated. Using your fingers, gently shred the stem; the irregular surface of these pieces will yield greater flavor and preserve the crisp texture. Similarly, shred the cap, beginning with the stem end, or cut into paper-thin slices with a sharp knife (these will look impressive scattered across the top of a dish).

NAMÉKO Small clusters of these slippery, orangey brown mushrooms are typically packed already trimmed in clear plastic bags kept on refrigerated shelves in markets or less often in small shelf-stable tins. The Japanese have a fondness for viscous foods and will often add these mushrooms to a sauce or soup to thicken it a bit. If you prefer, you can remove some of this natural stickiness by briefly blanching the mushrooms and letting them cool naturally.

SHIITAKÉ With a damp cloth or mushroom brush, dust fresh shiitaké mushrooms to remove residual dirt. After trimming away any gritty material clinging to the stems, twist and remove the stems and use them to enrich stock. Slice the caps lengthwise into narrow strips, or into 4 or 6 wedgelike pieces, depending on the recipe. (For information on dried shiitaké mushrooms, see page 262.)

SHIMÉJI If you are using cultivated, pearly gray *shiméji* mushrooms, also known as *shiméjitaké* or oyster mushrooms, they need to be rinsed briefly under cold running water and gently squeezed dry. Trim away the moldy parts of the stems and, with your hands, separate each mushroom from the larger mass. If the caps of the mushrooms are more than $1/2$ inch across, cut these in half lengthwise before slicing into $1/2$-inch lengths.

Naga negi

Japanese *naga negi*, literally "long onions," are similar to leeks, though far more slender and quite long: the white portion is usually 12 inches or longer; the green tops are at least 3 or 4 inches long. Dirt is rarely trapped between the tightly packed white layers, unlike leeks that require attention to rinsing. *Naga negi* are sweet when seared or grilled, though quite spicy when chopped or thinly sliced and served raw.

Available at many Asian groceries outside Japan, *naga negi* should be wrapped in damp newspaper and kept on a cool, dark pantry shelf, or refrigerated. If need be, to make them easier to store, cut in half where the green and white portions meet. Do not be alarmed when cut edges seem to regenerate from the inner layers; it's fine to thinly slice or mince these "extra" bits. Japanese leeks will keep well for 7 to 10 days in the refrigerator. Seeds are also available from many catalog companies; it is a fairly easy crop to grow, though it requires deep top soil.

Nattō

Nattō (sticky fermented soybeans) has been a staple food in the Japanese diet for at least a millennium. In recent years, the macrobiotic movement has done much to revive interest in this nutritious food and popularize its use in daily menu planning. *Nattō* is especially rich in vitamin K, a nutrient that aids in the clotting of blood, but it also contains ample pyrazine (an organic compound) and a special enzyme, nattokinase, which prevents or dissolves blood clots. Not surprisingly, *nattō* is considered an excellent food for anyone with circulatory problems.

You will find *nattō* in the refrigerated case of most Asian groceries and many health-food stores. Often three small containers, each holding about $1^1/2$ ounces, will be bundled together. Typically, each container will have an inner wrapper of plastic film covering the beans (peel back and discard) and a tiny packet of seasoned soy sauce and an even smaller packet of bright yellow mustard. Unfortunately, both the sauce and the mustard are usually loaded with chemical additives and I advise you to discard them.

Nigari

Nigari (the word derives from the Japanese word for "bitter") is a coagulant used to transform liquid soy milk into solid tōfu. It is made from seawater by removing the sodium chloride and evaporating the water. Chemically, it is mostly magnesium chloride with some magnesium sulfate and other trace elements.

Although traditionally processed as a powder (the sediment that remains after water evaporates), the liquid form is far more common and is what you will find in Asian groceries and health-food stores. Store on a cool, dark shelf, even after opening. Umi no Sei or Aranami are the two brands you will most likely encounter.

Nuka

A by-product of rice processing, *nuka* is the bran that is removed when brown rice (*genmai*) is transformed into polished white rice. Like so many by-products in the Japanese *kansha* kitchen, *nuka* is used, rather than discarded. Its primary use is in the making of a pickling paste, and because of that, packages often display photographs or designs that suggest pickling. A detailed recipe describing the creation and maintenance of a *nuka toko* (rice-bran pickling medium) can be found on page 214.

A secondary culinary use for *nuka* is in performing *aku nuki*, or removal of unwanted, naturally occurring chemicals, such as the hydrocyanic acid in fresh bamboo shoots. When *nuka* is added to fresh bamboo shoots as they boil, its starchy oil leaches out and neutralizes any possible toxic effects of the hydrocyanic acid. In Japan, fresh bamboo shoots are sold with a small packet of *nuka* (rice bran) or *iri nuka* (parched rice bran). Outside Japan, you may need to purchase *nuka* separately. If you buy brown rice and get the store to polish it for you, ask for the *nuka*.

The oils in *nuka* can go rancid within weeks if the *nuka* is not stored properly. A vacuum-sealed or tightly closed container kept in a cool, dry spot is the best way to prevent rancidity. To hedge your bets, dry-roast the *nuka* just before using it (page 245). If the *nuka* smells like old cooking oil at any point, it is beyond saving. Add it to your compost heap.

Okara

Okara (tōfu lees) is the fluffy, fiber-rich lees produced (in great quantities) when tōfu is made. It is highly perishable and therefore rarely sold in ordinary Asian grocery stores. If you can find a local source for artisanal tōfu, that shop might offer *okara* for sale. Or, better yet, make your own soy milk (page 156), and you will end up with both soy milk and *okara*. Whether homemade or store-bought, keep *okara* refrigerated and use it within a few days. The color of *okara* depends upon the variety of *daizu* (dried soybean) used; most often it is snowy white with occasional dark flecks and quite rough textured (with crushed bean skins). Before cooking with it, smell it—any hint of old, used oil is a sign of spoilage.

Pickles

You will find a whole chapter devoted to making pickles starting on page 190. For a discussion of commercially prepared pickled vegetables, see *tsukémono*, page 282.

Rice

Two kinds of rice are used in Japanese cooking. *Uruchi mai* is served most often at table and is prepared by simmering in a pot or rice cooker with water or flavored broth. *Mochi-gomé*, used primarily to make rice taffy and other confections and snack foods, is a sweet rice that is typically prepared by steaming and becomes quite sticky. It is often labeled "sticky rice" or "glutinous rice." When purchasing rice, it is important to distinguish between these two kinds.

In this book, I call *uruchi mai* "Japanese-style rice." It cooks up into moist, tender grains that cling to one another, making it easy to eat with chopsticks. In Japan, households will often have a preference for a particular variety of *uruchi mai*, claiming their preferred type is sweeter or silkier, or boasts a better sheen. The two most popular varieties are *sasa nishiki* and *koshi hikari*, which are ivory colored when raw. Both of them are grown in America, and sometimes you will find them identified by name on labels. Either one is fine to use. My preference for *koshi hikari* in Japan is based on price. My local supermarket in Tokyo buys directly from farmers in Uonuma (a district in Niigata Prefecture) and passes on the discount to its customers.

Although rice imported from Japan can be purchased in many Asian grocery stores, excellent American-grown Japanese-style rice is widely available in ordinary supermarkets and specialty stores. Medium- and short-grain Japanese-style rice is sold under many different names, including the unfortunate label of "sushi rice." I call it "unfortunate" because it is misleading. Rice that has been cooked and then dressed with seasoned vinegar as it cools is sushi rice. In this book, it is the name of a recipe, not an ingredient.

Raw rice should be stored at room temperature in a cool, dry spot. In Japan, special rice-storage bins are sold that hold 10 kilograms (22 pounds). These units include a *gō* (measuring cup equivalent to about ³/₄ cup) for measuring raw rice. In your kitchen, I suspect you will find it simplest to store rice in the original paper bag, and place that bag, loosely folded down, in a larger, lidded plastic container or large zippered plastic bag. I suggest you keep your rice-measuring cup in the container or bag with your rice. If you will be cooking your rice in an electric rice cooker, the cup should be the one that came with the appliance, so you can use the water lines marked on the rice-cooker bowl. If you will cooking your rice in a pot on the stove top, store a standard ¹/₂-cup measure with your rice.

Roots and tubers

An increasing number of urban and suburban farmers' markets outside Japan are selling burdock root, lotus root, Japanese sweet potatoes, and mountain yams. These, along with carrots (common orange or specialty Kyoto reds) and potatoes, find their way into stews, stir-fries, soups, noodles, and even desserts in the Japanese vegetarian kitchen. When preparing roots and tubers, some Japanese cooks will perform *aku nuki* (bitterness removal) to minimize the earthiness of them and to control discoloration; others abhor the practice.

If you prefer mild flavors and want to avoid graying or browning (or, in the case of lotus root, occasionally purplish) discoloration, you can treat the various roots and tubers to the different soaks described below.

BURDOCK ROOT Called *gobō* in Japanese, this long, slender, beige root (pictured on page 277) is often sold at markets with a thin layer of soil still clinging to it. Because its woodsy aroma and much of its nutritional value are concentrated in the outer layers, try to avoid heavy scraping when scratching soil away with the back of a knife. Burdock discolors quickly; do not be surprised when the surface turns pale brown, or even gray, as you scrape. Sometimes rusty-looking streaks will run the length of the scraped root.

If you like, soak the burdock root in plain cold water for about 2 minutes (the water will turn brown) to minimize its earthy flavor. If discoloration is an issue, soak burdock root in water to which vinegar has been added; this will bleach the root and lessen the astringency somewhat. Drain and cook immediately to preserve nutrients.

LOTUS ROOT Twice a year, in the spring and the fall, lotus root (pictured on page 277) comes to the market. Known as *renkon* and *hasu* in Japanese, it grows in swamps and sometimes arrives in still-muddy clusters. Most often, though, the root has been both rinsed and cut so that you can see the lacelike pattern of channels. Peek inside to make sure they are reasonably clean (they are difficult to clean without cutting the root into thin slices and soaking the slices). This is especially important if you will be grating the lotus root, rather than cutting it into slices or chunks. Grating changes the texture of the root from crisp and crunchy to rather chewy; Lotus Root Dumpling Soup (page 78) highlights this textural transformation. Lotus root can be boiled, steamed, stir-fried, or deep-fried, and has an affinity for salty, sweet-and-sour, or spicy flavors.

If you want to preserve lotus root's snowy white color, peel and soak for 5 or 6 minutes in water to which vinegar has been added. This acidulated bath not only bleaches the root but also draws out excessive starchiness; the water will turn quite cloudy, with sediment sometimes forming at the bottom of the bowl. Drain and pat dry, then prepare and eat right away to preserve the nutrients (lotus root is a fine source of vitamin C).

JAPANESE-STYLE SWEET POTATO Used in both sweet and savory dishes, these sweet potatoes called *Satsuma imo* (pictured on page 277) have red skins and golden yellow flesh. The entire tuber is eaten (the skins are especially delicious).

When peeled, the potatoes will begin to discolor, often turning grayish (sometimes tinted with blue). If you find this distressing, the most effective way to control color is with a solution of *yaki myōban* (page 284) and water. Soak for at least 10 minutes, then rinse thoroughly and pat dry. Plain water (without the alum) can also work well; soak for 10 to 15 minutes. Cook and eat soon after treating to preserve the nutrients.

YAMA IMO This tuber (pictured on page 277) is eaten raw (peeled, sliced, and shredded or peeled and grated). It can also be enjoyed cooked (sliced and seared, then sauced). Either way, the texture is most unusual. Raw slices and shreds are slippery on the exposed surfaces, yet crisp when bitten into. When *yama imo* is seared, it retains a certain degree of surface crispness while it becomes tender inside.

Raw and grated *yama imo* resembles egg whites. In fact, it is used as a binder, in lieu of eggs, in the vegan kitchen. Some *soba* noodles use ground *yama imo* to keep the noodles (which are made from gluten-free *soba* flour) from falling apart.

The yams need to be peeled before used. The tubers are often packed in a sawdustlike material; dust or shake off any bits that cling. The beige-colored hairy outer peel can easily be removed with a vegetable peeler (compost the peels). Be careful, though: the exposed inner white surfaces will be slippery. I suggest you wear thin latex gloves or hold the exposed end wrapped with paper towels. Sometimes the enzymes in these tubers can cause temporary irritation. If your hands begin to itch, rinse in cold water to which a few drops of vinegar or lemon juice have been added.

Saké

Often referred to as "rice wine," saké is an alcoholic beverage brewed from highly refined rice. The subject of making saké, and consuming it as a beverage, is vast. My goal here is to provide you with a few simple guidelines for purchasing saké for cooking.

Look at the label. Sugar should not be listed as an ingredient. In fact, only two ingredients, or possibly three, should appear: rice (not other grains), *komé kōji* (a "good" mold that converts the starch in rice to sugar, which in turn feeds the yeasts that are responsible for fermentation), and possibly alcohol, which assists the fermentation process. The *kōji* could be "defined" differently in English by different distributors. Its scientific name is *Aspergillus oryzae*; in Japanese, it is called *kōji kin*.

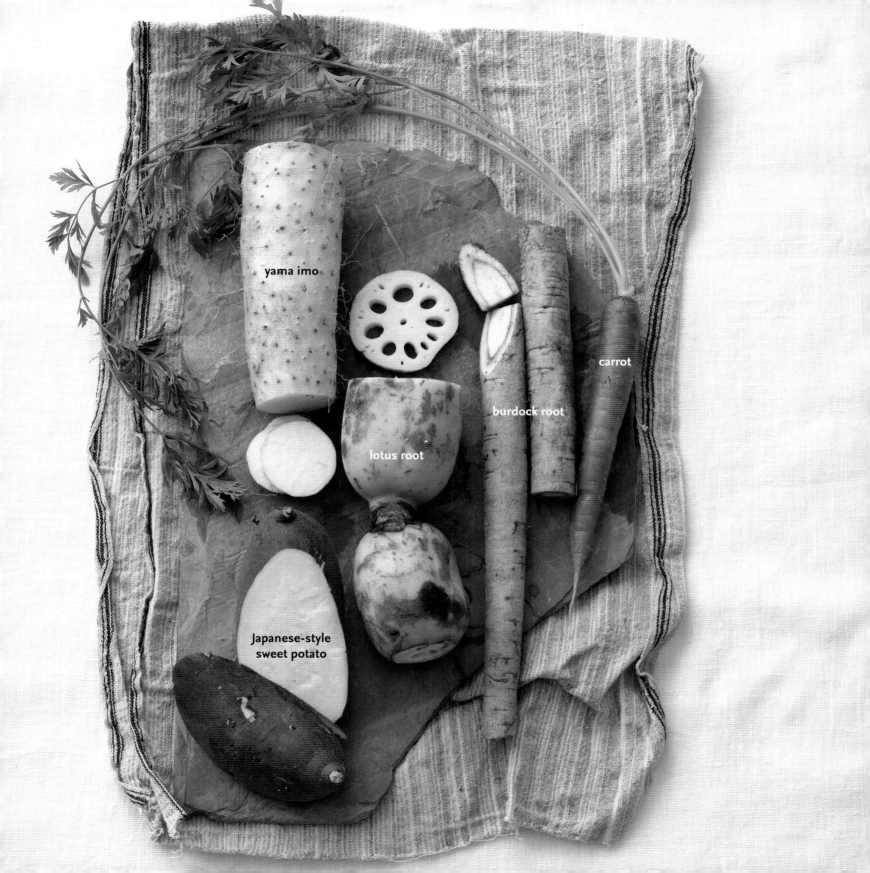

yama imo

lotus root

burdock root

carrot

Japanese-style
sweet potato

I suggest a *karakuchi* (dry) saké, rather than an *amakuchi* (sweet) saké, because the drier brews will interfere less with other flavors. An alcohol content between 12 and 14 percent by volume will perform the best with cooking.

Salt

A precious culinary mineral in every known cuisine, salt is certainly an important ingredient in the Japanese kitchen. It has traditionally been harvested from seawater by the *enden* method in Japan. Today, most Japanese kitchens stock two kinds of salt: table salt (fine granulated flakes that pour easily from a shaker) and *ara-jio*, or cooking salt (coarse-textured crystals used in food preparation, especially in making *tsukémono*).

For most purposes, what is sold as kosher salt in America will work well when a slightly abrasive salt is needed (for example, when making *tsukémono* or rubbing away the fuzz on fresh *édamamé* or okra). For general cooking, a fine-granulated salt will be fine. In Japan, I prefer to use *enden* salt from the Inland Sea (Setonaikai). One of my earliest culinary surprises in Japan was the extraordinary "mellow sweetness" of the salt my mother-in-law used. It had been processed locally, in Kannoji.

Sesame

A fine source of calcium, iron, and vitamin B₁, sesame (*goma*) provides a nutritional boost and a nutty richness to a wide variety of dishes. Both white sesame (*shiro goma*) and black sesame (*kuro goma*) are the seeds of a slender, flowering stalk that grows at least 3 feet high. A single plant will produce either white or black seeds. When the plants are mature, they are cut down and dried, and the seeds are thrashed from them.

SEEDS I strongly recommend that you purchase raw whole seeds, called *arai goma*, and dry-roast them yourself (see page 245). Depending on the recipe, you will be instructed

to leave the seeds whole, or to crack, crush, or grind them. Once sesame seeds have been roasted, their oils come to the surface, which is what makes them smell and taste so nutty. Once the oils have surfaced and are exposed to air, they can go rancid quickly.

Store raw sesame seeds in a closed container on a dry, cool shelf in your cupboard. All opened packages of pre-toasted sesame should be stored in the refrigerator, or other very cool, dry spot in your kitchen, if you want to keep them fresh for more than a few weeks. Crushed or cracked seeds and opened jars or tubes of paste go stale quickly. Refrigeration slows the process of deterioration.

SESAME PASTE Sesame paste, called *neri goma*, comes in both white (a beige color, really) and black (an inky color), ocassionally sold in tubes, but more often in glass jars. The oil easily separates out and floats to the top of the jar. This is not a sign of spoilage. Pour off excess oil to get a stiffer, more intense paste, or stir to recombine for a silkier, more unctuous texture. Opened packages are best refrigerated and used within a month of opening.

SESAME OIL Sesame oil (*goma abura*) comes in two types: dark aromatic sesame oil that is used as a flavor accent, and light-colored sesame oil that is used as any other vegetable oil might be, to dress salads, sauté, and fry foods. Commercially, both dark and light sesame oil are extracted from white sesame seeds, which are slightly richer in oil than black seeds.

Shira uri

Despite its name, which means "white gourd," this is a very pale green member of the Cucurbitaceae family, a botanically varied group of vegetables that includes squashes, pumpkins, gourds, and cucumbers. The Japanese have been eating *shira uri* for more than 1,000 years. It is the classic choice for pickling, especially for making *Nara-zuké* (see page 209), which is transformed by lengthy time submerged in saké lees. Scrape the seeds out of this bulbous gourd before pickling.

Shira uri is difficult to obtain fresh outside of Asia, so try substituting organically grown cucumbers (rather than zucchini).

Soy milk

Soy milk (tonyū) is increasingly available at supermarkets throughout the world, but vast differences exist among products. When you shop, check labels carefully before you buy.

The greater the percentage of soy solids (*kokéibun*), the richer (and more nutritious) the soy milk will be. The level affects the taste, texture, and nutrition of the soy milk and how it behaves in recipes. In Japan, all commercially sold soy milk lists the percentage of soy solids in the liquid. In the United States, no law requires the information be included on packages. Soy milk sold as a beverage typically contains 6 or 7 percent soy solids, though sometimes it is as low as 3 or 4 percent. You need soy milk with at least 8 percent, preferably 10 to 12 percent, soy solids to make good tōfu. *Yuba* is best when made from soy milk with more than 12 percent; the higher percentage of soy solids improves tensile strength. Some recipes suggest adding a drop of vegetable oil to increase the fat content of the soy milk.

In many recipes, soy milk is used in place of eggs, often as a binder. Any stabilizers that are added to packaged soy milk will change the way it behaves in cooking. They will interfere with coagulation when making tōfu and reduce the tensile strength of *yuba*.

Always buy unflavored soy milk, for both cooking and drinking. If you want a flavored beverage, you can add your own vanilla extract, cocoa powder, or other flavoring.

Soy sauce

A few distinct kinds of soy sauce are used in Japanese cooking, each for a slightly different purpose. The two types that I call for in recipes are regular soy sauce (*shōyu* or *koi kuchi shōyu*), which I simply call soy sauce, and light-colored soy sauce (*usukuchi shōyu*).

In most recipes, you will find that regular soy sauce is suitable. Sometimes the decision to use one or the other is an aesthetic one, not a culinary one. Regular soy sauce, for example, would make the Spring Breeze Aspic (page 95) look muddy, and it might stain the pale tōfu in Successively Simmered Kōya-Dōfu and Vegetables (page 140).

Often the choice is a matter of habit—or, perhaps, regional prejudice is a more accurate description. Residents of the Kansai (Kyoto, Nara, Osaka, and, to a lesser degree, Kobe) feel that the deep color of regular soy sauce "stains" and "muddies" the appearance of all food. People in the north and northeast (the Kanto area, with Tokyo at its center) appreciate the deep, burnished color of foods simmered or glazed with regular soy sauce, and often consider foods prepared with pale amber-colored *usukuchi shōyu* insipid.

Soy sauce labels can be confusing. Reduced-sodium products (sometimes with labels that read "lite soy sauce") are not necessarily lighter in color (it is hard to see the true color in the bottle), and pale-colored *usukuchi shōyu* soy sauce may actually be higher in sodium content than the standard product. Read the labels carefully, and calculate your own dietary needs.

The very dark tamari soy sauce is mainly employed for sashimi; in the vegan kitchen, it is often used with *nama yuba* (for a *nama yuba* recipe, see page 160) or drizzled on cold tōfu. Health-food stores will often sell tamari soy sauce as a wheat-free soy sauce. If consumption of wheat is a health concern for you, check the label to make sure wheat has not been used. Tamari is a generally more intense sauce, with a higher ratio of minerals, including sodium.

No matter what kind of soy sauce you purchase, small containers are probably best. Soy sauce does not spoil easily, but its subtle, full-bodied bean aroma fades within a few weeks of being opened. Keep opened bottles in the refrigerator, or tightly capped on a dark pantry shelf. You can restore verve to soy sauce that has lost its aroma over time by transforming it into Vegan Seasoned Soy Concentrate (page 131).

Sweeteners

The Japanese use various sweeteners in preparing savory foods to balance salty and sour flavors and when making confectionary. The kind of sugar commonly found in Japanese home kitchens today is processed from sugarcane. Japanese white sugar is moist, "packs" the way brown sugar does, and blends smoothly with other ingredients without applying heat. It is less intensely sweet than the granulated white sugar readily available in America. I have adjusted recipes in this cookbook, presuming that readers will use American sugar, or a granulated product similar to it. When a recipe in *Kansha* calls for sugar, use granulated white sugar. Powdered sugar (a mixture of finely pulverized cane sugar and cornstarch), sometimes called confectioners' sugar, is used in two recipes.

Honey is consumed by most Japanese who practice a *shōjin* lifestyle. However, honey is not acceptable to most people who adhere to a vegan diet. I have not used honey in recipes.

Four sweeteners in addition to sugar are called for, some or all of which may be new to you: *ama-zaké, kuro-zatō,* mirin, and *mizu amé.*

AMA-ZAKÉ To make *ama-zaké* (sweet rice mash), equal amounts of cooked rice, or rice porridge, and *komé kōji* (the same healthful mold spores used to ferment soybeans when making miso) are mixed and allowed to sit for a short while (*ama-zaké* is also known as *hitoya-zaké,* or "one-night rice wine"). During this time, "good" bacteria break down the rice starches and convert them into sugar. The result is a sweet mash, with bits of rice suspended in a thick, cloudy liquid. Because fermentation is not allowed to continue, the alcohol level is extremely low—so low that this rice mash is traditionally served to children at festival time. And so low that *ama-zaké* is not considered an alcoholic beverage in Japan.

Ama-zaké has been part of the Japanese pantry for thousands of years. During the Muromachi period (1392–1573), *ama-zaké* consumption took on a regional identity: in and around Kyoto, it was sipped in the summertime as a stamina drink to fortify a heat-weary metabolism; in the Edo plains (what is now Tokyo), it was drunk to ward off chills on frigid nights.

Refrigerate *ama-zaké* and consume it by the date indicated on the package. Shelf life can be extended for a month by freezing the unopened package. Recipes in this book call for blending *ama-zaké* to a creamy smoothness before using it as a binder and sweetener in frozen desserts. When purchasing, check labels to make sure no sugar or other flavoring has been added.

KURO-ZATŌ (Japanese brown sugar) Literally "black sugar," *kuro-zatō* is very dark brown. Its mild, malted flavor and rich deep color makes fabulous syrup (page 224). Because this product may not be readily available to all readers, I have called for brown sugar (the American term for dark-colored unrefined sugar) as an alternative to Japanese *kuro-zatō* in recipes.

In Japan, the most flavorful *kuro-zatō,* and the one richest in minerals (including significant amounts of calcium and iron), comes from Okinawa. It is worth the search to find this superior product. Store as you would any sugar, on a dry, dark shelf or cupboard away from heat.

MIRIN This naturally sweet product is used two ways in the Japanese kitchen: to balance the saltiness of soy sauce (especially light-colored *usukuchi shōyu*) and to glaze foods. Real mirin is naturally sweet. It is brewed from *mochi-gomé* (glutinous rice) in the same manner that saké is brewed from ordinary table rice (*uruchi mai*). Unfortunately, most products labeled "mirin" are syrupy mixtures of sugar and inexpensive rice wine. If you can source real mirin, you will be rewarded with a superior mellow, sweet flavor (what the Japanese call *maroyaka na aji*). Store true mirin at cool room temperature (it tends to crust and crystallize if refrigerated); it will darken after several months. Syrupy imitators can be refrigerated or stored on a dark, cool pantry shelf.

MIZU AMÉ A clear, thick syrup with a mild, sweet flavor, *mizu amé* is typically processed from barley (and therefore called "barley malt" on English-language labels), though some brands are made from other grains, including brown rice (*genmai*). *Mizu amé* has a viscous texture similar to that of honey. It can be stored at room temperature; indeed, refrigerating it makes it very stiff and difficult to pour or spoon. Corn syrup and maple syrup are sweeter than *mizu amé*; if you will be using either as a substitute, reduce the amount slightly.

Tōfu

Tōfu, or fresh soybean curd, is the single most important source of nonanimal protein in the Japanese vegan diet. If you want to try your hand at making tōfu from scratch, a detailed recipe (page 158) is devoted to doing just that. Throughout the book I have included dozens of recipes calling for tōfu products you can purchase. Unfortunately, many of these are poorly labeled (confusing and/or inaccurate). My goal in this entry is to help you source the correct product for whatever dish you are making. In the recipes in this book, I have given amounts in ounces and provided a range to allow for vast differences in packaging.

When shopping, look for the weight on any given package and purchase accordingly. I have included information about five fresh products: firm tōfu (*momen-dōfu*), silken tōfu (*kinugoshi-dōfu*), grilled tōfu (*yaki-dōfu*), thin fried tōfu (*abura agé*), and thick fried tōfu (*atsu agé*). Information on *okara* (tōfu lees) appears on page 274 and on *kōya-dōfu* (shelf-stable freeze-dried tōfu) on page 261.

FIRM TŌFU Firm tōfu (*momen-dōfu*) is formed in containers lined with *sarashi* (page 249). The cloth leaves a distinctive small-grid pattern on the surface of the tōfu loaves. Silken tōfu, in contrast, has a glass or mirrorlike surface.

In America, a wide range of "firm" tōfu products are available, from extremely dense Chinese-style blocks weighing nearly a pound (these are often made and packaged locally and sold in local Asian groceries) to small, semicompressed loaves weighing less than 6 ounces, packed in vacuum-sealed containers (these are produced by larger companies, most with national distribution).

Some manufacturers will offer their customers "firm" and "very firm" options (in addition to "soft" and "medium," among other descriptors). You may need to do some experimentation to find the product that suits you best. Here are a few guidelines for usage.

Extra-firm tōfu is best when you are mashing it for use in a mock-meat or -fish preparations (Tōfu-Tōfu Burgers, page 169; Glazed Eel Look-Alike, page 188). It can also be substituted for thick fried tōfu, *kōya-dōfu*, or grilled tōfu in slow-simmered preparations.

Medium-firm tōfu is best if you are cubing tōfu for adding to miso soup; it will better absorb the flavor of the broth (and vegetables). Medium-firm is also a better choice than extra-firm when mashing in sauces (page 99).

Store any unused portion of the tōfu covered with fresh cold water in a lidded container. Refrigerate for up to 3 days, changing water daily. (If at any time an oily film forms on the surface, discard the tōfu.)

SILKEN TŌFU As with firm tōfu, many products labeled "silken" or "soft" tōfu (*kinugoshi-dōfu* in Japanese) have very different textures. You can make your own silken loaf by following instructions for Steamed Soy Milk Custard (page 162) and using a square or rectangular heatproof container that fits in your steamer.

Although delicate and requiring greater care in handling, silken tōfu has a creamy texture that is unique—and key to the enjoyment of certain preparations, such as Crispy-Creamy Tōfu, Southern Barbarian Style (page 178). It is also the type to use if you want to make your own mock-meat Tōfu Chunks (page 164). If you do not use the entire package at once, store what remains in the same way you would firm tōfu.

GRILLED TŌFU To make grilled tōfu (*yaki-dōfu*), blocks of firm tōfu are compressed slightly before they are grilled. The dark markings top and bottom should be visible through the package label; the distinctive small-grid lines are evidence that *sarashi* cloth was used to line the container in which the firm tōfu was made.

Grilled tōfu makes a good base on which to place sauces or other ingredients, canapé style. It can be added to, or substituted for, the nama fu in Miso-Slathered Nama Fu (page 148), and it makes a good addition to many braised vegetable dishes, adding volume and protein (Two Kinds of Tōfu, Amber Braised with Carrots, page 174). Or, try adding it to the pan juices remaining after making Skillet-Seared Daikon with Yuzu (page 98). If you do not use the entire package at once, store what remains in the same way you would firm tōfu.

THIN FRIED TŌFU To make thin fried tōfu (*abura agé*), whole loaves of firm tōfu are pressed (to rid them of excess moisture), sliced horizontally, and then deep-fried. During the frying, a pocket of air forms in the center of each slice. The slices are sometimes pried open for stuffing (Good Fortune Bags, page 180), or they are opened to make a flat sheet and used to enclose other foods (Tricolored Vegetables Rolled in Fried Tōfu, page 182).

At Asian grocery stores, thin fried tōfu will be stored in a refrigerated case (or possibly the freezer if imported from Japan). If the sheets have a puffy appearance, they have probably been injected with air to make them easier to pry open. Thin fried tōfu is a highly perishable food that needs to be kept refrigerated and will stay fresh for only a few days. Do not refreeze.

The sheets are quite greasy (the oil keeps the sheets flexible, which is especially important if you will be making pouches to stuff). Blot well with paper towels and/or blanch briefly in boiling water to remove unwanted oil. Blanching is the preferred method when you want to use the tōfu as a pouch because the heat expands air trapped inside, making each slice puff up. Puffed slices are less likely to tear or rip as you pry them open.

THICK FRIED TŌFU To make thick fried tōfu (*atsu agé*), blocks of either firm or silken tōfu are deep-fried. The outer surfaces are golden brown and a bit crispy-chewy, and the center is snowy white and silky—and quite creamy if made with silken tōfu. Thick fried tōfu is used in many stir-fried and braised dishes. Look for it in the refrigerator case in Asian markets. The shelf life is short, usually only 2 or 3 days.

Tsukémono

Most English-language texts call *tsukémono* "pickles." I prefer to use the original Japanese term. In doing so, I hope readers will set aside preconceived notions of heavily preserved foods with a primarily sour taste. Japanese *tsukémono* run the gamut from mildly tart to intensely sweet and sour, barely fermented to quite heady, lightly salted to very briny. I have devoted an entire chapter to making a wide range of *tsukémono* at home. Some of the recipes, however, require a commitment of time (several months or longer to reach maturity), refrigerator or cool shelf space, and/or energy to source unusual ingredients. Many readers may want to purchase commercially prepared *tsukémono* instead of, or in addition to, making varieties at home. In this catalog, I have provided information on store-bought *tsukémono*, including pickled plums (*uméboshi*), sour plum paste (*bainiku*), and *yukari* (crushed dried *aka-jiso* leaves left over from making pickled plums) under the entry for *uméboshi*, which follows.

Uméboshi

Uméboshi (pickled plums) have a long culinary history in Japan. The first written records date back to the sixth century, though it is likely that the practice of brining and consuming salt-pickled plums originated on the Asian mainland long before that. A wide variety of health benefits have been, and continue to be, attributed to pickled plums. I make no particular claims in that regard, either for or against. In *Kansha*, you will find *uméboshi* and the by-products of its production—sour plum paste (discussed at the end of this entry), sour plum vinegar (see the next entry), and *yukari* herb (page 259)—used for their culinary virtues.

Because the pickling of *uméboshi* is difficult to do in small quantities, and the different stages require attention sporadically over a span of several months, I have not included a recipe for making them in this book. I have fond memories of community pickling parties in Japan—several households joining forces to make ten kilograms or more, and then divvying up the results. My share of two kilograms, about eighty-five softly wrinkled, dusty pink plums, would last a year, doled out slowly and each one savored.

When you go to purchase *uméboshi*, you will find a confusing array of products. Here is what I recommend: seek out the larger, softer, squishier-looking plums, rather than the small, hard, olivelike ones (unless you want to add

them to a martini cocktail, a recent craze in Japanese bars). I prefer (and I think you will, too) plums that have been brined with an herb called *aka-jiso* (a very distant botanical relative of mint); the deep purple-pink leaves impart an appetizing floral-fruity aroma and provide antibacterial benefits. If you have a dehydrator (page 241), you can use the leaves to make *yukari*: mince them, spread them on the dehydrator tray, and dehydrate them following the instructions for drying herbs.

No matter what type of plum you prefer—soft or firm—you will need to read the labels very carefully. To reduce the amount of salt used in the brining—so the manufacturers can claim the plums are "reduced sodium"—sweeteners (especially honey) or preservatives are added. The salt used in the brine is what preserves the plums, so if the amount is reduced, spoilage needs to be deterred through other means, usually chemical.

Store *uméboshi* that have been made in the traditional fashion at room temperature. If you need to reduce your intake of sodium, limit your consumption to an occasional plum (or portion of a plum). You can "thin" plum paste made from mashed plums by adding a few drops of water or *kombu* stock to it.

Although you can purchase plum paste, called *bainiku*, in jars and tubes (again, check labels for additives), you can also make a paste easily by pulling the flesh from the pits and mashing it.

Vinegar

Vinegar naturally fermented from rice is preferred in Japanese cookery. Today, in Japan and overseas, you will find a dizzying array of rice vinegar products on store shelves. Always read labels carefully; many of these products have chemical additives and many are preseasoned. To help you sort through your options, here is a brief description of each type.

PLUM VINEGAR A by-product of pickling plums, this vinegar, called *umé-zu*, is tart and salty. A little bit goes a long way. When cooking with plum vinegar, sugar (in fairly large quantities) is typically called for to balance the intensity of the sour and salty flavors. Two types of plum vinegar are sold: white (pale, clear gold) and red (bright pink from the addition of *aka-jiso* leaves to the pickling medium).

RICE VINEGAR I sometimes liken the degree of purity in rice vinegars to olive oils. The equivalent of "virgin" is *komé-zu*, or rice vinegar. It is brewed from rice only (no other grains or fruit), but could have alcohol added to assist in fermentation. This is fine for most cooking purposes. What I would term "extra virgin" is *junmai su*, literally "pure" rice vinegar—nothing but rice, naturally fermented. These vinegars are wonderfully rich and mild compared to the harsher flavors produced when fermentation is hastened with added alcohol. Although it is slightly darker (more golden, really) than ordinary *komé-zu*, pure rice vinegar will not alter the appearance of foods seasoned with it. "Unfiltered extra virgin" would be *genmai su*, or brown rice vinegar, or *kuro-zu*, or black vinegar, named for its dark color. Several large commercial operations make pure rice vinegar from polished rice and brown rice. Mellow and delicious brown rice vinegar can "stain" foods, so you will need to weigh the relative merit of appearance and flavor when choosing.

Bottles labeled *su* (vinegar) are likely to be mixtures of various grains (wheat, corn, and rice) and alcohol—harsh supermarket swill. Bottles labeled "seasoned rice vinegar" have been doctored with sugar, salt, and possibly chemical glutamates. These products are designed for seasoning the rice used in sushi. A few commercial brands include the natural flavor-enhancing properties of *kombu*, rather than chemicals; check labels if you want to buy preseasoned vinegar. I provide a recipe for making your own seasoned vinegar on page 17.

Yaki myōban

Yaki myōban, coarse white alum powder, either rubbed directly on vegetables (usually in a mixture with coarse salt) or dissolved in water in which vegetables (such as fiddlehead ferns) are soaked, is used in the Japanese traditional kitchen to keep the colors of certain vegetables vibrant. Packages of *yaki myōban* will often include a picture of eggplant, because the powder is used when pickling eggplants to keep their skins a deep, rich blue-purple. In this book, I also list it as an option for small red radishes. *Yaki myōban* is rinsed off before the vegetable is eaten.

You can instead opt for a Japanese folk remedy to keep natural vegetable dyes from bleeding: rusty nails (*sabi kugi*)! The oxidized iron, rather than the alum, works the chemical magic. Nowadays, small metal "eggplants" specifically designed to keep colors from bleeding are sold in the housewares sections of Japanese department stores.

Yuzu

This incredibly fragrant citrus fruit perfumes many winter dishes. It is the peel that is prized, both fresh and dried; the white pith is bitter and the fruit rather pulpy. The fresh fruits come to market in most of Japan as summer turns to autumn, though the fruits are still green at that time. They reach their peak of flavor late in the fall, after they have turned a sunny yellow.

If you are able to source fresh *yuzu*, rasplike graters are best for taking zest. For broad strips or thin slivers to add to *tsukémono* or float in a broth, use a knife to remove the peel (use the blade of the knife to shave off any pith). *Yuzu* juice can be extracted by squeezing fresh fruit, but it tends to be cloudy and not especially "fruity." It could be mixed with soy sauce to make a simple *ponzu* sauce, though truthfully other citrus, such as lemons or oranges, work as well, if not better.

If you do not want to waste the fruit and pulp, tie the peeled *yuzu* in cloth (the Japanese use *sarashi*, page 250; a double layer of cheesecloth would work well instead) and place it in the bathtub. The citrus oils do double duty: aromatherapy and soother of dry, chapped skin. Leisurely soaks in *yuzu-buro* (deep hot tubs filled with *yuzu* bobbing about) is a Japanese winter ritual. Dried *yuzu* peel is more readily available outside Japan than the fresh fruit is. It can be added to the brine of many *tsukémono* or floated in a clear soup.

Yuba

Yuba is the thin, delicate skin that forms on the surface of fresh, warm soy milk free of coagulants. In its fresh, warm state, this skin is called *nama yuba* and is most often served with a drizzle of soy sauce and perhaps a dab of wasabi. Creamy and yet chewy, it is similar to loosely shirred eggs. Directions for preparing and serving *nama yuba* can be found on page 160. Because it is highly perishable, it is not surprising that previous generations of Asian cooks developed methods of extending its shelf life, chiefly by drying it (see *hoshi yuba*, page 261).

INDEX